Daniel Trubey

of

Franklin County Pennsylvania

The First Four Generations

First Edition

Compiled by

Alycon Trubey Pierce

HERITAGE BOOKS
2015

HERITAGE BOOKS
AN IMPRINT OF HERITAGE BOOKS, INC.

Books, CDs, and more—Worldwide

For our listing of thousands of titles see our website
at
www.HeritageBooks.com

Published 2015 by
HERITAGE BOOKS, INC.
Publishing Division
5810 Ruatan Street
Berwyn Heights, Md. 20740

Copyright © 2000 Alycon Trubey Pierce

Heritage Books by the author:

Daniel Trubey of Franklin County, Pennsylvania: The First Four Generations

Selected Final [Revolutionary] Pension Payment Vouchers, 1818–1864: Alabama: Decatur–Huntsville–Mobile–Tuscaloosa

Selected Final Pension Payment Vouchers, 1818–1864: District of Columbia

Selected Final Pension Payment Vouchers, 1818–1864: Maryland–Baltimore

Selected Final Pension Payments Vouchers, 1818–1864: New Jersey–Trenton, Volume 1 (A–M) and *Volume 2 (N–Z)*

All rights reserved. No part of this book may be reproduced or transmitted in any form or by any means, electronic or mechanical, including photocopying, recording or by any information storage and retrieval system without written permission from the author, except for the inclusion of brief quotations in a review.

International Standard Book Numbers
Paperbound: 978-1-58549-626-6
Clothbound: 978-0-7884-6170-5

Contents

Preface i

Generation One 1

Generation Two 13

Generation Three 28

Generation Four 86

Appendix A: Barevias A. Trubey Manuscript 247

Appendix B: Letters 339

Index 361

Willow Bend Books and Family Line Publications offer the following other publications by Alycon Trubey Pierce, CG:

- *Selected Final Pension Payment Vouchers, 1818–1864, Alabama: Decatur, Huntsville, Mobile, Tuscaloosa* (1997)

- *Selected Final Pension Payment Vouchers, 1818–1864, Maryland: Baltimore* (1997)

- *Selected Final Pension Payment Vouchers, 1818–1864, District of Columbia* (1998)

- *Selected Final Pension Payment Vouchers, 1818–1864, New Jersey: Trenton* (2000)

Preface

Sometime in 1944, Barevias Augustus Trubey (1860–1949) completed work on a Trubey family genealogy which was never published. A typescript copy of this work, obtained by this compiler from Barevias's great-granddaughter, indicated that his correspondence and interviews with Trubey descendants between 1922 and 1944 formed the basis for the work. No public records were cited. A complete transcription of this manuscript appears in Appendix A with the permission of Hugh and Sharon K. (Trubey) Yoho, who held the original copy of the manuscript in 1984.

In an effort to test its veracity, the manuscript's claims were checked initially in the secondary sources available at the National Society, Daughters of the American Revolution (NSDAR) Library, in Washington, D.C., such as transcribed probate and tombstone records, published genealogies on the families intermarried with the Trubeys, documentation cited in NSDAR applications which shared portions of their lineages with that of the various Trubeys, and so on. This led to further research in courthouse records, and in Federal records including census, nonpopulation schedules, land records, passport and patent applications, and consular reports. Correspondence with distant courthouses and state archives produced a host of marriage, divorce, land, and probate records.

Correspondence with living descendants was deliberately avoided, as this would have produced a volume of twentieth-century anecdotal data which would have been extremely difficult for this compiler to document, given the lack of access afforded to researchers who are not immediate family members. Therefore, only the first four generations of this Trubey family have been targeted in this work. Members of the fifth generation appear, to the extent that they were identified in the manuscript or through their appearance in some other records, but they have not been documented or followed further in this publication.

ii   DANIEL TRUBEY OF FRANKLIN COUNTY, PENNSYLVANIA

The "Hessian"

This unpublished and undocumented 1940s genealogy manuscript claims that the progenitor of this branch of the Trubey family was *Jacob* Trubey, a German auxiliary or "Hessian" soldier serving with the British forces in the American Revolution, who died in Franklin County, Pennsylvania, circa 1805.[1] One of the claims in this simple beginning led to a long and circuitous path to evidence of its own invalidity.

Jacob was allegedly one of three brothers serving with the German troops, and, indeed, there were at least three Trubey men who came from the same town in Hesse Cassel, served in the same Erbprinz (Hereditary Prince) Regiment, and were imprisoned quite near Franklin County, Pennsylvania, toward the end of the America Revolution. Jakob, Andreas, and Augustin "Trube" served as privates in the Leib Company in 1775, and all were from the town of Kammerbach.[2] An "August Trube," also of Kammerbach, was a private in Col. Hachenberg's Company whose rolls of March 1782 and May 1783 carry August as a deserter.[3] The spacing of the birth dates attributed to these Trube men (presumably calculated from their ages as given in their service records) supports the possibility that they were siblings:

---

[1] Barevias Augustus Trubey, "Genealogy and History of Trubey Family from its first entry into the United States of America" (typescript, circa 1944), original in possession of Sharon Kay (Trubey) Yoho, Sunland, Calif. Transcript, with original pagination, reproduced as an appendix to this book.

[2] Veröffentlichungen Der Archivschule Marburg Institut Für Archivwissenschaft, *Hessische Truppen im Amerikanischen Unabhängigkeitskrieg (HETRINA), Index nach Familiennamen*, III (Marburg, Germany: 1976, by the Institute), entries 14861, 14866-14871. Hereinafter, this publication is cited as HETRINA. This index includes "place of origin" as a category without further distinction as to whether that was a place of the soldier's birth, residence, or enlistment.

[3] HETRINA, III: entries 14862-14865.

PREFACE   iii

Andreas born 1750/51; August born 1751/52; Augustin born 1755/56; and Jakob born 1754/55/56.

When this regiment was captured at Yorktown, the prisoners were sent to Frederick, Maryland, where they remained until May 1783. Several months later, a marriage license was recorded there for a "Jacob Truvey and Catherine Isenberger," on 15 September 1783.[4] This did not mesh at all with the manuscript's description of Jacob's wife as a Miss "Mack." Further, the Frederick County Jacob and Catherine (Isenberg) Trubey removed to Huntingdon County, Pennsylvania, with other members of the Isenberg family shortly after their marriage.[5]

The source for "Jacob" as the given name of the progenitor was a family Bible seen by the manuscript's compiler, Barevias A. Trubey, in 1936. The Bible is described as having originally belonged to Jacob M. Trubey [#15], a then-deceased grandson of the progenitor. No publication date was mentioned. That Bible described Jacob M. Trubey's father as "Jacob Trubey, son of Jacob Trubey." This piece of information appears to be in error, however. Pursuit of the claims that the Hessian soldier died in Franklin County, Pennsylvania, circa 1805, led to the identification of only one adult Trubey male in that county from 1789 through 1807: *Daniel* Trubey. The Federal census, state tax and militia lists, and county probate for this man all concur in referring to him as *Daniel*.

---

[4] Robert Barnes, *Maryland Marriages, 1778-1800* (Baltimore, Md.: Genealogical Publishing Co., Inc. [hereinafter GPC], 1978), 232.

[5] The Rev. J. M. S. Isenberg, B.D., *An Historical Sketch and Genealogical Record of the Isenberg Family of Pennsylvania* (n.p., 1900), 16; copies furnished by the Historical Society of Pennsylvania, Philadelphia, Pa. See also deed of sale from Jacob and Catharine Trube to Henry Coon, 29 May 1798 (recorded 7 June 1798), Huntingdon County, Pa., Deeds F-1: 578-581; one of the subscribing witnesses signed in German script but not the grantor Jacob Trube (Catharine "Trubey" made her mark). Note: this Jacob may not be the Kammerbach soldier either; he has been placed in another Trubey family by Mary Truby Graff in her *Early History of Truby-Graff and Affiliated Families* (1941), p. 1.

iv   DANIEL TRUBEY OF FRANKLIN COUNTY, PENNSYLVANIA

For those reasons, the progenitor will be referred to as "Daniel" in this genealogy. The fact that all of Daniel's children were yet minors when he died may account for the discrepancy in the remembrance of his given name. Further, Daniel's widow survived past 1820, by which time all their children were adults, yet her name was recalled only as "Miss Mawk."

No German auxiliary service record exists for a soldier named "Daniel Trube;" however, there is one record for a "Daniel Drube." Daniel "Drube" (born 1751/1752, of Ostuffeln) served in the von Bose Regiment No. 5, under the command of Major Friedrich Henrich von Scheer.[6] After their defeat at Yorktown on 19 October 1781, these men were marched as prisoners to Frederick, Maryland,[7] where the previously described quartet of "Trube" privates of the Erbprinz Regiment were housed as well. One of the two barracks buildings

---

[6] HETRINA, II: entry 3062. The document on which his name appears (a unit roll coded as "SR484;" not in Library of Congress collection and not seen) shows Drube served under the command of Major von Scheer in the von Bose Regt., Company 5, with a muster date of "1775," place of origin of "Ostuffeln," and the notation that he was "on leave" when this list was made (full date not apparent). A copy of the only other surviving von Bose document at the Marburg archives (coded "8826") is available at the Library of Congress, but does not include Daniel Drube. After capture at Yorktown in October 1781, Drube was brought to Frederick, Maryland, where he deserted, according to the von Scheer report (below). Other soldiers in this unit from the same town of Ostuffeln (so listed in Volume II of HETRINA) were Henrich Kohlschein (entry 2323), Anton Goette (entry 4257), Ludwig Heynemann (entry 5329), Henrich Leck (entry 6134), George Pfleging (entry 7934), Johannes Vaupel (entry 11098), and Henrich Waldrop (entries 11387 and 11388).

[7] Lion G. Miles, "After Yorktown - The Hessian Regiment von Bose," *Maryland Genealogical Society Bulletin*, 28 (Fall 1987): 400. Other Yorktown prisoners were marched to the barracks at Winchester, Virginia.

which were specially constructed there for war prisoners is yet standing.[8]

Major Scheer drafted a status report, including entries as late as May 1782 or 1783,[9] of all 177 men under his command in Virginia, indicating who had died, deserted, or had been paroled to New York. This report lists Private "Drube" as the ninth of 20 deserters belonging to von Scheer's company.[10]

---

[8] For more of their history, see Hazel K. McCanner's *The Hessian Barracks: A Witness to History* (Frederick, Md.: by the Maryland School for the Deaf, June 1976).

[9] Miles, "After Yorktown - The Hessian Regiment von Bose," 401.

[10] Ibid., 409. Miles's footnote 16: "The original three-page report is in the Hessisches Staatsarchiv at Marburg, West Germany, catalogued as Bestand 4h, Verzeichnis 411, no. 3: Relationes vom Nord-Amerikanischen Kriege unter dem Commandierenden General von Lossberg, 1782, 1783, 1784, vol. V. The author [Miles] used a photostat copy at the Library of Congress, catalogued as Marburg, Preussisches Staatsarchiv, Militaria O.W.S. 1248 Wilhelmshoeher Kriegsakten No. CXXIII, fos. 133-134. The document is listed as 'Rapport B' in Marion Dexter Learned, *Guide to the Manuscript Materials Relating to American Military History to the German State Archives* (Washington: Carnegie Institution of Washington, 1912), 115. At the top of the report is the notation: 'belonging to the reports of 17 and 31 May.' At the end is the endorsement: 'Report of the Illustrious Supreme Highness' Hessian Infantry Regiment of Lieut. General von Bose, Its Strength on 19 October last year at Yorktown, Losses during the Time in Captivity, and Its Present Strength on May of this year.'" This list, reviewed by the compiler, was located in the Manuscript Division of the Library of Congress as "Germany, Preussisches Staatsarchiv, Marburg, Hessen, Kabinettsminiterium, OWS 1248, No. CXXIII, (Part II) OWS 1249, 1783-1789 (a-i)," box 2415, in negative photostat format, folios 133, 133v, and 134 (which were stamped on the reverse as 194, 195, and 196, respectively).

Assuming this same Daniel Trubey settled in Franklin County, Pennsylvania, it seems he did not leave his military training behind him completely. A 1789-1790 muster roll for Captain Thomas Wallace's militia company lists Daniel Trubey among its strength.[11]

---

[11] Benjamin Matthias Nead, *Waynesboro* (Harrisburg, Pa.: Harrisburg Publishing Co., MCM), 394-396, Note 41, NSDAR Library, Washington, D.C.

Generation One - The "Hessian"

1. A Johann Daniel[1] Drube (Trubey) was baptized on 24 January 1750 in Burguffeln, Germany,[12] the son of Martha Elisabeth Trubey, a single woman. Martha Elisabeth, baptized on 8 December 1715, was the daughter of a Johann Drube, and her brother Johann Daniel Drube (baptized 8 August 1726) served as godfather at her son's 1750 baptism. The recording of Martha Elisabeth Drube's 21 September 1798 death in the churchbook mentions that she worked for 26 years as a *Totenfrau*, or preparer of the dead.[13]

The Daniel "Drube" who served in the von Bose Regiment No. 5 gave his "place of origin" in 1775 as "Ostuffeln,"[14] a small community which no longer exists, but the parish church in Burguffeln (formed in 1681) was found to contain references to many members of the Drube family of that area, including this Johann Daniel Drube.[15] It is likely, though not proven, that this Johann Daniel Drube is the Daniel "Drube" who slipped his military imprisonment in Frederick, Maryland, by May 1783. It is also likely, though not proven, this escapee is identical to the Daniel "Truby" who married **Margaret Mack** circa 1784 in the adjoining county of Franklin County, Pennsylvania.

---

[12] Letter (26 January 1989) from the office of the "Evangelisches Pfarramt;" in possession of compiler. This comports well with Daniel's age category of "over 45" (i.e., born before 1755) in the 1800 Census (cited below).

[13] Burguffeln Kirchenbucher photocopies in possession of compiler. The entry for Martha Elisabeth's death states she died in rural Bernsehen, unmarried, on the 21 September 1798 at 2 o'clock, approximately 82 years old.

[14] HETRINA, II: entry 3062.

[15] Letter from the minister of the Evangelical Parish Church of Grebenstein-South and Burguffeln to the compiler, dated 26 January 1989.

Margaret Mack was the daughter of Jacob and Hannah (Englehart) Mack,[16] and great-granddaughter of Alexander Mack (1679-1735) founder of the Church of the Brethren in America (or "Dunkards").[17] Margaret Mack was born 1 May 1756,[18] probably in Cumberland (now Franklin) County, Pennsylvania.

Daniel first appeared in Franklin County tax lists of 1787, and thereafter in all extant subsequent tax lists up through 1807, when his entry bears the suffix of "gone."[19] In 1790, the first Federal Census recorded him as the head of a household with two males under sixteen, and two females.[20] Listed five entries above Daniel's was Jacob "Mock," whom research shows was Daniel's father-in-law. Daniel

---

[16] Jacob Mack will, 11 July 1811 (recorded 30 March 1814), Franklin County, Pennsylvania, Will Book C: 176. Also see "Deed of Sale from the Executors of Jacob Mock [viz. Samuel Royer and John Benedict] to Samuel Needy," 2 April 1835 (recorded 14 January 1836), Franklin County, Pennsylvania, Deed Book 17: 34 ("...whereas Margaret Truby daughter of said Jacob Mock dec'd...").

[17] Rev. Freeman Ankrum, A.B., *Alexander Mack the Tunker and Descendants* (Scottdale, Pa.: Herald Press, 1943), 1, 6, 75.

[18] Ankrum, *Alexander Mack*, 56. Note, however, that Margaret's spouse is listed here incorrectly (i.e., as her brother-in-law John Miller instead of Daniel Trubey).

[19] "Tax and Exoneration Returns," 1787, 1788, 1789, Franklin County, Washington Township, Record Group 4, roll 223; "County Levies, Assessor's Duplications and Returns," 1794, 1796, 1797, 1798, 1799, 1801, 1806, 1807, Franklin County, Washington Township, Manuscript Group 4, rolls 58 and 59; "Septennial Census Returns," 1786 (Daniel not listed in 1786; 1793 return does not survive), 1800, 1807 (Daniel not listed) Franklin County, Washington Township, Record Group 7, roll 243; Pennsylvania State Archives, Harrisburg, Pennsylvania.

[20] 1790 U.S. census, Franklin County, Pennsylvania, p. 273; National Archives micropublication M637, roll 9.

GENERATION ONE - THE "HESSIAN"

Trubey does not appear as an owner, possessor, or occupier of the types of real property specified in the U.S. Direct Tax of 1798.[21]

"Septennial Census Returns" dated 1800 for Washington Township, Franklin County, list Daniel "Truby," but without occupation.[22] In the 1800 Federal Census, Daniel Trubey was enumerated immediately following Jacob "Mack."[23] Daniel's household then contained two males under 10, one male 10-16, a female 10-16, another female 26-45, and Daniel is assumed to have been the male over 45. Analysis of these 1790 and 1800 Federal Census entries suggests that one of the males who was under sixteen in 1790 was missing in 1800, and that two additional males had been born since 1790. However, evidence supports a total of four surviving children only, and it may be that Daniel's son Jacob, born in December 1789, was misconstrued as "under ten" in 1800.

No sample of Daniel's actual signature or mark has been located, nor even a clerk's interpretation thereof (e.g., as transcribed into county record books as a witness to a neighbor's deed or kinsman's will), so it is not known whether Daniel could write nor how he spelled his surname.

---

[21] Tax Lists for the State of Pennsylvania, U.S. Direct Tax of 1798, Records of the Internal Revenue Service (Record Group 58), National Archives micropublication M372, roll 18: Sixth Direct Tax Division, Volumes 550-616, Fourth Assessment District (Franklin County), Washington Township, Volumes 611-615: Particular Lists A, B, E, Lists No. 1 and 2, and single page of sales.

[22] "Septennial Census Returns," 1800, Washington Twp., entry #352, Franklin County (1786-1821), Pennsylvania; Record Group 7, microfilm roll 243; Pennsylvania State Archives, Harrisburg, Pennsylvania. Relatively few persons on this return have occupations listed for them.

[23] 1800 U.S. census, Franklin County, Pennsylvania, Washington Twp., p. 32; National Archives micropublication M32, roll 38.

DANIEL TRUBEY OF FRANKLIN COUNTY, PENNSYLVANIA

Daniel died intestate before 21 February 1807 in Franklin County, Pennsylvania.[24] No guardianship records are on file there although all of his children were under 21 when he died, suggesting Daniel did not own property of sufficient value to warrant protection by a guardian.

On the twenty first February 1807. Letters of Administration in common form were granted unto Michael Miller, of the estate of Daniel Truby late of Franklin County yeoman deceased.[25]

Franklin County, Pennsylvania
No. 879 - Inventory of the Estate of Daniel Trubee dec^d
Filed 8th August 1808
An Appraisement of the Estate of Daniel Truby Deceased

An Inventory of the goods and *chatels* belonging to the Estate of Daniel Truby Deceased of Washington township Franklin County Appraised by the under subscribers February 27th 1807

	$	cents
1 Black horse	60	0
1 Black mare	40	0
1 Gray horse	15	0
1 Old Brindled cow	11	0
1 dito dito dito with some white	9	0

---

[24] Franklin Co., Pennsylvania, Will Book B: 315. Franklin County Chapter DAR's *Franklin County Wills and Administrations* (1959), claims that Will Book B, page 315, also states the following: "Margaret N. Truby, widow, renounces her right to administer on the estate of her husband, February 12, 1807, and letters of administration on the estate of Daniel Truby were granted unto Michael Miller, February 21, 1807. Sureties: Philip Reed and Frederick Foreman," but those words are not recorded there. That DAR Chapter and the Kittochinny History Society were both contacted for assistance in locating this document, and the correct citation to it, but no such record was found. It is not among the loose probate records for Daniel Truby's estate #879 as microfilmed by the Family History Library (FHL microfilm 1465876).

[25] *Ibid.*

Generation One - The "Hessian"

1 cow with calf	10	0
1 small Brindled cow	8	0
1 Brindled hieffer	6	0
1 Black hieffer	5	0
1 Red hieffer	4	0
9 Sheep	18	0
Horse geers and Bridles	5	0
2 Ploughs and 1 Shovel plough	4	0
1 windmill	5	0
Old Iron	0	50
1 Old cuting box	0	25
1 dung hook and fork and pitch fork	1	25
15 Bundles of flax	1	0
1 dung fork and pitch fork and 2 rakes	1	0
7 Geese	2	0
9 Hogs	18	0
1 wagon and bed and longe laders	16	0
1 old sled and hogshead	1	25
3 New Bags and 3 old ones	4	0
1 Old sadle	1	50
1 old cradle and sythe	1	0
1 old Shot gun	3	0
Pewter ware	2	0
	252	75
Earthen ware	1	0
1 kitchen dresser	6	0
1 pair Stilliards	1	0
5 Split Bottomed Chairs	1	25
1 Walnut Table	2	0
1 Old chest	1	50
1 Looking Glass	--	25
1 Stove and pipe	11	0
1 Bed and Bedstead	15	0
1 Blue Be[d]stead and Bed	14	0
1 dito dito	8	0
2 spining wheels and check Reel	2	--
1 Dutch oven and pot and frying pan	1	50
1 Doughtry and three buckets	1	0
oats at 40 cents per bushel	6	60
370 lb of meat at 9 cents per lb	33	30
7½ bushel of wheat at 1 Dollar per bushel	7	50
15 Bushels of Rye at 73 cents per bushel	10	95
95 lb of hemp at 6 cents per lb	5	70

DANIEL TRUBEY OF FRANKLIN COUNTY, PENNSYLVANIA

1 Large washingtub	1	0
2 old cider barrels	1	0
1 old churn	0	25
8¼ bushels potatoes at 40 cents per bushel	3	30
1 meat tub and cabage tub and sausage bentch	1	0
8 Earthen crocks	0	30
1 Grind Stone	0	12
wheat in the ground 7$ per acre	25	83
Rye in the ground 5$ and 50 cents per acre	33	70
1 axe mall and wedg an Drawing knife	0	75
6½ bushels of corn at 53 cents per bushel	3	44 ½
3 cow chains	0	50
1 flaxbrake	0	50
1 half Bushel	0	50
1 Harrow	1	0
	$203	07 ½

Franklin County §

Personaly came before me one the subscriber one of the justices of the peace in and for said county John Weynant Philip Read and being *Duely* Sworn Deposeth and saith that the within Inventory of the goods and Chattels of the Estate of Daniel Truby late of Washington Deceased is a just and true valuation according to the best of their knowledge sworn and Subscribed this twenty second Day of August 1807 before me

            Wm Bleakney
            John Weyant
            Philip Reed

Amt of Inventory	1st page	$252	75	
	2nd ditto	203	07	½
	Total	$455	82	½

A *vandue* list of the Estate of Daniel Truby Deceased of Washington Township Franklin County, February the 28th 1806 [?]

Names		Chatels	
Jasper Hinkel		1 old Barrel with *Hundred*	0.16
David Stoner		1 mall and wedge and Drawing knife	0.95
Philip Reed		2 Bags	1.63
John Stamy		2 Dito	1.50
Jacob Bettis Jr.	Note	2 Do	1.75

Generation One - The "Hessian"

Michael Miller	1 axe	0.30
dito dito	1 ?? lambs	0.20
John Mann	5 cow chaines	1.00
Gasper Hinkel	1 old Sadle	3.00
Philip Reed	1 cradle and sythe	1.65
John Bornes	1 large washing tub	0.50
dito dito	1 meat tub	0.60
Samuel Royer Jr.	1 cabage tub	0.66
Lewis Steward	1 sausage *bentch*	0.05
Michael *Dawalt*	1 Barrel of vinegar	1.00
Dito Dito	1 Barrel Dito	0.50
John Welsh	8 1/2 bushels potatoes at 56 pr bush.	4.62
Frances Shober	1 old Barrel and *clear*	0.78
Lewis Steward	1 big wheel	0.17
David Snoberger	1 old plough	0.55
John Stamy	1 shovel plough	2.00
Jacob Peter	1 plough	2.45
David Truby	2 Rakes	0.34
Philip Holinger	1 Dung fork	0.62
Jacob Shockey	1 dito and Hook	1.41
Samuel Royer Jr.	1 hay fork	0.60
John Mann	1 dito	0.61
John Bourns	1 Cuting Box	1.00
Jacob Bettis Senr.	1 horse giers	1.90
John Welty	1 Dito	0.52
David Snoberger	1 dito	0.80
Jacob Bercedoll	2 Collars	0.51
		37.98
Samuel Royer jr.	1 Collar	0.80
Jacob Shockey	1 Dito and hems	1.50
David Snoberger	1 windmill	4.51
Samuel Royer jr.	1 halter	0.20
John Weyant	15 Bundles of flax	1.51
Elias Horn	1 harrow	1.56
Samuel Royer jr.	1 wagon and bed	20.00
John Walter	95 lb of hemp at 9½ cents pr lb	9.02½
John Bourns	7 ½ bushels of wheat at 1$15 cents	8.62
Dito Dito	15 Dito of Rye at 82 cents pr bush.	12.30

John Cochran	16 ½ Dito of oats at	
	54 cents pr bush.	8.75
Widow	1 old Brindle cow	12.25
John Welty	1 cow 2d choice	13.50
Jacob Bettis Jr.	1 Dito 3d choice	12.01
John Walter	2 hiefers	17.00
John Stamay	1 Red hiefer	5.50
Jasper Hinkel	2 hogs first choice	8.05
Jacob Bercedoll	2 Dito 2d choice	5.65
Philip Reed	2 Dito 3d choice	3.79
Widow	2 Dito 4th choice	2.00
Philip Reed	1 Dito 5th choice	1.00
John Stamay	2 sheep first choice	6.16
Dito	2 Dito 2d choice	6.00
Dito	5 Dito 3d choice	7.60
John Welsh	7 gees	2.79
Gasper Hinkel	1 gray horse	15.00
John Stamay	1 Black mare	42.00
Samuel Royer jr.	1 Black Horse	98.00
John Bourns	6 ½ Bushels of Corn at	
	67 cents pr bush.	4.35½
Vallentine Glass	1 Bed and bedstead	18.06
Widow	1 Bed and Be[d]stead	8.90
Michael Davault	19 lb of Bacon at	
	10 cents pr lb.	1.90
Dito Dito	22 ½ lb Dito at	
	14 cents pr lb.	3.15
Dito Dito	29 ½ lb Dito at	
	16 cents pr lb.	4.72
Henry Krabs	23 ½ lb Dito at 15 cents pr lb.	3.52
Dito Dito	25 ¾ lb Dito at 17 cents pr lb.	4.37
Michael Davault	20 lb Dito at 14 cents pr lb.	2.80
Henry Krabs	28 lb Dito at 15 cents pr lb.	4.20
		381.54
Henry Krabs	24 lb bacon at 13 cents pr lb.	3.12
Francis Shober	21 ½ lb Dito at	
	11½ cents pr lb.	2.47
George Fields	24 ½ lb Dito at 13 cents per lb.	3.18
John Welsh	30 lb Dito at 10 cents pr lb.	3.00
Dito Dito	25 lb. Dito at 9 cents pr lb.	2.25
Francis Shober	18 lb. Dito at 8½ cents pr lb.	1.53
Michael Davault	25 ¼ lb Dito at 8 cents pr lb.	2.02
John Welsh	34 lb. Dito at 9 cents pr lb.	3.06

GENERATION ONE - THE "HESSIAN"

Jacob Bercdoll	1 pair of Stilliards	1.05
Michael Reed	1 acr 12.½ per of wheat at	
	8$26 cents pr acr	10.35½
Gasper Hinkel	2 acr 12.30 per Dito at	
	8$30 cents pr acr	22.30
Dito Dito	2 lot of meat	0.50
David Stoner	2 acr and 1 perch of Rye at	
	7$ 1 cent per acr	14.08
Dito Dito	4 acres and 25 perches at	
	6$ 50 cents	27.01
Jacob Peter	6 sickels	0.2[ ]
John Stamy	1 half Bushel	0.[ ]
Jacob Shroyer	1 grindstone	0.34
		97.05
		37.98
		381.54
	Amount of vendue bill	516.57
	Amt retained by widow	
	at appraisement	53.80
		570.37
	Amount of Inventory	455.82
	Advance in Sales	114.55[26]

At an Orphans Court held at Chambersburg for Franklin County on the thirteenth day of September the year one thousand eight hundred and eight before James McDowell & James McCalmont Esquires Judges of our said court &c

The court took into consideration...the account of Michael Miller admr. of the estate of Daniel *Truble* decd. and approved thereof a ballance of four hundred & ninety seven dollars & 27½/100 appearing in the hand of said accountant.[27]

---

[26] "Vendue Paper of the Estate of David Trubee deceased, filed 8th February 1808," estate #879, Franklin County, Pennsylvania, Register of Wills, Estate Papers, 1807-1811, #874-#972; FHL microfilm 1465876.

[27] Orphans Court Docket, Volume A (1785-1813), 246; Franklin County, Pennsylvania; FHL microfilm 0323837.

No. 879
Administration account of the Estate of Daniel Trubee deceased Examined & approved 14 Sept 1808 by the Orphans court Ballance $497.27 E.C.

The account of Michael Miller Administrator of all & Singular, the goods and chattels, rights, and credits, which were of Daniel Trubee, late of Franklin County yeoman deceased.

The said accountant, chargeth himself with all and singular the goods and chattels, rights, & credits, which were of the said deceased as Dr. Inventory and appraisement filed in the Register's Office at Chambersburg,

amounting to	$455	82 ½
Also with the advances in sales	114	55
Cash received of Valentine Glass	- -	44
" received of Philip Reed	3	44
	$574	25 ½

The said accountant prays an allowance for the following payments and disbursements, to wit

	By cash paid Register for Letters of Administration	2	0
1.	By cash paid Daniel Royer Pr rec^t & account	- -	99
2.	By cash paid John Black do do	- -	42
3.	By cash paid John Royer funeral expenses Pr rec^t	2	40
4.	By cash paid Peter Stephens proven acct do	2	23
5.	By cash paid John Snowberger do do	6	13
6.	By cash paid John Coughran do do	4	13
7.	By cash paid John Wentling do do	4	20
8.	By cash paid William Miner for crying Vend. do	3	- -
9.	By cash paid Abraham Stoner proven acct & do	6	50
10.	By cash paid David Mentzer do do	2	65
11.	By cash paid D[r?] John Ollig do do	3	53
12.	By cash paid Philip Reed Pr rec^t for coffin, appraising & Clerk at Vendue	8	0
13.	By cash paid Henry Peges Pr rec^t	2	0
	By Register's fees in this account copy & Ca	3	5
	By Clerk's fees in the orphans court	1	95
	By an allowance to accountant	20	0
14.	By cash paid funeral expences per acct	3	80
		$76	98
	Ballance	497	27 ½
		574	25 ½

GENERATION ONE - THE "HESSIAN"   11

I certify that I have examined this account, exhibited by Michael Miller affirmed to the truth thereof, and also that the same has been duly filed & advertised for Settlement at the orphans court 13 Sep. 1808.   Edw Crawford Reg[r]

The widowed Margaret (Mack) Trubey continued to reside in Washington Township, Franklin County, Pennsylvania, where her father Jacob Mack devised a portion of his land to her by his will, dated 11 July 1811.[28] Tax records show Margaret was assessed on 60 acres of land in Washington Township from 1817 through 1821, after which the acreage was assessed to "Trubey's hears" [heirs]; this entry was followed by assessments for Jacob, David and Daniel Trubey.[29]

Daniel and Margaret (Mack) Trubey are likely buried in unmarked graves in the Mack cemetery in Washington Township, as Daniel did not own land, and other Mack daughters are interred there. An 1835 Franklin County deed identifies one child, Daniel, as the son of Margaret (Mack) Trubey.[30] No direct, primary source proof of parentage for Daniel and Margaret's other three children was located by this researcher, however, the fact that there was no other Trubey in this area after 1782 tends to add credence to the assertion that the following children were theirs.

---

[28] Franklin County Will Book C: 176.

[29] "County Levies, Assessor's Duplications and Returns," Washington Township, alphabetical listing [n.p.], Franklin County, Pennsylvania; Manuscript Group 4 (microfilm), Pennsylvania State Archives, Harrisburg, Pennsylvania. The lists for 1815 and 1816 are not filmed.

[30] "Deed of Sale from the Executors of Jacob Mock [viz. Samuel Royer and John Benedict] to Samuel Needy," 2 April 1835 (recorded 14 January 1836), Franklin County, Pennsylvania, Deed Book 17: 34.

The children of Daniel[1] Trubey and Margaret Mack:
+ 2. i. NANCY[2] TRUBEY, born 3 March 1786; m. Christian Welty
+ 3. ii. DAVID TRUBEY, born circa 1788; m. Catherine Motter/Mautter
+ 4. iii. JACOB TRUBEY, born 25 December 1789; m. Mary Welty
+ 5. iv. DANIEL TRUBEY, born 8 August 1793 or 1795; m. Mary Stoner

Generation Two 13

2. **Nancy**[2] **Trubey** (Daniel[1]) was born 3 March 1786[31] in either Maryland[32] or Pennsylvania.[33] A license for her marriage to **Christian Welty** was issued in Washington County, Maryland, on 29 January 1814[34] to the Rev. Henrich Jonathan Rahauser, who ministered to several German Reformed churches in the Pennsylvania/Maryland border area.[35]

Christian Welty, born 22 March 1788[36] in this border area, was the son of Jacob Welty who died intestate during October 1834 in Washington County, Maryland.[37]

---

[31] Dorothy Summer, compiler, editor, "Massillon Cemetery," *Stark County, Ohio, Cemetery Records*, sponsored by the Stark County Historical Society, 3 (typescript, 1955), 904. Birthdate calculated from age at death [hereinafter "calculated"].

[32] 1850 U.S. census, Stark County, Ohio, population schedule, Pike Twp, Dist. 138, p. 196/391; National Archives micropublication M432, roll 731.

[33] 1880 Census records of her children; citations given where applicable.

[34] "Index to Washington County Marriage Licenses," MdHR 50148-1, Maryland Hall of Records, Annapolis, Maryland.

[35] Frank and Rachael Schwartz, *Old Zion, A History of the First German Reformed Church in Hagerstown [Maryland] 1770-1970* (Chambersburg, Pa.: Craft Press, 1970), 63-64.

[36] Sommer, *Stark County Cemeteries*, 3: 904. Calculated.

[37] "Petition of Abraham Row, Administrator of the Estate of Jacob Welty," 12 August 1835, Franklin County, Pennsylvania, Orphans' Court Book C: 400. Also "Petition of John Welty to divide estate of Jacob Welty," 1839, Franklin County, Pennsylvania, Orphans' Court Book D: 214 and 229. The latter petition to divide Jacob Welty's land in Franklin County, Pennsylvania, was filed there in 1839 by Jacob's eldest son John, who listed the names of Jacob's

According to their son Jacob,[38] Christian and Nancy Welty and their four children left Franklin County, Pennsylvania, in 1835, settling in Pike Township, Stark County, Ohio. Two land ownership maps of this township[39] show that Christian Welty owned the Northwest ¼, Section 20, Township 9 North, Range 8 West, in the Ohio River Survey. Christian Welty was as "farmer" as late as 1860 and 1870.[40] Nancy died 30 June 1860[41] of "dropsy."[42] Christian died of "old age" in Pike Township on 26 December 1875,[43] and his last will and

---

children then living, including "Christian Welty of Starke [sic] Co., Ohio" (and "Mary Truby of Starke [sic] Co., Ohio," who is the spouse of Trubey descendant #4 Jacob² Trubey).

[38] William Henry Perrin, *History of Stark County, with an Outline Sketch of Ohio* (Chicago: Baskin & Battey, 1881), 643-644.

[39] "Land Ownership Map #677," Stark County, Ohio, 185?, published by Williams, Dorr & Co.; Geography and Map Division, Library of Congress, Washington, D.C. L. H. Everts & Co., *Combination Atlas Map of Stark County, Ohio* (Philadelphia: Everts & Co., 1875), 70.

[40] 1860 U.S. census, Stark County, Ohio, pop. sched., Pike Twp., P. O. Canton, p. 14/430; National Archives micropublication M653, roll 1038. 1870 U.S. census, Stark County, pop. sched., Pike Twp., P. O. Pierce, p. 5/542; National Archives micropublication M593, roll 1269. See also Appendix B letter #2.

[41] Sommer, *Stark County Cemeteries*, 3: 904.

[42] 1860 U.S. census, Stark County, Ohio (mortality schedule), Pike Twp., p. 1, line 3; National Archives micropublication T1159, roll 30.

[43] Stark County Chapter Ohio Genealogical Society, *Stark County, Ohio[,] Death Records* (N.p.: by the Society, 1991), 520-521 which cites original as Volume 1:176. Christian's birthplace is recorded here as "Pennsylvania." This death date is also supported

GENERATION TWO 15

testament identifies his four children.[44] The descendants of Nancy (Trubey) Welty are not presented in the Trubey manuscript.

The children of Nancy[2] Trubey and Christian Welty:
+ 6. i. JACOB T.[3] WELTY, born November 1815; m. Phianna Klinker
+ 7. ii. JOHN WELTY, born circa 1820; m. Mary Jane McWhinney
+ 8. iii. MARY ANN WELTY, born circa 1827; m. Francis P. Mills
+ 9. iv. ABRAHAM WELTY, born 10 June 1829; m. Mary Richards

3. **David[2] Trubey** (Daniel[1]) was born circa 1788,[45] probably in Franklin County, Pennsylvania. He married **Catherine Motter/ Mautter** by virtue of a license issued to Rev. Rahauser on 26 February 1814 in Washington County, Maryland.[46] The parentage of Catherine

---

by his tombstone inscription as transcribed by Sommer in *Stark County Cemeteries*, 3: 904.

[44] Christian Welty will, 11 March 1871 (recorded 4 January 1876), Stark County, Will Book B: 167-168, Office of Probate Judge, Canton, Ohio. Photocopy in possession of compiler.

[45] 1850 U.S. census, Tuscarawas County, Ohio, pop. sched., Auburn Twp., p. 26/5; National Archives micropublication M432, roll 734. 1860 U.S. census, Tuscarawas County, Ohio, pop. sched., Union Twp., p. 49/822; National Archives micropublication M653, roll 1042.

[46] "Index to Washington County Marriage Licenses," MdHR 50148-1, Maryland Hall of Records, Annapolis, Maryland.

Motter, born circa 1788-1789 in Maryland or Pennsylvania,[47] has not been determined.[48]

David first appears in the tax lists of Washington Township, Franklin County, Pennsylvania, in 1811 along with his brother Jacob and mother, who was listed as "Widow Truby". He is taxed again in 1812 but does not reappear until 1822, and his 1823 entry reads "David Trubey, laborer, gone."[49]

David Trubey and his family resided in Bethlehem Township, Stark County, Ohio, in 1830, and in Tuscarawas County, Ohio, in 1840 and 1850.[50] Sometime before 1860, David and Catherine removed to Union Township, Wells County, Indiana,[51] where they purchased land. David, also a farmer, did not leave a will, but the last deed recorded for him in Wells County reveals how he and his wife disposed of their property:

---

[47] 1850 U.S. census, Tuscarawas County, Ohio, Auburn Twp., p. 26/5, and 1860 U.S. census, Tuscarawas County, Ohio, Union Twp., p. 49/822.

[48] This Catherine is *not* the daughter of NSDAR-recognized Maryland private George Mattern (ca 1735 - March 1810) whose Franklin Twp., Huntingdon Co., Pa., will mentions a daughter "Cathrine Truby." David Trubey had not married Catherine Motter/Mautter by the date George Mattern wrote his will. George's daughter "Cathrine" married Andrew[3] Truby (Jacob[2], Christopher[1]), according to Mary Truby Graff's *Early History of Truby-Graff and Affiliated Families* (1941), 67.

[49] "County Levies," Harrisburg, Pennsylvania. No returns survive for 1808-1810.

[50] 1830 U.S. census, Stark County, Ohio, Bethlehem Twp., p. 333; National Archives micropublication M19, roll 140. 1840 U.S. census, Tuscarawas County, Ohio, Lawrence Twp., p. 317; National Archives micropublication M704, roll 430. 1850 census, Tuscarawas County, Ohio, Auburn Twp., p. 26.

[51] 1860 U.S. census, Wells County, Indiana, pop. sched., Union Twp., p. 49/822; National Archives micropublication M653, roll 309.

GENERATION TWO 17

By this deed, we David Truby and Catharine Truby his wife of Wells County in the state of Indiana convey and warrant to Catharine Trimble of Wells county in the state of Indiana for the sum of Six Hundred Dollars (for the payment she undertakes to keep them decently) the following Real Estate in Wells County in the State of Indiana to wit:
The North West quarter of the North West quarter of Section Twenty Eight (28) Township Twenty Eight (28) North of Range Eleven (11) East in the lands subject to sale at Fort Wayne Indiana containing forty acres more or less.
In witness whereof the said David Truby & Catharine Truby his wife have hereunto set their hands and seals this thirtieth day of January A.D. 1860.

David Truby (seal)
Catharine (+ her mark) Truby[52]

David died 11 April 1863, and Catherine died 18 August 1863; both were interred in the Zanesville Cemetery in Union Township, Wells County, Indiana.[53]

The children of David[2] Trubey and Catherine Motter:
+ 10. i. JACOB ANDREW[3] TRUBEY, born "22 November 1814;" m. Mary Ann Taylor
+ 11. ii. SUSANNAH TRUBEY, born circa 1819; m. John Arbaugh
+ 12. iii. MARY CATHERINE TRUBEY, born 12 August 1822; m. John Trimble
+ 13. iv. DAVID M. TRUBEY, born circa 1822-1826; m. (1) Mary Smutz, and (2) Anna M. Swihart

---

[52] "Deed of Sale from David and Catherine Truby to Catharine Trimble," 30 January 1860 (recorded 30 January 1860), Wells County Deed Book K: 414, Bluffton, Indiana. Photocopy in possession of the compiler.

[53] Ingabee Brineman Minniear, comp., "Zanesville Cemetery," *Wells County, Indiana, Cemetery Records*, 4 (typescript: Ft. Wayne Public Library, 1972), n.p.

4. Jacob² Trubey (Daniel¹) was born 25 December 1789,[54] probably in Washington Township, Franklin County, Pennsylvania. Like his brother and sister before him, Jacob was married in Washington County, Maryland. On 8 November 1817, a marriage license was issued for Jacob Trubey and **Mary Welty**, daughter of Jacob Welty.[55] She was born 2 February 1801[56] in Pennsylvania. The Rev. Kurtz performed the ceremony on 8 November 1817 at St. John's Evangelical Lutheran Church in Hagerstown.[57]

Franklin County, Pennsylvania, tax lists and the statements of his son in a county history concur that Jacob Trubey and his family left Pennsylvania in 1823, and settled in Sugar Creek Township, Stark County, Ohio,[58] the date set forth in the Trubey manuscript:

> Jacob Trubey emigrated from his native state of Pennsylvania to Stark County, Ohio[,] in 1823, taking up his abode on the farm in Sugar Creek Township, Ohio, which was later owned by his son Jacob M.

---

[54] Perrin, *Stark County*, 970; Sommer, *Stark County Cemeteries*, 3: 899.

[55] "Index to Washington County Marriage Licenses," MdHR 50148-1, Maryland Hall of Records, Annapolis, Maryland. Mary's parentage proven by "Petition of John Welty to divide estate of Jacob Welty," 1839, Franklin County, Pennsylvania, Orphans' Court Book D: 214 and 229. This petition sought to divide Jacob Welty's land in Franklin County, Pennsylvania, and was filed there in 1839 by Jacob's eldest son John, who listed the names of Jacob's children then living, including "Mary Truby of Starke [sic] Co., Ohio" (and "Christian Welty of Starke [sic] Co., Ohio," who is the spouse of Trubey descendant #2 Nancy² Trubey).

[56] Perrin, *Stark County*, 970.

[57] Maryland Daughters of the American Revolution, Genealogical Records Committee [hereinafter DAR GRC] *Records of St. John's Evangelical Church of Hagerstown, Washington County, Maryland*, 1 (typescript, 1935), 107: Jacob Druby & Mary Weltz.

[58] "County Levies;" Perrin, *Stark County*, 970.

Trubey. The land was partially cleared at the time it came into his possession, and a hewed log house was on the place into which they resided until a more substantial structure could be erected. He only lived about twelve years after his advent into this Stark County, dying at the early age of about forty five years, on March 1st, 1835. He was a very prominent man in his township, holding the office of Justice of Peace, and had so long been numbered among its leading citizens, that the news of his death came as a personal calamity to his many acquaintances. At his death he left his wife, and three children, viz., Nancy, Jacob M. and Samuel. Mary Welty Trubey, his wife, died September 13th, 1851 [*sic*].[59]

Documentary evidence supports Jacob's death date as 1 March 1835.[60] The cause of his death is unknown; however, among the claims against Jacob's estate is Dr. Alfred Heacock's bill. Apparently, Jacob's final illness began at the end of January. From the 27th until his death, the following procedures and medications were administered: bleeding, catharic, aperients, diaphoretics, chologogues, epispastics, tonics and rubefacients.

One month after Jacob's death, his infant daughter Ida Martha died.[61] On 9 November 1836, more than a year after Jacob's death, Charles Slutz was appointed guardian of Jacob and Mary's two minor

---

[59] Trubey manuscript, 21.

[60] Perrin, *Stark County*, 970; Sommer, *Stark County Cemeteries*, 3: 899; "Estate records of Jacob Truby," April 1835-July 1837, Stark County Probate Judge, Case #594 (inventory, claims, receipts, final account), Canton, Ohio. Photocopies (50 pages) in possession of compiler.

[61] Sommer, *Stark County Cemeteries*, 3: 899. The inscription "daughter of J & M Truby" is the *only* evidence that Ida Martha belonged to this family.

sons, Jacob and Samuel.[62] Their daughter Nancy had married in 1835, and was not mentioned in these records.[63]

The widow Mary (Welty) Trubey, was remarried on 24 August 1845 to James Thornsbury in Stark County.[64] Their 1850 Census entry suggests he was a widower with at least two children before he married Mary. There is no indication that any children were born to this second marriage. Mary died 13 September 1854, and was buried in the Massillon Cemetery beside her first husband, Jacob Trubey.[65]

The children of Jacob[2] Trubey and Mary Welty:

+   14.   i.   NANCY[3] TRUBEY, born circa 1818; m. Lewis May
+   15.   ii.   JACOB M. TRUBEY, born 7 May 1820; m. (1) Eliza Swan, (2) Elizabeth Pherson
+   16.   iii. SAMUEL J. TRUBEY, born 9 November 1822; m. Mary Groner
      17.   iv. IDA MARTHA TRUBEY, d. 12 April 1835 at age 1 year, 10 months, 10 days.

---

[62] "Appointment of Charles Slutz as Guardian to Jacob Truby and Samuel J. Truby," 9 November 1836, Docket A: 150, Stark County, Ohio. Abstract by Stark County District Library volunteer, Canton, Ohio, in possession of compiler.

[63] Perrin, *Stark County*, 970.

[64] Ohio DAR GRC, *Marriage Records of Stark County, Ohio, 1808-1865*, 3 (typescript, 1936): "Book B, p. 120." Also 1850 U.S. census, Stark County, Ohio, pop. sched., Sugar Creek Twp., p. 153; National Archives micropublication M432, roll 731.

[65] Sommer, *Stark County Cemeteries*, 3: 899.

GENERATION TWO 21

5. **Daniel² Trubey** (Daniel¹) was born 8 August 1793[66] or 1795[67] in Washington Township, Franklin County, Pennsylvania. He married his first cousin **Mary ("Polly") Stoner**, daughter of David and Maria (Mack) Stoner,[68] born 25 March 1799.[69] Washington County, Maryland, issued a license for this marriage to Rev. Rahauser on 11 June 1817.[70] Although his brothers left for Ohio in 1823, Daniel remained in Washington Township, Franklin County, Pennsylvania, another 10 years before following their lead.[71]

---

[66] Daniel Trubey tombstone, Independence Cemetery, Richland Township, Defiance County, Ohio; calculated. Photograph in possession of compiler.

[67] Family data, Daniel Trubey Family Bible (photostatic copy of two pages of birth records only), File Case folder labeled "Stoner, Abraham, b. 1745, d. 1824, PA," Library Office, NSDAR, Washington, D.C. "Family Record of Daniel Trubey," District of Columbia DAR GRC Report, 249 (typescript, 1954-1955), 163; this is a partial transcription of the Bible photostat, but contains errors. The GRC transcription includes the statement that the Bible was then in the possession of Mary (Altimus) Trubey of Long Island, Kansas. Its whereabouts were unknown to her children in 1985.

[68] Ankrum, *Alexander Mack*, 75, 77. Also "Petition of Daniel Truby to divide estate of David Stoner," not dated (recorded 9 April 1827), Franklin County Orphans' Court, Volume C: 112, Chambersburg, Pennsylvania.

[69] Mary Trubey tombstone, Silver Creek Cemetery, Richardson County, Nebraska; calculated. Transcript provided by Lydia Bruun Woods Memorial Library, Falls City, Nebraska.

[70] "Index to Washington County Marriage Licenses," MdHR 50148-1, Maryland Hall of Records, Annapolis, Maryland.

[71] "County Levies," Harrisburg, Pennsylvania.

On 30 October 1834, Daniel and Polly Trubey mortgaged a tract of land in Sugar Creek Township, Stark County, Ohio.[72] Here Daniel earned a reputation as one of the county's eminent bear hunters, and, "on one occasion, killed four bears in almost as many minutes."[73]

Sometime before 1848, Daniel and his family removed to Huntington County, Indiana. John Trubey, presumably Daniel's second son, entered 80 acres (S½, NE¼, Section 2, Township 27, Range 8) in Huntington County on 17 February 1848.[74] On 10 May 1848, John sold this land to (his father) Daniel Trubey, "of Huntington County, Indiana."[75] Ultimately, Daniel and Mary Trubey sold this parcel on

---

[72] "Mortgage from Henry Hess to Daniel Truby," 30 October 1834 (recorded 23 March 1836), Stark County Deed Book O: 385-386, County Recorder's Office, Canton, Ohio: north part of southeast ¼, Section 26, Township 11 North, Range 10 West. Photocopy in possession of compiler.

[73] William Henry Perrin, *History of Stark County, with an Outline Sketch of Ohio* (Chicago: Baskin & Battey, 1881), 524-525.

[74] Land Entry Book, p. 76, Huntington County, Indiana, and "Patent of John Trubey, 1 May 1849," (recorded 24 June 1862) Huntington County Deed Book Q: 284, Huntington, Indiana. Photocopies in possession of compiler.

[75] "Deed of Sale from John Trubey to Daniel Trubey *of Huntington County*," 10 May 1848 (recorded 24 June 1862), Huntington County Deed Book Q: 285, Huntington, Indiana. Photocopy in possession of compiler.

GENERATION TWO 23

15 November 1873 to a John Stouder;[76] the debt still owed by Stouder on this land appeared in Daniel and Mary Trubey's probate records.[77] Daniel Trubey was not located in the 1850 Census of Huntington County, Indiana; Stark County, Ohio; or Wyandot County, Ohio.[78] The only Trubey listed in the 1850 Agricultural Census of Huntington County, Indiana, was "Abram Truby"[79] (with 80 acres), which is more likely an error than a reference to Daniel's youngest son [#26] who was then just shy of 15 years old.

The 1860 Census of Huntington County confirms that Daniel Trubey owned property, then worth $1,500.[80] Barevias Trubey related

---

[76] "Deed of Trust from Daniel and Mary Truby to John Stouder," 15 November 1873 (recording date not given), Huntington County Deed Book and page were not indicated on the photocopy provided by the County Recorder, Huntington, Indiana..

[77] "Probate Records of Daniel Trubey, dec'd, and Mary Trubey, dec'd," 29 March 1876 - 3 February 1879, Defiance County Probate Case "TR 4 (Old)," Court of Common Pleas, Probate and Juvenile Divisions, Defiance, Ohio. Thirteen photocopied pages in possession of compiler.

[78] "Power of Attorney of Mary Truby, wife of Daniel Truby *of Wyandot County, Ohio*, to Jacob M. Truby [her nephew] of Stark County, Ohio," sworn 11 February 1857 in Stark County, Ohio (recorded 16 February 1857), Franklin County Deed Book 32: 353 ("...all my right and interest in the estate of my aunt Rebecca Stoner, late of Franklin County, Pa."), Chambersburg, Pennsylvania.

[79] 1850 U.S. census, Huntington Co., Indiana, agricultural schedule, Archives Division, Indiana Commission of Public Records, Indianapolis, Indiana. No volume or page citation furnished by the ICPR Archives Division supervisor in her typed abstract, sent to the compiler 6 December 1984.

[80] 1860 U.S. census, Huntington County, Indiana, pop. sched., Polk Twp., P. O. Antioch, p. 93; National Archives micropublication M653, roll 267.

in his manuscript that his grandfather Daniel remained in Huntington County, Indiana, until 1866,

> when he and grandmother came to live in one of our houses on the John Trubey farm in Defiance Co., Ohio, and lived there until after grandmother had a stroke in the fall of 1874 when they broke up housekeeping and grandfather went to live with his daughter, Mrs. Catharine Carr. Grandmother went to live with another daughter, Mrs. Nancy Yantiss in Nebraska."[81]

Daniel and Mary Trubey last appear together in the 1870 Census in Defiance County, Ohio.[82] Their probate records are recorded in Defiance County, Ohio,[83] even though Mary died and was buried in Richardson County, Nebraska. She died 18 December 1875 and is interred in the Silver Creek Cemetery.[84] Daniel Trubey died 8 October 1875, and is interred in the Independence Cemetery in Richland Township, Defiance County, Ohio.[85] The joint inventory of both estates included one bedstead, 13 yards carpet, 1 trunk, 1 rocking chair, 1 bureau, 1 table, 1 cupboard, 1 stove, 1 feathertick, 1 clock, bedding, and the notes owed by John Stouder.

Final distribution records were not among Daniel and Mary Trubey's probate records, however, Bible records prove the identity and birthdates of their eleven children.[86]

---

[81] Trubey manuscript, 43.

[82] 1870 U.S. census, Defiance County, Ohio, pop. sched., Richland Twp., p. 163; National Archives micropublication M593, roll 1195.

[83] Defiance County probate case TR 4 (Old).

[84] Mary Trubey tombstone, Silver Creek Cemetery, Richardson County, Nebraska.

[85] Daniel Trubey tombstone, Independence Cemetery, Richland Township, Defiance County, Ohio.

[86] Daniel Trubey Family Bible.

GENERATION TWO

The children of Daniel[2] Trubey and Mary Stoner:

+ 18. i. SUSAN[3] TRUBEY, born 1 March 1818; m. (1) Asa Harvey Hunt, (2) Henry McCullick, (3) James Bell
+ 19. ii. DAVID TRUBEY, born 27 November 1819; m. Keziah Klinker
+ 20. iii. JOHN TRUBEY, born 2 October 1821; m. (1) Sarah Jane Dougherty, (2) Jane Morse, (3) Lydia Moore
+ 21. iv. DANIEL TRUBEY, born 7 June 1824; m. Esther Heath
+ 22. v. NANCY TRUBEY, born 4 September 1826; m. Jacob Yantiss
+ 23. vi. REBECCA TRUBEY, born 15 December 1828; m. John Mohn
    24. vii. SAMUEL TRUBEY, born 21 January 1831. By the time of the 1860 Census, Samuel resided in Liberty Township, Henry County, Ohio, where he was employed as a laborer.[87] The next year this Samuel "Truby," age 28, was mustered in for Civil War service on 16 October 1861 in Napoleon, Henry County, Ohio, for three years as a private in Capt. Richards's Company, which became Company A, 68th Regiment Ohio Infantry. A Company Muster Roll and Descriptive Book both show Samuel Truby as a deserter; "Name not borne on sub[sequent?]. rolls." No further information.[88]
+ 25. viii. MARY ANN TRUBEY, born 9 April 1833; m. Andrew Scofield

---

[87] 1860 U.S. census, Henry County, Ohio, pop. sched., Liberty Twp., P. O. Napoleon, p. 75/312; National Archives micropublication M653, roll 985.

[88] Samuel Truby Compiled Service Records (Co. A, 68th Ohio Infantry), card abstracts 21805754, 21805870, and 34181082, Records of Volunteer Union Soldiers Who Served During the Civil War (Record Group 94), National Archives, Washington, D.C. Photocopies in possession of compiler.

+ 26. ix. ABRAHAM TRUBEY, born 20 July 1835[89] in Sugar Creek Township, Stark County, Ohio.[90] No 1850 Census entry for his family could be located in Huntington County, Indiana,[91] but, by 1860, 24-year-old Abraham and his 16-year-old sister Catherine were the last two offspring yet residing with their parents in Polk Township, Huntington County, Indiana.[92] After the Civil War, Abraham apparently followed his sister Nancy (Trubey) Yantiss to Nebraska as in 1870 he was living less than 6 miles from the Yantiss family in Richardson County,[93] but he did not remain there long.

In 1871, Abraham homesteaded in Jewell County, Kansas, according to the manuscript. There he married a widow, **Mrs. Martha M. (Gaines)**

---

[89] Daniel Trubey Family Bible. North Central Kansas Genealogical Society, *Kansas Mitchell County Cemeteries*, Volume 1 (Cawker City, Kans.: by the Society, 1981), 99.

[90] Daniel Trubey's mortgage from Henry Hess proves Abraham's parents were residents of Stark Co., Ohio, by 1834.

[91] However, the "Abram Truby" entry in the agricultural schedule of the 1850 U.S. census of Huntington County (owning 45 acres of improved land and 35 acres of woodland in an unspecified township) is believed to pertain to Daniel rather than his son Abraham Trubey, then 14 years old.

[92] 1860 U.S. census, Huntington County, Indiana, pop. sched., Polk Twp., P. O. Antioch, p. 93.

[93] 1870 U.S. census, Richardson County, Nebraska, pop. sched., Township 3 Range 16, p. 16/188, dwelling [113?]; National Archives micropublication M593, roll 832.

Knight, on 10 August 1887.[94] In this marriage record, Abraham's age was given as 52 and Martha's as 42. Their 1900 Census entry in Athens Township, Jewell County, Kansas, together with Martha's tombstone inscription show Martha was born 29 August 1845 in Illinois.[95] Martha's two sons by a previous marriage were enumerated in the household. Abraham and Martha apparently had no children together. Martha died on 23 March 1915, and Abraham died on 9 May 1922; both are interred at the Browns Creek Cemetery in Solomon Rapids Township in Mitchell County, Kansas.[96] The tombstone inscription shows Abraham served during the Civil War in Company I, 8th Kansas Veteran Volunteer Infantry, 3rd Division, but no Federal Pension records for Civil War service were found for him.

+ 27. x. ELIZABETH TRUBEY, born 19 November 1838; m. George Long
+ 28. xi. CATHERINE TRUBEY, born 7 July 1842; m. Franklin B. Carr

---

[94] DAR, *Jewell County., KS, Marriage Records* (typescript, no date; G.R.C. vol. 31825), 9: " Vol. C, p. 57." North Central Kansas Genealogical Society, *Kansas Mitchell County Cemeteries*, Volume 1 (Cawker City, Kans.: by the Society, 1981), 95 and 99, showing Martha née Gaines.

[95] 1900 U.S. census, Jewell County, Kansas, pop. sched., Athens Twp., ED 43, p. 5, dwelling 80; National Archives micropublication T623, roll 483. North Central Kansas Genealogical Society, *Kansas Mitchell County Cemeteries*, 1: 95, 99.

[96] North Central Kansas Genealogical Society, *Kansas Mitchell County Cemeteries*, 1: 95 and 99. Note, however, that the Trubey manuscript claims Abraham died on 20 April 1922 in Glen Elder, Kansas, at the home of his niece Mrs. J. W. Stump.

Generation Three

6. **Jacob T.**[3] **Welty** (Nancy[2] Trubey, Daniel[1]) was born in November 1815[97] in Maryland[98] or Pennsylvania.[99] He married **Phianna Klinker**, daughter of Jacob and Catherine (Schweickert) Klinker,[100] in Tuscarawas County, Ohio, on 15 February 1842.[101] Phianna was born in New York[102] or Pennsylvania[103] in May 1822.[104]

---

[97] Perrin, *Stark County, Ohio*, 643-644.

[98] 1880 U.S. census, Stark County, Ohio, pop. sched., city of Canton, ED 139, p. 4, dwelling 32; National Archives micropublication T9, roll 1067.

[99] 1850 U.S. census, Tuscarawas County, Ohio, pop. sched., Lawrence Twp., p.185/369, dwelling 4; National Archives micropublication M432, roll 734. 1860 U.S. census, Tuscarawas Co., Ohio, pop. sched., Lawrence Twp., p. 19/332, dwelling 133; National Archives micropublication M653, roll 1043. 1870 U.S. census, Tuscarawas Co., Ohio, pop. sched., Franklin Twp., p.111, dwelling 93; National Archives micropublication M593, roll 1273.

[100] Perrin, *Stark County, Ohio*, 644; and Donna R. Irish, *Marriages and Marriage Evidence in Pennsylvania German Churches*, "[Baptisms of] Hamilton Union Church 1763-1830, Hamilton Twp, formerly Northampton Co., Pa.," (Baltimore: Genealogical Publishing Co., Inc., 1982), 129, for name of Jacob Klinker's first wife.

[101] Tuscarawas County Genealogical Society, Inc., *Tuscarawas County, Ohio, Marriages 1808-1844*, Vol. 1 from Books 1-2-3 (New Philadelphia, Ohio: T.C.G.S. 1979), 82 and 104.

[102] 1880 U.S. census, Stark County, Ohio, Canton, ED 139, p. 4, dwelling 32.

GENERATION THREE

   As a single man, Jacob devoted "much of his time to teaching school and civil engineering."[105] Once married, he farmed extensively and successfully, owning $10,000 worth of real estate in 1860 and 1870.[106] Jacob T. Welty died in 1899, and was buried in the Massillon Cemetery.[107] In 1900, his widow "Fianna" was enumerated in the home of her only surviving daughter, "Ella" Naylor, in Lagrange County, Indiana.[108] Phianna died in 1907 and was buried by her husband and children in Stark County, Ohio.[109]

   Six children were born to this marriage according to cemetery records, Phianna's 1900 Census entry, and earlier census records, all previously cited. Of these six children, three were living in 1881, and only two survived to 1900.

---

   [103] 1850 U.S. census, Tuscarawas County, Ohio, Lawrence Twp., p.185/369, dwelling 4. 1860 U.S. census, Tuscarawas Co., Ohio, Lawrence Twp., p. 19/332, dwelling 133. 1870 U.S. census, Tuscarawas Co., Ohio, Franklin Twp., p.111, dwelling 93.

   [104] 1900 U.S. census, Lagrange County, Indiana, pop. sched., Bloomfield Twp., ED 70, p. 4; National Archives micropublication T623, roll 383.

   [105] Perrin, *History of Stark County, Ohio*, 644.

   [106] 1860 U.S. census, Tuscarawas Co., Ohio, Lawrence Twp., p. 19/332, dwelling 133. 1870 U.S. census, Tuscarawas Co., Ohio, Franklin Twp., p.111, dwelling 93. See also Appendix B letters #1, 2, 9, 10, 11.

   [107] Sommer, *Stark County, Ohio, Cemeteries*, 3: 904.

   [108] 1900 U.S. census, Lagrange County, Indiana, Bloomfield Twp., ED 70, p. 4.

   [109] Sommer, *Stark County, Ohio, Cemeteries*, 3: 904.

The children of Jacob T.³ Welty and Phianna Klinker:

+ 29. i. ALMON C.⁴ WELTY, born circa 26 October 1843; m. Mary E. Savage
    30. ii. CULLEN J. WELTY, 1846-1858[110]
+ 31. iii. ALVIRA "ELLA" N. OR M. WELTY, born September 1850; m. David Naylor
    32. iv. JOHN CULLEN WELTY, born 10 September 1852 in Tuscarawas County, Ohio.[111] The fact that John Cullen was born six years before the death of his older brother Cullen J. Welty suggests that his original name may have been something other than the apparent mirror-image of his deceased brother's.

          John was a prominent attorney, who held the elective offices of Canton (Stark County) City Solicitor and Prosecuting Attorney for Stark County, as well as other commercial directorships. His marriage on 11 October 1877 or 1878 to **Anna T. Graham** is cited in the 1897 edition of *Bench and Bar of Ohio*; Miss Graham was the daughter of Charles H. Graham, "a prominent capitalist of Philadelphia" (p. 175).

          No children were born to this couple, according to their 1900 Census entry.[112]

    33. v. FRANK WELTY, 1855 – 1858
    34. vi. LILLIE WELTY, 1856 – 1860

---

[110] See reference to his poor health in 1847 in Appendix B letter #2.

[111] George Irving Reed, editor, *Bench and Bar of Ohio, Compendium of History and Biography* (Chicago: The Century Publishing and Engraving Company, 1897), 173-176; *Progressive Men of Northern Ohio* (Cleveland: Plain Dealer Publishing Co., 1906), 13; and Hon. William B. Neff, *Bench and Bar of Northern Ohio, History and Biography* (Cleveland: The Historical Publishing Co., 1921), 711. Photographs appear in the last two sources.

[112] 1900 U.S. census, pop. sched., Stark County, Ohio, Canton, ED 97, p. 16; National Archives micropublication T623, roll 1321.

GENERATION THREE 31

7. **John³ Welty** (Nancy², Trubey, Daniel¹) was born on or around 10 February 1820[113] in Maryland or Pennsylvania.[114] He married **Mary Jane McWhinney**, daughter of John and Nancy (Wolf) McWhinney,[115] on 15 March 1853 in Stark County, Ohio.[116] John McWhinney was born 12 November 1786 in County Down, Ireland; his wife Nancy, daughter of John Wolf, was born near Chambersburg, Franklin County, Pennsylvania, on 4 July 1804,[117] and married John McWhinney in Stark County, Ohio, on 27 October 1829.[118]

According to his father's will,[119] John Welty and his family resided with and took care of his father Christian Welty from the time John was married until his father's death in 1875. Indeed, the 1870 Census[120]

---

[113] Stark County Chapter Ohio Genealogical Society, *Stark County, Ohio[,] Death Records* (No place: by the Society, 1991), 520-521: transcribed from original Volume 3: 574. John's age at death on 26 April 1889 (69 years, 2 months, 6 days) calculates to a birth date of 20 February 1820.

[114] 1850 U.S. census, Tuscarawas County, Ohio, Lawrence Twp., p.185/369, dwelling 4. 1860 U.S. census, Tuscarawas Co., Ohio, Lawrence Twp., p. 19/332, dwelling 133. 1870 U.S. census, Tuscarawas Co., Ohio, Franklin Twp., p.111, dwelling 93. John's death record gives "Pennsylvania" as his birthplace.

[115] 1850 U.S. census, Stark County, Ohio, pop. sched., Sugar Creek Twp., p. 153; National Archives micropublication M432, roll 731. See also Perrin, *Stark County, Ohio*, 926.

[116] DAR, *Stark County, Ohio, Marriages*, "Bk. C, p. 26."

[117] Perrin, *Stark County, Ohio*, 926.

[118] DAR, *Stark County, Ohio, Marriages*, "Bk. A, p. 64."

[119] Stark County, Ohio, Will Book E: 167-168.

[120] 1870 U.S. census, Tuscarawas Co., Ohio, Franklin Twp., p.111, dwelling 93.

shows that 83-year-old Christian Welty, owning $9600 in real estate, resided with 49-year-old John Welty, who owned no real estate.

John was a farmer until his death in Pike Twp., from palsy, on 26 April 1889;[121] he was buried in the Massillon Cemetery in Stark County, Ohio.[122] His widow Mary Jane lived with her son Cullen Welty in 1900 and 1910.[123] She died in 1921 and was buried beside her husband.[124] Mary Jane was the mother of two children, one of whom remains unknown and died before 1900.[125]

The children of John[3] Welty and Mary Jane McWhinney:
    35.   i.   unknown, died before 1900
+ 36   ii. CULLEN M.[4] WELTY, born 5 February 1858; m. Mary Amelia Lebold

8. Mary Ann[3] Welty (Nancy[2] Trubey, Daniel[1]) was born in Pennsylvania circa 1827.[126] No marriage record could be located in Stark County where she appears to have been married circa 1853 to

---

[121] Stark County Chapter Ohio Genealogical Society, *Stark County, Ohio[,] Death Records*, 520-521.

[122] Sommer, *Stark County, Ohio, Cemeteries*, 3: 904.

[123] 1900 U.S. census, Tuscarawas County, Ohio, pop. sched., Sandy Twp., ED 131, p. 16; National Archives micropublication T623, roll 1327. 1910 U.S. census, Tuscarawas County, Ohio, pop. sched., Sandy Twp., ED 145, p. 9A, dwelling 164, family 168, 30 April; National Archives micropublication T624, roll 1236.

[124] Sommer, *Stark County, Ohio, Cemeteries*, 3: 904.

[125] The 1900 census lists her as the mother of two children, but only one then living.

[126] 1850 U.S. census, Stark County, Ohio, pop. sched., Pike Twp., p. 196/391; National Archives micropublication M432, roll 731. 1860 U.S. census, Stark County, Ohio, pop. sched., Pike Twp., p.14/430; National Archives micropublication M653, roll 1038.

Francis P. Mills, son of Henry and Mary (Purdy) Mills[127] who were married on 27 May 1808 in Dutchess County, New York,[128] and resided in Bethlehem Township, Stark County, Ohio, in 1850.[129]

Mary Ann died before 23 September 1867, possibly in White County, Indiana, at which date and place her husband married a second time, to Sarah J. Hays.[130] After his remarriage, Francis, his new wife, and his two children by Mary Ann — Mary Ellen and Francis[131] — removed to Marquette County, Michigan,[132] where Francis, Sr., became the Superintendent of the Cleveland Iron Mining Company,[133] and was

---

[127] [Anonymous], *Counties of White and Pulaski, Indiana, Historical and Biographical* (1883, Rpt. Evansville, Ind.: Unigraphic, Inc., n.d.), 275-276. W. H. Hamelle, supervisor, *A Standard History of White County, Indiana* (Chicago & New York: Lewis Publishing Co., 1915), 862.

[128] Jean D. Worden, comp., *First Reformed Church, Fishkill; First Reformed Church, Hopewell, Dutchess County, New York* (No place: no publisher, 1981), 37.

[129] 1850 U.S. census, Stark County, Ohio, pop. sched., Bethlehem Twp., p. 101; National Archives micropublication M432, roll 731: son Francis in household.

[130] *Index to Marriage Record, White County [Indiana], 1850-1920*, Volume II, Letters L-Z (Indiana Works Progress Administration, 1938), 412: Book C-3, page 158. Note that *Counties of White and Pulaski, Indiana* (pp. 275-276) mistakenly estimates Mary Ann's death year as 1868.

[131] 1860 U.S. census, Stark County, Ohio, Pike Twp., p.14/430, and as named in their grandfather's will.

[132] 1870 U.S. census, Marquette County, Michigan, pop. sched., Ishpeming Twp., p. 274; National Archives micropublication M593, roll 689.

[133] *Counties of White and Pulaski, Indiana*, 275-276.

elected major of Ishpeming in 1873.[134] By 1880, Francis, wife Sarah J., and their four children lived in Prairie Twp, White County, Indiana.[135]

Neither Marquette County, Michigan, nor White County, Indiana, could locate marriage records for Francis and Mary Ann's two children who are last found in the 1870 Census of Marquette County, Michigan.[136] The son, Francis, was living in 1883 when a county history stated he was Superintendent of the Youngstown Iron Mining Company.[137] It is not clear from the 1883 text whether Francis and Mary Ann's daughter, Mary Ellen, was then living.

Francis is last found in Federal Census records in 1910, as a resident of Cedaridge, Delta County, Colorado,[138] where he died 19 June 1910.[139]

The children of Mary Ann³ Welty and Francis P. Mills:
37. i. MARY ELLEN⁴ MILLS, born circa 1856; living in 1870
38. ii. FRANCIS MILLS, born circa 1858; living in 1883

---

[134] Alvah L. Sawyer, *A History of the Northern Peninsula of Michigan and its People*, Volume 1 (Chicago: Lewis Publishing Co., 1911), 431.

[135] 1880 U.S. census, White County, Indiana, pop. sched., Prairie Twp., Brookston Town, ED 135, p. 12; National Archives micropublication T9, roll 323.

[136] White County, Indiana, marriage records (5W: 56158) list a marriage of a Mary Mills, 34, to William Philip on 15 April 1885 or 1886 who may be Mary Ann's daughter (FHL microfilm 1380343).

[137] *Counties of White and Pulaski, Indiana*, 275-276.

[138] 1910 U.S. census, Delta County, Colorado, pop. sched., Cedaridge, Precinct 7, ED 32, p. 8A, dwelling 79, family 71; National Archives micropublication T624, roll 114.

[139] Mrs. Donald E. Pyle and Tanya Pyle, compilers, *Cedaridge Cemetery* (No place: no publisher., 1992), 20.

GENERATION THREE 35

9. **Abraham³ Welty** (Nancy² Trubey, Daniel¹) was born 10 June 1829 (according to his tombstone in Massillon Cemetery)[140] in Pennsylvania.[141] He was married to **Mary Richards**, daughter of John and Elizabeth (Warner) Richards,[142] on 29 December 1852 in Stark County, Ohio.[143] Mary's parents migrated to Stark County, Ohio, from Frederick County, Maryland, where they were married on 3 September

---

[140] Sommer, *Stark County, Ohio, Cemeteries*, 3: 904.

[141] 1850 U.S. census, Stark County, Ohio, pop. sched., Pike Twp., p. 196/391; National Archives micropublication M432, roll 731. 1870 U.S. census, Stark County, Ohio, pop. sched., Pike Twp., p.5/542; National Archives micropublication M593, roll 1269. 1880 U.S. census, Stark County, Ohio, pop. sched., Lawrence Twp., ED 142, p. 70; National Archives micropublication T9, roll 1067. 1900 U.S. census, Wayne County, Ohio, pop. sched., Sugar Creek Twp., Village of Dalton, ED 159, p. 2, National Archives micropublication T623, roll 1332.

[142] "Will of John Richards," 16 March 1864 (recorded 27 March 1867), Stark County, Ohio, Will Bk. D, p.145-146, Stark County District Library microfilm collection. Photocopy in possession of compiler. See also 1850 U.S. census, pop. sched., Stark County, Ohio, Pike Twp., p.193, National Archives micropublication M432, roll 731.

[143] DAR, *Stark County, Ohio, Marriages*, 5, "Bk. C, p. 25."

1806.[144] Census records give Mary's birthplace as Pennsylvania or Ohio.[145]

Abraham, like his brothers, was a farmer. After his marriage, he remained in Pike Township through 1870,[146] lived in Lawrence Township in 1880,[147] and by 1900 was residing as a widower (occupation: "picture agent") with his daughter Iva in Sugar Creek Township, Wayne County, Ohio (adjacent to Stark County).[148] His wife Mary was buried in the Dalton Cemetery in this township. Her tombstone reads that she died on 25 December 1892, at age 64 years, 9 months, and 9 days, making her birth date 16 March 1828.[149]

---

[144] "Marriage Record of John Richards and Elizabeth Warner," 3 September 1806, Frederick County, Maryland, from letter, dated 12 December 1933, citing records received from the Clerk of the Circuit Court of Frederick County, Md., bound with National Number #283489, Volume 1415, on Revolutionary War Patriot John Richards (1760–1823, Md.), Office of the Registrar General, NSDAR Washington, D.C.

[145] 1860 U.S. census, Stark County, Ohio, pop. sched., Pike Twp., p.14/430; National Archives micropublication M653, roll 1038. 1870 U.S. census, Stark County, Ohio, Pike Twp., p.5/542. 1880 U.S. census, Stark County, Ohio, Lawrence Twp., ED 142, p. 70.

[146] 1860 U.S. census, Stark County, Ohio, Pike Twp., p.14/430. 1870 U.S. census, Stark County, Ohio, Pike Twp., p.5/542.

[147] 1880 U.S. census, Stark County, Ohio, Lawrence Twp., ED 142, p. 70.

[148] 1900 U.S. census, Wayne County, Ohio, Sugar Creek Twp., Village of Dalton, ED 159, p. 2.

[149] Genealogy Section of Wayne County [Ohio] Historical Society, comp., *Wayne County, Ohio, Burial Records* (Evansville, Ind.: Unigraphic, Inc., 1975), 609. Mary Welty's tombstone inscription — published incorrectly therein as "D. Dec. 25, 1832, 64

Abraham departed this life on 26 September 1903, and was interred in Stark County's Massillon Cemetery.[150] The seven children of Abraham and Mary Welty were identified from the census records previously cited.

The children of Abraham[3] Welty and Mary Richards:
+ 39. i. TILDEN[4] WELTY, born 29 September 1853; m. Selina A. McElhenie
    40. ii. IVA WELTY, born circa 1856; living in 1900
    41. iii. IDA WELTY, born May 1859[151] or after August 1860[152] in Ohio; m. John H. Howells on 26 January 1896 in Stark County.[153] In the 1910 Census[154] Ida indicated that her one child (born after 1900)[155] was no longer living.

---

yr." — was inspected and photographed by a Wayne County Genealogical Society volunteer in May 1985. Transcript and photograph in possession of compiler. Calculated.

[150] Sommer, *Stark County, Ohio, Cemeteries*, 3: 904.

[151] 1900 U.S. census, Stark County, Ohio, pop. sched., Tuscarawas Twp., ED 149, p. 11; National Archives micropublication T623, roll 1323.

[152] Not listed as a member of her parents' household as enumerated on 9 August 1860 (U.S. census, pop. sched., Stark Co., Ohio, Pike Twp., p. 14/430).

[153] Stark County Marriage Book 15: 411, "Ohio, Stark County, Marriage Index S-Z, (1858-1972)," FHL microfilm 897627.

[154] 1910 U.S. census, Stark County, Ohio, pop. sched., Tuscarawas Twp., ED 242, family 445; National Archives micropublication T624, roll 1232.

[155] 1900 U.S. census, Stark County, Ohio, Tuscarawas Twp., ED 149, p. 11: no children born to this mother.

+	42.	iv.	MINNIE WELTY, born March 1862; m. Amos Miller
+	43.	v.	NETTIE WELTY, born May 1864; m. Henry Bowers
+	44.	vi.	FRANKLIN WELTY, born April 1868; m. Mary Brannon
	45.	vii.	INA MAY WELTY, born circa 1870; living in 1880

10. Jacob Andrew³ Trubey (David², Daniel¹) was said to have been born on 22 November 1814, according to the Trubey manuscript, but no proof of this date has been located. His entry in the 1840 Census[156] lists his age as 20-30, which concurs with the above date. Jacob Andrew, more often appearing as "Andrew" in county records, was married in Tuscarawas County on 11 April 1833[157] to **Mary Ann Taylor**, probably the daughter of John Taylor and Mary Ann Musser although direct proof was not located. She was born circa 1815, and died of consumption at age 35 in *May* 1850, according to the 1850 Mortality Schedule.[158] A tombstone in Stone Creek Cemetery in Jefferson Township gives her death date as 24 *March* 1850.[159] The administrator of her estate was bonded on 27 July 1850.[160]

On 15 August 1850, the administrator of Mary Ann's estate, Thomas Dotts, petitioned the court to sell land owned by her at her

---

[156] 1840 U.S. census, Tuscarawas County, Ohio, Lawrence Twp., p. 321; National Archives micropublication M704, roll 430.

[157] Dickenson, *Tuscarawas County, Ohio, Marriages*, 64 and 192.

[158] 1850 U.S. census, Tuscarawas County, Ohio, mortality schedule, not paginated, entry 24; National Archives micropublication T1159, roll 15.

[159] T.C.G.S., *Tuscarawas County, Ohio, Cemeteries*, III: 28.

[160] Mary Ann Truby estate, Tuscarawas County case A1120-1-3-363, Office of Probate Judge, New Philadelphia, Ohio. Photocopies in possession of compiler. Letters of administration granted 27 July 1850 to Thomas Dotts.

death in order to cover administration costs.[161] Those 46 acres, described as being the NE¼ SW¼ Section 12, Township 7, Range 3, U.S. Military District, were purchased by John Taylor on 15 February 1851.[162] The Trubey manuscript indicates that Andrew

> emigrated with his parents to Tuscarawas County, Ohio, where he grew to manhood and was educated in German and English. He was professor of these languages in Scio College in or near New Philadelphia;[163]

however, independent research shows that Scio College began as "Rural Seminary" in 1856, some eight years after Andrew died.[164]

> Prof. Andrew Trubey was interested financially in coal lands in the vicinity in which he lived. He left this world of strife and toil Feb. 4, 1848[,] at the early age of 33 years, 2 months, and 9 days.[165]

---

[161] Final Record Chancery, Tuscarawas County, Ohio, Volume 8: 582, FHL microfilm 1303049. Here Dotts appears to be "Ditts."

[162] *Ibid.*

[163] Trubey manuscript, 4.

[164] Letter from Yost Osborne, Librarian (Mount Union College, Alliance, Ohio 44610) to compiler, dated 14 May 1985: "If [Jacob Andrew Truby] died in 1848, there is no way he could have taught at Scio College, for it did not start until some ten years later. Actually this college started in 1856 as Rural Seminary (near Carrollton, Ohio); was moved to Scio (or New Market, Ohio, as it was then known) shortly after the Civil War. The name of the town changed to Scio, and later so did the name of the college. It was merged with Mount Union College (Alliance, Ohio) in 1911."

[165] Trubey manuscript, 4.

There is a published tombstone inscription[166] for an Andrew "Truby," buried in Lawrence Township, but the data ("d. 18_1_8 ae _21_ yrs, 2 mo, ? d") does not seem to relate to this or any other known Trubey. It seems likely that the gravesite is that of Jacob Andrew Trubey, but that an accurate reading of the original tombstone inscription is no longer possible. The administrator of his estate was appointed on 25 April 1848 in Tuscarawas County, Ohio.[167]

Two children who died in infancy were mentioned in the manuscript for whom no other corroborating records could be found. They are included below despite lack of primary source evidence.

The children of Jacob Andrew[3] Trubey and Mary Ann Taylor:

+ 46. i.   MARY ANN[4] TRUBEY, born August 1833 or 1834; m. Henry Sprain
  47. ii. "JOHN TAYLOR TRUBEY, 5 February 1837 - 19 September 1845"
+ 48. iii. LYDIA CATHERINE TRUBEY, born circa 12 January 1839; m. Philip Profit
  49. iv. DAVID M. TRUBEY was allegedly born 27 April 1841[168] in Ohio.[169] David's occupation was listed as "rail roader" in the regimental descriptive book of Capt. Heath's Company A of the 46th Regiment Ohio Infantry, in which David enlisted on 10 September

---

[166] T.C.G.S., Inc, *Tuscarawas County, Ohio, Cemeteries*, IV: 45.

[167] Andrew Truby estate, Tuscarawas County case A994-1-3-318, Office of Probate Judge, New Philadelphia, Ohio. Photocopies in possession of compiler. Letters of administration granted 25 April 1848 to Abraham Taylor,

[168] Trubey manuscript, 4.

[169] 1850 U.S. census, Tuscarawas County, Ohio, pop. sched., Auburn Twp., p. 51/26; National Archives micropublication M432, roll 734. At this time the orphaned David and brother Abraham resided with their paternal grandparents David and Catherine Trubey. Guardianship records also support an 1841 birth date for him.

GENERATION THREE 41

1861 at Van Wert, Ohio.[170] Corporal Trubey died "of disease" at Camp Shiloh, Tennessee, on 29 March 1862.[171] There is no evidence that he married or left heirs.

+ 50. v. ABRAHAM M. TRUBEY, born 20 April 1843; m. Mary M. Frysinger
51. vi. "ANDREW HANIBEL TRUBEY, 6 February 1845 – 2 July 1845"

11. Susannah³ Trubey (David², Daniel¹) was born circa 1819[172] in Pennsylvania, and was married to **John Arbaugh**, of undetermined parentage, in Tuscarawas County, Ohio, on 30 March 1837.[173] John Arbaugh was born on 11 August 1813 (as calculated from his tombstone);[174] curiously his 1850 and 1860 Census entries, in Tuscarawas County, Ohio, and Wells County, Indiana, respectively, both list "Pennsylvania" as his place of birth, but the same hand

---

[170] David M. Truby Compiled Service Records (Corporal, Co. A, 46th Ohio Infantry), Records of Volunteer Union Soldiers Who Served During the Civil War (Record Group 94), National Archives, Washington, D.C.; photocopies in possession of compiler.

[171] *Ibid.* Note that the Trubey manuscript (p. 5) gives date of death as 22 April 1862.

[172] 1850 U.S. census, Tuscarawas County, Ohio, pop. sched., Dover, p. 65/130; National Archives micropublication M432, roll 734. 1860 U.S. census, Wells County, Indiana, pop. sched., Union Twp., p. 49/822; National Archives micropublication M653, roll 309. 1870 U.S. census, Wells County, Indiana, pop. sched., Union Twp., p. [2?]; National Archives micropublication M593, roll 372.

[173] T.C.G.S., *Tuscarawas County, Ohio, Marriages*, 11 and 120.

[174] Minniear, *Wells County, Indiana, Cemeteries*, 4, "Zanesville Cemetery."

appears to have crossed through this on both census entries, and substituted "born in Maryland."[175]

John Arbaugh's occupation was "carpenter" in 1850 and "farmer" in 1860. He died on 9 June 1866, and was buried in the Zanesville Cemetery, Union Township, Wells County, Indiana.[176] His widow Susan was listed as a farmer in the 1870 Census, the latest record in which she was found;[177] inexplicably, her tombstone transcription gives 10 January 1857 as her death date.[178]

The Trubey manuscript provides no information on Susannah or "Susan" other than her listing as the last of David Trubey's four children.

The children of Susannah[3] Trubey and John Arbaugh:

+ 52. i. SAMANTHA J.[4] ARBAUGH, born November 1840; m. William Holloway
+ 53. ii. CATHERINE ANN ARBAUGH, born November 1842; m. Joseph Mays
+ 54. iii. ELIZABETH J. E. ARBAUGH, born January 1845; m. John Nedrow
+ 55. iv. DAVID FRANKLIN ARBAUGH, born April 1847; m. Nancy E. Fry
+ 56. v. CAROLINE H. ARBAUGH, born September 1851; m. John W. Taylor

---

[175] 1850 U.S. census, Tuscarawas County, Ohio, Dover, p. 65/130. 1860 U.S. census, Wells County, Indiana, Union Twp., p. 49/822.

[176] Minniear, *Wells County, Indiana, Cemeteries*, 4, "Zanesville Cemetery."

[177] 1870 U.S. census, Wells County, Indiana, Union Twp., p. [2?].

[178] Minniear, *Wells County, Indiana, Cemeteries*, 4, "Zanesville Cemetery." A letter of inquiry to the compiler regarding this discrepancy was not answered. It may be that "1857" was an inadvertent transposition of "1875."

GENERATION THREE 43

57. vi. WILLIAM A. ARBAUGH, born circa 1858; no further information.

12. Mary Catherine³ Trubey (David², Daniel¹) was born 12 August 1822 in Pennsylvania.[179] She married **John Trimble** in Tuscarawas County, Ohio, on 14 June 1843.[180] He was born circa 1821 and died after the census of 1850,[181] reportedly drowned off Rochester, New York.[182] The 1850 Census confirms he was a boatman.[183]

---

[179] 1850 U.S. census, Tuscarawas County, Ohio, pop. sched., Dover, p. 65/130; National Archives micropublication M432, roll 734. 1860 U. S. census, Wells County, Indiana, pop. sched., Union Twp., p. 49/822; National Archives micropublication M653, roll 309. 1870 U. S. census, Morgan County, Missouri, pop. sched., Hough Creek Twp., p. 40/166; National Archives micropublication M593, roll 794. 1880 U.S. census, Lagrange County, Indiana, pop. sched., Lagrange Twp., ED 18, p. 3, National Archives micropublication T9, roll 290. Catherine Trimble, death certificate no. 3593[may be more numerals picked up on copy], Indiana State Board of Health; copy kindly furnished to compiler by descendant Pat Mundy Moburg of Brooklyn, Michigan, in 1986.

[180] T.C.G.S., *Tuscarawas County, Ohio, Marriages*, 78 and 120: "Catherine Truly [*sic*]."

[181] 1850 U.S. census, Tuscarawas County, Ohio, Dover, p. 65/130.

[182] Weston A. Goodspeed and Charles Blanchard, editors, *County of Williams, Ohio, Historical and Biographical* (Chicago: F. A. Battey & Co., 1882), 649.

[183] 1850 U.S. census, Tuscarawas County, Ohio, Dover, p. 65/130.

Catherine, his widow, moved quite often; in 1860 she was looking after her parents in Wells County, Indiana;[184] in 1870 she resided with her son and his wife in Morgan County, Missouri;[185] in 1880 she resided with another son in Lagrange County, Indiana;[186] in 1882 she moved with this family to Williams County, Ohio;[187] in 1891 she made a deposition for her son's Civil War pension while living in Cook County, Illinois, and her second deposition in 1897 (and last record found for her) proved her return to Montpelier, Williams County, Ohio.[188] Catherine died of heart trouble on 6 October 1918 in Fremont, Steuben County, Indiana.[189]

The children of Mary Catherine[3] Trubey and John Trimble:
+ 58. i. THOMAS BARKDOLL[4] TRIMBLE, born 11 February 1844; m. (1) Sarah Allman, (2) Mary Ann Selby
+ 59. ii. SUSAN K. TRIMBLE, born circa 1846; m. Ezra Taylor
+ 60. iii. DAVID A. TRIMBLE, born 29 January 1847; m. Mary Drake
+ 61. iv. MARY CAROLINE TRIMBLE, born 3 October 1849; m. Alanson Mundy

---

[184] 1860 U. S. census, Wells County, Indiana, Union Twp., p. 49/822. Wells County Deed Book K: 414.

[185] 1870 U. S. census, Morgan County, Missouri, Hough Creek Twp., p. 40/166.

[186] 1880 U.S. census,, Lagrange County, Indiana, Lagrange Twp., ED 18, p. 3.

[187] Goodspeed and Blanchard, *County of Williams, Ohio, Historical and Biographical*, 649.

[188] "Depositions of Catharine Trimble," Thomas (alias "Park") Trimble Pension, Civil War and Later Pension Files, Records of the Veterans Administration (Record Group 15), National Archives, Washington, D.C.

[189] Catherine Trimble, Indiana state death certificate 3593[?].

Generation Three 45

13. David M.[3] **Trubey** (David[2], Daniel[1]) was born circa 1822-1826[190] in Tuscarawas County, Ohio, where he married (1) **Mary Smutz**, on 9 November 1846.[191] She was born 24 March 1826 in the same county,[192] and was likely the daughter of Jacob (and Mary) Smutz,[193] a gunsmith originally from Bullskin Township, Fayette County, Pennsylvania,[194] who was last found in the 1860 Census in Dover Township, Tuscarawas County, Ohio.[195]

---

[190] 1850 U.S. census, Tuscarawas County, Ohio, pop. sched., Dover, p. 102/203; National Archives micropublication M432, roll 734. 1860 U.S. census, Wells County, Indiana, pop. sched., Union Twp., p. 49/822; National Archives micropublication M653, roll 309. 1870 U.S. census, Lagrange County, Indiana, pop. sched., Bloomfield Twp., p. 4; National Archives micropublication M593, roll 333.

[191] T.C.G.S., *Tuscarawas County, Ohio, Marriages*, 1845-1863, Volume II from Books 4 and 5 (New Philadelphia, Ohio: by the Society, 1991), 3 and 47: cites Book 4, p. 68, return #4672, married by Solomon Ritz, M.G., of Bolivar.

[192] David M. Trubey obituary, *Lagrange Standard*, Lagrange, Lagrange Co., Indiana, 26 July 1894 (page and column not given). Transcript from Lagrange County Public Library in possession of compiler.

[193] 1850 U.S. census, Tuscarawas County, Ohio, pop. sched., Dover, p. 103; National Archives micropublication M432, roll 734.

[194] Franklin Ellis, ed., *History of Fayette County, Pennsylvania with Biographical Sketches of many of its Pioneers and Prominent Men*, Part 2 (Philadelphia: L. H. Everts & Co., 1882), 491. This reference lists Bullskin Township property owners and their occupations in 1823, including Jacob Smutz, gunsmith.

[195] 1860 U.S. census, Tuscarawas County, Ohio, pop. sched., Dover, p. 147; National Archives micropublication M653, roll 1042.

The Trubey manuscript includes statements made by David's grandson, David Norvin Truby, explaining why this branch of the family dropped the "e" from Trubey. The tradition is that David was in debt, for which he could have been imprisoned, in Tuscarawas County, Ohio, in the late 1840's, so he fled to Indiana and "thought he would be safer by changing the spelling of his name."

Indeed the court records of Tuscarawas County show a suit brought in Chancery Court by George Oswald on 20 November 1850 against David and Mary Trubey.[196] David had defaulted on the mortgage of $144.00 on the NW¼ SW¼ Section 1 Township 8 Range 3 (of the unappropriated lands in the Military District) recorded 12 October 1848. Further, Oswald alleged that David had sold this parcel of land to Matthew Hubert, and, although the Trubeys and Hubert were subpoenaed, they failed to appear in court. The land in question was sold at sheriff's auction on 12 July 1851 to John Butler for $333.00. David may have been expecting to receive money from a suit of his own; on 23 April 1851, he gave power of attorney to Daniel Zimmerman to use whatever monies due him to "release, cansel [sic] or receipt any Mortegeage, Cansel the same in the name of myself..."[197]

By 1853, David Trubey and family relocated in Union Township, Wells County, Indiana.[198] About this time, David Trubey became a minister in the Church of the Brethren ("Dunkard") in Markle,[199] on the Wells-Huntington County line. The records of this church in Wells County reveal that David was one of two ministers who went with the

---

[196] *George Oswald vs. David M. and Mary Truby*, Appearance Docket, Vol. 9: 542, and Final Record, Chancery "R," Vol. 9: 248, Tuscarawas County Court of Common Pleas, New Philadelphia, Ohio. Photocopies in possession of compiler.

[197] Tuscarawas County Deed Book 36: 131, New Philadelphia, Ohio. Photocopy in possession of compiler.

[198] 1860 U.S. census, Tuscarawas County, Ohio, Dover, p. 147: daughter Sarah, age 7, first child born in Indiana.

[199] Otho Winger, *History of the Church of the Brethren in Indiana*, (Elgin, Ill.: Brethren Publishing House, 1917), 90.

Progressive Movement which split the denomination in 1881-1882, by which time he was living in in Lagrange County, Indiana.[200] In Lagrange, David was associated with the Shipshewana and English Prairie Brethren churches.[201]

The *Lagrange Standard* ran a full obituary for Mary Smutz Trubey, who died 8 April 1894 and was buried in the Greenwood Cemetery:[202]

> Mary Smutes was born in Tuscaraws [sic] County, Ohio, on the 24th day of March, 1826. She was united in marriage to David M. Truby, November 13, 1845, and with him removed to Wells County, Indiana[,] in 1848 and to Lagrange County in 1864, where they have since resided. Seven children were born to them, four sons and three daughters. Her husband, the sons, one daughter, one brother and two sisters survive. Jacob A., David, Joseph, George W., and Mrs. Mary C. Stauffer. About 34 years ago Mrs. Truby with her husband united with the German Baptist Church in Wells County, of which church Mr. Truby became an active and efficient minister. Mrs. Truby for two or three years had been in declining health. She was a woman of an amiable dispos[i]tion, industrious, and frugal, a kind and obliging neighbor, devoted to the care and welfare of her children and a faithful and affectionate wife, beloved and respected by a large circle of friends. She departed this life on Monday the 8th, resting in the full assurance of a blissfull [sic] immortal life. The funeral took place from the residence on Tuesday afternoon, two and one half miles north of Lagrange, conducted by Revs. J. P. Jones and J. R. Preston, and her burial in the cemetery near by.[203]

---

[200] Winger, *Brethren*, 39.

[201] Winger, *Brethren*, 137-138.

[202] Truby and Stauffer tombstones, Greenwood Cemetery, Lagrange County, Indiana; photographed and transcribed by J. Scott McKibben, Lagrange County Historical Society, Inc., August 1985.

[203] Mary Smutes Truby obituary, *Lagrange Standard*, Lagrange, Lagrange Co., Indiana, 19 April 1894, p. 1. Transcript from the Lagrange Public Library in possession of compiler.

David remarried on 10 June 1894 to (2) **Anna M. Swihart**,[204] but died just weeks later on 20 July 1894,[205] only eleven days after writing his will.[206] His obituary read simply: "David M. Truby, one of the old and respected citizens of the county died on Friday last after a long and painful affliction. He was for many years a minister in the Dunkerd [sic] Church."[207] David was also buried in the Greenwood Cemetery.[208]

The children of David and Mary (Smutz) Trubey are proved by census records, a regional history,[209] and David's will.[210]

The children of David³ Trubey and Mary Smutz:
+ 62. i.   JACOB A.⁴ TRUBEY, born 26 August 1846; m. Melissa Wyland
+ 63. ii. MARY C. TRUBEY, born 8 August 1846/1847; m. (1) Jacob Bear/Bare, (2) Peter Stauffer

---

[204] Lagrange County marriage, 10 June 1894, Lagrange County, Indiana. No volume or page indicated on photocopy (in possession of compiler) sent by the County Clerk.

[205] David Truby tombstone, Greenwood Cemetery, Lagrange County, Indiana. *Lagrange Standard*, 26 July 1894.

[206] Will of David M. Truby, 9 July 1894 (proved 23 July 1894), Lagrange County, Indiana, Will Book 2, pp. 530-531. See also Lagrange County Probate Order Book H: 248 (6 September 1895). Photocopies in the possession of the compiler.

[207] *Lagrange Standard*, 26 July 1894.

[208] David M. Truby tombstone, Greenwood Cemetery, Lagrange County, Indiana.

[209] *History of Northeast Indiana – Lagrange, Steuben, Noble and DeKalb Counties*, Volume II (Chicago & New York: The Lewis Publishing Company, 1920), 425.

[210] Lagrange County, Will Book 2: 530-531.

GENERATION THREE 49

+ 64. iii. DAVID A. TRUBEY, born circa 1849; m. Mary E. Summers
 65. iv. SARAH TRUBEY, born circa 1853; died before 1894.[211]
 66. v. JOSEPH B. TRUBEY, born January 1854 in Indiana;[212] married **Mary A. Moffett** on 12 July 1882 in Lagrange County, Indiana.[213] Mary was born in March 1860 in Indiana, and this couple resided in Bloomfield, Lagrange County, Indiana, where Jacob worked as a farmer, until at least 1910.[214] According to both the 1900 and 1910 Census, no children were born to this union. Both were interred in the Trubey plot at Greenwood Cemetery in Lagrange: Jacob died in 1934, and Mary in 1950.[215]
+ 67. vi. GEORGE TRUBEY, born 31 October 1856; m. (1) Hannah Slack, (2) Mrs. Minnie (Brown) Yergin

---

[211] *History of Northeast Indiana*, II: 425. 1860 U.S. census, Wells County, Indiana, Union Twp., p. 49/822. 1870 U.S. census, Lagrange County, Indiana, Bloomfield Twp., p. 4.

[212] 1900 U.S. census, Lagrange County, Indiana, pop. sched., Bloomfield, ED 69, p. 7; National Archives micropublication T623, roll 383.

[213] Lagrange County Marriage Book [not furnished]; 93, County Clerk's Office, Lagrange, Indiana. Photocopy of marriage license and return in possession of compiler.

[214] 1900 U.S. census, Lagrange County, Indiana, Bloomfield, ED 69, p. 7. 1910 U.S. census, Lagrange County, Indiana, pop. sched., Bloomfield, ED 94, p. 1; National Archives micropublication T624, roll 361.

[215] Joseph B. and Mary A. Truby tombstones, Greenwood Cemetery, Lagrange County, Indiana.

68. vii. EMILY TRUBEY, birth date unknown; died before 1894.[216]

14. Nancy³ Trubey (Jacob², Daniel¹) was born in Washington Township, Franklin County, Pennsylvania, circa 1818.[217] She was still at home when her father died on 1 March 1835 in Stark County, Ohio, but married **Lewis May** there on 3 December 1835,[218] and thus she does not appear in the guardianship records of 9 November 1836, when Charles Slutz was appointed guardian of her minor brothers Jacob and Samuel J. Trubey.[219]

Lewis and Nancy May left Stark County after 1840, and settled in Flat Rock Township, Henry County, Ohio.[220] Lewis May was born in 1815 in Pennsylvania,[221] and was a farmer up to his death sometime between 1870-1880, probably in Henry County, Ohio, where his widow

---

[216] *History of Northeast Indiana*, 2: 425; not found in any census enumeration of David's family.

[217] 1850 U.S. census, Henry County, Ohio, pop. sched., Flat Rock Twp., p. 12; National Archives micropublication M432, roll 693. 1860 U.S. census, Henry County, Ohio, pop. sched., Flat Rock Twp., p. 260; National Archives micropublication M653, roll 985. 1870 U.S. census, Henry County, Ohio, pop. sched., Flat Rock Twp., p. 269; National Archives micropublication M593, roll 1221.

[218] DAR, *Stark County, Ohio, Marriages*, 2, "Bk. A, p. __."

[219] Stark County Docket A: 150.

[220] 1850 U.S. census, Henry County, Ohio, Flat Rock Twp., p. 12. 1860 U.S. census, Henry County, Ohio, Flat Rock Twp., p. 260. 1870 U.S. census, Henry County, Ohio, Flat Rock Twp., p. 269.

[221] 1850 U.S. census, Henry County, Ohio, Flat Rock Twp., p. 12. 1860 U.S. census, Henry County, Ohio, Flat Rock Twp., p. 260. 1870 U.S. census, Henry County, Ohio, Flat Rock Twp., p. 269.

GENERATION THREE 51

continued to reside in 1880, in the home of their son Samuel.[222] Lewis and Nancy May's three children were proved by the 1850 and 1860 Census. The date and place of Nancy's death are unknown.

The children of Nancy[3] Trubey and Lewis May:
+ 69. i. MARY MARGARET[4] MAY, born September 1836; m. (1) Jeremiah H(o)uston, (2) Joel A. Edwards
+ 70. ii. HARRISON T. MAY, born 22 October 1839; m. Sophrona Hester D. Cole
+ 71. iii. SAMUEL W. MAY, born November 1841; m. "Mrs. Catherine (Dancer) Kaylor"
+ 72. iv. ALSETTA MAY, born circa 1845; m. Philip Huston

15. Jacob M.[3] Trubey (Jacob[2], Daniel[1]) was born on 7 May 1820 in Washington Township, Franklin County, Pennsylvania.[223] Jacob married (1) **Eliza Swan** (daughter of Nicholas D. Swan and Mary A. [—?—])[224] on 12 December 1844 in Stark County, Ohio.[225] She was born in Holmes County, Ohio, on 9 April 1824,[226] and died on 7 (or

---

[222] 1880 U.S. census, Henry County, Ohio, pop. sched., Flat Rock Twp., ED 115, p. 18; National Archives micropublication T9, roll 1032.

[223] *Portrait and Biographical Record of Stark County, Ohio* (Chicago: Chapman Brothers, 1892), 281-282 plus lithograph portrait. The statement about his great-grandfather serving as a patriot in the Revolutionary War is without foundation. Also William Henry Perrin, *History of Stark County, Ohio* (Chicago: Baskin & Battey, Historical Publishers, 1881), 970.

[224] *Portrait and Biographical Record of Stark County*, 282. *History of Stark County*, 970.

[225] *Marriage Records of Stark County, Ohio: From 1808-1865*, Volume 3 (typescript: Canton, Alliance, and Massillon Chapters, DAR, 1936): "Book B, p. 112."

[226] Perrin, *Stark County, Ohio*, 970.

14)[227] June 1858, at age 34 years, 1 month and 29 days, and was buried in the Massillon Cemetery, Stark County, Ohio.[228]

Jacob was married to (2) **Elizabeth Pherson** (daughter of Theophilus Pherson and Eliza Tate)[229] on 12 December 1858 in Stark County by D. B. Wyant, J.P.[230] She was born in Stark County on 24 February 1833,[231] and was living with her husband in Sugar Creek Township, Stark County, Ohio, in June 1900;[232] but her post-1900 death date is not known.

The county history data verify that Jacob was a farmer, as indicated in his census entries, but also point out that he served as Justice of the Peace for 18 years and as County Commissioner for three years, and held other civil positions in the county. Mention was made of the seven hundred acres he owned (circa 1892), "the greater portion of

---

[227] *Portrait and Biographical Record of Stark County, Ohio*, 282.

[228] Sommer, *Stark County, Ohio, Cemeteries*, 3: 899. Perrin's county history agrees with this date; the 1892 county history gives "14 June 1858."

[229] *Portrait and Biographical Record of Stark County, Ohio*, 282. Perrin, *History of Stark County*, 964 and 970.

[230] *Stark County Marriages*, I: "Book 5, p. 6."

[231] *Portrait and Biographical Record of Stark County, Ohio*, 282.

[232] 1900 U.S. census, Stark County, Ohio, pop. sched., Sugar Creek Twp., ED 147, p. 14; National Archives micropublication T623, roll 1323.

which is located in Lagrange County, Ind."[233] His portrait and an engraving of his residence have been published.[234]

Jacob was living as late as 1900 when the Federal Census enumerated him and his second wife residing in Sugar Creek Twp., Stark County, Ohio.[235] The Trubey manuscript furnishes Jacob's death date as 25 May 1902,[236] but his county death record shows Jacob died of paralysis in Sugar Creek Township on 10 June 1902.[237] Jacob's children by both wives were proved by the county histories cited, cemetery records,[238] and census records of 1850, 1860, 1870, and 1880.[239]

---

[233] *Portrait and Biographical Record of Stark County, Ohio*, 282.

[234] [Anonymous], *Combination Atlas Map of Stark County, Ohio* (Philadelphia: L. H. Everts & Co., 1875), 105.

[235] 1900 U.S. census, Stark County, Ohio, pop. sched., Sugar Creek Twp., ED 147, p. 14; National Archives micropublication T623, roll 1323.

[236] Trubey manuscript, 24.

[237] Stark County Chapter Ohio Genealogical Society, *Stark County, Ohio[,] Death Records*, 496-497: transcribed from original Volume 4: 272. Jacob's birthplace is recorded here as "Franklin, Pa.," and his age at death is ten years off: 72 [*sic*: 82] years, 1 month, 3 days.

[238] Sommer, *Stark County, Ohio, Cemeteries*, 3: 899.

[239] 1850 U.S. census, Stark County, Ohio, pop. sched., Sugar Creek Twp., p. 153; National Archives micropublication M432, roll 731. 1860 U.S. census, Stark County, Ohio, pop. sched., Sugar Creek Twp., p. 88; National Archives micropublication M653, roll 1037. 1870 U.S. census, Stark County, Ohio, pop. sched., Sugar Creek Twp., p. 616; National Archives micropublication M593, roll 1269. 1880 U.S. census, Stark County, Ohio, pop. sched., Sugar

The children of Jacob M.³ Trubey and Eliza Swan:
- 73. i. FERDINAND⁴ TRUBEY, born 26 July 1845; died 8 August 1845
- 74. ii. ISABELLA TRUBEY, born and died April 1846
- + 75. iii. NATHAN TRUBEY, born 29 November 1847; m. Melissa Knepper
- + 76. iv. HARMON TRUBEY, born September 1850; m. Mary A. Augustine
- + 77. v. ESDRAS TRUBEY, born circa 1853; m. (1) Mary A. Sheline, (2) Elizabeth Williamson, (3) "Mrs. Luella Marchand," (4) "Rose Lewallyn"
- 78. vi. MARY ANN TRUBEY, born circa 1856, likely in Stark County, Ohio.[240] Mary Ann was married on 20 December 1877 in Stark County, Ohio, to **Josiah H. Jones**,[241] whose parentage is not known.[242] The only mention of Mary Ann in the Trubey manuscript is "Mary Ann married Josiah Jones, having lived twenty nine years."[243] If, as this suggests, Mary Ann died circa 1885, the latest census in which she can be found is the 1880 Census, in which she and her husband were enumerated with no children in their

---

Creek Twp., ED 157, p. 30; National Archives micropublication T9, roll 1068.

[240] 1860 U.S. census, Stark County, Ohio, Sugar Creek Twp., p. 88. 1870 U.S. census, Stark County, Ohio, Sugar Creek Twp., p. 616. 1880 U.S. census, Lagrange County, Indiana, pop. sched., Bloomfield Twp., ED 17, p. 7; National Archives micropublication T9, roll 290.

[241] Stark County Marriages, Volume 8: 690; FHL microfilm 0897627.

[242] His 1880 Census entry indicates that his father was born in Massachusetts and his mother in Vermont.

[243] Trubey manuscript, 22.

GENERATION THREE

household.[244] No other evidence was seen which indicates that this couple had children.
+ 79. vii. FREEMAN TRUBEY, born 23 May 1858; m. Anna Mary Minnick

The children of Jacob[3] Trubey and Elizabeth Pherson:
+ 80. i. ELLSWORTH J. TRUBEY, born 25 November 1861; m. Satira Kilgore
   81. ii. PRISCILLA TRUBEY, born in 1863; died 10 July 1866
+ 82. iii. JENNIE ETTA TRUBEY, born June 1865; m. Samuel Muskopf
   83. iv. ROLLIN LINCOLN TRUBEY, born 1866; died on 12 April 1890, at age 23 years, 11 months, and 24 days.[245]
+ 84. v. ASA HARVEY TRUBEY, born May 1868; m. Ida Elnora Wolf
+ 85. vi. IRA T. TRUBEY, born 26 July 1870; m. Arie L. McFarren
   86. vii. LUELLA MAY TRUBEY, born on or about 19 February 1873, died 11 April 1876[246]
+ 87. vii. ALVAH P. TRUBEY, born 31 March 1876; m. Emma Belle Caler

---

[244] 1880 U.S. census, Lagrange County, Indiana, Bloomfield Twp., ED 17, p. 7.

[245] Stark County Chapter The Ohio Genealogical Society, *Cemetery Inscriptions, Stark County, Ohio*, Volume VI (No place: by the Society, 1985), 187: Perry Township, Massillon City Cemetery #126.

[246] Stark County Chapter Ohio Genealogical Society, *Stark County, Ohio[,] Death Records*, 496-497: transcribed from original Volume 1: 206. She was recorded here as "Truella May," who died of "inflammation of the bowels." Luella's death date also supported by her tombstone as transcribed in Sommer, *Stark County, Ohio, Cemeteries*, 3: 899.

16. Samuel J.³ Trubey (Jacob², Daniel¹) was born 9 November 1822[247] in either Pennsylvania or Ohio.[248] He married **Mary Groner** in Stark County, Ohio, on 17 January 1850.[249] In the Federal Census of that year, he and his wife were enumerated in the same household as his brother Jacob's family along with his mother and her second husband James Thornsbury.[250]

Samuel died on 9 April 1852, at the age of 29 years and 5 months, according to his tombstone.[251] His only son Samuel died in infancy that same year.[252]

The only child of Samuel⁴ Trubey and Mary Groner:
   88. i. SAMUEL⁴ TRUBEY, born 17 March 1851; died 6 November 1852

18. Susan³ or Susannah Trubey (Daniel²,¹) was born 1 March 1818[253] in Washington Township, Franklin County, Pennsylvania, and was about 17 years old when her family moved to Stark County, Ohio. The

---

[247] Sommer, *Stark County, Ohio, Cemeteries*, 3: 899. Calculated.

[248] 1850 U.S. census, Stark County, Ohio, Sugar Creek Twp., p. 153. However, Perrin's county history states that Samuel's father Jacob lived in Pennsylvania until 1823.

[249] DAR, *Stark County, Ohio, Marriages*, 3, "Bk. B, p. 176."

[250] 1850 U.S. census, Stark County, Ohio, Sugar Creek Twp., p. 153.

[251] Sommer, *Stark County, Ohio, Cemeteries*, 3: 899.

[252] *Ibid.*

[253] Daniel Trubey Family Bible.

Trubey manuscript furnished only the surnames of her three husbands,[254] but this facilitated further identification of these men.

Susan's first husband was (1) **Asa Harvey Hunt**,[255] born 17 October 1817[256] in New York.[257] No marriage record was found in Stark nor in adjacent counties of Wayne and Tuscarawas. The first four of her five children by Asa Harvey Hunt were born in Ohio, and their first child Minerva was born circa 1838, according to census and probate records,[258] so the marriage likely occurred circa 1836.

Between 1846 and 1849 this family removed to Jackson Township, Blackford County, Indiana, where Harvey worked as a farmer.[259] He

---

[254] Trubey manuscript, 44.

[255] Harvey Hunt estate, Jay County probate, Box 5-Estates, Court of Common Pleas, Portland, Indiana: "Petition to sell real estate of Harvey Hunt, deceased, by Administratrix Susan Hunt," sworn 5 June 1854. Photocopy in possession of compiler. Indiana DAR, *Partial List of Tombstone Inscriptions from Cemeteries Located in Jay County, Indiana*, 2 (typescript: 1956-1957), 93.

[256] Indiana DAR, *Partial List of Tombstone Inscriptions from Cemeteries Located in Jay County, Indiana*, 2: 93.

[257] 1850 U.S. census, Blackford Co., Indiana, pop. sched., Jackson Twp., p. 37; National Archives micropublication M432, roll 136.

[258] 1850 U.S. census, Blackford Co., Indiana, Jackson Twp., p. 37. Jay County probate Box 5-Estates.

[259] 1850 U.S. census, Blackford Co., Indiana, Jackson Twp., p. 37: Nancy, age 4, born in Ohio, Harvey, age 1, born in Indiana. However, they may have been in Stark or Tuscarawas County as late as 7 August 1847, when a letter of that date mentions that Harvey purchsased a colt from brother-in-law Daniel Trubey there; see Appendix B letter #1. A later letter dated 7 August 1849 confirms the Hunts' presence in Blackford County, Indiana (Appendix B letter #3).

died on 24 December 1852, and was buried in the Old Camden Cemetery in Penn Township, Jay County, Indiana.[260] His probate records show he owned 68 53/100 acres (fractional SW¼, Section 5, Township 23 North, Range 12 East) in Blackford County, Indiana, and Lots 4, 5, 6, Block 5, Original Plot of town of Camden, Jay County, Indiana.[261]

As administratrix of her husband's estate, Susan Hunt petitioned the court for an order to sell the real estate to settle Harvey's indebtedness. She also named Harvey's heirs and gave their ages. The entry identifying the youngest child as "Harvey A. Hunt" was crossed through before the account was signed on 5 June 1854,[262] suggesting his death before that date. The records of Jay County show Mrs. Susan (Trubey) Hunt married (2) **Henry McCullick** on 3 July 1854.[263] On 9 November 1854, as "Susan McCullick" she petitioned the Jay County court to appoint an administrator *de bonis non* to settle her first husband's estate as she was then living in adjoining Wells County.[264]

---

[260] Indiana DAR, *Partial List of Tombstone Inscriptions from Cemeteries Located in Jay County, Indiana*, 2: 93.

[261] Jay County probate Box 5-Estates.

[262] Estate petition (above).

[263] Jay County Marriage Book C-B: 199, Clerk of the Circuit Court's Office, Portland, Indiana. Photocopy in possession of compiler.

[264] Jay County probate Box 5-Estates: "Final account and request for appointment of an administrator *de bonis non* for the estate of Harvey Hunt, deceased," sworn 9 November 1854. Photocopy in possession of compiler.

GENERATION THREE 59

Henry McCullick was born 31 December 1794[265] in Pennsylvania, and was said to have been a veteran of the War of 1812,[266] though evidence of this was not found. His first wife was Martha Twibell, by whom he had nine children.[267] Martha died 27 February 1847 and was buried in the Twibell Cemetery in Harrison Township, Blackford County.[268] Henry's second wife was Esther Slusher, whom he married in Wells County, Indiana, on 16 December 1847.[269] The date of her decease and burial site are unknown. One child was born to Henry McCullick and his third wife, Mrs. Susan (Trubey) Hunt.[270] Henry died on 10 October 1863, at age 68 years, 10 months, and 10 days, and he was buried in the aforementioned Twibell Cemetery.[271]

---

[265] DAR, *Cemeteries in Blackford County, Indiana, from County Records*[?], (typescript, 1955), 17. Calculated.

[266] [Anonymous], *Biographical Memoirs of Wells County, Indiana* (Logansport, Ind.: B. F. Bowen, 1903), 379.

[267] [Anonymous], *Wells County, Indiana*, 378.

[268] DAR, *Cemeteries in Blackford County, Indiana, from County Records*[?], 17.

[269] Mary Penrose Wayne Chapter DAR, *Marriage Records of Wells County, Indiana, Marriages 1837-1900*, (typescript, 1956-1957), 13.

[270] 1860 U.S. census, Wells County, Indiana, pop. sched., Chester Twp., p. 108/1029; National Archives micropublication M653, roll 309. 1870 U.S. census, Wells County, Indiana, pop. sched., Chester Twp., p. 12/24; National Archives micropublication M593, roll 372. *Wells County, Indiana*, p. 379.

[271] DAR, *Cemeteries in Blackford County, Indiana, from County Records*[?], 17.

Susan married a third time on 1 May 1870 in Wells County, Indiana, to (3) **James Bell**.[272] Susan predeceased him, dying on 29 April 1873; she was interred in the Miller Cemetery. Mr. Bell, a widower before his marriage to Susan, was born 25 November 1811 in Pennsylvania, and died 30 November 1894.[273] He was interred beside Susan in the Miller Cemetery. According to census records, he was a farmer,[274] and a freight agent.[275] No children were born to this last marriage.

The children of Susan[3] Trubey and Asa Harvey Hunt:
- 89. i. MINERVA[4] HUNT, born circa 1838; m. Levi Kimble 28 September 1876 in Wells County, Indiana.[276] Allegedly Minerva "married late in life and only lived a short while after."[277] No further information.
- 90. ii. MARY A. HUNT, born circa 1841; m. (1) Bardin Stewart 5 July 1855, Wells County, Indiana.[278] By this union were born *(a)* Henry Stewart, *(b)* James Stewart, *(c)* William Stewart, and *(d)* Elizabeth

---

[272] DAR, *Wells County, Indiana, Marriages*, 131.

[273] Minniear, *Wells County, Indiana, Cemeteries*, 3, Chester Twp, "Miller Cemetery."

[274] 1870 U.S. census, Wells County, Indiana, Chester Twp., p. 12/24.

[275] 1880 U.S. census, Wells County, Indiana, pop. sched., Chester Twp., ED 146, dwelling 245, family 249; National Archives micropublication T9, roll 323.

[276] *Wells County Marriages*, 186.

[277] Trubey manuscript, 44.

[278] *Wells County Marriages*, 42.

GENERATION THREE

Stewart.[279] Mary married (2) John Dixon, by whom were born *(e)* George Dixon, *(f)* Nellie Dixon, and *(g)* Clarabelle Dixon.[280]

91.   iii.   GEORGE D. HUNT, born circa 1844; living in 1854. No further information.
+ 92.   iv.   NANCY MARIA HUNT, born circa 1846-1848; m. William Jones
93.   v.   ASA HARVEY HUNT, born circa 1849; died before 5 June 1854.

The child of Susan[3] Trubey and Henry McCullick:
+ 94.   i.   ELLEN MCCULLICK, born 29 August or September 1858; m. Edward Terhune

19. David[3] Trubey (Daniel[2,1]) was born 27 November 1819[281] in Washington Township, Franklin County, Pennsylvania. He was married in Tuscarawas County, Ohio, on 12 May 1845 at the First Presbyterian Church in Canal Dover to **Keziah Klinker**,[282] daughter of Jacob Klinker

---

[279] Trubey manuscript, 44.

[280] Trubey manuscript, 44. No record other than Mary's 1855 marriage to a Bardin Stewart was found to corroborate these data. Census records and Civil War pension records for men of this name were examined, but none fit the known profiles of these families. The Indiana Civil War pensioner Barton Stewart was not this man.

[281] Daniel Trubey Family Bible.

[282] Tuscarawas County Marriage Record Vol. 4: 29, #4372, Office of the Probate Judge, New Philadelphia, Ohio. Certified copy in possession of compiler.

and Catherine Schweickert.[283] Keziah was born 12 June 1818 in Hamilton Township, Northampton County, Pennsylvania.[284]

This family was enumerated in Liberty Township, Hancock County, Ohio, in the 1850 Census,[285] and had been there since at least August 1847.[286] They likely resided on the land deeded to Keziah by her father before her marriage.[287]

---

[283] Baptism of Cassia [Keziah] Klinker, daughter of Jacob and Cath. Klinker, born 12 June 1818, baptized October [day and year not recorded]," Hamilton Union Church, Hamilton, Pa. Photocopy in possession of compiler. See also Rev. A. S. Leiby, compiler, *The Hamilton Township Union Church Record Located in Hamilton Township Northampton County Pa. Now Monroe County Pa. Contains Baptismal, Communicant and Confirmation Records from 1768 - 1830* (typescript, 1936), 134. Tuscarawas County Deed Book 47: 332-333, Office of County Recorder, New Philadelphia, Ohio: "Deed of Mary A. Klinker to Jacob Klinker's Heirs," 12 August 1863 (recorded 18 January 1864). Tuscaraway County Deed Book 47: 607-608: "Deed of John Higgins, Keziah Truby and James Klinker to Jacob T. Welty," selling the land described in the first deed, 3 September 1863 (recorded 2 May [?] 1864). Photocopies in possession of compiler.

[284] Baptism (October 1818), Hamilton Union Church, Hamilton, Pa.

[285] 1850 U.S. census, Hancock County, Ohio, pop. sched., Liberty Twp., p. 395; National Archives micropublication M432, roll 692.

[286] See Appendix B letter #1.

[287] Deed of Jacob Klinker to Hezekiah [sic] Klinker (recorded 21 Sep 1844 in Deed Bk. 5, p.211), Hancock County, Ohio, S½, SE¼, Section 19, Township 1, Range 10, 80 acres; from photocopy of deed book index to grantors, Office of the County Recorder, Findlay, Ohio. Photocopy in possession of compiler. See also the numerous letters from Keziah (Klinker) Trubey's father Jacob Klinker

David's grandson, George W. Trubey, wrote in a letter dated 12 May 1959 that David died "from an overdose of calomel (mercurous chloride), Hg_2Cl_2 — a bit of an error on the part of an M.D. My father [William David Trubey #98] was about 6 weeks old at the time."[288] This places David's death in March 1855, although notes written by David's granddaughter Grace (Shepherd) Martin give August 1856 as his death date in Wyandot County, Ohio.[289] David's tombstone[290] in McCutchenville (bordering Wyandot and Seneca Counties) gives 1855 as his death year, but the stone also bears an inscription for Keziah ("1818 – 1894"), suggesting this stone was erected nearly forty years after David's death. Although David did not leave a will, there is an estate for him on file in Wyandot County.[291]

There are guardianship records in Wyandot County dated 25 December 1858 appointing William Brayton as the guardian of David Trubey's four minor children, giving their complete names and birth

---

and brother-in-law Jacob T. Welty (Appendix B letters #2, 4, 5, 8-11). Keziah's own letter to her daughter Arabella appears as Appendix B letter #15.

[288] "Letter of George W. Trubey to his son David K. Trubey," 12 May 1959, published in *The Forgotten Friend, Grandmother Ran's Story, Eurannah Hass Trubey Staffeldt (1869-1952), with Some Trubey Family History and Genealogy*, comp. by David K. Trubey (No place: by the compiler, Jan 1979), 45.

[289] Undated notes in the handwriting of [#331] Grace Darling (Shepherd) Martin [1877-1948]. Originals in possession of compiler.

[290] David Trubey tombstone, McCutchenville, Ohio. Photograph of tombstone, in possession of compiler, taken by David Keith Trubey in 1978: "1819-1855."

[291] Letter from the Wyandot County Courts (Common Pleas, Probate and Juvenile), Upper Sandusky, Ohio. No photocopies could be made of these records, nor were the citations to them provided in the clerk's 1987 letter.

dates.[292] The widow Keziah remarried in Wyandot Couny on 18 July 1858 to Joseph Morgan, a widower with two children;[293] the ceremony was performed by the Trubey children's guardian William Brayton, J.P.[294] Apparently, Keziah's six-month delay in announcing her second marriage to her family was not well-received by her father.[295]

One child was born to this marriage, but the couple soon divorced.[296] The child, Lyman,[297] remained with Keziah and assumed the Trubey surname.[298] Joseph Morgan, born circa 1805-1808 in Pennsylvania or Virginia,[299] moved to Bartlow Township, Henry

---

[292] Wyandot County probate [no volume or page indicated on the photocopy],Office of the Probate Judge, Upper Sandusky, Ohio. Photocopy in possession of the compiler.

[293] 1850 U.S. census, Hancock County, Ohio, Liberty Twp., p. 395.

[294] Wyandot County Marriage Vol. 2: 244, #732, Office of the Probate Judge, Upper Sandusky, Ohio. Certified copy in possession of compiler.

[295] Appendix B letter #10.

[296] Wyandot County Complete Record, Vol. 3 (1859-1861): 447-451 (26 October 1860), Common Pleas Court, Upper Sandusky, Ohio, FHL microfilm 1017145.

[297] 1860 U.S. census, Wyandot County, Ohio, pop. sched., Crawford Twp., p. 468; National Archives micropublication M653, roll 1054.

[298] 1870 U.S. census, Wyandot County, Ohio, pop. sched., Crawford Twp., p. 21/685; National Archives micropublication M593, roll 1284.

[299] 1850 U.S. census, Hancock County, Ohio, Liberty Twp., p. 395. 1880 U.S. census, Henry County, Ohio, pop. sched., Bartlow Twp., ED 120, p. 19; National Archives micropublication T9, roll 1032.

GENERATION THREE 65

County, Ohio, where he resided with his son Charles in 1880.[300] No probate records were found for him in Henry County nor has his parentage been determined.

Keziah amassed a great deal of land in Hancock, Wyandot, Stark and Tuscarawas Counties, Ohio. By 1870, her real estate holdings were worth $16,000.[301] Keziah resided in Nottawa Township, St. Joseph County, Michigan, in 1880 (mistakenly listed as "Elizabeth" in the census).[302] She returned to Crawford Township, Wyandot County, Ohio, where she died on 19 May 1894 of Bright's disease.[303]

The children of David[3] Trubey and Keziah Klinker:
+ 95. i. ARABELLA SERENA[4] TRUBEY, born 17 May 1846; m. Elmore Shepherd
+ 96. ii. ERASTUS SEABURY TRUBEY, born 16 March 1848; m. (1) Martha Liddle; (2) unknown
+ 97. iii. MARY CATHERINE TRUBEY, born 14 August 1850; m. Jasper Van Nette
+ 98. iv. WILLIAM DAVID TRUBEY, born 26 January 1855; m. Eurannah Hass

20. John[3] Trubey (Daniel[2, 1]) was born 2 October 1821[304] in Washington Township, Franklin County, Pennsylvania. The manuscript states

---

[300] 1880 U.S. census, Henry County, Ohio, Bartlow Twp., ED 120, p. 19.

[301] 1870 U.S. census, Wyandot County, Ohio, Crawford Twp., p. 21/685.

[302] 1880 U.S. census, St. Joseph County, Michigan, pop. sched., Nottowa Twp., ED 199, p. 24; National Archives micropublication T9, roll 603.

[303] Keziah Truby entry, Wyandot County Deaths, Vol. 1890-1900, p. 189, Court of Common Pleas, Upper Sandusky, Ohio. Certified copy in possession of compiler.

[304] Daniel Trubey Family Bible.

he was bound out when a lad, and learned the wagon makers trade. When his time was out, becoming of age, he came to Ohio, to where his parents and family had moved. The great canal system was being built going through Canal Dover where he took to boating and also boated on the Wabash and Cincinnati branches.[305]

A county history confirms that John Trubey engaged in wagonmaking about 1844 in Flatrock Township, Henry County, Ohio.[306] He was enumerated here in the 1850 Census in the household of Joseph Stout, a tavernkeeper, and was listed as a "Waggonmaker."[307] He first married (1) **Sarah Jane Dougherty** in Henry County on 23 March 1851;[308] she appears to be the daughter of Nathan and Sarah (Dickey) Dougherty, of Maryland and Ohio respectively,[309] married in Butler County, Ohio, on 11 August 1813.[310] Sarah Jane died on 29 May 1852,

---

[305] Trubey manuscript, 52.

[306] Lewis Cass Aldrich, editor, *History of Henry and Fulton Counties, Ohio* (Syracuse: D. Mason & Co., 1888), 224.

[307] 1850 U.S. census, Henry County, Ohio, pop. sched., Flat Rock Twp., p. 9/17; National Archives micropublication M432, roll 693.

[308] Henry County Marriage Volume A: 22 (license 22 March), Napoleon, Ohio; FHL microfilm 0423620. Ruth Bowers and Anita Short, compilers, "Henry County, Ohio, Marriages 1847-1851," *Ohio Gateway to the West*, Volume 1 (Baltimore, Md.: Genealogical Publishing Co., Inc., 1989), 604: "The following marriages were taken from 'Marriage Record A' located in the Probate Court House at Napoleon."

[309] 1850 U.S. census, Butler County, Ohio, pop. sched., Wayne Twp., p. 369/737; National Archives micropublication M432, roll 663.

[310] DAR, *Early Marriage Records of Butler Co, Ohio*, Vol. 1: 1803-1823 (typescript, 1940), 49.

eight days after their son, Nathan John, was born.[311] A family letter dated 25 June 1852 confirms both the recent death of John's wife and the existence of a surviving infant.[312]

For his second wife, John wed (2) **Jane Morse** in Defiance County, Ohio, on 18 September 1853, with Thomas Parker officiating.[313] No evidence has been seen of any children of this union.

John was married a third time in Butler County, Ohio, on 3 August 1859 to (3) **Lydia Moore**,[314] daughter of Louis and Susannah Moore.[315] Lydia was born 29 November 1823, according to her tombstone.[316] They settled in Richland Township, Defiance County, Ohio, where their three children were born.[317] During the Civil War, John moved to the city of Defiance to make wagons, according to the manuscript. After the war, he reputedly planted the first peach orchard in the county.

---

[311] Henry County Genealogical Society, *Cemeteries Henry County, Ohio, Flatrock Township* (Deshler, Ohio: by the Society, 1990), 32: Florida Village Cemetery, Row 3, #12, John Trubey [*sic*: Mrs. John Trubey], d. 29 May 1852, at age 24 years, 9 months, 3 days.

[312] Appendix B letter #6.

[313] Defiance County Marriage Volume 1 (1845-1861), p. 88, Defiance, Ohio; FHL microfilm 1977639.

[314] Butler Cournty Marriage Volume 3 (1847-1862), p. 324, #2833, Hamilton, Ohio; FHL microfilm 0355779. Officiated by Rev. E. K. Lovell,

[315] Mary H. Motley, "Personal Histories, Defiance County, Ohio, Richland Township," in *Historical Atlas Illustrated*, edited by Charles H. Jones (Chicago: H. H. Hardesty & Co., 1876), 13.

[316] Defiance Chapter Ohio Genealogical Society, Harold H. Rulman, editor, *Cemeteries of Defiance County, Ohio* (typescript, not dated), 5: "Independence Cemetery."

[317] Motley, *Historical Atlas Illustrated*, 13.

John died in Defiance County on 18 March 1907; his wife Lydia died on 26 July 1904.[318] Both are buried in the Independence Cemetery in Richland Township. John's children were proved by census records[319] and the biographical sketch cited.

The children of John[3] Trubey and Sarah Jane Dougherty:
+ 99. i. NATHAN JOHN[4] TRUBEY, born 21 May 1852; m. (1) Nettie J. Ely; (2) Lillian A. Gilbert; (3) Virginia C. Gilbert

The children of John[3] Trubey and Lydia Moore:
+ 100. i. BAREVIAS AUGUSTUS TRUBEY, born 25 February 1860; m. Zeruia Goodenough
+ 101. ii. JUSTIN A. TRUBEY, born 1 October 1861; m. Sarah J. Kimberly
+ 102. iii. AMBROSE E. TRUBEY, born 5 September 1863; m. Catherine Osborn

21. Daniel[3] Trubey (Daniel[2, 1]) was born 7 June 1824[320] in Washington Township, Franklin County, Pennsylvania. As a single man, Daniel penned two letters to his married brother David in 1847 and 1852, which yet survive.[321]

---

[318] Rulman, *Cemeteries of Defiance County, Ohio*, 5.

[319] 1870 U.S. census, Defiance County, Ohio, pop. sched., Richland Twp., p. 163; National Archives micropublication M593, roll 1195. 1880 U.S. census, Defiance County, Ohio, pop. sched., Richland Twp., ED 231, p. 22; National Archives micropublication T9, roll 1011.

[320] Daniel Trubey Family Bible.

[321] See Appendix B letters #1 and #7; #6 is an 1852 letter written to him by his sister Mary Ann Trubey. Although Daniel enjoyed a long and healthy life, the only two letters which survive for him were both written when he was ill.

His Civil War pension[322] contains a certified abstract of his marriage to **Esther D. Heath** on 14 November 1852 "by E. Carr, Henry County, p. 10, Record of Marriages."[323] Esther, daughter of Joseph and Mary Heath,[324] was born in July 1832 in New York, according to her 1900 Census entry.[325]

Daniel enlisted for Civil War service at Toledo, Ohio, and served less than one year in Company D, 55th Regiment. His pension questionnaire, completed on 19 April 1898, gives the names and birth dates of his children.[326] This family yet resided in Henry County, Ohio,

---

[322] Daniel Trubey Pension (Co. D, 55th Ohio Infantry), application 441384, certificate 351986, Civil War and Later Pension Files, Records of the Veterans Administration (Record Group 15), National Archives, Washington, D.C.

[323] Marriage Records, Henry County, Ohio, Volume I, pp. 9-10, license 12 November; FHL microfilm 0423620. The county clerk was unable to locate this marriage record; a published volume of abstracts — *The 1st Marriage Records of Henry County[,] OH[,] 1847-1898* (Warsaw, Ind.: Scheuer Publications, 1992) — offers one clue why, insofar as the compilers, at least, read and published the groom's surname as "Freeby" rather than "Truby."

[324] 1850 U.S. census, Henry County, Ohio, pop. sched., Flat Rock Twp., p. 8; National Archives micropublication M432, roll 693.

[325] 1900 U.S. census, Mitchell County, Kansas, pop. sched., Glen Elder Twp., ED 83, p. 11; National Archives micropublication T623, roll 491.

[326] Daniel Trubey pension.

in 1870,[327] but removed to Kansas by November 1872,[328] settling in Glen Elder Twp., Mitchell County by 1880.[329]

Daniel's wife Esther died on 11 October 1903,[330] and by 19 March 1907, Daniel resided in Oakland, Shawnee County, Kansas.[331] His death was reported to the U.S. Pension Agency as having occurred on 2 September 1910.[332]

The children of Daniel[3] Trubey and Esther Heath:

+ 103. i. JOSEPH ANDREW[4] TRUBEY, born 13 November 1853; m. Saphronia Day
+ 104. ii. MARY JANE TRUBEY, born 9 September 1855; m. (1) William T. Pilcher, (2) Andrew T. Taylor
+ 105. iii. JOHN A. TRUBEY, born 13 January 1858; m. Sarah A. Morgan
+ 106. iv. LEWIS FRANCIS TRUBEY, born 2 June 1859 or 1860; m. Lavina Amanda Dudley a.k.a. Ferguson
+ 107. v. MELISSA A. TRUBEY, born 29 January 1862 m. Benjamin F. Hutchi(n)son

---

[327] 1870 U.S. census, Henry County, Ohio, pop. sched., Bartlow Twp., p. 246/3; National Archives micropublication M593, roll 1221.

[328] 1880 U.S. census, Mitchell County, Kansas, pop. sched., Glen Elder Twp., ED 83, p. 11; National Archives micropublication T9, roll 389: "Kansas" given as the birthplace of their eighth child, George.

[329] *Ibid.*

[330] Trubey manuscript, 68; however, Daniel was not located in a search of Glen Elder Township schedules of the 1910 U.S. Census of Mitchell County, Kansas.

[331] Pension records.

[332] Pension records. The Trubey manuscript (p. 68) gives "10" September 1910.

108. vi. DANIEL A. TRUBEY was born 2 June 1864[333] in Henry County, Ohio.[334] As with Daniel's sister Mary Jane, the Trubey manuscript is silent on the subject of Daniel's life. At age 24, Daniel married **Hannah E. McFarland** on 6 December 1888 in Maher, Montrose County, Colorado.[335]

Daniel was located in San Miguel County, Colorado, in 1900, at which time he was a farmer with wife Hannah E., an adopted son Clyde M. Stanley, and a servant. Daniel is said to have separated from Hannah, and to have married (2) Ida Mae Casteel on 14 February 1901.[336] They allegedly lived in St. Louis, Missouri, in 1909, and in Topeka, Kansas, circa 1912-1913.[337] Daniel died 6 December 1958, after which his widow married a

---

[333] His father's pension.

[334] 1870 U.S. census, Henry County, Ohio, pop. sched., Bartlow Twp., p. 246/3; National Archives micropublication M593, roll 1221. 1880 U.S. census, Mitchell County, Kansas, pop. sched., Glen Elder, ED 179, p. 4; National Archives micropublication T9, roll 389. 1900 U.S. census, San Miguel County, Colorado, pop. sched., Precinct 15, Sawpit, ED 122, p. 9; National Archives micropublication T623, roll 129.

[335] Colorado Marriage Record Report #150, Montrose County, performed by minister George O. States; FHL microfilm 1690143. 1962 Trubey manuscript, p. 37, identifies her as Hannah Elma McFarland (her birth name) or Slack (her step-father's name).

[336] 1962 Trubey manuscript, 37; place not given.

[337] 1962 Trubey manuscript, 37.

Mr. Townsend; she was living in Bolckow, Missouri, in 1962.[338]

+ 109. vii. DAVID C. TRUBEY, born 4 October 1866; m. Lulie A. Pratt
+ 110. viii. GEORGE TRUBEY, born 22 November 1872; m. Mary B. Altimus

22. Nancy³ Trubey (Daniel[2, 1]) was born 15 December 1826[339] in Washington Township, Franklin County, Pennsylvania. Nancy's letters to her married brother David in 1847 and 1849 each make reference to David's recently born daughter [Arabella] and son [Erastus] respectively.[340] According to the latter letter, Nancy resided with her married sister Susan(nah) (Trubey) Hunt in Blackford County, Indiana, where Nancy taught school in the summer of 1849: "girl's wages are not much, from 50 cents to 75."

Nancy became the second wife[341] of **Jacob Yantiss** in Huntington County, Indiana, on 13 April 1851.[342] Jacob was born on 8 October

---

[338] Clarence O. Trubey, copyist, *History of the Trubey Family* (typescript, 1962), 37. Photocopy in possession of compiler. Hereinafter "1962 Trubey manuscript." This entry claims Daniel and Ida had four children, the eldest of whom was Clyde. It is not known whether this Clyde is identical to the son adopted by Daniel and his first wife Hannah. The other three children attributed to Daniel and Ida are (a) George A., (b) Walter, and (c) Violet who married Mr. Meyers.

[339] Daniel Trubey Family Bible.

[340] See Appendix B letters #1 and #3.

[341] John Wesley Stump (of Long Island, Kansas) Family Record. *Our Family, Its Record and Guide to Greatness and Honor* (No place: no publisher, not dated),16; found in File Case folder labeled "Stoner, Abraham, Pa., b. abt. 1745-6, d. 9-__-1824 Franklin Co., Pa.," Library Office, NSDAR, Washington, D.C.

[342] Huntington County Marriage Book D: 110, as appears on p. 113 of a typed volume of marriage record abstracts (title page not sent) furnished by the Indiana Room of the Huntington Public

GENERATION THREE 73

1817 in Frederick County, Maryland, according to his son-in-law's family record,[343] although his census entries give his birthplace as Ohio.[344] These Bible records give his first wife as Arminda Iden, and their marriage date as 16 December 1840.[345]

Jacob and Nancy's six children were born in Polk Township, Huntington County, Indiana, after which, circa 1867, they removed to Richardson County, Nebraska.[346] Jacob, Nancy and their first child Melissa were members of the First Methodist Church in Falls City in the late 1860's and "transferred to Salem" by letter on 24 February 1890.[347]

Nancy's death is described in the manuscript as an accident occuring after Jacob and Nancy's visit to the gravesites of their daughter, Effie Yantiss, and of Nancy's mother, Mary (Stoner) Trubey. "On their way home, the horse became frightened, throwing her

---

Library, Huntington, Indiana.

[343] John Wesley Stump Family Record.

[344] 1850 U.S. census, Huntington County, Indiana, pop. sched., Dist. 52, p. 53; National Archives micropublication M432, roll 152. 1860 U.S. census, Huntington County, Indiana, pop. sched., Polk Twp., p. 90; National Archives micropublication M653, roll 267. 1870 U.S. census, Richardson County, Nebraska, pop. sched., Township 2 Range 16, p. 6/175 [listed as "John" instead of Jacob]; National Archives micropublication M593, roll 832. 1880 U.S. census, Richardson County, Nebraska, pop. sched., Ohio Pct., ED 311, p. 30; National Archives micropublication T9, roll 754.

[345] John Wesley Stump Family Record.

[346] 1860 U.S. census, Huntington County, Indiana, Polk Twp., p. 90. 1870 U.S. census, Richardson County, Nebraska, Township 2 Range 16, p. 6/175.

[347] Nebraska DAR, *Records of the First Methodist Church, Falls City, Nebraska* (typescript: Lone Willow Chapter, 1983), 45, 64.

[Nancy] out on her head unconscious. She died on 30 September 1892...and was buried in Silver Creek Cemetery."[348]

Jacob was a farmer, and died 16 April 1897 in Smith County, Kansas, where several of his children lived. He was buried in Silver Creek Cemetery, Richardson County, Nebraska.[349]

The children of Nancy[3] Trubey and Jacob Yantiss:

+ 111. i. MELISSA[4] YANTISS, born 30 September 1851; m. Emanuel D. Heyde
    112. ii. GEORGE YANTISS, born 1 March 1853, died 7 January 1937
+ 113. iii. LANDON YANTISS, born 26 November 1854; m. Mary Merriam
    114. iv. JOSEPH J. YANTISS, born 26 June 1857, died 23 June 1934
+ 115. v. DANIEL D. YANTISS, born July 1859; m. Lillie A. Meyers
    116. vi. infant, died at birth 15 June 1861
+ 117. vii. MARY ELIZABETH YANTISS, born 25 November 1863; m. John W. Stump
    118. viii. EFFIE D. YANTISS, 14 January 1866 – 11 August 1891

23. Rebecca[3] Trubey (Daniel[2, 1]) was born 15 December 1828[350] in Washington Township, Franklin County, Pennsylvania. She became the wife of **John Mohn** on 2 June 1850 in Huntington County, Indiana.[351]

---

[348] Trubey manuscript, 81.

[349] John Wesley Stump Family Record.

[350] Daniel Trubey Family Bible.

[351] Huntington County Marriage Book B: 89, as appears in a typed volume of marriage record abstracts (title page not sent) furnished by the Indiana Room of the Huntington Public Library, Huntington, Indiana. Their household was enumerated in the census on 14 September 1850; the presence of a 6-month-old daughter raises the possibility that John Mohn had an earlier wife who died in this year, although no candidate appears in a published transcript of the

GENERATION THREE 75

Rebecca's husband John Mohn, probably the son of John and Mary Mohn,[352] was born circa 1819 in Baden, Germany.[353] Census records show he was a farmer.[354] He died sometime after 1880 and before 1900, when Rebecca was enumerated as a widow living at 1305 South 9th Street, St. Joseph, Buchanan County, Missouri, where she was a boarding house keeper.[355]

Mortality Schedule (1850 U.S. census, Huntington County, Indiana, pop. sched., p. 56, National Archives micropublication M432, roll 152. Lowell M. Volkel, *1850 Indiana Mortality Schedule* (No place: by the transcriber, 1971).

[352] 1850 U.S. census, Huntington County, Indiana, p. 56: German-born John M. Mohn, age 68, and Mary Mohn, age 62, also living in this household.

[353] 1860 U.S. census, Huntington County, Indiana, pop sched., Huntington Twp., p. 28/211; National Archives micropublication M653, roll 267. In this entry, John's surname is given as "Moon," and his wife's first name as "Truby." 1870 U.S. census, Huntington County, Indiana, pop. sched., Polk Twp., p. 1;, National Archives micropublication M593, roll 325. 1880 U.S. census, Huntington County, Indiana, pop. sched., Polk Twp., ED 201, p. 21; National Archives micropublication T9, roll 285.

[354] 1850 U.S. census, Huntington County, Indiana, p. 56. 1860 U.S. census, Huntington County, Indiana, Huntington Twp., p. 28/211. 1870 U.S. census, Huntington County, Indiana, Polk Twp., p. 1. 1880 U.S. census, Huntington County, Indiana, Polk Twp., ED 201, p. 21.

[355] 1900 U.S. census, Buchanan County, Missouri, pop. sched., Washington Twp., St. Joseph City, ED 72, p. 19; National Archives micropublication T623, roll 843.

76   DANIEL TRUBEY OF FRANKLIN COUNTY, PENNSYLVANIA

Rebecca gave her age as 77 in her 3 February 1906 deposition in support of her sister's Civil War widow's pension application.[356] Soon thereafter, Rebecca died "of old age" at this boarding house on 12 June 1909.[357] Her death record states she had resided in St. Joseph 20 years (i.e., since circa 1889). A brief death notice appeared in the *St. Joseph Gazette* on 13 June 1909, giving the names and residences of her surviving children;[358] she was interred at the Mt. Mora Cemetery in St. Joseph.[359]

The children of Rebecca[3] Trubey and John Mohn:
119.   i.   CAROLINE C.[4] MOHN, a probable daughter, born January or March 1850, probably in Huntington County, Indiana;[360] not in the parents' household after

---

[356] Frank B. Carr Pension (Co. D, 124th Ohio Infantry), application 901216, certificate 701028, and Kate Carr widow's application 827155, certificate 607618, Civil War and Later Pension Files, Records of the Veterans Administration (Record Group 15), National Archives, Washington, D.C.

[357] Rebecca Mohn entry, City of St. Joseph Deaths [no volume or page indicated on transcript]; photocopy sent to the compiler by the St. Joseph Public Library, St. Joseph, Missouri.

[358] Rebecca Mohn obituary, *St. Joseph Gazette*, St. Joseph, Buchanan Co., Missouri, 13 June 1909, [no page, no column]. Photocopy from the St. Joseph Public Library, St. Joseph, Missouri, in possession of compiler.

[359] M. M. Downs and M. M. Thompson, *Mt. Mora Cemetery, Buchanan Co., St. Joseph, Missouri* (typescript, 1975), 76, NSDAR Library, Washington, D.C.

[360] 1850 U.S. census, Huntington County, Indiana, p. 56. 1860 U.S. census, Huntington County, Indiana, Huntington Twp., p. 28/211. Caroline appears as a six-month-old in the 1850 household of John and Rebecca, who were married just three months earlier. It is possible Caroline was a daughter of John Mohn's by an

GENERATION THREE 77

1860, and not mentioned in Rebecca's 1909 obituary; may be one of the three children who died before 1900.
120. ii. unknown; born before June 1852;[361] died before 1900.
+ 121. iii. JOHN FREDERICK MOHN, born March 1854; m. Mrs. Sarah C. (Jones) Bradshaw
+ 122. iv. MARY JANE MOHN, born 21 November 1856; m. John I. Dille
123. v. CLARISSA ELIZABETH MOHN was born 5 March 1859 in Indiana.[362] She married 14 June 1897 in Cleveland, Ohio, **Alexander Hazen**,[363] apparently as his second wife.[364] Alexander Hazen was son of Samuel Wilder Hazen and Eliza McGuinness, who was born 16 October 1852 in Oil Creek Townhip, Crawford County, Pennsylvania.[365] "Clara" and her husband were both living in St. Joseph, Missouri, as

---

earlier marriage.

[361] See Appendix B letter #6: according to this 25 June 1852 family letter, Rebecca (Trubey) Mohn offered to nurse her infant nephew [#99 Nathan John Trubey] whose mother had just died.

[362] 1900 U.S. census, Buchanan County, Missouri, pop. sched., Washington Twp., St. Joseph, E.D. 72, p. 19; National Archives micropublication T623, roll 843. Trubey manuscript, 87.

[363] Marriage Records, Cuyahoga County, Ohio, Volume 45: 113; FHL microfilm 0877931.

[364] Tracy Elliot Hazen, *The Hazen Family in America* (Thomaston, Conn.: Robert Hazen, M.D., 1947), 723-724. 1900 Census (above) states she then had been married for three years, but her married name of Hazen is not listed. The Trubey manuscript, p. 87, gives their marriage date as 12 June 1897.

[365] Hazen, *The Hazen Family*, 723-724.

late as 1910.[366] The Hazen genealogy claims that Alexander "was a railroad man, serving as brakeman, machinist, engineer, and shop foreman; res. St. Joseph, Mo., but later prospected for gold in Colorado, and res. (1915) at St. Louis, Mo.[367] There are no known children from this union.

124. vi. AMANDA CATHERINE MOHN, born 28 December 1861 in Indiana.[368] On 28 June 1885 in Huntington County, Indiana, Amanda married John F. Falck,[369] from whom she was divorced.[370] While the Trubey manuscript states that Amanda was married but that her (unknown) husband and children predeceased her,[371] Amanda's 1900 Census entry shows that she

---

[366] 1900 U.S. census, Buchanan County, Missouri, Washington Twp., St. Joseph, E.D. 72, p. 19. 1910 U.S. census, Buchanan County, Missouri, pop. sched., St. Joseph City, ED 86, p. 20; National Archives micropublication T624, roll 772: both Alexander and Clara living at her deceased mother's address of 1305 9th Street, although a 1909 city directory for St. Joseph lists Alexander Hazen residing at 303 N. 5th St. The 1920 Soundex for Missouri does not include Alexander or Clara/Clarissa Hazen.

[367] Hazen, *The Hazen Family*, 723-724.

[368] 1900 U.S. census, Buchanan County, Missouri, St. Joseph, ED 72, p. 19. Trubey manuscript, 87.

[369] Ruth M. Slevin, *Huntington County, Indiana, Marriage Records 1883-1900*, Volume 2 (1970), Brides, 61.

[370] Clerk of Huntington County, Indiana, confirms this divorce is the subject of Cases #21534 and #2814.

[371] *Index to Birth Records Huntington County, Indiana, 1875 - 1920 Inclusive, Volume 2, Letters M - Z* (typescript: Indiana Works Progress Administration, 1942), 24, and *Index to Death Records, Huntington County, Indiana, 1882 - 1920 Inclusive, Letters A - Z*

GENERATION THREE 79

was then divorced (no married name listed), and had no children living or dead.[372] Rebecca (Trubey) Mohn's 1909 obituary seems to refer to Amanda as "Miss Mamie Mohn" of 1305 S. Ninth St., St. Joseph, Missouri, and she appears by that name in the 1910 Census as well.[373] She was said to have been living in Los Angeles, California, in 1941.[374]

+ 125. vii. DANIEL ANDREW MOHN m. Mary "May" J. Hancock
126. viii. CHARLES G. MOHN, born 24 October 1867[375] or 1868[376] in Indiana. A Charles G. Mohn, a barber, boarded at Daniel A. Mohn's address in Toledo, Ohio, in 1897-1898, and at the same address as Daniel's widow May Mohn in 1899,[377] and those entries likely

---

(typescript: Indiana W.P.A., 1942), 197, show that Amanda Mohn had a daughter Mamie Belle Mohn, born 7 December 1883 (Book H-22: 6) who died in Andrews Twp. at age two months on 24 February 1884 (Books H-29: 3 and A-1: 304).

[372] Amanda may have divorced prior to 4 November 1891, as another marriage is recorded in Huntington County on that date for a John F. Falck (possibly her ex-husband).

[373] 1910 U.S. census, Buchanan County, Missouri, pop. sched., St. Joseph, ED 86, p. 20; National Archives micropublication T624, roll 772.

[374] Trubey manuscript, 87.

[375] Trubey manuscript, 87.

[376] 1900 U.S. census, Buchanan County, Missouri, pop. sched., St. Joseph, ED 72, p. 19; National Archives micropublication T623, roll 843.

[377] *Toledo City Directory...1897* (R. L. Polk & Co., 1897), 899, and *Toledo City Directory...1898*, 940; Library of Congress, U.S. City Directories 1882-1901, rolls 8 and 9, Microform Reading Room,

refer to this Charles. Charles gave a deposition in 1901 which appears in his aunt Catherine (Trubey) Carr's application for a Civil War widow's pension, and he was living in St. Joseph, Missouri, at the time of his mother's death in 1909. The 1910 Census confirms that he operated a barbershop in St. Joseph at that time, and that he had married circa 1899 a **Mrs. Minnie M. [—?—] Mertens**, who had only one surviving child then residing with the couple.[378] Charles apparently had no children, and was living in Inglewood, California, in 1941.[379]

25. Mary Ann³ Trubey (Daniel², ¹) was born 9 April 1833[380] in Franklin County, Pennsylvania, apparently just before the family's removal to Ohio. The only census in which Mary Ann could be found (1860)[381] gives her birthplace as "Pennsylvania," and her only surviving

---

Washington, D.C. Trubey manuscript, 88.

[378] 1910 U.S. census, Buchanan County, Missouri, pop. sched., Washington Twp., St. Joseph, ED 54, p. 6A; National Archives micropublication T624, roll 771. Their marriage record is not recorded in Buchanan County.

[379] Trubey manuscript, 88.

[380] Daniel Trubey Family Bible.

[381] 1860 U.S. census, Henry County, Ohio, pop. sched., Flat Rock Twp., p. 253; National Archives micropublication M653, roll 985.

GENERATION THREE 81

child gave "Pennsylvania" as Mary Ann's birthplace in the 1880[382] and 1900 Census.[383]

A letter penned by Mary Ann in 1852 survives, written upon learning of the death of her brother John's wife.[384] This letter also reveals that the Trubey parents were separated during this time; Mary Ann and sister Elizabeth apparently resided on their father's farm in Huntington County, Indiana, whereas their mother and younger sister Catherine were residing in Henry County, Ohio, with brother Daniel.

Mary Ann Trubey's only husband was **Andrew W. Scofield**, son of Jared and Susannah Scofield,[385] born circa 1819 in New York.[386] This couple was married in Henry County, Ohio, on 20 or 21 March 1853.[387] The Trubey manuscript states that Mary Ann died on 15 September 1865 in Florida, Henry County, Ohio, at the age of 32 years, 5 months and 6 days but no proof of this death date was located.

---

[382] 1880 U.S. census, Henry County, Ohio, pop. sched., Flat Rock Twp., ED 115, p. 29; National Archives micropublication T9, roll 1032.

[383] 1900 U.S. census, Henry County, Ohio, pop. sched., Flat Rock Twp., ED 24, p. 12; National Archives micropublication T623, roll 1286.

[384] See Appendix B letter #6.

[385] Genevieve Eicher, editor and compiler, *Henry County, Ohio*, 3 (Napoleon, Ohio: Henry County Historical Society, 1979), 68.

[386] 1870 U.S. census, Henry County, Ohio, pop. sched., Flat Rock Twp., p. 7; National Archives micropublication M593, roll 1221. See also 1860 U.S. census, Henry County, Ohio, Flat Rock Twp., p. 253, and 1880 U.S. census, Henry County, Ohio, Flat Rock Twp., ED 115, p. 29.

[387] Henry County Marriage Book 1: 15; citation furnished by the Office of the Probate Judge, Napoleon, Ohio. *The 1st Marriage Records of Henry County[,] Ohio[,] 1847-1898* (Warsaw, Ind.: Scheuer Publications, 1992), gives an earlier date of 20 March 1853.

Andrew Scofield married (2) Catharine Gunn or Grimm,[388] and died between 1880 and 1900.[389]

The children of Mary Ann[3] Trubey and Andrew Scofield:
    127. i.   HELEN S.[4] SCOFIELD, "1854 – 1862"
    128. ii.   NELSON E. SCOFIELD, "1856 – 1864"
    129. iii. ELIZABETH J. SCOFIELD, "1858 – 1862"
    130. iv. "MARY E. SCOFIELD," "1861 –1862"
+ 131. v.   EFFIE S. SCOFIELD, born 11 June 1863; m. Abraham Lose

27. Elizabeth[3] Trubey (Daniel[2, 1]) was born 19 November 1838[390] in Sugar Creek Township, Stark County, Ohio. On 19 December 1858[391] in Henry County, Ohio, Elizabeth became the second wife of **George Long**, son of Armel Long and Hannah Grundel.[392] George was born 17 November 1819 in Butler County, Ohio.[393] George's first wife, Elizabeth Weaver, died in 1858 leaving three children: John, Noah and Lavina.[394]

---

[388] Eicher, *Henry County, Ohio*, 3: 68. *The 1st Marriages...of Henry County,*: 2 May 1869; gives the surname of this second bride as Grim(m), and both surnames occur in this county.

[389] 1900 U.S. census, Henry County, Ohio, pop. sched., Flat Rock Twp., ED 24, p. 13; National Archives micropublication T623, roll 1286. "Cathrin Scofield" a widow in 1900. See also 1880 U.S. census, Henry County, Ohio, Flat Rock Twp., ED 115, p. 29.

[390] Daniel Trubey Family Bible.

[391] Henry County Marriage Book 1: 115; from a citation furnished by the Office of the Probate Judge, Napoleon, Ohio.

[392] Aldrich, *Henry and Fulton Counties, Ohio*, 682.

[393] Eicher, *Henry Co., Ohio*, 3: 191.

[394] *Ibid.*

GENERATION THREE 83

The manuscript and the above county history state that George and Elizabeth (Trubey) Long were parents of seven children, three of whom died in infancy. Elizabeth reportedly died on 27 July 1878, but proof of this date has not been found. Her husband George married a third time to Mrs. Rebecca [—?—] Ice[395] before the 1880 Census.[396] George is said to have died on 26 February 1898.

The children of Elizabeth[3] Trubey and George Long:
    132. i.   WILLIAM H.[4] LONG ,"15 March 1860;" living in 1880
    133. ii.   GEORGE LONG, "21 May 1863" – died young
    134. iii. FRANKLIN LONG, "29 March 1865 – ca 1869"
+ 135. iv. CHARLES R. LONG, born 13 July 1869; m. Josephine Heckler
+ 136. v.   HERMAN LONG, born 1 April 1872 or 1873; m. Frances Menninger
+ 137. vi. [twin] CAREY MAY "NETTIE" LONG, born February 1876; m. John Palmer Blank
    138. vii. [twin] REUBEN LONG, b. February 1876 - d. young[397]

28. Catherine[3] Trubey (Daniel[2, 1]) was born 7 July 1842 in Sugar Creek Township, Stark County, Ohio.[398] She was married to **Franklin B. Carr** in Defiance County, Ohio, by the Rev. W. V. Thomas on 5 June 1869.[399] Franklin Carr, born in Ohio circa 1842, was a Civil

---

[395] *Ibid.*

[396] 1880 U. S. census, Henry Co., Ohio, pop. sched., Flat Rock Twp., ED 115, p. 26; National Archives micropublication T9, roll 1032.

[397] Eicher, *Henry Co., Ohio*, 3: 191.

[398] Daniel Trubey Family Bible.

[399] Frank B. Carr Pension (Co. D, 124th Ohio Infantry), application 901216, certificate 701028, and Kate Carr widow's application 827155, certificate 607618, Civil War and Later Pension Files, Records of the Veterans Administration (Record Group 15),

War veteran (Co. D, 124th Ohio Infantry) and pensioner who died of dysentery 16 October 1904 in Mercy Hospital in McAlester, Choctaw Nation, Central District, Indian Territory (later Oklahoma).[400]

Catherine, known as "Kate," was deserted by her husband Frank Carr in March 1898, according to her widow's pension deposition.[401] Kate and her children moved to St. Joseph, Buchanan County, Missouri, near her sister Rebecca Mohn [#23]. Rebecca Mohn provided an affidavit in 1906 in support of Kate's pension application, as did her son Charles Mohn in 1901.[402]

In the 1900 Census of St Joseph, Missouri, Kate gave her occupation as "dressmaker." Three daughters and one granddaughter then resided with her.[403]

Kate died of typhoid fever and a fractured hip 15 November 1914 in Denver, Colorado, where three of her children (Charles, Eugenie and Pansy) then lived.[404] She was buried in the Fairmont Cemetery in Denver.

National Archives, Washington, D.C. Marriage records of Defiance County confirms this (Volume 2: 153; FHL microfilm 0909336).

[400] Carr pension. The 1900 U.S. census (Choctaw Nation, Indian Territory, pop. sched., Twp. 6, ED 79, p. 14B; National Archives micropublication T623, roll 1851) lists a Frank Carr who may be this man, but whose age does not comport with other census records found for Kate's husband: age 46, born May 1854, in Pennsylvania, to German-born parents, widowed, occupation "marine engineer." This Frank was a boarder in the household of Marion Lynch.

[401] Carr pension.

[402] *Ibid.*

[403] 1900 U. S. census, Buchanan County, Missouri, pop. sched., St. Joseph City, ED 62, p. 21; National Archives micropublication T623, roll 842.

[404] Carr pension.

GENERATION THREE 85

The children of Catherine³ Trubey and Franklin Carr:
- 139. i. CHARLES H.⁴ CARR, born in May 1870 in Defiance, Ohio.⁴⁰⁵ Charles was last known to be living in Denver, Colorado, at the time of his mother's death in 1914.
- 140. ii. WILLIAM A. CARR, born 4 May 1871 in Defiance, Ohio;⁴⁰⁶ living in Defiance, Ohio, in 1880. His mother's 1900 Census entry does not indicate any of her five children were deceased by that date, but nothing further is known about William.
- \+ 141. iii. NETTIE E. CARR, born August 1874; m. Edward Graves
- 142. iv. EUGENIE E. CARR, born 12 April 1879⁴⁰⁷ in Defiance, Ohio.⁴⁰⁸ She was yet living in Denver, Colorado, in 1914.
- 143. v. PANSY CARR, born 15 July 1882 in Defiance, Ohio.⁴⁰⁹ She was living in Denver, Colorado, in 1914.

---

⁴⁰⁵ 1870 U.S. census, Defiance County, Ohio, pop. sched., Defiance, p. 50/46, 29 July; National Archives micropublication M593, roll 1195: gives "May" as his birth month and 1/12 of a year as his age, although his father's Civil War pension gives "10 June 1869." 1880 U.S. census, Defiance County, Ohio, pop. sched., Defiance, ED 233, p. 46; National Archives micropublication T9, roll 1011.

⁴⁰⁶ His father's pension gives full birth date as well as the family's residence in Defiance until 1885.

⁴⁰⁷ Her father's pension.

⁴⁰⁸ 1880 U.S. census, Defiance County, Ohio, Defiance, ED 233, p. 46.

⁴⁰⁹ Her father's pension.

Generation Four

29. Almon C.[4] **Welty** (Jacob T.[3], Nancy[2] Trubey, Daniel[1]) was born on or around 26 October 1843 in Bolivar, Lawrence Twp., Tuscarawas County, Ohio.[410] A letter written by Almon's father Jacob T. Welty on 27 July 1863 [see Appendix B letter #11] reveals that the latter refused to allow Almon to be recruited along with other service-aged neighbors during the Civil War. As a result, unknown persons fired shots at the Welty house in the middle of the night, yet Jacob remained steadfast in his desire "to hold Allman at the risk of my [Jacob's] own life."

Almon married in Tuscarawas County, Ohio, on 15 December 1864, **Mary E. Savage**,[411] daughter of Almon Savage and Maria Stout.[412] Mary was born circa 1841, possibly in Wayne Twp.,

---

[410] Stark County Chapter Ohio Genealogical Society, *Stark County, Ohio[,] Death Records* (No place: by the Society, 1991), 520-521: transcribed from original Volume 3: 590. A. C. Welty's age at death recorded here (51 years, 9 months, 7 days) calculates to a birth date of 26 October 1843. That approximate birth date is supported by his ages in the following census entries: 1850 U.S. census, Tuscarawas County, Ohio, pop. sched., Lawrence Twp, p. 185/369; National Archives micropublication M432, roll 734; 1860 census, Tuscarawas County, Ohio, pop. sched., Lawrence Twp, p. 332/19; National Archives micropublication M653, roll 1043; 1880 census, Stark County, Ohio, pop. sched., Sugar Creek Twp, ED 157, p. 32; National Archives micropublication T9, roll 1068.

[411] *Tuscarawas County, Ohio, Marriages 1864-1880, Volume III from Books 6 and 7* (New Philadelphia, Ohio: Tuscarawas County Genealogical Society, Inc., May 1990), 76: the celebrant U. Jesse Knisely, Ph. D., M.G., served the Lutheran church St. Paul's at Newcomerstown 1864-1865. The county marriage record is cited above as appearing in Book 6: 58, return #9989. Bride's surname rendered "Savidge."

[412] *Tuscarawas County, Ohio, Marriages 1808-1844, Volume I from Books 1-2-3* (New Philadelphia, Ohio: Tuscarawas County Genealogical Society, Inc., 1979), 68. The county marriage record is

GENERATION FOUR 87

Tuscarawas County, Ohio.[413] By the time of the 1880 Census, the couple and their two sons resided in Sugar Creek Township, Stark County, Ohio. This census entry is the last known living date and residence for Almon C. Welty. He died in Beach City of "constitutional disease" at age 51 years, 9 months, and 7 days, on 2 August 1895.[414] Mary's date and place of death are not known.

The children of Almon C.[4] Welty and Mary E. Savage:
- 144. i. CULLEN F.[5] WELTY, born February 1866; last known to be living as a single man in Cleveland, Ohio, in 1900.[415]
- 145. ii. PERLER OR PERLEE L. WELTY, born July 1870, married circa 1896 to Belle H. [—?—], and last known to be living in Canton, Ohio, in 1900, at which date the couple had two children: *(a)* James A. Welty, born August 1897, and *(b)* Walter H. Welty, born August 1899.[416]

31. Alvira N. or M.[4] Welty (Jacob T.[3], Nancy[2] Trubey, Daniel[1]) appears variously as "Ella" and "Ellen" in Federal Census records; she

---

cited above as appearing [Book not given]: 311, return #2481. 1860 U.S. census, Tuscarawas County, Ohio, pop. sched., Franklin Twp, P. O. Strasburg, p. 240/239; FHL microfilm 805043.

[413] Almon Savage indexed as appearing on page 396 of that locale's schedules of the 1840 Census.

[414] *Stark County Death Records*, 520-521.

[415] 1900 U.S. census, Cuyahoga County, Ohio, pop. sched., Cleveland, ED 12, p. 2; National Archives micropublication T623, roll 1252: boarder of Robert L. Grant on Bond Street.

[416] 1900 U.S. census, Stark County, Ohio, pop. sched., Canton, ED 95, p. 6; National Archives micropublication T623, roll 1321.

was born in Ohio in September 1850.[417] The date of her marriage to **David Naylor** appears in Stark County, Ohio, records as 26 February 1880[418] although David's Civil War pension contains both this and a second version (23 September 1882, by Dr. Kuns, English Lutheran Church).[419]

This pension furnished David Naylor's birth data as 17 March 1846 in "Newbury Twp., Lagrange County, Indiana." The 1850 and 1860 Census of that locality enumerated a family which does contain an appropriately-aged male named David; David's presumed parents from those entries are Thomas Naylor (born circa 1806 in Indiana or Scotland) and wife Margaret (born circa 1815 in Scotland).[420]

David enrolled for Civil War service on 28 September 1864, and was discharged on 28 June 1865 at Nashville, Tennessee, after serving with Co. G of the 142nd Indiana Infantry. His invalid pension application was based upon an injury received in Tennessee where he slipped on ice and injured his hip joint. This resulted in lameness in his left ankle and foot, compelling him to drag his leg. This 5' 5" tall, blue-eyed veteran resided in Sturgis, Michigan, and Lagrange, Indiana, after the war, and his occupation was as a merchant.

In addition to the aforementioned variations in Ella's given name, the census enumerator in 1880 — in St. Joseph County, Michigan —

---

[417] 1850 U.S. census, Tuscarawas County, Ohio, pop. sched., Lawrence Twp., p. 369/185; National Archives micropublication M432, roll 734.

[418] Stark County, Ohio, Marriages, Vol. 9: 282; FHL microfilm 0897627.

[419] David Naylor Pension (Co. G, 142nd Indiana Infantry), application 1306986, certificate 1087913, C2,513,239, Civil War and Later Pension Files, Records of the Veterans Administration (Record Group 15), National Archives, Washington, D.C.

[420] 1850 U.S. census, Lagrange County, Indiana, pop. sched., Newberry Twp., p. 42; National Archives micropublication M432, roll 157. 1860 U.S. census, Lagrange County, Indiana, pop. sched., Newberry Twp., p. 136/581; National Archives micropublication M653, roll 274.

GENERATION FOUR 89

recorded her name as "Welty."[421] By 1900, dry goods merchant David Naylor and family had removed to Lagrange County, Indiana.[422] It was in this Naylor household in Indiana that Ella's widowed mother Phianna (Klinker) Welty resided in 1900. Mrs. Ella (Welty) Naylor predeceased her husband, and at her death in 1915, her remains were interred in the Jacob T. Welty family plot in Stark County's Massillon City Cemetery.[423] David Naylor died on 8 January 1925 in Lagrange, Indiana.[424]

The children of Alvira/Ella[4] Welty and David Naylor:
146. i. ROGER WELTY[5] NAYLOR, born 16 March 1882 or 1883 in Michigan;[425] last known to be living on 2 March 1922.[426]
147. ii. unknown; this family's 1900 Census entry shows that "Ella" was the mother of two children, one of whom was deceased by that date.

---

[421] 1880 U.S. census, St. Joseph County, Michigan, pop. sched., Sturgis Village, ED 202, p. 50; National Archives micropublication T9, roll 603.

[422] 1900 U.S. census, Lagrange County, Indiana, pop. sched., Bloomfield, ED 70, p. 4; National Archives micropublication T623, roll 383.

[423] Sommer, *Stark Co., Ohio, Cemeteries*, 3: 877.

[424] "Drop Report" in David Naylor's pension furnishes this death data.

[425] Naylor pension. 1900 U.S. census, Lagrange County, Indiana, Bloomfield, ED 70, p. 4.

[426] Pension records include a questionnaire completed on this date by David Naylor which lists Roger as his only child (living or dead), and states Roger was then living. Neither David nor Roger were not found in a search of the 1920 Soundex to Indiana's census schedules.

36. Cullen M.[4] **Welty** (John[3], Nancy[2] Trubey, Daniel[1]) appears to have been born 5 February 1857[427] in Pike Township, Stark County, Ohio.[428] Cullen was a farmer in 1880 in Stark County and in 1900 in Tuscarawas County,[429] where he had married on 1 December 1897 **Mary Amelia Lebold**.[430] Amelia, daughter of Jacob R. Lebold and Mary Merchant, was born on 6 August 1871 in Fairfield Township, Tuscarawas County, Ohio.[431]

By 1900, there was one child of this couple in their household, as well as Cullen's widowed mother Mary Jane (McWhinney) Welty.

---

[427] Cullen M. Welty, death certificate no. 74677 (1931), Ohio Department of Health; FHL microfilm 1992480: birth date given as 5 February 18_6_7, yet his age at death of 74 years, 10 months, and 2 days places his birth at 18_5_7. See also 1860 U.S. census, Stark County, Ohio, pop. sched., Pike Twp, p. 14/430; National Archives micropublication M653, roll 1038. 1870 U.S. census, Stark County, Ohio, pop. sched., Pike Twp., p.6/542; National Archives micropublication M593, roll 1269. 1880 U.S. census, Stark County, Ohio, pop. sched., Pike Twp., ED 154, p. 2; National Archives micropublication T9, roll 1068/ 1900 U.S. census, Tuscarawas County, Ohio, pop. sched., Sandy Twp., ED 131, p. 16, dwelling 357, family 365; National Archives micropublication T623, roll 1327: born February 1860, and married two years at this time.

[428] Cullen M. Welty, Ohio state death certificate 74677.

[429] 1900 U.S. census, Tuscarawas County, Ohio, Sandy Twp., ED 131, p. 16, dwelling 357, family 365.

[430] Marriage Records, Tuscarawas County, Ohio, Volume 10 (1894-1899): 323, #22453; FHL microfilm 0890367. Ceremony officiated by J. N. *Beall*, M.G. The bride's name is given here as "Amelia," as it is most other places; however, it appears as "Mary A." on her death certificate for which her husband gave the information.

[431] Mary A. Welty, death certificate no. 19520 (1922), Ohio Bureau of Vital Statistics; FHL microfilm 1991915.

GENERATION FOUR 91

Tombstone inscriptions located for Cullen's family in Sandyville Greenlawn Cemetery, Sandy Township, Tuscarawas County, reveal a second child.[432]

Mary Amelia died on 19 March 1922 of appoplectic stroke at age 50; Cullen succumbed to valvular heart disease with lobar pneumonia and Bright's disease on 7 December 1931.[433]

The only known children of Cullen[4] Welty and Mary Amelia Lebold:
- 148. i. JOHN J.[5] WELTY, born October 1898; living in Tuscarawas County, Ohio, in 1910.[434] No further information.
- 149. ii. ALVIN CULLEN WELTY, born 12 February 1906 in Sandy Township, Tuscarawas County, Ohio; while a college student, Alvin accidentally drowned in Sandy Township on 15 July 1927, at age 21 years, 5 months, and 3 days.[435]

39. Tilden[4] Welty (Abraham[3], Nancy[2] Trubey, Daniel[1]) was born on 29 September 1853,[436] probably in Pike Twp, Stark County, Ohio.[437]

---

[432] Tuscarawas County Genealogical Society, Inc., *Tuscarawas County, Ohio, Cemeteries,* Volume IV (New Philadelphia, Ohio: by the society, not dated), 110.

[433] Cullen M. Welty, Ohio state death certificate 74677. Mary A. Welty, Ohio death certificate 19520.

[434] 1910 U.S. census, Tuscarawas County, Ohio, pop. sched., Sandy Twp., Precinct Two, ED 145, p. 94, dwelling 164, family 168, 30 April; National Archives micropublication T624, roll 1236.

[435] Alvin Cullen Welty, death certificate no. #43746, Ohio Division of Vital Statistics; FHL microfilm 1985114. See also his appearance in the 1910 U.S. census, Tuscarawas County, Ohio, Sandy Twp., Precinct Two, ED 145, p. 94, dwelling 164, family 168.

[436] Tilden Welty death certificate no. 63262, Ohio Department of Health; FHL microfilm 1992276.

Tilden was married on 8 February 1888 in Wayne County, Ohio, to **Selina A. McElhenie**,[438] the daughter of Joe McElhenie and Elizabeth Stinson.[439] Selina was born on 30 December 1858 in Ohio.[440]

Tilden apparently remained and farmed in Wayne County through at least 1900, at which time the census recorded him, his wife, and three children. No later census records were searched for him, but published tombstone inscriptions show Tilden, Selina, and one of their

---

[437] 1860 U.S. census, Stark County, Ohio, pop. sched., Pike Twp, p. 196/391; National Archives micropublication M653, roll 1038. 1870 U.S. census, Stark County, Ohio, pop. sched., Pike Twp., p. 14/430, National Archives micropublication M593, roll 1269. 1880 U.S. census, Stark County, Ohio, pop. sched., Lawrence Twp, ED 142, p. 70; National Archives micropublication T9, roll 1067. 1900 U.S. census, Wayne Co., Ohio, pop. sched., Baughman Twp., ED 139, p. 12; National Archives micropublication T623, roll 1331.

[438] Wayne County Marriage Volume 11: 26, according to a letter from David J. Skelly, 31 December 1985, reporting results of searches for seven Welty marriages in Wayne County. Original in possession of the compiler.

[439] Selina A. Welty death certificate no. 6495, Ohio Department of Health; FHL microfilm 1992988. *Wayne County, Ohio, Marriage Index 1813-1898* (Wooster, Ohio: Wayne County Genealogical Society, 1977), 164, shows Joseph McElhenie married Elizabeth Stinson there on 20 November 1838, volume 4A: 237, by J. McKee, minister.

[440] Selina A. Welty death certificate gives "1858;" however "1859" is given in her 1900 Census entry (1900 U.S. census, Wayne County, Ohio, pop. sched., Sugar Creek Twp., Village of Dalton, ED 159, p. 2; National Archives micropublication T623, roll 1332).

children were interred in the cemetery in Dalton, Wayne County.[441] Tilden died in Dalton on 9 October 1930 from cerebral apoplexy, and Selina died in Dalton on 8 January 1934 from carcinoma of the stomach.[442]

The known children of Tilden[4] Welty and Selina A. McElhenie:
- 150. i. BLANCHE JENETTIE[5] WELTY, born in Baughman Township, Wayne County, Ohio, on 26 February 1889;[443] no further information.
- 151. ii. WALTER E. WELTY, born in Baughman Township, Wayne County, Ohio, on 25 May 1892;[444] no further information.
- 152. iii. ALVA MCKINLEY WELTY, born in Baughman Township, Wayne County, Ohio, on 10 October 1899;[445] died in 1916, buried in the Dalton, Wayne County, Ohio, cemetery.

42. Minnie[4] Welty (Abraham[3], Nancy[2] Trubey, Daniel[1]) was born circa March 1862, according to her 1900 Census entry.[446] In Wayne County,

---

[441] Genealogical Section of the Wayne County Historical Society, compilers, *Wayne County, Ohio, Burial Records* (Evansville, Ind.: Unigraphic, Inc., 1975), 609.

[442] Tilden Welty, Ohio death certificate no. 63262. Selina A. Welty, Ohio death certificate 6495.

[443] *Probate Court Birth Records of Wayne Co., Ohio*, Volume 1: Original Birth Records in Volumes 1 - 4, 1867-1908 (No place: no publisher, 1991), p. 257: cites original record at 3: 62.

[444] *Ibid.*; cites original record at 3: 125.

[445] *Ibid.*; cites original record at 3: 243.

[446] 1900 U.S. census, Stark County, Ohio, pop. sched., Lawrence Twp., ED 118, p. 14; National Archives micropublication T623, roll 1322.

Ohio, she was married on 15 April 1885 to **Amos Miller**.[447] Amos was born in Ohio circa November 1858, and died sometime between 1900 and 1910, predeceasing his wife.[448] Minnie was last known to be living in 1910 at 212 West Creedmore Avenue, Barberton, Summit County, Ohio, with her two surviving children.

The children of Minnie[4] Welty and Amos Miller:
- 153. i. ROGER OSCAR[5] MILLER was born in December 1887, and worked as a machinist in a "match machine shop" in 1910 as a single 22-year-old man. No further information.
- 154. ii. MARY GERTRUDE MILLER was born in February 1892, and was employed as an organist at a Barberton Methodist Episcopal Church in 1910. No further information.
- 155. iii. unknown; died before 1900.

43. Nettie[4] Welty (Abraham[3], Nancy[2] Trubey, Daniel[1]) was born in May 1864 in Ohio.[449] Although she was married in Wayne County, Ohio, on 18 November 1891 to **Henry A. Bowers**,[450] she was enumerated as a resident of Stark County, Ohio, in every extant Federal Census from 1870 through 1910.[451] Henry Bower, born in December

---

[447] Wayne County Marriage Volume 10: 322, per Skelly letter.

[448] 1900 U.S. census, Stark County, Ohio, Lawrence Twp., ED 118, p. 14. 1910 Miracode, Summit County, Ohio, Barberton, ED 194, visitation number 170/265; National Archives micropublication T1272, roll 249, in which Minnie was listed as a widow.

[449] 1900 U.S. census, Stark County, Ohio, pop. sched., Perry Twp., Massillon, ED 136, p. 1; National Archives micropublication T623, roll 1322.

[450] Wayne County Marriage Volume 11: 433, per Skelly letter.

[451] 1870 U.S. census, Stark County, Ohio, pop. sched., Pike Twp., p. 5/542; National Archives micropublication M593, roll 1269. 1880 U.S. census, Stark County, Ohio, pop. sched., Lawrence Twp.,

1860 in Ohio,[452] made his living as a "grocer" in 1900, and as a "lumberman" in 1910, which is the date of the last census in which this family was sought. In that year they resided at 24 South Locust Street in Massillon, Stark County, Ohio.

The children of Nettie[4] Welty and Henry A. Bowers:
156. i.   RAYMOND[5] BOWERS was born in October 1892; yet living in Massillon in 1910; no further information.
157. ii. HELEN BOWERS was born in May 1894; yet living in Massillon in 1910; no further information.
158. iii. LAURA BOWERS was born in March 1896; yet living in Massillon in 1910; no further information.

44. Franklin[4] Welty (Abraham[3], Nancy[2] Trubey, Daniel[1]) was born about April 1868, likely in Stark County.[453] On 28 February 1893, Franklin married **Mary A. Brannon** in adjacent Wayne County.[454]

ED 142, p. 70; National Archives micropublication T9, roll 1067. 1900 U.S. census, Stark County, Ohio, Perry Twp., Massillon, ED 136, p. 1. 1910 Miracode, Stark County, Ohio, Perry Twp., Massillon, ED 231, visitation number 164/159; National Archives micropublication T1272, roll 37.

[452] 1900 U.S. census, Stark County, Ohio, pop. sched., Perry Twp., Massillon, ED 136, p. 1.

[453] 1900 U.S. census, Wayne County, Ohio, pop. sched., Sugar Creek Twp., Dalton, ED 159, p. 1; National Archives micropublication T623, roll 1332. 1870 U.S. census, Stark County, Ohio, pop. sched., Pike Twp., p. 5/542; National Archives micropublication M653, roll 1269.

[454] Wayne County Marriage Volume 11: 575, per Skelly letter. Surname appears here as "Brauneu," but birth records for their children render it "Brannon."

Mary was born in Pennsylvania in February 1873 to Irish and English parents.[455]

In 1900, Franklin was working as a day laborer in Dalton, where he resided with his family. Although this family was not sought in Federal Census records later than 1900, tombstone inscriptions indicate Franklin lived until 1924, and Mary until 1946; they were interred in the Dalton Cemetery in Wayne County.[456]

The children of Frankin[4] Welty and Mary A. Brannon:
- 159. i. HAZEL M.[5] WELTY, born in Dalton, Wayne County, on 17 July 1893;[457] no further information.
- 160. ii. GRETCHEN WELTY, born in Dalton, Wayne County, on 8 December 1895;[458] no further information.
- 161. iii. PAULENE WELTY, born in Dalton, Wayne County, on 30 March 1900;[459] no further information.
- 162. iv. CHARLES HENRY WELTY, born in Dalton, Wayne County, on 10 April 1905;[460] no further information.

---

[455] 1900 U.S. census, Wayne County, Ohio, pop. sched., Sugar Creek Twp., Dalton, ED 159, p. 1.

[456] Genealogical Section of the Wayne County Historical Society, compilers, *Wayne County, Ohio, Burial Records* (1975), 614.

[457] *Probate Court Birth Records of Wayne Co., Ohio*, 1: 257: cites original record at 3: 144. Her 1900 Census entry gives "August" as her month of birth.

[458] *Ibid.*; cites original record at 3: 180.

[459] *Ibid.*; cites original record at 3: 243.

[460] *Ibid.*; cites original record at 4: 54 - I313.

GENERATION FOUR 97

46. Mary Ann⁴ Trubey (Jacob Andrew³, David², Daniel¹) was born in Ohio in August 1833[461] or 1834.[462] Her birth likely occurred in Tuscarawas County, where her parents were married in early 1833. Proof of her 10 August 1856 Tuscarawas County marriage to **Henry Sprain** was obtained from the latter's Civil War pension records.[463] According to those records, the ceremony was performed by John Ruff or Rueff, Justice of the Peace. Henry's birth date in Germany can be calculated to 4 February 1829,[464] and he was in Van Wert County by 1850, when his census entry shows he resided with Hoffman and Hei individuals, the latter of whom appeared in his pension records with his surname spelled "High."[465] At his enlistment with Co. H, 139th Ohio Infantry, Henry was 28 years old, 5' 8" tall, fair complected, with blue eyes and dark hair.[466]

Henry Sprain was a farmer, and census records indicate he owned considerable property in Van Wert County; there was even a land

---

[461] 1900 U.S. census, Van Wert County, Ohio, pop. sched., York Twp., ED 99, p. 13; National Archives micropublication T623, roll 1329.

[462] Van Wert County Chapter of the Ohio Genealogical Society, *Van Wert County, Ohio, Cemetery Inscriptions*, Volume IV (by the Society, 1990), 172: Tomlinson Cemetery tombstone inscription gives "1834" as her birth year.

[463] Henry Sprain Pension (Co. H, 139th Ohio Infantry), application 355833, certificate 498733, Civil War and Later Pension Files, Records of the Veterans Administration (Record Group 15), National Archives, Washington, D.C.

[464] Pension records state Henry died on 4 May 1883 at age 54 years and 3 months.

[465] 1850 U.S. census, Van Wert County, Ohio, pop. sched., York Twp., p. 200/399; National Archives micropublication M432, roll 736.

[466] Henry Sprain pension.

certificate in the pension file indicating his ownership of the W½ SE¼, the E½ SW¼, and the SW¼ NW¼ of Section 30 in York Township. It was here in York Township, Van Wert County, Ohio, that Henry died on 4 May 1883;[467] Mary Ann died in 1916, and was interred beside Henry in the Tomlinson Cemetery in Union Township, Mercer County, Ohio.[468]

The children of Mary Ann[4] Trubey and Henry Sprain:[469]

163. i. SOPHIA ELLEN[5] SPRAIN, born circa 1857 in Ohio; no further information.

164. ii. HENRY CLARK SPRAIN, born October[470] 1858;[471] married Sally Pritchard (1867-1896); children *(a)* Abie [son] 1890-1898, *(b)* Goldie born September 1892, married Carl B. Fisher, died 1949, *(c)* Maudie 1895-1896. Clark died 1920.

165. iii. LYDIA C. SPRAIN, born 1861; died 1890 at age 29 years, 2 months, and 20 days.

166. iv. MARY SPRAIN, born circa 1863; no further information.

---

[467] Henry Sprain pension.

[468] *Van Wert County, Ohio, Cemetery Inscriptions*, IV: 172.

[469] 1860 U.S. census, Van Wert County, Ohio, pop. sched., York Twp., Auglaize, p. 85/394; National Archives micropublication M653, roll 1045. 1870 U.S. census, Van Wert County, Ohio, pop. sched., York Twp., Auglaize, p. 459/15; National Archives micropublication M593, roll 1275. 1880 U.S. census, Van Wert County, Ohio, pop. sched., York Twp., ED 156, p. 17; National Archives micropublication T9, roll 1074. Henry Sprain pension. All death years are taken from *Van Wert County, Ohio, Cemetery Inscriptions*, IV: 172, except where noted.

[470] 1900 Census for month.

[471] *Van Wert County, Ohio, Cemetery Inscriptions*, IV: 168, for birth year, and for data identifying his wife and three children.

167.	v.	ELMINA "MINA L." SPRAIN, born in April 1864 or 1865; died in 1935 at age 70 years, 9 months, and 18 days.
168.	vi.	MARTHA SPRAIN, born circa June 1866/1868; no further information.
169.	vii.	JANE ETTA SPRAIN, born 16 April 1868; living in December 1941.[472]
170.	viii.	PHILLIP AUGUSTUS SPRAIN, born 27 August 1870; died 1911 at age 40 years, 6 months, and 18 days.
171.	ix.	EMMA A. SPRAIN, born 1872; died 1879 at age 7 years, 8 months, and 24 days.
172.	x.	ABRAHAM F. SPRAIN, born 1874; died 1879 at age 5 years, 6 months, and 8 days.
173.	xi.	SAMANTHA ELIZABETH "BESSIE" SPRAIN, born 16 October 1875; died 1952 at age 76 years, 9 months, and 12 days.
174.	xii.	IDA FLORENCE SPRAIN, born 17 December 1878; died 1957 at age 78 years, 11 months, and 5 days.

48. Lydia Catherine[4] **Trubey** (Jacob Andrew[3], David[2], Daniel[1]) was born in Ohio on or near 12 January 1839,[473] and became the second wife of **Philip Profit** on 3 June 1870 in Van Wert County, Ohio.[474]

---

[472] Trubey manuscript, 5.

[473] 1850 U.S. census, Tuscarawas County, Ohio, pop. sched., Dover, p. 130/65; National Archives micropublication M432, roll 734. Tuscarawas County Guardianship case no. A618-1-3-206, Vol. 2: 67. *Van Wert County, Ohio, Cemetery Inscriptions*, IV: 180 (Tomlinson Cemetery): the date of birth for Lydia is calculated from her age at death given here as 36 years, 7 months, and 29 days on 10 September 1875.

[474] Van Wert County Marriage Volume 3: 507, #961, Office of Probate Judge, Van Wert, Ohio. Copy in possession of compiler.

100 DANIEL TRUBEY OF FRANKLIN COUNTY, PENNSYLVANIA

Philip Profit was a shoemaker, born in Bavaria circa 1828.[475] There is a record of his earlier marriage in Van Wert County to a Dorothy Maisch on 19 September 1854,[476] but she died on 28 November 1867.[477]

There is some uncertainty about the children of Philip Profit by both of his wives. There were no children surviving in 1860, six years after Philip's first marriage to Dorothy Maisch, yet by 1870 an 11-year-old "Donday" [female] and a 9-year-old John were in Philip's household. Three days after the official date of this census, Philip married Lydia Catherine Trubey. By 1880, *another* "unaccounted for" child — Susan, age 16 — appears in their household (along with five others who were born in or after 1870), yet Susan did not appear as a 6-year-old in Philip's 1870 household. To further complicate matters, Philip's wife in 1880 was not Lydia (born 1839 in Ohio) but rather "Catherine," born circa 1837 in Indiana. Lydia's tombstone in the Tomlinson Cemetery of Union Township, Mercer County, Ohio, gives her date of death as 10 September 1875;[478] this concurs with the Trubey manuscript which further states that Lydia Catherine (Trubey) Profit had three children by Philip Profit: "Charles, Margaret and Mary."[479]

---

[475] 1860 U.S. census, Van Wert County, Ohio, pop. sched., Van Wert, p. 459; National Archives micropublication M653, roll 1045. 1870 U.S. census, Van Wert County, Ohio, pop. sched., Pleasant Twp., Van Wert Village, p. 332/3; National Archives micropublication M593, roll 1275. 1880 U.S. census, Van Wert County, Ohio, pop. sched., Pleasant Twp., ED 151, p. 26; National Archives micropublication T9, roll 1073.

[476] *Data of the Van Wert County, Ohio, Marriage Record: Book 1* in Ohio DAR GRC (typescript, 1948), 46.

[477] *Van Wert County, Ohio, Cemetery Inscriptions*, IV: 180 (Tomlinson Cemetery). "Dorothea's" age at death was 40 years, 9 months, and 24 days.

[478] *Ibid.*

[479] Trubey manuscript, 5.

GENERATION FOUR   101

To reconcile the 1870 findings with that statement, Emma may also have been known as Mary, and Theodore may have died young or simply been overlooked by the supplier of Profit data to the manuscript's compiler. Philip Profit died 1 September 1885, at age 57 years, 6 months, and 25 days, and was buried by his first and second wives in the Tomlinson Cemetery.[480]

The children of Lydia Catherine[4] Trubey and Philip Profit:

- 175. i. EMMA[5] ["MARY?"] PROFIT, born circa 1870; no further information known.
- 176. ii. CHARLES PROFIT, born circa 1871.
- 177. iii. THEODORE PROFIT, born circa 1872.
- 178. iv. MARGARET "MAGGIE" PROFIT, born circa 1873.

50. Abraham M.[4] Trubey (Jacob Andrew[3], David[2], Daniel[1]) was born 20 April 1843 near Bolivar, Tuscarawas County, Ohio, according to his Civil War pension, granted in consideration of the gunshot wound he received as a soldier in Co. A of the 46th Ohio Infantry.[481] These pension records also confirm that Abraham was a 5' 8½" tall, fair-complected, dark-haired farmer with hazel eyes.

Abraham enlisted on 10 September 1861, and was first hospitalized when he contracted typhoid fever in Holly Springs, Mississippi, in December 1862; he was taken to the regional hospital at Grand Junction. He was later in the battle of Shiloh, Tennessee, where on 6 April 1863, he received his leg wound and was hospitalized at Keokuk Tower. On 15 October 1864, he was hospitalized again for inflammation of his wound, this time in Chattanooga, Tennessee. Abraham received his discharge from the army on 29 July 1865.

This Civil War pension also contains proof of Abraham's 11 May 1874 marriage to **Mary M. Frysinger** performed by Jayson Young in

---

[480] *Van Wert County, Ohio, Cemetery Inscriptions*, IV: 180 (Tomlinson Cemetery).

[481] Abraham Trubey Pension (Co. A, 46th Ohio Infantry), application 158599, certificate 114206, Records of the Veterans Administration (Record Group 15), National Archives, Washington, D.C.

Celina, Mercer County, Ohio, as well as proof of their five children. A published history claims that Mary (born August 1856)[482] was the daughter of Nathan and Jane (Ryan) Frysinger, whose genealogical history is given in great detail there.[483] Abraham and his family resided in Dublin Township, Mercer County, Ohio, from 1880 through 1910.[484] The pension check dated 4 March 1918 for Abraham M. Trubey of Rockford, Ohio, was returned to the pension office "with the information that the pensioner died December 31, 1917."[485] Mary's death date and place are not known.

The children of Abraham M.[4] Trubey and Mary M. Frysinger:
- 179. i. BERTHA V.[5] TRUBEY, born 16 August 1879, and was married to a Mr. Fair by 1898, according to the pension records. She may have died by 1900, when her mother's census entry recorded that of her five children, only four were living, and four children were then in her household.
- 180. ii. MINNIE L. TRUBEY, born 27 March 1885 or 1886; no further information.
- 181. iii. ELIDA TRUBEY, born 9 June 1887 or 1889.
- 182. iv. RALPH A. TRUBEY, born 8 February 1891.

---

[482] 1900 U.S. census, Mercer County, Ohio, pop. sched., Dublin Twp., Rockford Village, ED 78, p. 11; National Archives micropublication T623, roll 1303.

[483] [Anonymous], *A Portrait and Biographical Record of Mercer and Van Wert Counties, Ohio* (Chicago: A. W. Bowen & Co., 1896), 323-325.

[484] 1880 U.S. census, Mercer County, Ohio, pop. sched., Dublin Twp., ED 182, p. 22; National Archives micropublication T9, roll 1048. 1900 U.S. census, Mercer County, Ohio, Dublin Twp., Rockford Village, ED 78, p. 11. 1910 Miracode, Mercer County, Ohio, ED 111, visitation number 130/63; National Archives micropublication T1272, roll 373.

[485] Abraham Trubey pension.

GENERATION FOUR

183. v. REGENAL [REGINALD?] TRUBEY, born 25 May 1895.

52. Samantha J.[4] **Arbaugh** (Susannah[3] Trubey, David[2], Daniel[1]) was born in Ohio in November 1840,[486] the first of John and Susannah (Trubey) Arbaugh's children, and the one who would travel the most in her lifetime. Her marriage in Wells County, Indiana, on 28 August 1858 to **William Holloway** suggests that her family had settled there at least two years before the 1860 Federal Census enumerated them in that locale.[487]

William Holloway served in the Civil War in Company G of the 101st Indiana Infantry, and was wounded in the thigh in the Battle of Chickamauga, Georgia, on 19 September 1863. He was captured in a field hospital on 20 September 1863, and paroled in Chattanooga on 29 September 1863.[488] Information in these files proves William was born 15 January 1840 in Randolph County, Indiana, and died on 13 March 1910 in Enterprise, Wallowa County, Oregon.

William appears to have been the last child born to former-Quaker Pleasant Holloway, whose birth was recorded in Quaker records of Bedford and Campbell Counties, Virginia, as occurring on the 23rd day of the 4th month of 1795;[489] Pleasant was disowned on the 15th

---

[486] 1900 U.S. census, Wallowa County, Oregon, pop. sched., Lost Prairie Precinct, ED 103, p. 8, dwelling/family 209; National Archives micropublication T623, roll 1352.

[487] Mary Penrose Wayne Chapter DAR, compilers, *Marriage Records of Wells County, Indiana, 1837-1900* (G.R.C. 1956-1957), 57.

[488] William Holloway Pension (Co. G, 101st Indiana Infantry), application 363688, certificate 161501, and Samantha Holloway widow's application 942181, certificate 710788, Civil War and Later Pension Files, Records of the Veterans Administration (Record Group 15), National Archives, Washington, D.C.

[489] William W. Hinshaw, compiler, *Encyclopedia of American Quaker Genealogy*, Volume 6: Virginia (Ann Arbor, Mich.: Edwards Brothers, 1950), 314 ; Volume 5: Ohio, 248, 339, 446. 1850 U.S.

day of the 12th month of 1821 for marrying "out of unity." Presumably this was his marriage to the similarly-aged Samaria, who was enumerated in Pleasant's household in 1850. William Holloway's 1910 responses to the pension questionnaires revealed his post Civil War residences as Indiana until 1869, Kansas until 1882, Choctaw Nation until 1884, then Oregon.[490] This file contains many statements made by relatives and in-laws of William Holloway. His widow's death date is not known, although there is evidence in his pension file that Samantha resided in San Francisco circa 1914.

The children of Samantha[4] Arbaugh and Willliam Holloway:[491]

184. i. CATHERINE ELIZABETH[5] HOLLOWAY, born in Indiana circa 1859,[492] and married a Mr. Oliver sometime before 1898, according to her father's pension records.

185. ii. PHEBY KEZIAH HOLLOWAY, born circa 1861, and married a Mr. Reed before 1898.

---

census, Randolph County, Indiana, pop. sched., Stoney Creek Twp., p. 10; National Archives micropublication M432, roll 292.

[490] Part of this migration is supported by the 1870 U.S. census, Marion County, Kansas, pop. sched., Center Twp., p. 286/10; National Archives micropublication M593, roll 438, and 1880 U.S. census, Chase County, Kansas, pop. sched., ED 144, p. 5/22; National Archives micropublication T9, roll 375. Note that a 4-year-old "Amey A. Halloway" died in May 1870 of diphtheria; she may have been a child of William's whom he did not list in his pension, or she may have been his niece, as there is another Holloway family enumerated after William's family in 1870 (1870 U.S. census, Marion County, Kansas, mortality schedule, Center Twp.; National Archives micropublication T1130, roll 3).

[491] Approximate birth dates and places taken from the 1870, 1880, and 1900 Census records previously cited.

[492] 1860 U.S. census, Wells County, Indiana, pop. sched., Union Twp., p. 61/234; National Archives micropublication M653, roll 309, 23 June: "Catharine E." age 9/12.

GENERATION FOUR 105

186. iii. SUSAN CAROLINE HOLLOWAY, born in May 1868 or 1869 in Indiana, and married circa 1886 Luis Nicson or Nicoson.[493]
187. iv. NORA LOUETHA HOLLOWAY, born in July 1871 in Kansas, and married John Wakefield circa 1897.[494]
188. v. WILLIAM BARKDOLL HOLLOWAY, born May 1877 in Kansas, and married Texas-born Emma L. [—?—] circa 1897.[495]
189. vi. JOHN TIPTON HOLLOWAY, born March 1882 in Kansas; living in Wallowa County, Oregon, in 1900.

53. Catherine Ann[4] **Arbaugh** (Susannah[3] Trubey, David[2], Daniel[1]) was born in November 1842[496] in Ohio.[497] It may have been with her

---

[493] 1900 U.S. census, Wallowa County, Oregon, Lost Prairie Precinct, ED 103, p. 8, dwelling/family 216.

[494] *Ibid.*, dwelling/family 195.

[495] *Ibid.*, dwelling/family 219.

[496] 1900 U.S. census, Creek Nation, Indian Territory, pop. sched., Township 17 North, Range 9 East, ED 54, p. 4B; National Archives micropublication T623, roll 1853.

[497] 1850 U.S. census, Tuscarawas County, Ohio, pop. sched., Dover Twp., p. 130; National Archives micropublication M432, roll 734. 1860 U.S. census, Wells County, Indiana, pop. sched., Union Twp., p. 49/822; National Archives micropublication M653, roll 309. 1870 U.S. census, Wells County, Indiana, pop. sched., Union Twp., p. 2; National Archives micropublication M593, roll 372. 1880 U.S. census, Morris County, Kansas, pop. sched., Clark's Creek Twp., ED 130, p. 19; National Archives micropublication T9, roll 390. 1900 U.S. census, Creek Nation, Indian Territory, Township 17 North, Range 9 East, ED 54, p. 4B. 1910 U.S. census, Creek County, Oklahoma, pop. sched., Depew Twp., ED 40, p. 9; National Archives micropublication T624, roll 1249.

brother David F. Arbaugh that Catherine migrated to Morris County, Kansas, where on 12 May 1872[498] she became the second wife[499] of

---

[498] Joseph Mays Pension (Co. M, 9th Kansas Cavalry), application 388787, certificate 348675, C2,575,137, Civil War and Later Pension Files, Records of the Veterans Administration (Record Group 15), National Archives, Washington, D.C.

[499] 1910 U.S. census, Creek County, Oklahoma, Depew Twp., ED 40, p. 9. Joseph's first wife Margaret Ann Atkinson (per pension) died 12 November 1869 at age 19 years, 7 months and 12 days (*Morris County Kansas Cemetery Inscriptions*, Volume 2 [Council Grove, Kansas: 1990] listed as Kansas DAR GRC 1991 Series 2, volume 14 [1991], 127). However, she was recorded with Joseph "Maze" and their two children William 2, and Isaac 8/12 in the 1870 U.S. census, Morris County, Kansas, pop. sched., Clark's Creek Twp., p. 679/4; National Archives micropublication M593, roll 439. Margaret was also listed in the mortality schedule of that year, which lists her death date as December [1869], and cause as pneumonia (Helen Franklin and Thelma Carpenter, compilers, *1870 Mortality Schedule of Kansas* [by the Topeka Genealogical Society, 1974], 143, entry #27). Joseph's pension mentions this first wife, and identifies his first two children (which were born to this first wife) as William Wesley, born 24 November 1867, and Isaac Dickenson, born 3 October 1869.

GENERATION FOUR

Joseph Mays, son of David Mays and Mrs. Mary (Archer) Atkinson.[500] Joseph was born 23 March 1845 in Monroe County, Ohio.[501] Joseph Mays enrolled for service in the Civil War with the 9th Kansas Cavalry on 1 July 1861 at Council Grove, Kansas.[502] He was wounded in the left arm on 24 July 1864 ten miles below Little Rock, Arkansas, and was discharged on 17 July 1865 at Duvall's Bluff, Arkansas. Following the war, Joseph lived in Council Grove and Kingman, Kansas, in panhandle Texas, in Payne and Lincoln Counties, Oklahoma Territory, and, finally, in the part of Creek Nation, Indian Territory, which would become Creek County, Oklahoma.

Joseph was a farmer who owned his own farm in Creek County, Oklahoma, by 1910,[503] and still held 500 acres of land there at his death on 2 March 1936 in Bristow, Oklahoma.[504] Catherine died sometime after 1910 and before 1920, at which latter date Joseph was enumerated

---

[500] Death certificate in his pension file. See also Catharine Foreaker Fedorchak, *Monroe County, Ohio, Genealogical Records*, Vol. XI (Gary, Indiana: 1974), 110: "Record Book 7, p. 106, Petition to sell lands filed 8 June 1844, Martin Troy admr of the estate of Abel Atkinson vs. Mary Mays and David her husband and Matilda Atkinson. The said decedent died leaving Mary Atkinson his widow, since intermarried with David Mays and Matilda Atkinson his heir."

[501] Joseph Mays pension. This information supported by the 1880 and 1910 Census, and 1920 Soundex (Creek County, Kansas, Bristow Twp., ED 16, p. 3; National Archives micropublication M1563, roll 100) at which time he had a third wife Minerva.

[502] Joseph Mays pension.

[503] *Ibid.*

[504] Joseph Mays pension, plus Nancy Green Chapter NSDAR, *Creek County [Oklahoma] Burials - Hutchins-Maples Funeral Home, Bristow, Ok. September 1929 - December 1956* (Sapulpa, Oklahoma: November 1990), 31.

with a (third) wife Minerva.[505] Catherine's 1900 Census entry shows she was the mother of six children, all six of whom were then living, but Joseph's pension records identify only the youngest four.[506]

The children of Catherine[4] Arbaugh and Joseph Mays:
190. i. WALTER FRANKLIN[5] MAYS, born 6 May 1873 in Kansas;[507] he married circa 1893 Pearl [—?—] (born circa 1877 in Kansas to a New York-born father and Indiana-born mother).[508] Of the three children born to them by 1910, only two were then living: *(a)* Ethel (born circa 1895 in Oklahoma), and *(b)* Lloyd (born circa 1900 in Oklahoma).[509]

---

[505] 1910 U.S. census, Creek County, Oklahoma, Depew Twp., ED 40, p. 9. 1920 Soundex, Creek County, Kansas, Bristow Twp., ED 16, p. 3. Minerva predeceased Joseph as well, as he was listed as a widower on his death certificate.

[506] 1900 U.S. census, Creek Nation, Indian Territory, Township 17 North, Range 9 East, ED 54, p. 4B.

[507] Joseph Mays pension. 1880 U.S. census, Morris County, Kansas, Clark's Creek Twp., ED 130, p. 19. 1910 U.S. census, Creek County, Oklahoma, Depew Twp., ED 40, p. 9.

[508] 1910 U.S. census, Creek County, Oklahoma, Depew Twp., ED 40, p. 9. This family was sought but not found in the 1900 Soundex to both Oklahoma and Kansas under codes for both May and Mays.

[509] 1900 U.S. census, Creek Nation, Indian Territory, Township 17 North, Range 9 East, ED 54, p. 4B. 1910 U.S. census, Creek County, Oklahoma, Depew Twp., ED 40, p. 9.

GENERATION FOUR 109

191. ii. NORMA GERTRUDE MAYS, born 9 October 1874 or 1875 in Kansas.[510] Norma was married circa 1893 to James G. Wilson, who was born May 1864 in Missouri.[511] One of Norma's six children born prior to 1900 had died, the survivors being *(a)* Walter F. Wilson (born circa 1896 in Oklahoma), *(b)* Alford E. (born circa 1902 in Oklahoma), *(c)* Loren C. (born circa 1906 in Missouri), and twins *(d)* and *(e)* both unnamed as of 29 April 1910 (born circa January 1910).[512]

192. iii. ANNA BELL MAYS, born 26 September 1876 in Kansas;[513] no further information.

193. iv. JOSEPH ARCHER MAYS, born 14 June 1878 in Kansas;[514] living in Creek Nation in 1900.

---

[510] Joseph Mays pension. 1880 U.S. census, Morris County, Kansas, Clark's Creek Twp., ED 130, p. 19. 1910 U.S. census, Creek County, Oklahoma, Depew Twp., ED 40, p. 9. The 1880 and 1910 Census support 1875, but 1900 Census gives 1874 (1900 U.S. census, Creek Nation, Indian Territory, Township 17 North, Range 9 East, ED 54, p. 4B).

[511] 1900 U.S. census, Creek Nation, Indian Territory, Township 17 North, Range 9 East, ED 54, p. 4B. 1910 U.S. census, Creek County, Oklahoma, Depew Twp., ED 40, p. 9.

[512] 1910 U.S. census, Creek County, Oklahoma, Depew Twp., ED 40, p. 9.

[513] Joseph Mays pension. 1880 U.S. census, Morris County, Kansas, Clark's Creek Twp., ED 130, p. 19.

[514] *Ibid.*

194. v. EMMA J. MAYS, born July 1884 in Kansas;[515] living in Creek Nation in 1900.

54. Elizabeth J. E.[4] Arbaugh (Susannah[3] Trubey, David[2], Daniel[1]) was born in Indiana in January 1845, according to her 1900 Federal Census entry.[516] Her 7 January 1866 Wells County, Indiana, marriage to Civil War veteran **John D. [or W.] Nedrow** (Co. G, 58th and 101st Indiana Infantry) is confirmed by both county marriage records and her husband's pension records.[517]

A death certificate for John Nedrow is part of his pension file, and it shows that he died on 9 October 1937 in Joseph, Wallowa County, Oregon, at age 93 years, 9 months and 9 days. John's parents are listed as Simon and Rebecca [—?—] Nedrow, both born in Pennsylvania, and John's birth data are recorded thereon as 31 January 1844 in Ohio. A questionnaire completed by John in his lifetime furnished "Tuscarosa County, Ohio" as his birthplace; with this information it was possible to locate the 22 August 1841 marriage in *Tuscarawas* County, Ohio, of his parents Simon Nedrow and Rebecca Crites.[518] Further research indicates that Rebecca was the granddaughter of Revolutionary War

---

[515] 1900 U.S. census, Creek Nation, Indian Territory, Township 17 North, Range 9 East, ED 54, p. 4B. Emma is *not* mentioned in her father's pension records.

[516] 1900 U.S. census, Wallowa County, Oregon, pop. sched., Lost Prairie Precinct, ED 103, p. 7; National Archives micropublication T623, roll 1352.

[517] *Wells County Marriages*, p. 96. John W. Nedrow Pension (Co. G, 58th and 101st Indiana Infantry), application 459224, certificate 462319, Civil War and Later Pension Files, Records of the Veterans Administration (Record Group 15), National Archives, Washington, D.C.

[518] Margaret Dickinson, compiler, Katherine R. Scott, copyist, *Tuscarawas County, Ohio, Marriage Records 1808-1845* (Massillon Chapter Ohio DAR, 1967), 136.

GENERATION FOUR   111

soldier Jacob Crites (1740-1820), through his son John (1785-1859), per wills of both of these men.

Census records show the John Nedrow family resided in Wells County, Indiana, in 1870,[519] although his pension indicates they removed [perhaps later] that year to Kansas, where they remained through 1878. The pension responses identify Colorado as their next home, from 1878 to 1885, yet the census-recorded birthplaces of their children and the 1880 Census itself show this family was in Missouri during at least some of these years.[520] By 1900, farmer John Nedrow's family was enumerated only a few households away from Mrs. Elizabeth (Arbaugh) Nedrow's sister Mrs. Samantha (Arbaugh) Holloway in Wallowa County, Oregon.

No death date for Elizabeth was found in John's pension files, but she was living on 13 June 1910 when she deposed, for her sister's pension application, that she attended both William Holloway's wedding and funeral. Elizabeth was likely living as late as 10 June 1912 when John completed a questionnaire which included data about his marriage, and she was not described as deceased.

The children of Elizabeth[4] Arbaugh and John Nedrow:[521]

195. i.   MARY C.[5] NEDROW, born 27 September 1866 in Indiana; as Mary C. Turner, her 1938 deposition in her father's pension identifies her residence then as 1244 19th Street, Boulder, Colorado.
196. ii. JOSEPH FRANKLIN NEDROW, born 18 September 1871 in Kansas; no further information.
197. iii. JOHN ALLEN NEDROW, born 6 November 1873 in Kansas; he appears in the 1900 Census of Wallowa

---

[519] 1870 U.S. census, Wells County, Indiana, pop. sched., Union Twp., dwelling 18; National Archives micropublication M593, roll 372.

[520] 1880 U.S. census, Ozark County, Missouri, pop. sched., Bridger Twp., ED 109, p. 15/26; National Archives micropublication T9, roll 707.

[521] All names and complete birth dates obtained from the John W. Nedrow pension.

County, Oregon, with a wife Carrie B., whom he married that year.

198. iv. WILLIAM HENRY NEDROW, born 29 May 1878 in Missouri. William was single in 1900, but married and left two daughters Jane (born circa 1922) and Leona (born circa 1927) at his death prior to 1938, according to sister Mary C. Turner's deposition of that date.

199. v. JESSE(Y) WESLEY NEDROW, born 19 March 1881 or 1882 in Missouri; Jesse was interviewed in 1936 for his father's pension, as was his daughter Mrs. Glen M. Tetrick (of 1002 14th Street, LaGrande, Oregon).

55. David Franklin[4] **Arbaugh** (Susannah Trubey[3], David[2], Daniel[1]) was born in April 1847 in Ohio,[522] probably Tuscarawas County. His family removed to Indiana by 1860, and to Kansas by 1870.[523]

On 10 October 1879, "Franklin" was married to **Nancy Ellen Fry** in Morris County, Kansas.[524] Nancy was born in July 1852 in Indiana, to parents born in Kentucky and Ohio, respectively.[525] The couple

---

[522] 1900 U.S. census, Chautauqua County, Kansas, pop. sched., Little Caney Twp., ED 9, p. 9; National Archives micropublication T623, roll 473.

[523] 1870 U.S. census, Marion County, Kansas, pop. sched., Center Twp., p. 286/10; National Archives micropublication M593, roll 438.

[524] Letter from Morris County District Court Deputy, 6 June 1985; in possession of compiler.

[525] 1900 U.S. census, Chautauqua County, Kansas, Little Caney Twp., ED 9, p. 9.

GENERATION FOUR   113

resided in Morris County, Kansas, in 1880,[526] and by 1900 had settled in Little Caney Township, Chautauqua County, Kansas.[527]

"Frank" Arbaugh gave depositions for Civil War pension applications of two of his brothers-in-law: John Nedrow and William Holloway. On 6 November 1883, Frank was a resident of Cascade, Chautauqua County, Kansas, when he deposed that he had earlier lived within two miles of John Nedrow.[528] Frank's 14 July 1894 deposition in William Holloway's pension file indicates that he then resided in Caney, Montgomery County, Kansas, and furnishes background data that he resided with the Holloways until the fall of 1870, which is corroborated by that family's 1870 Census entry in Marion County, Kansas.[529] He further stated that Holloway was "my father's nearest neighbor," and that the families moved from Indiana to Kansas in 1869.

D. F. and N. E. Arbaugh's 1900 Census entry indicates that Nancy was the mother of five children, four of whom were then living. One newlywed and childless daughter lived in the household, and the grandson in the household appears to belong to the second Arbaugh daughter listed. The couple yet resided in Little Caney Township,

---

[526] 1880 U.S. census, Morris County, Kansas, pop. sched., Highland, ED 134, p. 1; National Archives micropublication T9, roll 491.

[527] 1900 U.S. census, Chautauqua County, Kansas, Little Caney Twp., ED 9, p. 9.

[528] John W. Nedrow pension. David Franklin Arbaugh did not claim service in the Civil War in his 1910 Census enumeration, nor was any pension record found for him.

[529] William Holloway pension (Co. G, 101st Indiana Infantry), application 363688, certificate 161501; widow's application 942181, certificate 710788, Civil War and Later Pension Files, Records of the Veterans Administration (Record Group 15), National Archives, Washington, D.C. See 1870 Census cited above.

Chautauqua County, Kansas, by the time of the 1920 Census;[530] their death dates and places are not known.

The known children of David Franklin[4] Arbaugh and Nancy Ellen Fry:

200. i. SUSAN[5] ARBAUGH, born September 1882 in Kansas, and married to a Mr. Whipple circa 1899.[531]
201. ii. ELSIE ARBAUGH, born March 1886 in Kansas, mother of one child by 1900: Dennis Arbaugh, who was born in March 1900.[532]
202. iii. MAUD ARBAUGH, born November 1890 in Kansas; living at home in 1910;[533] no further information.
203. iv. BENJAMIN HARRISON ARBAUGH, born April 1894 in Kansas; living and working on his parents' farm in 1920 as a single man;[534] no further information.
204. v. unknown; died before 1900.

---

[530] 1920 U.S. census, Chautauqua County, Kansas, pop. sched., Little Caney Township, ED 8, page 7, dwelling and family 151, 1 March; National Archives micropublication T625, roll 522.

[531] 1900 U.S. census, Chautauqua County, Kansas, Little Caney Twp., ED 9, p. 9.

[532] Dennis is enumerated as a "son" (rather than "grandson") of Frank and Nancy Arbaugh in 1910 (1910 U.S. census, Chautauqua County, Kansas, pop. sched., Little Caney Township, ED 8, page 10-A, visitation 64, family 64, 21 April; National Archives micropublication T624, roll 433).

[533] 1910 U.S. census, Chautauqua County, Kansas, Little Caney Township, ED 8, page 10-A, visitation 64, family 64.

[534] 1920 U.S. census, Chautauqua County, Kansas, Little Caney Township, ED 8, page 7, dwelling and family 151.

56. Caroline Harriet[4] Arbaugh (Susannah[3] Trubey, David[2], Daniel[1]) was born in Ohio in September 1851.[535] She married **John W. Taylor** (son of David Taylor and [P]A[r]melia A. Smith)[536] on 11 September 1869 in Wells County, Indiana.[537] This family remained in Rock Creek Township, Wells County, Indiana, through 1900 (the last census searched for this family), where John worked as a farmer or farm laborer.[538] John's post-1900 death date is not known, but Caroline died in 1923, at age 72, and was buried in the Zanesville Cemetery in Wells County along with one of her children who died young.[539]

---

[535] 1900 U.S. census, Wells County, Indiana, pop. sched., Rock Creek Twp, ED 153, p. 5; National Archives micropublication T623, roll 413.

[536] 1860 U.S. census, Wells County, Indiana, pop. sched., Rock Creek, p. 42/814; National Archives micropublication M653, roll 309. Willard Heiss, compiler, *Warren County, Ohio, Marriage Records* (Indianapolis: no publisher, 1977), Volume 2: 70: #7401 - p. 292.

[537] *Wells County Marriages*, 127.

[538] 1870 U.S. census, Wells County, Indiana, pop. sched., Rock Creek Twp., P. O. Murray, p. 148; National Archives micropublication M593, roll 372. 1880 U.S. census, Wells County, Indiana, pop. sched., Rock Creek Twp., ED 143, p. 25; National Archives micropublication T9, roll 323. 1900 U.S. census, Wells County, Indiana, Rock Creek Twp, ED 153, p. 5.

[539] Ingabee Brineman Minnear, compiler, *Wells County, Indiana, Cemetery Records* (Fort Wayne, Ind.: Fort Wayne Public Library, 1972), Volume 4 (Zanesville Cemetery).

The children of Caroline Harriet[4] Arbaugh and John W. Taylor:

205. i. ANNIE D.[5] TAYLOR, born circa 1871; married I. Freeman Taylor in Wells County on 28 November 1891.[540]
206. ii. CALVIN G. TAYLOR, born circa 1873, and married Clara A. Myers in Wells County on 17 July 1897.[541]
207. iii. IDABELLA TAYLOR, born circa 1876, and married William Bushnell in Wells County on 7 July 1894.[542]
208. iv. ELI M. TAYLOR, born August 1885; last known living in 1900.
209. v. LEVI TAYLOR, possible twin of Eli M., as his tombstone gives his birth date as "1885," and death date as "1888;" he is buried with mother Caroline in the Zanesville Cemetery.

58. Thomas Barkdoll[4] Trimble (Mary Catherine[3] Trubey, David[2], Daniel[1]) was born 11 February 1844 in Tuscarawas County, Ohio,[543] but spent some of his childhood in Wells County, Indiana, where his widowed mother cared for his maternal grandparents.[544] Thomas married (1) **Sarah E. Allman** (daughter of Nicholas Allman and

---

[540] *Wells County Marriages*, 347.

[541] *Wells County Marriages*, 421.

[542] *Wells County Marriages*, 379.

[543] Thomas Barkdoll Trimble, alias "Park" Trimble, Pension (Co. G, 101st Indiana Infantry), application 584222, certificate 866469, Civil War and Later Pension Files, Records of the Veterans Administration (Record Group 15), National Archives, Washington, D.C.

[544] 1860 U.S. census, Wells County, Indiana, pop. sched., Union Twp., p. 49/822; National Archives micropublication M653, roll 309.

GENERATION FOUR 117

Margaret Clark)[545] on 13 January 1870 in Lagrange County, Indiana,[546] after which this couple, plus Thomas's widowed mother, set out for Morgan County, Missouri.[547] Sarah died at Marion Centre, Marion County, Kansas, on 6 July 1877,[548] leaving only one known child. Thomas and his daughter apparently returned to Indiana following Sarah's death, as they were enumerated in the household of his former sister-in-law in Lagrange County in 1880.[549] Here Thomas married (2) **Mary Ann Selby** (daughter of Luke Selby and Mary A. [—?—])[550] on 23 February 1881.[551] One son was born to this union.[552] Mary Ann

---

[545] *Counties of Lagrange and Noble, Indiana, Historical and Biographical* (Chicago: F. A. Battey & Co., Publishers, 1882), 435: biography of James Kennedy's wife [Barbara]. 1850 U.S. census, Noble County, Indiana, pop. sched., Noble Twp., p. 238; National Archives micropublication M432, roll 162. 1880 U.S. census, Lagrange County, Indiana, pop. sched., Clay Twp., ED 19, p. 26; National Archives micropublication T9, roll 291.

[546] Slevins, *Lagrange County Marriages*, Brides index p. 11, Grooms index p. 76 (cites original record as Book 3: 554).

[547] 1870 U.S. census, Morgan County, Missouri, pop. sched., Hough Creek Twp., P. O. Versailles, p. 40/166; National Archives micropublication M593, roll 794.

[548] Thomas B. Trimble pension.

[549] 1880 U.S. census, Lagrange County, Indiana, Clay Twp., ED 19, p. 26.

[550] 1870 U.S. census, Lagrange County, Indiana, pop. sched., Bloomfield, p. 27/146; National Archives micropublication M593, roll 333. 1880 U.S. census, Lagrange County, Indiana, pop. sched., Bloomfield, ED 17, p. 22; National Archives micropublication T9, roll 290.

[551] Thomas B. Trimble pension. *Index to Marriage Records of Lagrange County, Indiana, 1850-1920 Inclusive, Letters A-Z Inclusive* (Indiana Works Progress Administration, 1940), 194: cites original record at Book 5: 27.

died in 1908, and her husband Thomas died in 1926; both are buried in Greenwood Cemetery in Lagrange.[553]

Thomas Barkdoll Trimble's Civil War enlistment officer misunderstood his nickname "Bark" and recorded him as "Park" Trimble, thus records were generated for him under that name. He enlisted on 20 August 1862 in Wabash, Indiana, served with Co. G of the 101st Indiana Infantry, and developed diphtheria as well as heart disease during his participation in Sherman's march through Georgia. His pension mentions the loss of sight in his left eye among other disabilities he suffered in the service. His file contains depositions from his mother (in Cook County, Illinois, 30 May 1891; Montpelier, Ohio, 14 June 1897), brother David A. Trimble (Cook County, Illinois, 30 May 1891; Kansas City, Missouri, 14 June 1897), brothers-in-law Alanson Mundy (Lagrange, Indiana, 30 July 1887) and Ezra Taylor (Montpelier, Ohio, 1 October 1901), and from Jacob Trubey (Lagrange, Indiana, 16 April 1889 and 23 May 1892).

The child of Thomas Barkdoll[4] Trimble and Sarah E. Allman:
 210. i. HELEN ARDETTA[5] TRIMBLE, born 5 October 1871 in Missouri; married on 12 June 1901 in Lagrange Co., Indiana, to Charles C. Stroup;[554] was still living in 1924.[555]

---

[552] 1900 U.S. census, Lagrange County, Indiana, pop. sched., Bloomfield Twp., ED 70, p. 11; National Archives micropublication T623, roll 383. Thomas B. Trimble pension.

[553] Grace Libey and Mrs. Fred G. (Carlie) Deal, compilers, *Lagrange County, Indiana* (for Lagrange de LaFayette Chapter DAR, 1949), 73.

[554] *Index to Lagrange Marriages*, 194: cites original record at Book 7: 146.

[555] Thomas B. Trimble pension: half-brother Foss's 1924 deposition stated that his pensioner father resided part time with the latter's daughter, presumably Helen Ardetta.

The child of Thomas Barkdoll[4] Trimble and Mary Ann Selby:
211. i. FOSS S. TRIMBLE, born 9 September 1883 or 1884 in Indiana; married on 15 June 1910 in Lagrange Co., Indiana, to Elizabeth M. Floring;[556] he was still living in 1924.

59. **Susan K.**[4] **Trimble** (Mary Catherine[3] Trubey, David[2], Daniel[1]) was born circa 1846 in Ohio.[557] On 19 January 1862 in Wells County, Indiana,[558] Susan married **Ezra Taylor** (son of Isaac Taylor and Sarah A. Cox/Cocks).[559] Ezra Taylor served in the Civil War in Company G of the 101st Indiana Infantry, and received an invalid pension for which he applied on 18 December 1868.[560]

However, the National Archives and Veterans Administration staffs searched unsuccessfully for Ezra Taylor's pension file for more than 16

---

[556] *Index to Lagrange Marriages*, 194: cites original record at Book 10: 94.

[557] 1850 U.S. census, Tuscarawas County, Ohio, pop. sched., Dover Twp., p. 130; National Archives micropublication M432, roll 734. 1860 U.S. census, Wells County, Indiana, pop. sched., Union Twp., p. 49/822; National Archives micropublication M653, roll 309. 1870 U.S. census, Wells County, Indiana, pop. sched., Union Twp., p. 2; National Archives micropublication M593, roll 372.

[558] *Wells County Marriages*, 74.

[559] 1850 U.S. census, Warren County, Ohio, pop. sched., Wayne Twp., p. 373; National Archives micropublication M432, roll 737. *Biographical Memoirs of Wells County, Indiana* (Logansport, Ind.: B. F. Bowen, Publisher, 1903), 587-588.

[560] Ezra Taylor Pension (Co. G, 101st Indiana Infantry), application 37585, certificate 59,800, and widow's application 1134288 (dated 4 November 1918), certificate 894867, General Index to Pension Files, 1861-1934, Records of the Veterans Administration (Record Group 15), National Archives micropublication T288, roll 464, National Archives, Washington, D.C.

months.[561] The personal information in that pension would serve to enhance any present description of this family; however, the widow of Ezra who applied for a widow's pension in 1918 was not Susan K. (Trimble) Taylor, as she was deceased prior to 1900. In that year's census, Ezra appeared as the husband of Fanny, to whom he had been married only two years, and they resided in Montpelier, Williams County, Ohio.[562]

The children of Susan K.[4] Trimble and Ezra Taylor:
- 212. i. MARION B.[5] TAYLOR, born circa 1864 in Indiana, and was last known to be living in 1880 with his parents in Rock Creek Township, Wells County, Indiana.[563]
- 213. ii. HARRISON A. TAYLOR, born circa 1866; living in 1870.
- 214. iii. LAURETTA TAYLOR, born circa 1871; living in 1880.
- 215. iv. FRANKLIN TAYLOR, born circa 1873; living in 1880.
- 216. v. JOHN TAYLOR, born circa 1876; living in 1880.

---

[561] *Ibid.* This pension file as indexed carries an "XC-2-702-608," indicating it was filed with other Veterans Administration records, then at the Washington National Records Center. However, it was not found there, nor was it located within the "Veterans Administration records system" despite a 16-month search for it by the Veterans Administration office 1984-1986; still unavailable at National Archives in 1999. Correspondence in possession of compiler. U.S. Pension Bureau, *List of Pensioners on the Roll, January 1, 1883*, Volume 4 (1883, Rpt. Baltimore: Genealogical Publishing Co., 1970), 89: Huntington County, Indiana, Markle, Ezra Taylor, loss of finger.

[562] 1900 U.S. census, Williams County, Ohio, pop. sched., Superior Twp., Montpelier, ED 118, p. 6; National Archives micropublication T623, roll 1332.

[563] 1870 U.S. census, Wells County, Indiana, pop. sched., Union Twp., p.2; National Archives micropublication M593, roll 372. 1880 U.S. census, Wells County, Indiana, pop. sched., Rock Creek Twp., ED 143, p. 24; National Archives micropublication T9, roll 323.

GENERATION FOUR 121

60. David A.[4] **Trimble** (Mary Catherine[3] Trubey, David[2], Daniel[1]) was born 29 January 1847 in Tuscarawas County, Ohio.[564] He was married in Lagrange County, Indiana, on 25 January 1870[565] to **Mary Drake** (daughter of James L. Drake and Susannah Hayward),[566] who was born in March 1849 in Loudonville, Ashland County, Ohio.[567] Within months of their marriage, this couple removed to Morgan County, Missouri, where the Federal Census enumerated them in sequence with David's brother and sister-in-law Thomas Barkdoll and

---

[564] [Anonymous], *County of Williams, Ohio, Historical and Biographical* (Chicago: F. A. Battey & Co., Publishers, 1882), 649. 1900 U.S. census, Jackson County, Missouri, pop. sched., Kaw Twp., Kansas City, ED 134, p. 5; National Archives micropublication T623, roll 864.

[565] Ruth M. Slevin, compiler, *Lagrange County, Indiana, Marriages, 1832-1880* (Kokomo, Ind.: Selby Publishing and Printing, 1984), 76: cites original record at Book 3: 556. *Williams County History*, 649. 1870 U.S. census, Morgan County, Missouri, pop. sched., Hough Creek Twp., P. O. Versailles, p. 40/166; National Archives micropublication M593, roll 794: lists "January" as the month in which this couple was married.

[566] *Williams County History*, 649; *Lagrange and Noble Counties*, 1: 273-274. Also, James L. Drake served as Captain of Company H, 23rd Regt. Ohio Volunteers, and Provost Marshall, September 1862 - January 1865. He received a pension (application 163333, certificate 113715) as did his second wife and widow Harriet Filson (application 442910, certificate 480702), dated 10 July 1890. Records in this pension file indicate that James L. Drake was born circa 1818 in Holmes County, Ohio, and died 10 March 1886; his first wife Susannah died 23 May 1878, according to deposition of Lewis D. (age 59) and Ellen Hughes (age 54).

[567] 1900 U.S. census, Jackson County, Missouri, Kaw Twp., Kansas City, ED 134, p. 5. *Williams County History*, 649.

Sarah (Allman) Trimble.[568] Both Trimble brothers had been married in January, owned $1500 worth of real estate, and were farmers. Both brothers were enumerated in Lagrange County, Indiana, in 1880, at which time David A. Trimble had three children and his mother in his household.[569] However, an 1882 county history suggests that the David Trimble family had resided in Wolcottville, Noble County, Indiana, 1873-1879, and that, after establishing himself in the hardware business in Lagrange, he removed in 1881 to Williams County where he continued in that trade.[570] David was still a resident of Williams County as of July 1883, when he deposed for Alanson Mundy's Civil War pension, but was in Kansas City, Missouri, both in February 1887, when he deposed for Jacob A. Trubey's pension, and in 1897, when he deposed for his brother Thomas Trimble's pension.

The last census seen for David A. Trimble shows that his family was still living in Kansas City, Missouri, in 1900, and that he was employed there as a "commission merchant."[571] His wife Mary was yet living, and, although only one child, Nettie, was residing with them, Mary's entry shows that all of her three children were alive in 1900.

The children of David A.[4] Trimble and Mary Drake:
- 217. i. NETTIE E.[5] TRIMBLE, born November 1871 in Missouri, and was a single stenographer in Kansas City in 1900.
- 218. ii. CORA TRIMBLE, born circa 1872 in Missouri; living in 1900, according to mother's census entry.

---

[568] 1870 U.S. census, Morgan County, Missouri, Hough Creek Twp., P. O. Versailles, p. 40/166.

[569] 1880 U.S. census, Lagrange County, Indiana, pop. sched., Lagrange, ED 18, p. 3; National Archives micropublication T9, roll 290.

[570] *Williams County History*, 649.

[571] 1900 U.S. census, Jackson County, Missouri, Kaw Twp., Kansas City, ED 134, p. 5.

GENERATION FOUR 123

219. iii. PEARL S. TRIMBLE, born circa 1878 in Indiana; living in 1900, according to her mother's census entry.

61. Mary Caroline[4] **Trimble** (Mary Catherine[3] Trubey, David[2], Daniel[1]) was born in 3 October 1849,[572] probably in Tuscarawas County, Ohio.[573] In her first appearance in a Federal Census, she was recorded as "Nancy C.," although all subsequent census records in which she was found recorded her as either Mary or Caroline.[574] On 24 September 1865 in Steuben County, Indiana, Mary Caroline Trimble married (1) **Alanson Mundy**,[575] son of Lewis Mundy and first wife Polly Stevenson.[576] Mary married (2) **William Hills** at Fremont,

---

[572] 1900 U.S. census, Steuben County, Indiana, pop. sched., Fremont Twp, Fremont, ED 97, p. 1; National Archives micropublication T623, roll 404: the enumerator of the "Mundy's" district recorded full dates of birth; her death certificate gives 3 *November* 1849.

[573] Her family was enumerated in the 1850 Federal Census there (in Dover, p. 65/130).

[574] 1860 U.S. census, Wells County, Indiana, pop. sched., Union Twp., p. 49/822; National Archives micropublication M653, roll 309: Caroline. 1870 U.S. census, Steuben County, Indiana, pop. sched., Jackson Twp., P. O. Angola, p. 13; National Archives micropublication M593, roll 359: Mary. 1880 U.S. census, Lagrange County, Indiana, pop. sched., Springfield Twp., ED 16, p. 17; National Archives micropublication T9, roll 290: Mary. 1900 U.S. census, Steuben County, Indiana, Fremont Twp, Fremont, ED 97, p. 1: Caroline.

[575] Mrs. Charles E. Kensill, compiler and typist, *Steuben County, Indiana, Marriage Records, 1862-1889* (Pokagon Chapter Indiana DAR, 1974), 10.

[576] [Anonymous], *History of Steuben County, Indiana* (Chicago: Inter-State Publishing Co., 1885), 713-714.

Steuben County, Indiana, on 30 May 1907, but was divorced from him on 8 September 1908.[577]

Alanson Mundy served in the Civil War in both Company F of the 152nd Regiment, and Company K of the 44th Regiment of the Indiana Infantry, and both he and his widow received a pension therefor.[578] Alanson enlisted on 17 January 1862, and was hurt on 10 April 1862 at Pittsburgh Landing, Tennessee, when a sack of corn he was unloading fell on him, causing injury to his kidney and heart. Among the affiants furnishing testimony in his pension file were his three brothers-in-law, Thomas B. Trimble, David A. Trimble, and Ezra Taylor.

This soldier's birthplace was listed as Seneca County, Ohio, and he was described as being 5' 7" tall with blue eyes and auburn hair at the time of his application, although later data (1883, 1886, and 1895) describe Alanson as 5' 10" or 11" tall. Alanson was born in July 1845,[579] and died from heart disease on 18 February 1904 in Fremont, Steuben County, Indiana.[580] Mary Caroline (Trimble) Mundy, who told the pension office that she resumed use of her first husband's name after her divorce, was not sought in Federal Census records after last known living date of 9 September 1908, when she furnished information about her divorce to the pension office.[581] Her death certificate shows her names as "Mary Callie Hills," and she died of

---

[577] Alanson Mundy Pension (Co. F, 152nd Indiana Infantry and Co. K, 44th Indiana Infantry) application 483039, certificate 338157, and widow's application 800879, certificate 572680, Civil War and Later Pension Files, Records of the Veterans Administration (Record Group 15), National Archives, Washington, D.C.

[578] Alanson Mundy pension.

[579] 1900 U.S. census, Steuben County, Indiana, Fremont Twp, Fremont, ED 97, p. 1.

[580] Alanson Mundy pension.

[581] *Ibid.*

GENERATION FOUR 125

stomach cancer on 5 August 1918 in Fremont, Steuben County, Indiana; she was buried at Flint, Indiana.[582]

The children of Mary Caroline[4] Trimble and Alanson Mundy:
- 220. i. JOHN ALLEN[5] MUNDY, born 13 January 1867,[583] was a widower living in his parents' household in 1900, and may be the father of *(a)* Harry, born "30 June 1890," and *(b)* Glen, born "4 September 1892," also in that census entry.[584]
- 221. ii. WILLIAM ELLIS MUNDY, born 16 February 1870;[585] living in 1880.
- 222. iii. NETTIE ELLEN MUNDY, born 16 May 1872;[586] living in 1880.
- 223. iv. MERTIE MUNDY, born circa 1874; living in 1880 but may be one of the two children of Mary Caroline's who were deceased by 1900. Mertie is not listed in Alanson's pension application.
- 224. v. unknown; the second of two children who were deceased by 1900.

---

[582] Mary Callie Hills, death certificate no. 27425[?], Indiana State Board of Health; copy kindly furnished to the compiler by descendant Pat Mundy Moburg of Brooklyn, Michgan, in 1986.

[583] Complete birthdate from both Alanson Mundy pension, and 1900 Census (Steuben County, Indiana, Fremont Twp, Fremont, ED 97, p. 1).

[584] 1900 U.S. census, Steuben County, Indiana, Fremont Twp, Fremont, ED 97, p. 1.

[585] Complete birth date from Alanson Mundy pension.

[586] Alanson Mundy pension.

62. Jacob A.[4] **Trubey** (David[3,2], Daniel[1]) was born on 26 August 1846 in Tuscarawas County, Ohio.[587] Jacob married **Melissa Wyland** (daughter of Levi Wyland and Emily Mills)[588] on 14 October 1866 in Lagrange County, Indiana.[589] Jacob was an 18-year-old resident of Flint, Steuben County, Indiana, when he enlisted for Civil War service, with Co. A of the 44th Indiana Infantry, at Kendallville, Indiana. He was described as 5' 8" tall with grey eyes, brown hair, and a dark complexion. In 1885, Jacob stated that he had lived in Lagrange since the war ended, except between September 1872 and January 1875 when he resided in Republic County, Kansas. Jacob was enumerated twice in the 1870 Census of Bloomfield, Indiana: once in his father's household, and again as the head of his own young family.[590] In 1880, the family was again enumerated in Bloomfield, apparently after their brief residence

---

[587] Jacob A. Trubey Pension (Co. A, 44th Indiana Infantry), application 554848, certificate 394861, and widow's application 1114157 (dated 28 January 1918), certificate 852158, Civil War and Later Pension Files, Records of the Veterans Administration (Record Group 15), National Archives, Washington, D.C.

[588] Reah Lloyd McGaffey and Lucille Gibson Jackson, arrangers, *Marriage Records for Elkhart County, Indiana, 1830 through 1849* (typescript: submitted by William Tufts Chapter Indiana DAR, 1971), 108. 1850 U.S. census, Elkhart County, Indiana, pop. sched., Jackson Twp., p. 150; National Archives micropublication M432, roll 144 ("Malisse," age 5). 1880 U.S. census, Lagrange County, Indiana, pop. sched., Bloomfield Twp., ED 17, p. 7; National Archives micropublication T9, roll 290 (on same page with married daughter).

[589] Slevins, *Lagrange County Marriages*, 76. Jacob A. Trubey pension (although this erroneously cites Steuben County as the place of marriage).

[590] 1870 U.S. census, Lagrange County, Indiana, pop. sched., Bloomfield, pp. 4 and 6; National Archives micropublication M593, roll 333.

GENERATION FOUR 127

in Kansas.[591] Melissa's 1900 Census entry notes that only four of her seven children were then living.[592]

Jacob's pension file contains a copy of his death certificate, indicating that he died 16 January 1918 in Markle, Huntington County, Indiana;[593] the transcribed tombstones for this couple show that Jacob was interred in Greenwood Cemetery, Lagrange County, Indiana, as was his wife Melissa (1845-1922).[594]

The children of Jacob A.[4] Trubey and Melissa Wyland:[595]
    225. i.   DAVID N.[5] TRUBEY, born 14 November 1867 in Indiana; living in Woodland, Illinois, circa 1940.[596]
    226. ii.   LEVI F. TRUBEY, born 29 April 1869 in Indiana; tombstone gives 1870-1895.[597]

---

[591] 1880 U.S. census, Lagrange County, Indiana, pop. sched., Bloomfield, ED 17, p. 7; National Archives micropublication T9, roll 290.

[592] 1900 U.S. census, Wells County, Indiana, pop. sched., Union Twp., ED 155, p. 14; National Archives micropublication T623, roll 413.

[593] Jacob A. Trubey pension.

[594] Letter from Lagrange County Historical Society, 3 August 1985, in possession of the compiler.

[595] All names and complete birth dates taken from the Jacob A. Trubey pension.

[596] Trubey manuscript, 12.

[597] Transcription in letter from Lagrange County Historical Society, 3 August 1985, in possession of the compiler.

227. iii. EMILY TRUBEY, born 1 February 1871 in Indiana; this may be the daughter who married Wilson Maddox, and was living circa 1940 in Uniondale, Indiana.[598]

228. iv. MARY TRUBEY, born 5 May 1872 in Indiana; she married [J. W.?] Nicholson circa 1900,[599] and lived in Markle, Indiana, circa 1940.[600]

229. v. IRA W. TRUBEY, born 27 September 1876; tombstone gives 1879-1879.[601]

230. vi. FREEMAN A. TRUBEY, born 6 September 1879; living in Markle, Indiana, circa 1940.[602]

231. vii. CHAUNCY J. TRUBEY, born 22 March 1881; tombstone gives 1881-1881.[603]

63. Mary C.^{4} Trubey (David$^{3, 2}$, Daniel^1) was born on 8 August 1846 (more likely 1847)[604] in Ohio, and upon her death 8 March 1901, was interred in the Trubey plot at Greenwood Cemetery, Lagrange,

---

[598] Trubey manuscript, 12. Only the husbands' names of Jacob's two daughters are given in the manuscript; however, Jacob's 1900 census entry clarifies that Mrs. Nicholson was Mary.

[599] 1900 U.S. census, Wells County, Indiana, pop. sched., Union Twp., ED 155, p. 14: in household of parents as Mary "Nickelson," married "0" years. Trubey manuscript (p. 12) is the only source for Mary's husband's initials as "J. W."

[600] Trubey manuscript, 12.

[601] Letter from Lagrange County Historical Society.

[602] Trubey manuscript, 12.

[603] Letter from Lagrange County Historical Society.

[604] Mary's ages in Federal Census records support 1847; further, her brother Jacob gave his birthdate as August 1846 in his Civil War pension application.

GENERATION FOUR   129

Lagrange County, Indiana.[605] Mary married (1) **Jacob Bear**, as his second wife, on 7 March 1872 in Lagrange County, Indiana.[606] Further records were not located for Jacob Bear, but a later census entry of one of his sons which indicates Jacob was born in Indiana.[607] By 1880, Mary C. "Bare" was the widowed or divorced head of a household containing three young children, and "Bare" emerges as the more consistent spelling from this point.

The next year, (Mrs.) Mary C. (Trubey) Bare married (2) **Peter Stauffer** in Lagrange County on 18 December 1881.[608] The 1900 Soundex of Indiana, Ohio, and Michigan were examined for this couple without success, yet her tombstone indicates Mary was yet living in 1900. Only one of her three Bare children was located in 1900, but that household did not include either of the Stauffers. It is not known whether there were any children by Mary's second marriage to Peter Stauffer.

---

[605] Transcriptions in letter from Lagrange County Historical Society, 3 August 1985, in possession of the compiler.

[606] *Lagrange County Marriages*, 5. Jacob was first married on 24 May 1866 in Lagrange County (although his divorce petition stipulates "DeKalb" County, Indiana) to Permelia Canon, who deserted him 7 November 1867; at the March 1869 term of the Lagrange County Circuit Court, Jacob Bear presented these facts in his successful divorce suit. Photocopy provided by the court to the compiler without further citation.

[607] 1900 U.S. census, Lagrange County, Indiana, pop. sched., Bloomfield, ED 69, p. 7; National Archives micropublication T623, roll 383.

[608] Photocopy of marriage license and return supplied by the county clerk without further citation.

The children of Mary C.⁴ Trubey and Jacob Bear/Bare:⁶⁰⁹

232. i. DAVID⁵ BEAR/BARE, born circa 1874 in Indiana; no further information.
233. ii. MARY BEAR/BARE, born circa 1876 in Indiana; no further information.
234. iii. CHARLES BEAR/BARE, born January 1878 in Indiana; married circa 1895 to Bertha [—?—] (born May 1876, Indiana) by whom he had one known son Clarence (born September 1897).⁶¹⁰

64. David A.⁴ Trubey (David³´², Daniel¹) was born circa 1849, probably in Tuscarawas County, Ohio.⁶¹¹ David married **Mary Elizabeth Summers** on 22 October 1876 in Branch County, Michigan.⁶¹² Mary appears to have been born in November 1846 in Pennsylvania.⁶¹³ A compiled genealogy identifies Mary's parents as

---

⁶⁰⁹ 1880 U.S. census, Lagrange County, Indiana, pop. sched., Bloomfield Twp., ED 17, p. 7/46, dwelling 77, family 78; National Archives micropublication 9, roll 290.

⁶¹⁰ 1900 U.S. census, Lagrange County, Indiana, Bloomfield, ED 69, p. 7.

⁶¹¹ His family resided there in 1850 (1850 U.S. census, Tuscarawas County, Ohio, Dover Twp., p. 102/203).

⁶¹² Branch County Genealogical Society, *Early Marriage Records of Branch County, Michigan [Book II], 1876-1887* (Decorah, Iowa: Anundsen Publishing Co., for the society, 1995), 198: "Trubey, David A., 27, b. Ohio, of Lagrange Co., Ind., and Mary E. Summers, 29, b. Pa., of Noble [Twp.], on 22 Oct 1876 @ Noble by Jacob Trayer J.P., E175 - 6190." Letter from county clerk gives citation as Book E: 175.

⁶¹³ 1900 U.S. census, Kalamazoo County, Michigan, pop. sched., Ross Twp., ED 130, p. 13; National Archives micropublication T623, roll 720.

GENERATION FOUR 131

Jacob Summers and his second wife Frances S. Wilson.[614] Although he had children born in Indiana before and after 1880, David A. Trubey was not found in the 1880 Soundex of that state nor of Michigan. An obituary for David was printed in an Augusta, Michigan, newspaper on 19 March 1925:

> Buried Here - David Trubey, for many years a resident of Augusta and vicinity, died March 11 at Ft. Wayne, Ind. The remains were brought here where burial took place last Saturday.
> He leaves three sons, Oscar and Fred of Augusta, and Carl in Washingon state, and one daughter, Mrs. L. J. Charles, of Battle Creek.[615]

Mrs. Mary (Summers) Trubey predeceased her husband, and was interred at her death in 1917 in the Augusta Cemetery in Ross Township, Kalamazoo County, Michigan, where David and three of their children were also interred.[616]

---

[614] Hugh F. Gingerich and Rachel W. Kreider, *Amish and Amish Mennonite Genealogies* (Gordonville, Pa.: Pequea Publishers, 1986), 441-442; gives further lineage of Jacob[3] Summers (1790-1873) as Peter[2] Summers (1761-1836) who married Sarah Yoder, and John[1] Summers who married Catherine [—?—].

[615] David Trubey obituary, *Augusta Beacon*, Augusta, Michigan, Thursday, 19 March 1925, page 1, column 2, as provided by the Western Michigan University's Archives and Regional History Collections via letter dated 29 August 1985 in possession of the compiler. The 1917 issues of this newspaper were not in their collection, making a search for Mary E. (Summers) Trubey's obituary in their collection impossible. Obituaries for both David and Mary Trubey were sought by the WMU staff without success in the *Kalamazoo Gazette*.

[616] Kalamazoo Valley Genealogical Society, *Tombstone Inscriptions in Kalamazoo County, Michigan*, I: 112, 127, 278; publication data not apparent on photocopies provided by Western Michigan University's Archives and Regional History Collections staff.

132   DANIEL TRUBEY OF FRANKLIN COUNTY, PENNSYLVANIA

The children of David A.[4] Trubey and Mary E. Summers:[617]

   235. i. OSCAR D.[5] TRUBEY, born 15 August 1878 in Indiana, married Lula M. [—?—] (20 March 1883 - 7 August 1960), and died 26 November 1949; interred in Augusta Cemetery.[618]

   236. ii. EFFIE P. TRUBEY, born 1880, married Robert A. Johnston probably before 1900, and died 1922.[619]

   237. iii. WILMA V. TRUBEY, born March 1882 in Indiana, married L. J. Charles, and resided in Battle Creek, Michigan, in March 1925.[620]

   238. iv. FRED H. TRUBEY, born October 1884 in Indiana, married Trixie E. [—?—] (1892-1931), and died in 1934; interred in Augusta Cemetery.[621]

---

staff.

[617] 1900 U.S. census, Kalamazoo County, Michigan, Ross Twp., ED 130, p. 13, except for Effie who was listed in the Trubey manuscript (p. 17) as Effie Pearl Johnston, born 1880; an Effie P. Johnston (1880-1922) was buried two plots away from David and Mary Trubey in the Augusta Cemetery (Kalamazoo Valley Genealogical Society, *Tombstone Inscriptions in Kalamazoo County, Michigan*, I: 112).

[618] Kalamazoo Valley Genealogical Society, *Tombstone Inscriptions in Kalamazoo County, Michigan*, I: 112. The Trubey manuscript (p. 18) identifies Oscar's wife as Lulu Piper.

[619] Kalamazoo Valley Genealogical Society, *Tombstone Inscriptions in Kalamazoo County, Michigan*, I: 112.

[620] 1900 U.S. census, Kalamazoo County, Michigan, Ross Twp., ED 130, p. 13. *Augusta Beacon*, 19 March 1925.

[621] Kalamazoo Valley Genealogical Society, *Tombstone Inscriptions in Kalamazoo County, Michigan*, I: 112.

GENERATION FOUR   133

239.   v.   CARL E. TRUBEY, born May 1890 in Indiana; living in
            Washington state in March 1925.[622]

67. **George W.**[4] **Trubey** (David[3,2], Daniel[1]) was born 31 October 1856 in Huntington County, Indiana.[623] On 31 October 1880 in Lagrange County, Indiana, he married (1) **Hannah E. Slack**[624] (daughter of Abraham Slack and Hannah [—?—]).[625] Hannah was born in March 1860, probably in Johnson Township, Lagrange County, Indiana.[626]

---

[622] 1900 U.S. census, Kalamazoo County, Michigan, Ross Twp., ED 130, p. 13. *Augusta Beacon*, 19 March 1925.

[623] [Anonymous], *History of Northeast Indiana - Lagrange, Steuben, Noble and DeKalb Counties*, Volume II (Chicago and New York: The Lewis Publishing Company, 1920), 425.

[624] Photocopy of marriage license and return provided by county clerk. *History of Northeast Indiana*, 425.

[625] *History of Northeast Indiana*, p. 425; Ruth M. Slevin, *Lagrange County, Indiana, Will Records, 1842-1896* (Rpt. [original date not given], Kokomo, Indiana: Selby Publishing & Printing, 1982), 113: 1878 will of Abraham Slack naming daughter Hannah E. Slack). 1860 U.S. census, Lagrange County, Indiana, pop. sched., Johnson Twp., p. 42; National Archives micropublication M653, roll 274. 1870 U.S. census, Lagrange County, Indiana, pop. sched., Johnson Twp., p. 229; National Archives micropublication M593, roll 333. 1880 U.S. census, Lagrange County, pop. sched., Lagrange, ED 18, p. 9; National Archives micropublication T9, roll 291: Hannah Slack, 20, working in household of William Hudson. The birthplaces listed for Hannah and her parents here match those of Mrs. Hannah E. (Slack) Trubey in 1900 and 1910.

[626] 1860 U.S. census, Lagrange County, Indiana, pop. sched., Johnson Twp., p. 42: Anna, four months old. 1900 U.S. census, Lagrange County, Indiana, pop. sched., Bloomfield Twp., ED 69, p. 4; National Archives micropublication T623, roll 383.

A 1920 regional history identifies five children born to George and Hannah,[627] but by the time of the 1900 Census, two of them had died.[628] George, a farmer, lost his first wife on 25 May 1911, and married (2) **Mrs. Minnie (Brown) Yergin** in 1912.[629] No children are known to have been born to this union. George survived his second wife, who died in 1929, and upon his own death in 1938 was interred beside both of his former wives in Greenwood Cemetery in Lagrange.[630]

The children of George[4] Trubey and Hannah E. Slack:[631]

240. i. CLETURAH[5] TRUBEY, born in October 1881 in Indiana, and married George L. Schadle.
241. ii. GEORGE LESTER TRUBEY, born April 1886 in Indiana; discharged from the service in 1919.
242. iii. HAZEL TRUBEY, born August 1888, married after 1910 to Charles Routsong by whom she had four children (as of 1920), *viz.*, *(a)* George W., *(b)* Ruth, *(c)* Retha, and *(d)* Lois.
243. iv. EVA TRUBEY; died in infancy.
244. v. NEVA TRUBEY; died in infancy.

---

[627] *History of Northeast Indiana*, 425.

[628] 1900 U.S. census, Lagrange County, Indiana, Bloomfield Twp., ED 69, p. 4. 1910 U.S. census, Lagrange County, Indiana, pop. sched., Bloomfield Twp., ED 93, p. 13; National Archives micropublication T624, roll 361: confirms that Hannah was the mother of five children total (three of whom were living), as in the 1900 Census that figure of total children appears to be six.

[629] *History of Northeast Indiana*, 425.

[630] Letter from Lagrange County Historical Society.

[631] *History of Northeast Indiana*, 425. 1900 U.S. census, Lagrange County, Indiana, Bloomfield Twp., ED 69, p. 4.

GENERATION FOUR   135

69. Mary Margaret[4] **May** (Nancy[3] Trubey, Jacob[2], Daniel[1]) was born in September 1836, probably in Stark County, Ohio.[632] Her family had relocated to and bought land in Henry County, Ohio, by 1850,[633] and it was here that Mary was married to (1) **Jeremiah H(o)uston** (son of Jeremiah Houston and Catherine Baird)[634] on 16 November 1856 by James E. Scofield, J.P.[635] Jeremiah was born circa 1832-1834, probably in Ashland County, Ohio.[636] The couple had three children before the beginning of the Civil War, in which Jeremiah served with the 68th Ohio Infantry.[637] Jeremiah contracted Camp Fever at Pea Ridge,

---

[632] 1900 U.S. census, Henry County, Ohio, pop. sched., Flat Rock Twp., ED 24, p. 1; National Archives micropublication T623, roll 1286. Stark County is where her parents were married in 1835.

[633] 1850 U.S. census, Henry County, Ohio, pop. sched., Flat Rock Twp., p. 12; National Archives micropublication M432, roll 693.

[634] Lewis Cass Aldrich, editor, *History of Henry and Fulton Counties, Ohio* (Syracuse, N.Y.: D. Mason & Co., Publishers, 1888), 674. Henry County Historical Society, *Henry County, Ohio: A Collection of Historical Sketches and Family Histories*, Volume Three (Napoleon, Ohio: by the society, 1979), 171-172. 1850 U.S. census, Ashland County, Ohio, pop. sched., Clear Creek Twp., p. 3; National Archives micropublication M432, roll 658.

[635] Henry County Marriages, Book 1: 75-76, Napoleon, Ohio; photocopy of marriage license and return in possession of compiler. Copy also in the Civil War pension file of Jeremiah Huston's heirs.

[636] Aldrich, *History of Henry and Fulton Counties, Ohio*, 674. 1850 U.S. census, Ashland County, Ohio, pop. sched., Clear Creek Twp., p. 3; National Archives micropublication M432, roll 658. 1860 U.S. census, Henry County, Ohio, pop. sched., Flat Rock Twp., p. 260; National Archives micropublication M653, roll 985.

[637] 1860 U.S. census, Henry County, Ohio, Flat Rock Twp., p. 260. *Henry County, Ohio*, 171.

Tennessee, and died on a boat enroute home on sick leave on 10 June 1862.[638]

As "Mrs. Mary M. Huston," the widow married (2) a 20-year-old **Joel A. Edwards**, whose (unidentified) father filed his written consent to this 15 November 1862 marriage in Henry County.[639] Joel, whose father and mother were from Connecticut and Pennsylvania respectively, was employed during his marriage to Mary as a farm laborer and an employee in a stove factory.[640] At least eight children were born to them by 1880, after which Joel A. Edwards is not found in census records.[641]

Mary married a third time on 26 March 1890 in Henry County, Ohio, to **Amos Mitchell**;[642] the 1900 Census indicates Amos was 33 years her junior.[643] According to this same census, Mary was the

---

[638] Minors of Jeremiah Huston Pension (Co. F, 68th Ohio Infantry), application 144597, certificate 103086, Civil War and Later Files, Records of the Veterans Administration (Record Group 15), National Archives, Washington, D.C.

[639] Henry County Marriages, Book 2: 132, Napoleon, Ohio; photocopy of marriage license and return in possession of the compiler; this information also in pension granted to Jeremiah Huston's heirs.

[640] 1870 U.S. census, Henry County, Ohio, pop. sched., Flat Rock Twp., p. 269; National Archives micropublication M593, roll 1221. 1880 U.S. census, Henry County, Ohio, pop. sched., Napoleon Twp., ED 112, p. 18; National Archives micropublication T9, roll 1032.

[641] *Ibid.*

[642] Marriage Records, Henry County, Ohio, Volume 6 (1886-1890), 310; licensed and married 26 March 1890, Lewis A. Bulharz, J.P., officiating; FHL microfilm 0423622.

[643] 1900 U.S. census, Henry County, Ohio, Flat Rock Twp., ED 24, p. 1: Amos born April 1870, age 30.

mother of 12 children total, eight of whom were then living. Although three others in this household were enumerated as Amos's step-children, only one (Daisy) can be attributed to Mary, and the fact that the other two were born in 1892 and 1894 (during the span of Amos and Mary's marriage) makes it seem as though the enumerator erred in recording some aspect of this household's description. No 1910 Census entry could be located for this couple in the Miracode or in a search of schedules of Flat Rock Township.

The children of Mary Margaret[4] May and Jeremiah Huston:
245. i. SAMUEL D.[5] HUSTON, born 7 May 1857[644] in Ohio; living in 1880 as a single farmer.
246. ii. LOUISA J. HUSTON (recorded as "Susanna" in 1860), born 16 October 1858[645] in Ohio; living in 1880 as a single domestic.
247. iii. LEWIS R. HUSTON, born 19 November 1860[646] in Ohio; living in 1880 as a single farmer.

The children of Mary Margaret[4] May and Joel A. Edwards:
248. i. HARRISON ROYAL EDWARDS, born circa 1865 in Ohio; living in 1880 as a factory worker.
249. ii. NANCY EDWARDS, born circa 1867 in Ohio; not in 1880 household.
250. iii. R(E)UBIN A. EDWARDS, born February 1870 in Ohio; not in 1880 household.
251. iv. WILLIAM S. EDWARDS, born circa 1872 in Ohio; living in 1880.
252. v. LESTER A. EDWARDS, born circa 1874 in Ohio; living in 1880.
253. vi. GO[L?]DIE M. EDWARDS, born circa 1875 in Ohio; living in 1880.

---

[644] Jeremiah Huston pension.

[645] *Ibid.*

[646] *Ibid.*

254. vii.   BARBARA J. EDWARDS, born circa 1877 in Ohio; living in 1880.
255. viii. DAISY A. EDWARDS, born February 1879 in Ohio; living in 1900.
256. ix.   unknown; may be child by either husband; deceased by 1900.

70. Harrison T.[4] **May** (Nancy[3] Trubey, Jacob[2], Daniel[1]) was born 22 October 1839, in Stark County, Ohio.[647] Harrison married in Henry County, Ohio, on 24 December 1867 **Sophrona Hester D. Cole**[648] (probable daughter of Amos Cole and Nancy [—?—]).[649] Although Harrison's wife appears as "Sophrona" on their marriage record and in an earlier census record when single, she appears as "Hester" or "Hester D." in the 1880 and 1900 Census.[650]

During his service with the 68th Ohio Infantry in the Civil War, Harrison sustained a severe gunshot wound to his right leg at Champion

---

[647] Harrison T. May Pension (Co. F, 68th Ohio Infantry), application 448635, certificate 726344, Civil War and Later Files, Records of the Veterans Administration (Record Group 15), National Archives, Washington, D.C. 1900 U.S. census, Defiance County, Ohio, pop. sched., Defiance Twp., ED 232, p. 10; National Archives micropublication T623, roll 1263.

[648] Henry County Marriages, Book 3: 41, Napoleon, Ohio; photocopy of marriage license and return in possession of compiler.

[649] 1860 U.S. census, Henry County, Ohio, pop. sched., Flat Rock Twp., p. 262; National Archives micropublication M653, roll 985: Amos Cole (57, N.Y.), Nancy (58, Ohio)...Sophrona (16, Ohio). Also, the marriage of Harrison and Hester took place at the home of Amos Cole, according to Harrison's statements in his Civil War pension.

[650] 1880 U.S. census, Defiance County, Ohio, pop. sched., Defiance, ED 232, p. 10; National Archives micropublication T9, roll 1011. 1900 U.S. census, Defiance County, Ohio, pop. sched., Defiance, ED 8, p. 1; National Archives micropublication T623, roll 1263. Their 1870 Census entry was not located.

Hill, Mississippi, on 16 May 1863, but was not discharged until 10 July 1865.[651] His pension records show that he and his family removed from Henry County to Defiance County in October 1876. Harrison worked in a wheel factory in the city of Defiance, Ohio, in 1880, but he also served as a watchman, a merchant, and finally a rural mail carrier for 15-20 years.[652] Hester Sophron(i)a died 21 March 1922, and Harrison was yet living in 1925.[653]

The children of Harrison T.[4] May and Hester Sophron(i)a D. Cole:[654]

257. i. MAX WALTER[5] MAY, born 17 September 1869 or 1871[655] in Ohio; living in 1880.
258. ii. RALPH CAREY MAY, born 12 December 1871 or 1873[656] in Ohio; living in 1880.
259. iii. FRANK LEE MAY, born 2 April 1877[657] in Ohio; living in 1880.
260. iv. PAUL ERNEST MAY, born 22 July 1879[658] in Ohio; living as a single day laborer in 1900.

---

[651] Harrison T. May pension.

[652] *Ibid.*

[653] *Ibid.*

[654] 1880 U.S. census, Defiance County, Ohio, Defiance, ED 232, p. 10. 1900 U.S. census, Defiance County, Ohio, Defiance, ED 8, p. 1.

[655] Both birth years appear in Harrison's pension.

[656] Both birth years appear in Harrison's pension.

[657] Harrison T. May pension.

[658] Harrison T. May pension. 1900 U.S. census, Defiance County, Ohio, Defiance, ED 8, p. 1.

71. Samuel W.[4] **May** (Nancy[3] Trubey, Jacob[2], Daniel[1]) was born in November 1841 in Ohio. A modern day county history claims that Samuel married the widow of Samuel Kaylor[659] on 15 October 1867 in Henry County, yet neither the marriage license nor return[660] indicate that **Catherine Kaylor** was Mrs. Kaylor or née Dancer as the history states. There also exists the possibility that Samuel was married previously, insofar as there was a three-year-old Jennie in Samuel and Catherine's 1870 household whose birth may pre-date their marriage; further, five more "children" appear in this couple's later census enumerations although Catherine claims to be the mother of only five children total in 1900.

If Mrs. May's identity is as the history states, she was born on 2 January 1848 in Ashland County, Ohio, to John Dancer and wife Margaret Houston (sister of Jeremiah Houston – brother-in-law to Samuel May).[661] Samuel and Catherine resided and farmed in Flat Rock, Henry County, Ohio, until at least 1900, and their death dates are not known.

The children of Samuel W.[4] May and (Mrs.?) Catherine (Dancer?) Kaylor:
- 261. i. DORA[5] MAY, born circa 1871 in Ohio; no further information.
- 262. ii. GEORGE C. MAY, born circa 1872 in Ohio; no further information.
- 263. iii. CARRIE M. MAY, born circa 1878 in Ohio; no further information.

---

[659] *Henry County, Ohio*, 3: 171-172. This gives Catherine's parentage as John Dancer and Margaret Huston [sister of Jeremiah]; their 5 November 1846 marriage record is found in Ohio DAR GRC, *Early Marriage Bonds of Ohio*, Ashland County, Volume I: A-K (typescript, 1936), no pagination.

[660] Henry County Marriages, Book 3. 31, Napoleon, Ohio; photocopy of marriage license and return in possession of compiler.

[661] *Henry County, Ohio*, 3: 171-172.

GENERATION FOUR 141

264. iv. CHARLES L. MAY, born November 1879 in Ohio; no further information.
265. v. BESSIE MAY, born September 1887 in Ohio; "married Frank Leonhardt of Florida, Ohio, and had two children, Donald and Catharine Leonhardt."[662]

72. Alsetta F.[4] **May** (Nancy[3] Trubey, Jacob[2], Daniel[1]) was born circa 1845 in Ohio.[663] She married Civil War veteran[664] **Philip H(o)uston** (son of Jeremiah Houston and Catherine Baird)[665] in Henry County, Ohio, on 28 September 1865.[666] Philip was born circa 1838, probably in Ashland County, Ohio.[667]

---

[662] *Henry County, Ohio*, 3: 172.

[663] 1850 U.S. census, Henry County, Ohio, pop. sched., Flat Rock Twp., p. 12; National Archives micropublication M432, roll 693. 1860 U.S. census, Henry County, Ohio, pop. sched., Flat Rock Twp., p. 260; National Archives micropublication M653, roll 985. 1870 U.S. census, Henry County, Ohio, pop. sched., Flat Rock Twp., p. 269; National Archives micropublication M593, roll 1221. 1880 U.S. census, Henry County, Ohio, pop. sched., Flat Rock Twp., ED 115, p. 17; National Archives micropublication T9, roll 1032.

[664] *Henry County, Ohio*, 3: 171: 14th Ohio Infantry.

[665] 1850 U.S. census, Ashland County, Ohio, pop. sched., Clear Creek, p. 3; National Archives micropublication M432, roll 658: "Phillip" (12, Ohio). *Henry County, Ohio*, 3: 171. Aldrich, *History of Henry and Fulton Counties, Ohio*, 674. Philip's older brother Jeremiah married Alsetta's sister Mary Margaret.

[666] Henry County Marriages, Book 2: 247, Napoleon, Ohio; photocopy of marriage license and return in possession of the compiler.

[667] 1850 U.S. census, Ashland County, Ohio, Clear Creek Twp., p. 3. Aldrich, *History of Henry and Fulton Counties, Ohio*, 674.

Philip worked as a carpenter and a farmer in Henry County up through 1880.[668] This family was not located in the 1900 Federal Census, and it is possible that other children were born to Alsetta, who was 35 in 1880.

The children of Alsetta F.[4] May and Philip H(o)uston:
266. i. FRANK B.[5] HUSTON, born circa 1869 in Ohio; living in 1880. A modern county history did not identify Frank (or any son) among Philip and Alsetta's children.[669]
267. ii. LUSETTA HUSTON, born circa 1871; no further information.
268. iii. NANCY M. HUSTON, born circa 1875; no further information.

75. Nathan[4] Trubey (Jacob[3, 2], Daniel[1]) was born on 29 November 1847,[670] probably in Stark County, Ohio.[671] Nathan was not enumerated in the Federal Census with his birth family in 1870, but was found in

---

[668] 1870 U.S. census, Henry County, Ohio, Flat Rock Twp., p. 269. 1880 U.S. census, Henry County, Ohio, Flat Rock Twp., ED 115, p. 17.

[669] *Henry County, Ohio* 3: 171: "They had two daughters."

[670] Stark County Chapter of the Ohio Genealogical Society, *Cemetery Inscriptions, Stark County, Ohio*, Volume VI (No place: by the Society, 1985), 188: Perry Township, Massillon City Cemetery #126. The month and year given on his tombstone match those listed in his 1900 Census entry (1900 U.S. census, Lonoke County, Arkansas, pop. sched., Carlisle Twp., ED 76, p. 10-B; National Archives micropublication T623, roll 66).

[671] 1850 U.S. census, Stark County, Ohio, pop. sched., Sugar Creek Twp., p. 153; National Archives micropublication M432, roll 731. 1860 U.S. census, Stark County, Ohio, pop. sched., Sugar Creek Twp., p. 88; National Archives micropublication M653, roll 1037.

GENERATION FOUR 143

schedules for Gallatin County, Montana.[672] There Nathan was recorded as a school teacher, residing in the household of Ohio-born Enos Swan's family.

Nathan apparently returned to Stark County, Ohio, to marry **Melissa Knepper** on 21 September 1876.[673] Melissa was located in the 1860 Census as a 4-year-old in the household of Godfrey (born circa 1796, Pennsylvania) and Mary A. Knepper (born circa 1816, Pennsylvania);[674] a 20 February 1853 marriage is recorded in Stark County for Godfrey Knepper and a Mary A. Young.[675] Melissa's parents were listed on her 16 November 1930 Oklahoma City death certificate as Godfrey Knepper and Miss Spankel,[676] suggesting that Melissa's mother may have been Mrs. Mary A. (Spankel) Young at her 1853 marriage to Godfrey.[677]

---

[672] 1870 U.S. census, Gallatin County, Montana, pop. sched.m West Gallatin Precinct, P. O. Hamilton, p. 1/124-125; National Archives micropublication M593, roll 827.

[673] Stark County Marriages, Volume 8: 543; FHL microfilm 0897627.

[674] 1860 U.S. census, Stark County, Ohio, pop. sched., Sugar Creek Twp., p. 89; National Archives micropublication M653, roll 1037. 1870 U.S. census, Stark County, Ohio, pop. sched., Sugar Creek Twp., p. 36/618; National Archives micropublication M593, roll 1269: Melissa (13).

[675] Stark County Marriages, "Book C from 1851 to 1865," 14.

[676] Description of death certificate given in letter from Leo Trubey, Venice, California, 17 December 1985; in possession of the compiler.

[677] Godfrey's tombstone gives his death date as 9 October 1877 (*Cemetery Records, Stark County*, Vol. 1 (1955), Bose Cemetery, 147, at age 82 years, 3 months, 5 days), and his will (written on 21 April 1876) was recorded in Will Record Volume E: 317, probated 18 October 1877, with Jacob M. Trubey, executor (FHL microfilm

Nathan and Melissa's first two children were born in Ohio, but the family had removed to Nathan's former residence in Montana by 1880, where Nathan was then engaged in farming.[678] Land records prove that Nathan Trubey purchased 160 acres in Carlisle, Lonoke County, Arkansas, on 12 May 1885.[679] Nathan and Melissa sold three acres of this parcel in 1890.[680] No entry for Nathan could be located in the Soundex to the 1900 Census of Arkansas, but his family's entry was located in the actual schedules.[681] Nathan died at age 59 years, 10 months, and 6 days, from paralysis in Massillon on 5 October 1907 in

---

0892411). See also *Williams County, Ohio*, 638-639, giving Godfrey's birthplace as Fayette County, Pennsylvania. Ohio DAR GRC, *Early Marriage Bonds of Ohio, Columbiana County* (typescript, 1938?), 177: married (1) Magdalena Ithnier, 9 July 1818. 1850 U.S. census, Stark County, Ohio, pop. sched., Sugar Creek Twp., p. 300; National Archives micropublication M432, roll 731.

[678] 1880 U.S. census, Gallatin County, Montana, pop. sched., Upper Yellowstone Valley, ED 14, p. 4; National Archives micropublication T9, roll 742.

[679] Transcription of Lonoke County, Arkansas, Deed Book Y: 618 (12 May 1885), deed from William and Mary M. Harris (then in McLean County, Illinois) to Nathan Trubey, 160 acres, SW¼ Section 4, Township 1 North, Range 7 West of the 5th Principal Meridian; furnished by grandson Leo D. Trubey of Venice, California, on 17 December 1985.

[680] Transcription of Lonoke County, Arkansas, Deed Book 33: 467, 8 March 1890 (recorded 7 October 1890), Nathan and Melissa Trubey to Frederick Rife; provided by grandson Leo D. Trubey.

[681] 1900 U.S. census, Lonoke County, Arkansas, pop. sched., Carlisle Twp., ED 76, p. 10-B; National Archives micropublication T623, roll 66.

Beach City, Ohio.[682] Melissa was living in Stark County, Ohio, in 1910 with three of her children;[683] at her death on 16 November 1930, she was buried beside her husband in the Massillon City Cemetery.[684]

The children of Nathan[4] Trubey and Melissa Knepper:
- 269. i. JACOB MARION[5] TRUBEY, born November 1878 in Ohio;[685] no further information.
- 270. ii. ELVA TRUBEY, born June 1879 in Ohio;[686] married Mr. Kuns, and died 4 August 1933.[687]

---

[682] Stark County Chapter Ohio Genealogical Society, *Stark County, Ohio[,] Death Records* (No place: by the Society, 1991), 496-497: transcribed from original Volume 4: 274. Nathan's birthplace appears here as "New York," and his age at death calculates to a birth date of 29 November 1847. Nathan's tombstone in Massillon City Cemetery gives his death date as 3 October 1907 (see publication cited for his widow's tombstone inscription).

[683] 1910 Miracode, Stark County, Ohio, ED 241, visitation #193, p. 9; National Archives micropublication T1272, roll 374.

[684] Stark County Chapter The Ohio Genealogical Sociy, *Cemetery Inscriptions, Stark County, Ohio*, VI: 188: Perry Township, Massillon City Cemetery #126.

[685] 1880 U.S. census, Gallatin County, Montana, Upper Yellowstone Valley, ED 14, p. 4. 1900 U.S. census, Lonoke County, Arkansas, Carlisle Twp., ED 76, p. 10-B. Trubey manuscript (p. 25) gives "4 November 1877."

[686] 1880 U.S. census, Gallatin County, Montana, Upper Yellowstone Valley, ED 14, p. 4. 1900 U.S. census, Lonoke County, Arkansas, Carlisle Twp., ED 76, p. 10-B: apparently in error when it states "June 1880" as her birthdate, as she was 11 months old in June 1880. Trubey manuscript (p. 25) gives "27 June 1879."

[687] Trubey manuscript, 25.

271.	iii.	MYRTLE MAE TRUBEY, born 4 November 1881 or 1882 in Ohio,[688] married Mr. Kirk.[689]
272.	iv.	MARY WINONA TRUBEY, born 29 April[690] or November 1884[691] in Indiana,[692] married Arthur E. Van Eman, 2 September 1915, Stark County, Ohio.[693] Winona's tombstone inscription in Massillon City Cemetery indicates she had married a Mr. Ratt sometime before her death on 19 November 1951.[694]
273.	v.	NEBBIE DON TRUBEY, born 24 January 1887,[695] died 27 June 1910.[696]
274.	vi.	ALLIE TRUBEY, born 20 September 1891, died 21 October 1892.[697]

---

[688] Trubey manuscript gives "1881," and 1900 Census gives "1882."

[689] Trubey manuscript, 25.

[690] *Ibid.*

[691] 1900 U.S. census, Lonoke County, Arkansas, Carlisle Twp., ED 76, p. 10-B.

[692] *Ibid.*

[693] Stark County Marriages, Vol. 27: 441; FHL microfilm 0897627.

[694] Stark County Chapter The Ohio Genealogical Society, *Cemetery Inscriptions, Stark County, Ohio*, Volume VI: 187: Perry Township, Massillon City Cemetery #126.

[695] 1900 U.S. census, Lonoke County, Arkansas, Carlisle Twp., ED 76, p. 10-B. Trubey manuscript, 25.

[696] Trubey manuscript, 25.

[697] *Ibid.*

GENERATION FOUR 147

275. vii. ROBERT B. TRUBEY, 13 November 1894[698] in Arkansas; living in Stark County, Ohio, in 1910.[699]
276. viii. SELMA RUTH TRUBEY, 2 July 1901 in Arkansas; married Mr. Goodman.[700]

76. Harmon[4] **Trubey** (Jacob[3, 2], Daniel[1]) was born September 1850 in Stark County, Ohio.[701] There on 2 March 1876 he married **Mary Anne**

---

[698] 1900 U.S. census, Lonoke County, Arkansas, Carlisle Twp., ED 76, p. 10-B. Trubey manuscript, 25.

[699] 1910 Miracode, Stark County, Ohio, ED 241, visitation #193, p. 9.

[700] Trubey manuscript, 25.

[701] 1900 U.S. census, Stark County, Ohio, pop. sched., Tuscarawas Twp., ED 148, p. 21; National Archives micropublication T623, roll 1323. 1850 U.S. Census, Stark County, Ohio, pop. sched., Sugar Creek Twp., p. 153; National Archives micropublication M432, roll 731. Trubey manuscript (p. 26) gives "2 September 1850."

Augustine[702] (daughter of William Augustine and Martha Jane Cole),[703] who was born in January 1860 in Ohio.[704] Harmon was a farmer, who was enumerated in Stark County in all extant census records from 1850 through 1900, although the birthplaces given for some of this children in those records reveal an Indiana residence from about 1885 until 1897.[705] Five of his eight children by

---

[702] Stark County Marriages, Vol. 8: 484; FHL microfilm 0897627.

[703] Ohio DAR GRC, *Early Marriage Bonds of Ohio, Stark County* (typescript, 1936), Volume 5 (1851-1865): "Book C, p. 19:" William Augustine married Martha Jane Cole on 15 September 1852. 1860 U.S. census, Stark County, Ohio, pop. sched., Sugar Creek Twp., p. 73; National Archives micropublication M653, roll 1037: Mary A. (5/12). 1870 U.S. census, Stark County, Ohio, pop. sched., Sugar Creek Twp., p. 40/621; National Archives micropublication M593, roll 1269: Mary (10). 1880 U.S. census, Stark County, Ohio, pop. sched., Sugar Creek Twp., ED 157, p. 13; National Archives micropublication T9, roll 1068. Owned 40 acres in the SW¼ NW¼ Section 2, Township 11, Range 10 in Sugar Creek Township per plat in *Combination Atlas Map of Stark County, Ohio* (Philadelphia: Everts & Co., 1875), 103.

[704] 1860 U.S. census, Stark County, Ohio, Sugar Creek Twp., p. 73. 1900 U.S. census, Stark County, Ohio, Tuscarawas Twp., ED 148, p. 21. Trubey manuscript (p. 26) states that "Anne May" Augustine was born "9 January 1861."

[705] 1850 U.S. census, Stark County, Ohio, Sugar Creek Twp., p. 153. 1860 U.S. census, Stark County, Ohio, pop. sched., Sugar Creek Twp., p. 88; National Archives micro-publication M653, roll 1037. 1870 U.S. census, Stark County, Ohio, pop. sched., Sugar Creek Twp., p. 616; National Archives micro-publication M593, roll 1269. 1880 U.S. census, Stark County, Ohio, pop. sched., Sugar Creek Twp., ED 157, p. 19; National Archives micropublication T9, roll 1068. 1900 U.S. census, Stark County, Ohio, Tuscarawas Twp., ED 148, p. 21.

GENERATION FOUR 149

Mary Anne are identified by the 1880, 1900, and 1910 Census, and the other three are as taken from the Trubey manuscript, which also identified Harmon's death date as 25 December 1904.[706]

The children of Harmon[4] Trubey and Mary Anne Augustine:

277. i. MELVIN JAY[5] TRUBEY, born 16 June 1878 in Ohio.[707] He married Mary Olive Diller at Grants Pass, Oregon, on 8 June 1917, by whom he had a daughter Doris Oneida (born 27 November 1919) and a son Forest Cole (born 24 September 1924). In about 1940, "Mr. Melvin Trubey [was] an attorney-at-law, and real estate broker in Portland, Oregon."[708]

278. ii. DAISY ODETTA TRUBEY, 11 October 1881,[709] married Erastus DeWitt Ott on 20 February 1906, in Stark County, Ohio.[710] They were the parents of *(a)* Myron Dwight (2 July 1907), *(b)* Warren Franklin (21 April 1909), and *(c)* Edward Bryce (29 August 1915).[711]

279. iii. ELDA MARTHA TRUBEY, 18 June 1883; died 18 April 1885.[712]

---

[706] 1910 Miracode, Stark County, Ohio, Sugar Creek Twp., ED 241, visitation #61, National Archives micropublication T1272, roll 374. Trubey manuscript, 26.

[707] 1880 U.S. census, Stark County, Ohio, Sugar Creek Twp., ED 157, p. 19. Trubey manuscript, 26.

[708] Trubey manuscript, 26.

[709] *Ibid.*

[710] Stark County Marriages, Volume 21: 381; FHL microfilm 0897627.

[711] Trubey manuscript, 26-28; these three children are given individual treatment on page 28.

[712] Trubey manuscript, 26.

280. iv. JENNIE BLANCHE TRUBEY, 6 October 1885, married Benjamin F. Fairless at Pittsburgh, Pennsylvania, at an unknown date, and had one child Blaine Fairless. Mrs. Fairless "wrote a book and was also an artist of good repute." She died 29 September 1942.[713]

281. v. GOLDEN ONEIDA TRUBEY, born 20 June 1901[714] [sic: 1891],[715] married Oscar E. Barkey in Stark County by license issued 20 June 1916.[716] Two daughters were born to them, *(a)* Charity June (8 March 1920), and *(b)* Gloria Marie (6 December 1922).[717]

282. vi. WILLIAM COLE TRUBEY, 28 October 1893, died 11 August 1896.[718]

283. vii. SYLVESTER BRICE TRUBEY, 15 September 1897, married at Ft. Collins, Larimer County, Colorado, on 3 June 1923 to Lola Pearl Kunkel,[719] and had one son Dale (born 13 December 1928).[720]

---

[713] Trubey manuscript, 26 and 29.

[714] Trubey manuscript, 26 and 29.

[715] 1900 U.S. census, Stark County, Ohio, Tuscarawas Twp., ED 148, p. 21: Golden born June 1891, age 8. 1910 Miracode, Stark County, Ohio, Sugar Creek Twp., ED 241, visitation #61: Golden age 18.

[716] Stark County Marriages, Volume 28: 227; FHL microfilm 0897627.

[717] Trubey manuscript, 29.

[718] Trubey manuscript, 26.

[719] Colorado Marriage Record Report #7193, Larimer County; FHL microfilm 1690143. Minister H. S. Weaver officiating.

[720] Trubey manuscript, 26 and 29.

GENERATION FOUR   151

284. viii.   WILDA GALE TRUBEY, 2 October 1899; died
             15 February 1901.[721]

77. Esdras[4] Trubey (Jacob[3, 2], Daniel[1]) was born circa 1853, likely in Stark County, Ohio.[722] Esdras was first married on 11 May 1876 in New Philadelphia, Tuscarawas County, Ohio,[723] to **Mary Ann Sheline** (daughter of David Sheline by his probable second wife Cassandra).[724] After the birth of two children, Mary died of typhoid fever in Beach

---

[721] Trubey manuscript (p. 26) gives those full dates. 1900 U.S. census, Stark County, Ohio, Tuscarawas Twp., ED 148, p. 21: "Wildy," 9 months old, born Oct. 1899. Yet her recorded death record gives her death date as 1 October 1900, at age 1 year, 4 months, and 14 days (Stark County Chapter Ohio Genealogical Society, *Stark County, Ohio[,] Death Records* 496-497: transcribed from original Volume 3: 540).

[722] *Stark County Cemeteries*, I: 149 Bose Cemetery. Trubey manuscript (p. 30) gives 18 June 1852.

[723] Tuscarawas County Genealogical Society, *Tuscarawas County, Ohio, Marriages, 1864-1880, Volume III, from Books 6 and 7* (New Philadelphia, Ohio: by the Society, 1990), 207: Book 7: 274, return #13851, married by Elias Lower, V[erbi]. D[ei]. M[inister]. of the United Brethren Church. 1880 U.S. census, Tuscarawas County, Ohio, pop. sched., Wayne Twp., ED 235, p. 23; National Archives micropublication T9, roll 1072.

[724] Carroll County Genealogical Society, *Carroll County, Ohio, Early Marriages, 1833-1849*, Volume 1 (Carrollton, Ohio: by the society, 1984), #849, David Sheline to Susanna Kintner, February 1839. 1850 U.S. census, Carroll County, Ohio, pop. sched., Augusta Twp., p. 137; National Archives micropublication M432, roll 664. 1860 U.S. census, Tuscarawas County, Ohio, pop. sched., Wayne Twp., P.O. Dundee, p. 407; National Archives micropublication M653, roll 1043: Mary A. (5). 1870 U.S. census, Tuscarawas County, Ohio, Wayne Twp., p. 15/427: "Ann" (16). 1880 U.S. census, Tuscarawas County, Ohio, Wayne Twp., ED 235, p. 23.

City on 30 October 1881,[725] and was buried in the Bose Cemetery in Sugar Creek Township, Stark County, Ohio.[726]

On 9 November 1882 in Stark County, Esdras married (2) **Elizabeth "Lizzie" Williamson**[727] (probable daughter of George and Rachel Williamson).[728] Lizzie also gave birth to two children before predeceasing Esdras in 1898.[729] The Trubey manuscript states that Esdras married (3) **Mrs. Luella B. Marchand** in April 1902 (place not given), and, following her death circa 1904, married (4) **Rose Lewallyn** on 4 September 1910.[730] Rose survived her husband, who died 23 June 1917 and was buried beside his first two wives in the Bose Cemetery.[731]

---

[725] Stark County Chapter Ohio Genealogical Society, *Stark County, Ohio[,] Death Records*, 496-497: transcribed from original Volume 2: 169. Mary's birthplace was recorded here as "Tuscarawas County," and her age at death (27 years, 11 months, 11 days) calculates to a birth on 19 November 1853.

[726] Stark County Chapter Ohio Genealogical Society, *Stark County, Ohio[,] Death Records*, 496-497. *Stark County Cemeteries*, I: 149 Bose Cemetery.

[727] Stark County Marriages, Volume 10: 154; FHL microfilm 0897627.

[728] 1850 U.S. census, Stark County, Ohio, pop. sched., Lawrence Twp., p. 149; National Archives micropublication M432, roll 731. 1860 U.S. census, Stark County, Ohio, pop. sched., Lawrence Twp., p. 232; National Archives micropublication M653, roll 1037: Elizabeth (9).

[729] *Stark County Cemeteries*, I: 149 Bose Cemetery. Trubey manuscript, 30. Esdras was not indexed in the Soundex/Miracode to the 1910 or 1920 Census of Ohio, nor the 1920 Census of Indiana.

[730] Trubey manuscript, 30.

[731] *Stark County Cemeteries*, I: 149 Bose Cemetery. Trubey manuscript, 30.

GENERATION FOUR 153

The children of Esdras⁴ Trubey and Mary Ann Sheline:
285.   i.   ELIZA CASSANDRIA⁵ TRUBEY, born 2 January 1876; no further information.[732]
286.   ii. DAVID JACOB TRUBEY, born 27 March 1881,[733] possibly in Minnesota; no further information.

The children of Esdras⁴ Trubey and Elizabeth Williamson:
287.   i.   EUNICE BESSIE TRUBEY, born 2 August 1885 in Minneapolis, Minnesota.[734] Eunice married "Dr. John M. Luttenberger of Chicago, Ill., who passed on 7 January 1941."[735]
288.   ii. GEORGE ESDRAS TRUBEY, born 11 May 1888 in Minneapolis, Minnesota; married Clara C. Myer on 19 June 1908 at Circleville, Pickaway County, Ohio. Two children, not named in the manuscript, were born to this union. George died at age 25 on 8 March 1914.[736]

---

[732] 1880 U.S. census, Tuscarawas County, Ohio, Wayne Twp., ED 235, p. 23. Trubey manuscript, 30.

[733] Trubey manuscript, 30. 1900 U.S. census, Lagrange County, Indiana, pop. sched., Bloomfield, ED 69, p. 7; National Archives micropublication T623, roll 383: a David Truby, born April 1881 in Minnesota (to Minnesota-born parents), resided in the household of Frank B. Cline. This may be this David insofar as the age is quite close, and two of his next younger siblings were allegedly born in Minnesota, although the birthplaces of his parents would have to be erroneous.

[734] Trubey manuscript, 30.

[735] *Ibid.*

[736] Trubey manuscript, 30.

79. Freeman⁴ Trubey (Jacob[3, 2], Daniel[1]) was born 23 May 1858 in Stark County, Ohio.[737] Lagrange County, Indiana, marriage records list a license issued on 27 February 1885 for Freeman and **Anna Mary Minnick**[738] (daughter of William R. Minnick and Hannah L. Cain),[739] which was returned in August 1886 by Methodist Episcopal pastor J. B. Carns, stating the couple had been married by him on 1 March 1886.

Freeman worked as a farmer in Lagrange County, where all of his six children were born. Two of these children died without ever appearing in Federal Census records, but their births are documented by the total number of children born to their mother Anna recorded in the 1900 Census, and the Trubey manuscript furnished their uncorroborated birth and death dates.

---

[737] 1860 U.S. census, Stark County, Ohio, pop. sched., Sugar Creek Twp., p. 88; National Archives micropublication M653, roll 1037. 1870 U.S. census, Stark County, Ohio, pop. sched., Sugar Creek Twp., p. 616; National Archives micropublication M593, roll 1269. 1880 U.S. census, Stark County, Ohio, pop. sched., Sugar Creek Twp., ED 157, p. 30; National Archives micropublication T9, roll 1068. 1900 U.S. census, Lagrange County, Indiana, pop. sched., Bloomfield, ED 69, p. 3; National Archives micropublication T623, roll 383. 1910 U.S. census, Lagrange County, Indiana, pop. sched., Bloomfield, ED 93, p. 17; National Archives micropublication T624, roll 361. Trubey manuscript, 31.

[738] Photocopy of the single-page Lagrange County marriage license and return shows license granted on 27 February 188<u>5</u>, the couple married on 1 March 188<u>6</u>, and the certificate filed with the county on 31 August dated 188<u>6</u>; in possession of the compiler.

[739] *History of Lagrange and Noble Counties, Indiana*, I: 302. 1880 U.S. census, Lagrange County, Indiana, pop. sched., Bloomfield, ED 17, p. 15; National Archives micropublication T9, roll 290.

GENERATION FOUR 155

Anna Mary Minnick was born in February 1866,[740] and is said to have died on 6 November 1926.[741] Freeman's death date is given as 27 March 1937.[742]

The children of Freeman[4] Trubey and Anna Mary Minnick:
289. i.   ROXIE/ROXIA B.[5] TRUBEY, born 3 February 1886;[743] living in Lagrange County in 1910.[744]
290. ii. WILLIAM A. TRUBEY, born 20 May 1888 (or 1887).[745] William married Bessie Belle Sisson on 16 September 1906; their children included *(a)* Kenneth Devere, born 27 October 1910; *(b)* Lloyd William, born 18 December 1912 and died 24 January 1919; *(c)* Monroe S., born 25 July 1916, and *(d)* Homer Ray, born 9 December 1920. William died 29 September 1941.[746]
291. iii. unknown, born March 1889 and died as an infant.[747]

---

[740] 1900 U.S. census, Lagrange County, Indiana, Bloomfield, ED 69, p. 3.

[741] Trubey manuscript, 31.

[742] *Ibid.*

[743] *Ibid.*

[744] 1910 U.S. census, Lagrange County, Indiana, Bloomfield, ED 93, p. 17.

[745] Trubey manuscript (p. 31) versus 1900 Census.

[746] Trubey manuscript, 32. Fuller treatment of William's children and their families is given on this page.

[747] Trubey manuscript, 31. The 1900 census indicates two of Anna's six children had died by June 1900.

292. iv. NATHAN RAY TRUBEY, born 31 October 1890.[748] On 24 February 1915, Nathan married Avah Gooden, born 31 October 1893. Their children were *(a)* Nellie Virginia, born 2 January 1918, and *(b)* Russell Norris, born 27 June 1921.[749]

293. v. [twin] COR JACOB TRUBEY, born 24 February 1893, married Lulu Anderson by whom he had a child Stanley Rogers.[750]

294. vi. [twin] DOR ESDRAS TRUBEY, said to have died about age two and one half years.[751]

---

[748] Trubey manuscript, 31.

[749] Trubey manuscript, 33. Fuller treatment of Nathan's children is given on this page.

[750] Trubey manuscript, 34; however, correspondence from Stanley's wife in 1994 corrects "Lulu *Belle* Anderson," and "Stanley Ro*d*gers Trubey." Cor appears with his parents in the 1900 and 1910 census.

[751] Trubey manuscript, 31. Again, Anna's 1900 census data on children born and living takes into account this sixth birth and second death.

80. Ellsworth J.[4] **Trubey** (Jacob[3, 2], Daniel[1]) was born in November 1861 in Stark County, Ohio.[752] On 1 June 1886 in Stark County, Ellsworth married **Satira Eunice Kilgore**[753] (daughter of William B. Kilgore and Henrietta Books),[754] who was born 14 April 1866,[755] probably in Stark County, Ohio.[756] Two children were born to this couple, although the Trubey manuscript lists only the first son described below. Ellsworth worked as a farm laborer, and died on 26 September 1941[757] at nearly 80 years

---

[752] 1870 U.S. census, Stark County, Ohio, pop. sched., Sugar Creek Twp., p. 616; National Archives micropublication M593, roll 1269. 1880 U.S. census, Stark County, Ohio, pop. sched., Sugar Creek Twp., ED 157, p. 30; National Archives micropublication T9, roll 1068. 1900 U.S. census, Stark County, Ohio, pop. sched., Sugar Creek Twp., ED 147, p. 14; National Archives micropublication T623, roll 1323. 1910 U.S. census, Stark County, Ohio, pop. sched., Sugar Creek Twp., ED 241, visitation #286; National Archives micropublication T625, roll 1232.

[753] Stark County Marriages, Volume 11: 351; FHL microfilm 0897627.

[754] 1870 U.S. census, Stark County, Ohio, pop. sched., Sugar Creek Twp., p. 14/607; National Archives micropublication M653, roll 1269. Ohio DAR GRC, *Early Marriage Bonds of Ohio*, Stark County, Volume 1: "Book 5, p. 12:" Wm. B. Kilgore and Henrietta Books, 12 May 1859.

[755] Stark County Chapter of the Ohio Genealogical Society, *Cemetery Inscriptions, Stark County, Ohio,* Volume VI: 187: Perry Township, Massillon City Cemetery #126.

[756] Her parents were married here, and Satira's census entries support an "Ohio" birthplace.

[757] Stark County Chapter of the Ohio Genealogical Society, *Cemetery Inscriptions, Stark County, Ohio,* Volume VI: 187. Trubey manuscript (p. 35) gives 27 September 1941.

of age. At her death on 13 April 1945, Satira was interred beside her husband and son in the Massillon City Cemetery.[758]

The children of Ellsworth[4] Trubey and Satira Eunice Kilgore:
- 295. i. CLARENCE[5] TRUBEY, born in May 1887; living with his wife "Susa" in Stark County in 1910.[759]
- 296. ii. CLAYTON TRUBEY, born 18 October 1889[760] or 1890;[761] he died 21 April 1913.[762]

82. Jennie Etta[4] Trubey (Jacob[3, 2], Daniel[1]) was born in June 1865[763] in Stark County, Ohio. She was married in Stark County on 2 June

---

[758] Stark County Chapter of the Ohio Genealogical Society, *Cemetery Inscriptions, Stark County, Ohio,* Volume VI: 187.

[759] 1900 U.S. census, Stark County, Ohio, Sugar Creek Twp., ED 147, p. 14. 1910 U.S. census, Stark County, Ohio, Sugar Creek Twp., ED 241, visitation #286. Trubey manuscript, 35.

[760] Stark County Chapter of the Ohio Genealogical Society, *Cemetery Inscriptions, Stark County, Ohio,* Volume VI: 187. 1910 U.S. census, Stark County, Ohio, Sugar Creek Twp., ED 241, visitation #286.

[761] 1900 U.S. census, Stark County, Ohio, Sugar Creek Twp., ED 147, p. 14.

[762] Stark County Chapter of the Ohio Genealogical Society, *Cemetery Inscriptions, Stark County, Ohio,* Volume VI: 187.

[763] 1900 U.S. census, Stark County, Ohio, pop. sched., Sugar Creek Twp., ED 147, p. 14; National Archives micropublication T623, roll 1323: Jennie's age has been amended from 35 to 34, and the enumeration date was 21 June — the reader might infer that she was actually 35 on that date, but was 34 on the official census date of 1 June 1900. The Trubey manuscript (p. 36) gives her birth date as 16 June 1864.

GENERATION FOUR 159

1887 to **Samuel Muskopf**[764] (son of John Muskopf and his second wife Mary Magdalena Zintmeister, both born in Germany).[765] Samuel Muskopf, a farmer, was born 17 September 1861 in Ohio, and died 12 September 1912;[766] no death date is known for Jennie, who was not sought in Federal Census records later than 1910, at which date she and her husband yet resided in Sugar Creek Township, Stark County, Ohio.[767]

---

[764] Stark County Marriages, Volume 11: 551; FHL microfilm 0897627.

[765] *Stark County Marriages*, Volume 3: "Book B, p. 105: John Muskoff and Elizabeth Freymire, 6 February 1844." *Tuscarawas County Marriages 1845-1863*, Volume II: 213: "John Muskoff and Magdela [sic] Singmaster, 30 May 1850." 1850 U.S. census, Stark County, Ohio, pop. sched., Bethlehem, p. 109; National Archives micropublication M432, roll 731. 1870 U.S. census, Stark County, Ohio, pop. sched., Sugar Creek Twp., p. 44/622; National Archives micropublication M593, roll 1269. 1880 U.S. census, Stark County, Ohio, pop. sched., Sugar Creek Twp., ED 157, p. 31; National Archives micropublication T9, roll 1068. John H. Lehman, *A Standard History of Stark County, Ohio* (Chicago: The Lewis Publishing Company, 1939?), 815 and 824. Samuel's widowed mother "Mary M." (age 82) resided in his 1910 household (Stark County, Ohio, Sugar Creek Twp., ED 241, visitation #270, family #271, National Archives micropublication T624, roll 1232).

[766] Trubey manuscript, 36.

[767] 1910 U.S. census, Stark County, Ohio, Sugar Creek Twp., ED 241, visitation #270, family #271, lists her as "Jane E."

160　Daniel Trubey of Franklin County, Pennsylvania

The children of Jennie Etta[4] Trubey and Samuel Muskopf:
- 297. i. MARCELLUS[5] MUSKOPF, born 11 January 1889,[768] he was living in Cleveland, Ohio, circa 1940.[769]
- 298. ii. EMMA MUSKOPF, born 7 May 1890;[770] she was a school teacher in 1910,[771] and later married H. B. Ward.[772]
- 299. iii. HOMER MUSKOPF, born in January 1894;[773] living with parents circa 1940.[774]
- 300. iv. GLEN WILLIAM MUSKOPF, born 22 March 1906, died 15 or 19 August 1907 of cholera at age 1 year, 6 months, and 5 days.[775]

---

[768] 1900 U.S. census, Stark County, Ohio, Sugar Creek Twp., ED 147, p. 14. Trubey manuscript, 36.

[769] Trubey manuscript, 36.

[770] 1900 U.S. census, Stark County, Ohio, Sugar Creek Twp., ED 147, p. 14. Trubey manuscript, 36.

[771] 1910 U.S. census, Stark County, Ohio, Sugar Creek Twp., ED 241, visitation #270, family #271.

[772] Trubey manuscript, 36.

[773] 1900 U.S. census, Stark County, Ohio, Sugar Creek Twp., ED 147, p. 14. The Trubey manuscript (p. 36) describes a Homer A. Trubey born 31 January 1904, yet there is clearly a Homer born in January 1894 who was six years old at the time of the 1900 Census. If he died and another son was born and given his name in 1904 is not known and has not been pursued.

[774] Trubey manuscript, 36.

[775] Stark County Chapter, The Ohio Genealogical Society, *Stark County, Ohio, Death Records*, 344-345. Trubey manuscript, 36.

GENERATION FOUR

84. Asa Harvey⁴ Trubey (Jacob³,², Daniel¹) was born in May 1868 in Stark County, Ohio.[776] He was married in Lagrange County, Indiana, on 1 August 1891 to **Ida Elnora Wolf**[777] (daughter of Charles Wolf and Matilda [—?—]).[778] Ida Elnora was born on 7 February 1873 in Indiana, and died on 9 March 1929.[779]

Asa had located in Branch County, Michigan, by 1900 where he was employed as a cement works laborer.[780] No death date was given for him in the Trubey manuscript.

The children of Asa Harvey⁴ Trubey and Ida Elnora Wolf:
   301. i.   JENNIE ETHEL⁵ TRUBEY, born 8 June 1892 in Indiana.[781] She married Leon Maynard on 20 January 1916; they separated on 6 June 1932.[782]

---

[776] 1900 U.S. census, Branch County, Michigan, pop. sched., Bronson Twp., ED 4, p. 1; National Archives micropublication T623, roll 703. Trubey manuscript (p. 37) gives his full date of birth as 13 May 1868.

[777] Photocopy of Lagrange County marriage license and return furnished by the county clerk without further citation; in possession of the compiler.

[778] 1880 U.S. census, Lagrange County, Indiana, pop. sched., Clear Spring Twp., ED 22, p. 15; National Archives micropublication T9, roll 291: Elnora and Udora apparent twins (both age 6).

[779] 1880 U.S. census, Lagrange County, Indiana, Clear Spring Twp., ED 22, p. 15. Trubey manuscript, 37.

[780] 1900 U.S. census, Branch County, Michigan, Bronson Twp., ED 4, p. 1.

[781] 1900 U.S. census, Branch County, Michigan, Bronson Twp., ED 4, p. 1. Trubey manuscript, 37.

[782] Trubey manuscript, 37.

302. ii. CHARLES OTHA TRUBEY, born 10 December 1893 in Indiana.[783] He married (1) on 1 August 1915, wife's name not known, and one daughter was born to this union. Charles married (2) Myrtle Little on 4 July 1935, and they resided in Detroit, Michigan, circa 1940.[784]

303. iii. ASA ALVAH TRUBEY, born 12 October 1894/1896 in Indiana;[785] deceased before 1940.[786]

304. iv. ALBERT JASON TRUBEY, born 9 January 1900 in Michigan;[787] he married LaReine Curby of Buffalo, New York, on 16 March 1926. Their children were *(a)* June Ethel, born 9 March 1928; *(b)* Elnora LaReine, born 2 April 1929; *(c)* Lillian May, born 16 September 1932, and *(d)* Joice Mable, born 22 June 1935. This family resided in Grand Blanc, Michigan, circa 1940.[788]

305. v. ROBERT HENRY TRUBEY, born 17 January 1904 at Stroh, Indiana; he married Flossie McPhee on 16

---

[783] 1900 U.S. census, Branch County, Michigan, Bronson Twp., ED 4, p. 1. Trubey manuscript, 37.

[784] Trubey manuscript, 38.

[785] Trubey manuscript (p. 37) gives birth date as 12 October 1896, but 1900 census gives October 1894 plus birthplace as Indiana (1900 U.S. census, Branch County, Michigan, Bronson Twp., ED 4, p. 1).

[786] Trubey manuscript, 37.

[787] 1900 U.S. census, Branch County, Michigan, pop. sched., Bronson Twp., ED 4, p. 1, for birthplace. Trubey manuscript (pp. 37 and 38) for full birth date and name.

[788] Trubey manuscript, 38.

April 1931. This couple lived in Alpena, Michigan, in 1942.[789]

306. vi. CARL HARRISON TRUBEY, born 5 June 1908, "died at the age of 11 months."[790]

85. Ira T.[4] **Trubey** (Jacob[3, 2], Daniel[1]) was born on 26 July 1870 in Stark County, Ohio.[791] He was married in Stark County, Ohio, on 15 June 1892 to **Arie L. McFarren**[792] (daughter of Daniel McFarren and Jemima Shettler),[793] who was born circa 1875 in Ohio.[794]

Although Ira's family was not located in the 1900 Federal Census of Ohio or Indiana, their 1910 Census entry in Canal Dover,

---

[789] Trubey manuscript, 37 and 38.

[790] Trubey manuscript, 37.

[791] Trubey manuscript, 35. 1880 U.S. census, Stark County, Ohio, pop. sched., Sugar Creek Twp., ED 157, p. 30; National Archives micropublication T9, roll 1068. 1910 Miracode, Tuscarawas County, Ohio, Canal Dover, ED 111, visitation #85; National Archives micropublication T1272, roll 374. A search for Ira's entry in the 1900 Census via the Soundex for Ohio and Indiana was unsuccessful.

[792] Stark County Marriages, Volume 14: 63; FHL microfilm 0897627.

[793] John Danner, *Old Landmarks of Canton and Stark County, Ohio*, Volume 2 (Logansport, Ind.: B. F. Bowen, Publisher, 1904), 1011-1012. 1880 U.S. census, Stark County, Ohio, pop. sched., Sugar Creek Twp., ED 157, p. 14; National Archives micropublication T9, roll 1068.

[794] 1880 U.S. census, Stark County, Ohio, Sugar Creek Twp., ED 157, p. 14. 1910 U.S. census, Tuscarawas County, Ohio, pop. sched., Canal Dover, ED 111, visitation #85, 510 Front Street, National Archives micropublication T624, roll 1236. Stark County Marriages gives her age at marriage as 17.

Tuscarawas County, Ohio, identifies the same four children ascribed to them by the Trubey manuscript, and identifies Ira's occupation in that year as "grocer."[795]

Arie died on 20 November 1974, at age 99 years, according to a published transcription of her tombstone in the Maple Grove Cemetery in Dover; it is not known when or where Ira died.[796]

The children of Ira T.[4] Trubey and Arie L. McFarren:

307.   i.   NELLIE[5] TRUBEY, born circa 1893 in Ohio;[797] no further information.
308.   ii.   JOYCE M. TRUBEY, born circa 1899 in Ohio;[798] no further information.
309.   iii.   DANIEL F. TRUBEY, born circa 1904 in Ohio; "of Birmingham, Alabama" circa 1940.[799]
310.   iv.   LESTER E. TRUBEY, born circa 1908 in Ohio;[800] no further information.

---

[795] 1910 U.S. census, Tuscarawas County, Ohio, Canal Dover, ED 111, visitation #85.

[796] *Tuscarawas County, Ohio, Cemeteries, Vol. II, Dover, Dover Twp.* (New Philadelphia, Ohio: Tuscarawas County Genealogical Society, Inc., 1983), 231. Also transcribed from this cemetery are tombstones for two Trubey minors whose parentage is not known: Ira Truby, died 7 April 1911 at age 14 months (p. 224), and Zelda M. Truby, died 9 April 1911 at age 11 months (p. 228).

[797] 1910 U.S. census, Tuscarawas County, Ohio, Canal Dover, ED 111, visitation #85.

[798] *Ibid.*

[799] *Ibid.* Trubey manuscript, 35.

[800] 1910 U.S. census, Tuscarawas County, Ohio, Canal Dover, ED 111, visitation #85.

GENERATION FOUR 165

87. Alvah P.[4] **Trubey** (Jacob[3, 2], Daniel[1]) was born 31 March 1876[801] in Stark County, Ohio. He was married in Stark County, Ohio, on 1 January 1902 to **Emma B. Caler**[802] (daughter of George Caler and Susannah Elizabeth Mase), who was born in November 1879 in Ohio.[803] Alvah's death date is given as 17 November 1941,[804] and his widow Emma died less than a year later, on 23 September 1942.[805]

The children of Alvah P.[4] Trubey and Emma B. Caler:[806]
- 311. i. PAUL PERLEE[5] TRUBEY, born 1 June 1904;[807] no further information.
- 312. ii. MARY E. TRUBEY, born 27 December 1905; married a Mr. Keener.[808]

---

[801] Trubey manuscript (p. 39) for full date. 1880 U.S. census, Stark County, Ohio, pop. sched., Sugar Creek Twp., ED 157, p. 30; National Archives micropublication T9, roll 1068.

[802] Stark County Marriages, Volume 19: 93; FHL microfilm 0897627.

[803] 1880 U.S. census, Stark County, Ohio, pop. sched., Tuscarawas Twp., ED 241, p. 9; National Archives micropublication T9, roll 1068. 1900 U.S. census, Stark County, Ohio, pop. sched., Sugar Creek Twp., ED 146, p. 11; National Archives micropublication T623, roll 1323.

[804] Trubey manuscript, 39 and 40.

[805] *Ibid.*

[806] This couple's entries in the 1910 and 1920 census were not found, thus any data on their children is undocumented and as found in the Trubey manuscript (pp. 39-40) and the 1962 Trubey manuscript (p. 18).

[807] *Ibid.*

[808] *Ibid.*

313. iii. DWIGHT WILLIS TRUBEY, born 20 January 1908;[809] no further information.
314. iv. RUTH TRUBEY, born 22 June 1912; married a Mr. Render;[810] no further information.
315. v. RAYMOND CHARLES TRUBEY, born 24 November 1919;[811] no further information.

92. Nancy Maria[4] **Hunt** (Susan[3] Trubey, Daniel[2, 1]) was born circa 1846[812]-1848[813] in Ohio. She was married in Wells County, Indiana, on 25 December 1866 to **William A. Jones**[814] (son of Benjamin Jones and Elizabeth [—?—]).[815] William, born in June 1844 in Ohio,[816] was a

---

[809] *Ibid.*

[810] *Ibid.*

[811] Trubey manuscript, pp. 39 and 40.

[812] 1850 U.S. census, Blackford County, Indiana, pop. sched., Jackson Twp., p. 37; National Archives micropublication M432, roll 136.

[813] 1870 U.S. census, Wells County, Indiana, pop. sched., Chester Twp., p. 12/24; National Archives micropublication M593, roll 372. 1880 Soundex, Clay County, Kansas, Highland Twp., ED 33, p. 11; National Archives micropublication T749, roll 24.

[814] Mary Penrose Wayne Chapter DAR, compilers, *Index to and a Continuation of Marriage Records of Wells County, Indiana, 1837-1900* (typescript: DAR GRC 1956-1957), 104.

[815] 1850 U.S. census, Wells County, Indiana, pop. sched., Chester Twp., p. 335; National Archives micropublication M432, roll 181: Benjamin born in Maryland circa 1801, and Elizabeth born in Kentucky circa 1815.

GENERATION FOUR 167

farmer who removed his family from Indiana to Kansas between 1870 and 1874.[817]

William and Nancy settled on a farm in Highland Township, Clay County, Kansas,[818] and it is here Nancy is presumed to have died shortly after the birth of a daughter in April 1883.[819] The records of the District Court of Clay County were found to contain proof of William A. Jones's second marriage to Mary A. Shore (born circa 1858) on 1 December 1886.[820] This family's 1910 Census entry in Highland Township correctly records that William was in his second marriage, and wife Mary in her first, and that the couple had been married 23

---

[816] 1900 U.S. census, Clay County, Kansas, pop. sched., Highland Twp., ED 11, p. 7; National Archives micropublication T623, roll 474.

[817] Based upon birthplaces of consecutive children Ulysses and Ellen: 1880 U.S. census, Clay County, Kansas, pop. sched., Highland Twp., ED 33, p. 11; National Archives micropublication T9, roll 376.

[818] 1880 Soundex, Clay County, Kansas, Highland Twp., ED 33, p. 11.

[819] 1900 U.S. census, Clay County, Kansas, Highland Twp., ED 11, p. 7, gives this birth date. It also lists William with his second wife, but mistakenly records the number of years married as "30 years." Further, the number of children born to Mary was entered once as "6" and marked over as "4."

[820] Marriage license #1711 and return, recorded 3 December 1886, Clay County, Kansas; photocopy provided by the deputy clerk without further citation; in possession of compiler.

years.[821] Mary was listed as the mother of four children, all then living. William's post-1910 death date is not known.[822]

The children of Nancy Maria[4] Hunt and William A. Jones:

316. i. OSCAR B.[5] JONES, born circa 1868 in Indiana;[823] no further information.
317. ii. ULYSSES S. JONES, born December 1869 in Indiana;[824] was yet single in 1900 when living on his father's farm in Clay County, Kansas.
318. iii. ELLEN JONES, born circa 1874 in Kansas;[825] no further information.

---

[821] 1910 U.S. census, Clay County, Kansas, pop. sched., Highland Twp., ED 14, page 7A, visitation 114, family 115; National Archives micropublication T624, roll 434. William's entry herein does not include any information in the column marked "survivor of the Union or Confederate Army or Navy."

[822] His children by second wife Mary A. Shore are identified by the 1900 and 1910 Census as (a) John W., born August 1887 in Kansas; (b) Jessie H., born December 1888 in Kansas; (c) Emma P., born March 1891 in Kansas; and (d) Myrtle M., born July 1895 in Kansas.

[823] 1870 U.S. census, Wells County, Indiana, Chester Twp., p. 12/24. 1880 Soundex, Clay County, Kansas, Highland Twp., ED 33, p. 11.

[824] 1870 U.S. census, Wells County, Indiana, Chester Twp., p. 12/24. 1880 Soundex, Clay County, Kansas, Highland Twp., ED 33, p. 11. 1900 U.S. census, Clay County, Kansas, Highland Twp., ED 11, p. 7.

[825] 1880 Soundex, Clay County, Kansas, Highland Twp., ED 33, p. 11.

319. iv. DORA JONES, born circa 1876 in Kansas;[826] no further information.

320. v. DONA [?] J. JONES, born April 1883 in Kansas; living on father's farm in Clay County in 1900.[827]

94. Ellen[4] **McCullick** (Susan[3] Trubey, Daniel[2, 1]) was born 29 August[828] or September[829] 1858 in Indiana.[830] On 12 June 1880 in Wells County, Ellen became the second wife of **Edward Terhune**[831]

---

[826] *Ibid.*

[827] 1900 U.S. census, Clay County, Kansas, Highland Twp., ED 11, p. 7.

[828] *Biographical Memoirs of Wells County, Indiana*, 303.

[829] *Wells County Cemeteries*, Voume 3: Miller Cemetery.

[830] 1870 U.S. census, Wells County, Indiana, pop. sched., Chester Twp., p. 12/24; National Archives micropublication M593, roll 372. 1880 U.S. census, Wells County, Indiana, pop. sched., Chester Twp., ED 146, p. 1/112; National Archives micropublication T9, roll 323. 1900 U.S. census, Wells County, Indiana, pop. sched., Chester Twp., ED 138, p. 6; National Archives micropublication T623, roll 413.

[831] DAR GRC, *Marriage Records of Wells County, Indiana, 1837-1900*, 224. *Terhune vs. Terhune*, Wells County Circuit Court, Box 4180, Cause #565, April Term 1880, and Civil Order Book L: 510 (photocopies provided by Circuit Court, Bluffton, Indiana), provide background on Edward's first marriage to Rebecca J. Rausch in Wells County on 26 July 1876, his petition for divorce, his wife's cross complaint, and final decree dated 11 May 1880. Edward had one daughter by Rebecca, named Ida Belle Terhune, born by April 1877, per the divorce records.

(son of Garrett Terhune and Mary Bingham),[832] born on 11 January 1854 in Miami County, Indiana.[833]

Edward was a farmer and breeder of "Poland China hogs and shorthorn cattle;" his farm in Chester Township, Wells County, was located over an oil field, and had "nine very good wells" operating in 1903.[834] Ellen predeceased her husband, dying on 28 December 1906; Edward died 20 May 1941, and both are interred near his parents in the Miller Cemetery in Chester Township, Wells County, Indiana.[835]

---

[832] 1880 U.S. census, Wells County, Indiana, pop. sched., Chester Twp., ED 146, families #4 and #56; National Archives micro-publication T9, roll 323. *Biographical Memoirs of Wells County, Indiana*, 303 and 379. Indiana GRC, *General Index, Marriages, Montgomery County, Indiana, 1823-1860* (typescript, 1953), 153 lists Garrett W. Terhune and Mary J. Bingham married on 10 September 1848, Book 2: 428.

[833] *Biographical Memoirs*, 303.

[834] *Ibid.*

[835] *Wells County Cemeteries*, Volume 3.

GENERATION FOUR 171

The children of Ellen[4] McCullick and Edward Terhune:
- 321. i. EDITH[5] TERHUNE, born 13 August[836] or October[837] 1879 in Kansas[838] or Indiana;[839] she married James M. Mitchell[840] in Wells County on 26 September 1900.[841]
- 322. ii. CHARLES TERHUNE, born 21 March 1881, died 26 February 1897 or 1899.[842]
- 323. iii. CLAYTON TERHUNE, born 22 December 1882 in Indiana;[843] he appears to have married Jennie Iness Mounsey in Wells County on 16 January 1904.[844]

---

[836] *Biographical Memoirs*, 303.

[837] 1900 U.S. census, Wells County, Indiana, Chester Twp., ED 138, p. 6.

[838] *Ibid.*

[839] 1880 U.S. census, Wells County, Indiana, Chester Twp., ED 146, family #56.

[840] *Biographical Memoirs*, 303.

[841] Hilda Thrailkill Higgins, compiler, *Marriage Records 1899 thru 1974, Wells County, Indiana* (Bluffton, Ind.: by the compiler, 1976), Volume 4: Mc-Q.

[842] *Wells County Cemeteries*, Volume 3, gives 1897; *Biographical Memoirs*, 303, gives 1899.

[843] *Biographical Memoirs*, 303. 1900 U.S. census, Wells County, Indiana, Chester Twp., ED 138, p. 6.

[844] Higgins, *Wells County Marriages*, Volume 6: T-Z. There is another marriage listed here for a Clayton Terhune which may be this man, to a Mrs. Minnie (Brown) Davis on 27 May 1934.

324. iv. WILLIAM OSCAR TERHUNE, born 1 November 1884 in Indiana;[845] married Gladys Popejoy in Wells County on 24 February 1906.[846]

325. v. HENRY TERHUNE, born 17 August 1886 in Indiana;[847] married Renie Mendenhall in Wells County on 20 April 1907.[848]

326. vi. BERTHA TERHUNE, born 27 July 1889 in Indiana;[849] no further information.

327. vii. EDWARD RUSSELL TERHUNE, born 21 December 1893 in Indiana;[850] no further information.

328. viii. GRACE TERHUNE, born 31 January 1900 in Indiana;[851] no further information.

95. Arabella Serena[4] Trubey (David[3], Daniel[2, 1]) was born 17 May 1846[852] probably in Liberty Twp., Hancock County, Ohio.[853] Less than

---

[845] *Biographical Memoirs*, 303. 1900 U.S. census, Wells County, Indiana, Chester Twp., ED 138, p. 6.

[846] Higgins, *Wells County Marriages*, Volume 6: T-Z.

[847] *Biographical Memoirs*, 303. 1900 U.S. census, Wells County, Indiana, Chester Twp., ED 138, p. 6.

[848] Higgins, *Wells County Marriages*, Volume 6: T-Z.

[849] *Biographical Memoirs*, 303. 1900 U.S. census, Wells County, Indiana, Chester Twp., ED 138, p. 6.

[850] *Ibid.*

[851] *Ibid.*

[852] "Appointment of Guardian in the matter of the minor heirs of David Truby, deceased," 25 December 1858, Wyandot County, Ohio, no volume or page indicated on the photocopy furnished to the compiler by the office of the Probate Judge, Upper Sandusky, Ohio.

GENERATION FOUR   173

ten years later, her family was residing in adjacent Wyandot County when her father David Trubey died. Here Arabella was married on 9 April 1868 to **Elmore P. Shepherd**[854] (son of Thomas N. Shepherd and Eliza Fisher),[855] who was born 19 April 1846 in Carey, Wyandot County, Ohio.[856]

Elmore had served in the Civil War with the U.S. Signal Corps on Sherman's "March to the Sea,"[857] yet the only surviving correspondence "Belle" received from a Signal Corpsman was written by a self-

---

[853] See Appendix B letter #1, which proves the Trubeys' residence in Hancock County in 1847. Hancock County Deed Book 5: 211 proves that Arabella's mother Keziah Klinker was sold 80 acres in Section 19, Township 1 North, Range 10 South, Liberty Twp., by her father Jacob Klinker in 1844.

[854] Wyandot County Marriages, Volume 4: 8, #584; photocopy in possession of compiler.

[855] Hancock County Marriages, 36, #143: Thomas M. [sic] Shepherd to Eliza Fisher, 16 April 1835. "Application to Admit Will to Probate," Re: Thomas N. Shepherd, Wyandot County, 19 February 1886, Probate Judge, Upper Sandusky, Ohio: identifies son Elmore P. Shepherd then of Kinsley, Kansas.

[856] Elmore P. Shepherd Pension (Signal Corps, U.S. Volunteers) application 219706, certificate 221487, and widow's application 1215682, certificate 947105, Civil War and Later Pension Files, Records of the Veterans Administration (Record Group 15), National Archives, Washington, D.C. Pension file contains Elmore's own declaration of his birth date, plus his brother's sworn extract from the family Bible record.

[857] Elmore P. Shepherd Compiled Service Records (Signal Corps, U.S. Volunteers), Records of the Adjutant General's Office, 1780s-1917 (Record Group 94), National Archives, Washington, D.C.

proclaimed childhood friend, Curtis B. Hare.[858] After the war, Elmore wrote a letter to Arabella from Bureau County, Illinois, where he apparently attended school just two months prior to their marriage.[859] After their marriage, this couple lived briefly in Bureau County, Illinois.[860] From 1871 to 1878 they resided in Mendon, Michigan, according to information later supplied on Elmore's Civil War pension application papers.[861] On 18 March 1878 Arabella wrote her mother, "[w]e are going to pack for Kansas today."[862] The family, including two young children, removed to Comanche County, where their final child was born. Elmore worked as a farmer, and had 404 sheep by 1880.[863] Elmore applied for land in Comanche and Edwards Counties under a

---

[858] See Appendix B letter #12. "Curt" was a neighbor of Arabella's in Crawford Twp., Wyandot County, per their 1860 U.S. Census entries (pp. 468 and 469). Curtis enlisted in the Signal Corps on the same day (17 March 1864), at the same place (Madison Twp., Franklin County, Ohio), and under the same recruiting officer (Lt. Cyrus M. Roberts) as Arabella's future husband Elmore P. Shepherd. Curtis B. Hare Compiled Service Records (Signal Corps, U.S. Volunteers), Records of the Adjutant General's Office, 1780s-1917 (Record Group 94), National Archives, Washington, D.C.

[859] See Appendix B letter #13.

[860] 1870 U.S. census, Bureau County, Illinois, pop. sched., Milo Twp., P. O. Boyd's Grove, p. 14/385; National Archives micropublication M593, roll 190.

[861] Elmore P. Shepherd pension. However, son Clarence's place of birth in 1874 was recorded on his first marriage license as "St. Joseph."

[862] See Appendix B letter #14.

[863] 1880 U.S. census, Comanche County, Kansas, agricultural schedule, ED 375, p. 8; National Archives micropublication T1130, roll 18.

variety of land entry auspices.[864] A brief response to a later residency query in one such land entry file summarizes the difficulties of frontier life in general and the specific effect it had on this family: "I [Elmore] have resided continuously...my wife lives in Michigan and refuses to live in Kansas."[865]

Arabella and her children returned to her mother's home in Michigan, apparently during the summer of 1880, as she was enumerated twice in the Federal Census of that year.[866] The couple was divorced on 10 May 1892,[867] and Arabella continued to reside in Michigan[868] until her death in Kalamazoo on 25,[869] 26,[870] or 27[871]

---

[864] "Larned, Kansas, Homestead Final Certificate 5920," "Osage Trust and Diminished Reserve Lands, 5164-14926," and "Larned, Kansas, Cash Certificate 10671: Timber-Culture Application 3102," Records of the Bureau of Land Management, Record Group 49, National Archives, Washington National Records Center, Suitland, Maryland; photocopies in possession of compiler. This geographical area included present-day Kiowa County.

[865] "Homestead Proof - Testimony of Claimant," 28 November 1891, Larned, Kansas, Homestead Final Certificate 5920.

[866] 1880 U.S. census, Comanche County, Kansas, pop. sched., ED 375, p. 6-7; National Archives micropublication T9, roll 377. 1880 U.S. census, St. Joseph County, Michigan, pop. sched., Nottowa Twp., ED 199, p. 24; National Archives micropublication T9, roll 603.

[867] *Shepherd vs. Shepherd*, petition for alimony, 16 September 1891, District Court of Ford County, Kansas, and divorce case #1568, 1 December 1891, District Court of Edwards County, Kansas; photocopies in possession of compiler.

[868] 1900 U.S. census, St. Joseph County, Michigan, pop. sched., Colon, ED 106, p. 9; National Archives micropublication T623, roll 742.

August 1901. Elmore remarried on 25 November 1899 in Edwards County, Kansas, to the widowed Mrs. Sarah Catherine (Kochenderfer) Allen,[872] and died on 3 February 1924 in Kinsley, Edwards County, Kansas.[873]

The children of Arabella Serena[4] Trubey and Elmore P. Shepherd:
329.   i.   unknown; died when an infant.[874]

---

[869] Belle Sheapard [sic] obituary, *Kalamazoo Gazette-News*, Kalamazoo, Michigan, 27 August 1901, p. 5, as transcribed by the staff of Western Michigan University's Archives and Regional History Collections, Kalamazoo, Michigan; in possession of compiler.

[870] Records of the Kalamazoo Regional Psychiatric Hospital, Kalamazoo, Michigan; letter in possession of compiler.

[871] Abstract of death certificate as provided by the Deputy County Clerk of Kalamazoo County, cited as appearing in Book 3: 17; in possession of compiler.

[872] Elmore P. Shepherd pension.

[873] Elmore P. Shepherd, death certificate no. 24-739 (1924), Kansas State Department of Health and Environment, Topeka.

[874] Transcript of an uncited Colon, Michigan, obituary published for Arabella Serena (Trubey) Shepherd (in possession of compiler) states this child was male, yet a 1941 letter from Arabella's daughter Grace Darling (Shepherd) Martin to Barevias Augustus Trubey states it was "a girl [who] lived only a few hours after birth" (both documents in possession of compiler). No 1870 Mortality Schedule could be located for Milo Twp., Bureau County, Ill., where Elmore and Arabella then lived, which might have identified this firstborn child if it were born before 1870 and died between 1 June 1869 and 31 May 1870 (National Archives micropublication T655).

GENERATION FOUR 177

330. ii. CLARENCE CLARE[5] SHEPHERD, born 10 January 1874 in St. Joseph County, Michigan.[875] Clarence married (1) Harriet "Hattie" A. Patterson on 26 July 1905 in Jackson, Jackson County, Michigan.[876] Clarence married (2) Mrs. Tyrannus (Goe) Morton, on 22 November 1924, Finney County, Kansas.[877] By this second marriage was born one son Robert Earl, born 11 March 1927. Clarence died 24 August 1940, and was buried at Garden City, Kansas.[878]

331. iii. GRACE DARLING SHEPHERD, born 5 September 1877 in St. Joseph County, Michigan; married Tono E. Martin on 31 October 1915, by whom three children were born: *(a)* Samuel Page, born 13 February 1917, *(b)* Maribelle, born 10 September 1918, and *(c)* Tono Shepherd, born 6 May 1921 and died 24 July 1921.[879]

---

[875] Jackson County marriage license #274 - 1905, Jackson, Michigan; photocopy in possession of compiler. Trubey manuscript, 45.

[876] *Ibid.* This license gives birthplaces, fathers' names and mothers' maiden names for both bride and groom. This couple was divorced, although no record of it is on file in New Orleans (their 1912 residence), Ford County, Kansas (his residence in 1920), or Jackson County, Michigan (Hattie's residence circa 1940).

[877] Finney County Marriage Book E: 273, Clerk of the District Court, Garden City; photocopy in possession of compiler.

[878] Memorial card in possession of compiler.

[879] Trubey manuscript, 45-46.

178 DANIEL TRUBEY OF FRANKLIN COUNTY, PENNSYLVANIA

332. iv. EARL IRVIN SHEPHERD, born 27 July 1879 in then-Comanche County, Kansas;[880] married in Laramie, Wyoming, on 12 January 1912[881] to Anna Schermer. Two children, *(a)* Virginia Louise, and *(b)* Melba Helen. Earl died on 29 April 1960 in LaGrande, Oregon.[882]

96. Erastus Seabury[4] **Trubey** (David[3], Daniel[2, 1]) was born 16 March 1848[883] in Hancock County, Ohio. He was married in St. Joseph County, Michigan, on 25 November 1874 to **Martha Dawson Liddle**[884] (daughter of Gilbert Van Deusen Liddle and his second wife Rebecca

---

[880] 1880 U.S. census, Comanche County, Kansas, ED 375, p. 6-7. 1880 U.S. census, St. Joseph County, Michigan, Nottowa Twp., ED 199, p. 24. Earl Irvin Shepherd, death certificate no. 5547 (1960), Oregon Board of Health, Portland. Trubey manuscript, 45-46.

[881] Albany County Marriage Book E: 271, Office of the County Clerk, Laramie.

[882] Earl Irvin Shepherd, Oregon state death certificate no. 5547.

[883] Wyandot County guardianship records, 25 December 1858.

[884] *Trubey vs. Trubey* divorce case #867, bill of complaint filed 5 October 1891, St. Joseph County Circuit Court; photocopies (in possession of compiler) provided by the Western Michigan University's Regional History Collections curator. Martha Liddle Gifford, *Genealogy of the Liddle Family* (Vineland, N.J.: by the author, 1923), 16.

GENERATION FOUR

Bradley Watson), who was born on 29 September 1855,[885] in Michigan.[886]

Erastus worked as a farmer and stockman in Colon, St. Joseph County, Michigan, at least through 1900.[887] He was divorced from Martha in 1891,[888] and married a second time. On 19 May 1919 in Jackson, Jackson County, Michigan, 71-year-old Erastus married 66-year-old Canadian-born Betsy (Perrin) Patterson Fitch, the daughter of Joseph and Susan Perrin.[889] Erastus succumbed to arterioschlerosis at age 79 on 27 March 1927 in Colon[890] or Leonidas Township, St. Joseph

---

[885] *Liddle Family*, 15-16.

[886] 1880 U.S. census, St. Joseph County, Michigan, pop. sched., Colon, ED 190, p. 2; National Archives micropublication T9, roll 603.

[887] 1880 U.S. census, St. Joseph County, Michigan, Colon, ED 190, p. 2. 1880 U.S. census, St. Joseph County, Michigan, agric. sched., Colon, p. 1; National Archives micropublication T1164, roll 56. 1900 U.S. census, St. Joseph County, Michigan, pop. sched., Colon, ED 106, p. 15; National Archives micropublication T623, roll 742.

[888] *Trubey vs. Trubey* divorce case #867, St. Joseph County, Michigan.

[889] Jackson County Marriage License and Certificate no. 293 (1919); copy from microfilm furnished by the Jackson County Genealogical Society, Jackson, Michigan. Officiated by H. D. Skinner, M.G.

[890] Erastus S. Trubey obituary, *Jackson City Patriot*, Jackson, Michigan, 29 March 1927, page 18. Located by Beverly Boehmer of Jackson, Michigan; transcription made by David K. Trubey from photocopy (from microfilm) furnished him by the Jackson County Public Library. This obituary gives the residences of his two married daughters, and identifies his step-children as Mrs. William Welch, Mrs. Harriet Shepherd, Mrs. C. N. Neilson, and Mr. F. J.

County, Michigan.[891] Interment was in Woodland Cemetery on the south side of Jackson, Michigan.[892] The death date and place of his widow are not known.

The children of Erastus[4] Trubey and Martha Dawson Liddle:
- 333. i. HALLE BELLE[5] TRUBEY, born 17 August 1875 at Beach City, Ohio;[893] she married James K. Hirst in Camden, New Jersey, on 11 August 1906. Four children were born to them: *(a)* Edgar Delalia, born 19 April 1908, died 5 May 1918, *(b)* Martha Helene, born 27 August 1910, *(c)* James Vincent, born 20 October 1912, and *(d)* Halle Laveda, born 12 March 1915.[894] Living in Petaluma, California, in 1927.[895]
- 334. ii. VALERIE ANITA TRUBEY, born 18 April 1882 at Colon, Michigan;[896] married at Vineland, New Jersey, on 27 June 1906 to William Homer Walker, by whom she had *(a)* William H., *(b)* Robert, *(c)*

Patterson of Jackson, and Mr. C. L. Patterson of Winnetka, Illinois.

[891] Erastus S. Trubey entry, St. Joseph County Deaths, Volume 3: 174, no. 4, Office of County Clerk, Centreville, Michigan; copy furnished by David K. Trubey, who advised that this death was not located by the state vital records office in Lansing, Michigan.

[892] *Jackson City Patriot*, 29 March 1927.

[893] *Liddle Family*, 21. Trubey manuscript, 47.

[894] *Liddle Family*, 21 and 25-26, provide more information on these families.

[895] *Jackson City Patriot*, 29 March 1927.

[896] *Liddle Family*, 21.

GENERATION FOUR 181

Francis, and *(d)* Joseph.[897] Living in Pittsburgh, Pennsylvania, in 1927.[898]

97. **Mary Catherine**[4] **Trubey** (David[3], Daniel[2, 1]) was born 14 August 1850[899] in Hancock County, Ohio.[900] At age 27 and while a resident of Adrian, Ohio, Mary was married in Sturgis, St. Joseph County, Michigan, on 9 December 1878 to **Jasper Van Nette**[901] (son of Abel Van Nette and Sarah A. Schuyler),[902] then a 31-year-old inventor

---

[897] *Liddle Family*, 21. Trubey manuscript, 48.

[898] *Jackson City Patriot*, 29 March 1927.

[899] Wyandot County guardianship records, 25 December 1858.

[900] 1850 U.S. census, Hancock County, Ohio, pop. sched., Liberty Twp., p. 395B; National Archives micropublication M432, roll 692.

[901] Record of Marriages, Volume E, 1867-1884, St. Joseph County, Michigan, p. 231, #12 (Jasper "Vandette"); FHL microfilm 1295529.

[902] *Early Marriage Bonds of Ohio, Seneca County*, Volume 2 (typescript: DAR, 1936), n.p.: Abel Vannette and Sarah A. Schuyler; 1850 U.S. census, Seneca County, Ohio, pop. sched., Clinton Twp., p. 471/941; National Archives micropublication M432, roll 728. 1860 U.S. census, Seneca County, Ohio, pop. sched., Clinton Twp., p. 71/359; National Archives micropublication M653, roll 1035. 1870 U.S. census, Seneca County, Ohio, pop. sched., Clinton Twp., P. O. Tiffin, dwelling 177, family 182; National Archives micropublication M593, roll 1266. D. J. Stewart, *Comination Atlas Map of Seneca County, Ohio* (Philadelphia: no published., 1874), 4: W½ SE¼ Section 22: Abel [Van Nette].

residing in Tiffin, Ohio.[903] Jasper was born in May 1847,[904] likely in Clinton Township, Seneca County, Ohio.[905]

The next autumn, on 12 September 1879, Mary's mother Keziah in Mendon, Michigan, wrote a letter to daughter Arabella in Kansas, referring to Mary as residing elsewhere, and mentioning "Van Nette" traveling south with Keziah "to see about his machine."[906] Jasper was employed as a sewing machine agent in 1880,[907] which may explain this passage in Keziah's letter. In 1900, Jasper's occupation was again given as "inventor,"[908] and, in fact, he had three patents registered with the U.S. Patent Office by this date.[909] This couple was not sought in

---

[903] St. Joseph County Marriages, Volume E: 231.

[904] 1900 U.S. census, Seneca County, Ohio, pop. sched., Clinton Twp., Tiffin, ED 98, p. 10; National Archives micropublication T623, roll 1320.

[905] As cited above, his parents (who were married in Seneca County on 5 May 1846) resided in Clinton Township from at least 1850 through 1880.

[906] See Appendix B letter #15 (12 Sep 1879). The March 1878 letter, appearing as Appendix B letter #14, also mentions Arabella's desire to see "Van Nette" before leaving for Kansas.

[907] 1880 U.S. census, Wyandot County, Ohio, Crawford Twp., ED 159, p. 20; National Archives micropublication T9, roll 1079.

[908] 1900 U.S. census, Seneca County, Ohio, Clinton Twp., Tiffin, ED 98, p. 10.

[909] *Annual Report of the Commissioner of Patents for the Year 1895* (Washington, D.C.: Govt. Printing Office, 1896), 360: Jasper Vannette, Tiffin, Ohio, assignor to Singer Manufacturing Co. of New Jersey (1) feeding mechanism for sewing-machines, patent #543,068, 23 July, *Official Gazette* 72: 450, (2) sewing-machine, patent #545,924, 10 Sept., 72: 1523. *Annual Report...1897*, 373: Jasper Vannette, Tiffin, Ohio, assignor to Standard Sewing Machine Co.,

GENERATION FOUR 183

Federal Census records later than 1900, and their death data are unknown.

The children of Mary Catherine⁴ Trubey and Jasper Van Nette:
335. i. VERNE V.⁵ VAN NETTE, born in June 1881 in Ohio;[910] he married May Clark, and at his death was buried in Tiffin, Ohio.[911]
336. ii. ADAIR B. VAN NETTE, born in April 1888 in Ohio;[912] he married Frieda Coe, by whom he had *(a)* Thelma (Van Nette) Schaal, 1913-1959, *(b)* Carmen (Van Nette) Bretz, born 1916, *(c)* Adair B., born 1918, and *(d)* Joanne (Van Nette) Berkel, born 1920.[913]

98. William David⁴ Trubey (David³, Daniel²,¹) was born 26 January 1855[914] in Hancock or Wyandot County, Ohio. At age 36, while a resident of Colon, Michigan, William was married in Coldwater, Branch County, Michigan, on 19 September 1891 to 22-year-old **Eurannah Hass**[915] (daughter of George B. Hass and Rachel Narber),[916] of

---

Cleveland, Ohio, sewing-machine, patent #575,580, 19 Jan, *Official Gazette* 78: 435. Jasper's brother Wesley, of Poplar, Crawford County, Ohio, also had a patent registered in 1902 for a musical instrument (patent #694,589, 4 March, *Official Gazette* 98: 1815).

[910] 1900 U.S. census, Seneca County, Ohio, Clinton Twp., Tiffin, ED 98, p. 10.

[911] *The Forgotten Friend*, 47.

[912] 1900 U.S. census, Seneca County, Ohio, Clinton Twp., Tiffin, ED 98, p. 10.

[913] *The Forgotten Friend*, 47-48.

[914] Wyandot County guardianship records, 25 December 1858.

[915] Trubey manuscript, 50.

Sherwood, Branch County, Michigan.[917] Eurannah was born in October 1869 in Indiana.[918]

Like his older brother Erastus, William was a farmer and stockman, and the two worked in partnership as the Trubey Brothers Stock Brockers in Colon, Michigan, until 1890.[919] Two stud service advertising fliers published after their partnership was dissolved (dated 1891 and 1894) were reprinted in *The Forgotten Friend*, and list W. D. Trubey as the owner of the horses being advertised.[920]

William died 11 March 1899 on his farm in Branch County, Michigan.[921] His widow Eurannah remarried sometime between 1900 and 1911.[922]

---

[916] 1880 U.S. census, Branch County, Michigan, pop. sched., Girard Twp., ED 33, p. 18; National Archives micropublication T9, roll 573. *The Forgotten Friend*, 51.

[917] Record of Marriages, Volume G, 1887-1906, page 68, #10996, Branch County, Michigan; FHL microfilm 0930798.

[918] 1900 U.S. census, Branch County, Michigan, pop. sched., Matteson Twp., ED 15, p. 7; National Archives micropublication T623, roll 704.

[919] *The Forgotten Friend*, iii. Answer of Erastus Trubey, *Trubey vs. Trubey* divorce case #867, filed 16 March 1892, St. Joseph County Circuit Court, re: business partnership with brother dissolved in summer of 1890.

[920] *The Forgotten Friend*, 52.

[921] Trubey manuscript, 50. *The Forgotten Friend*, p. iv, gives an account of this accidental death.

[922] 1900 U.S. census, Seneca County, Ohio, Clinton Twp., Tiffin, ED 98, p. 10. A daughter (Rachel) by second husband born in 1911, per *The Forgotten Friend* (pages 48-49) which also claims Eurannah and her second husband divorced (p. iv.). Undocumented identification of Eurannah's second husband as William Staffeldt, and

GENERATION FOUR 185

The children of William David[4] Trubey and Eurannah Hass:
- 337. i. GEORGE WILLIAM[5] TRUBEY, born 1 May 1893[923] in Michigan; married Charlotte Ambs, and had *(a)* Charles William, born 1925, *(b)* David Keith, born 1928, and *(c)* George Gaylord, born 1930.[924]
- 338. ii. MYSTIA NAFEESIE TRUBEY, born 11 April 1896 in Michigan;[925] she married Charles Reginald Farnsworth by whom she had a daughter, Mystia Nafeesie (Farnsworth) Heuer, born 1929.[926]

99. Nathan John[4] Trubey (John[3], Daniel[2, 1]) was born 21 May 1852[927] probably in Florida, Henry County, Ohio, where his father ran a wagonmaking shop.[928] The Trubey manuscript indicates that Nathan

---

her second marriage date as 1902, from the Branch County Historical Society's *History of Branch County, Michigan*, I (Dallas, Texas: printed by Taylor Publishing Co., 1980), 468.

[923] 1900 U.S. census, Seneca County, Ohio, Clinton Twp., Tiffin, ED 98, p. 10: gives May 1892. Trubey manuscript, 50.

[924] *The Forgotten Friend*, 48.

[925] *The Forgotten Friend*, 48. Trubey manuscript, 50.

[926] *The Forgotten Friend*, 48.

[927] Trubey manuscript, 55. 1900 U.S. census, Butler County, Ohio, pop. sched., Middletown, ED 21, p. 2; National Archives micropublication T623, roll 1244. Appendix B letter #6, dated 25 June 1852, refers to the recent death of John's wife and his efforts to find someone to nurse "the child."

[928] Aldrich, *History of Henry and Fulton Counties, Ohio*, 224. Trubey manuscript, 52.

was taken by his maternal grandmother to Butler County, Ohio, to be raised; the 1860 Federal Census bears this out.[929]

The Trubey manuscript indicates that Nathan was married three times, and divorced twice.[930] Nathan married (1) **Nettie J. Ely** of "near Lafayette, Indiana,"[931] on 23 October 1881 in Tippecanoe County, Indiana.[932] No divorce record for this couple is on file in that county.[933] Nathan married (2) in Defiance County, Ohio, on 31 August 1887 **Lillian A. Gilbert**[934] (daughter of W. P. Gilbert and Susana [—?—]),

---

[929] 1860 U.S. census, Butler County, Ohio, pop. sched., Wayne Twp., p. 35/286; National Archives micropublication M653, roll 941: Nathan J. "Toby" (sic), age 8, in household of S. Daugherty, age 61, male [probably listed as a male in error as this should be Sarah Daugherty, who was 51 in the 1850 U.S. census, Butler County, Ohio, pop. sched., Wayne Twp., p. 369/737, National Archives micropublication M432, roll 663]. Trubey manuscript, 55.

[930] Trubey manuscript, 55.

[931] Trubey manuscript, 55.

[932] *Index to Marriage Record, Tippecanoe County [Indiana], 1850-1920 Inclusive*, Vol. IV, Rog-Z (typescript: WPA, no date), 174: recorded in Book C-16: 472.

[933] Response from the Clerk of the Circuit Court in possession of compiler.

[934] Marriage Records, Defiance County, Ohio, Volume 1 (1885 - May 1892), 149; FHL microfilm 1977640. Officiated by J. L. Philips.

born circa 1868.⁹³⁵ Within two years, this couple had separated, but no divorce record was found on file in Defiance County, Ohio.⁹³⁶

Nathan married (3) in Athens County, Ohio, on 4 September 1889 to **Virginia Carrie Gilbert**,⁹³⁷ born on 29⁹³⁸ April 1871 in West Virginia.⁹³⁹ Nathan worked as a painter or "house painter" in Butler County, Ohio, in 1900, and in Defiance County, Ohio, in 1910. Nathan died 7 June 1933, and his wife Carrie died 14 October 1943.⁹⁴⁰

The child of Nathan John⁴ Trubey and Lillian Gilbert:
    339.   i.   ROY⁵ TRUBEY, about whom no birth information was given in the Trubey manuscript, and for whom no Federal Census record was found.⁹⁴¹ Presumably born circa 1888.

---

⁹³⁵ 1880 U.S. census, Defiance County, Ohio, pop. sched., Hicksville, ED 237, p. 46-47; National Archives micropublication T9, roll 1011.

⁹³⁶ Response from the Clerk of the Court; in possession of compiler.

⁹³⁷ Photocopy of marriage license and return provided by the Deputy Clerk without further citation; in possession of compiler.

⁹³⁸ Trubey manuscript, 55.

⁹³⁹ 1900 U.S. census, Butler County, Ohio, pop. sched., Middletown, ED 21, p. 2; National Archives micropublication T623, roll 1244, for birth month and year. 1910 U.S. census, Defiance County, Ohio, Defiance, ED 5, dwelling 107, family 112, 318 Harrison Street, 18 April; National Archives micropublication T624, roll 1177, for birthplace as West Virginia. The 1900 Census entry for Carrie B. lists "Virginia" as her birthplace although her children's entries list "West Virginia" for her.

⁹⁴⁰ Trubey manuscript, 55.

⁹⁴¹ *Ibid.*

188   Daniel Trubey of Franklin County, Pennsylvania

The children of Nathan John[4] Trubey and Virginia Carrie Gilbert:

340.   i.   MARY E. TRUBEY, born May 1893;[942] no further information.
341.   ii. JOHN EARL NATHAN TRUBEY, born November 1894; living in 1910.[943]
342.   iii. EDITH ROSELLE TRUBEY, born February 1896; living in 1910.[944]
343.   iv. IDA BELLE TRUBEY, born March 1897; living in 1910.[945]
344.   v.   EMMA TRUBEY, born April 1900;[946] no further information.
345.   vi. ALBERT SIDNEY TRUBEY, born 5 March 1902;[947] married Loretta Dudlow in 1925, to whom two children were born: *(a)* Richard, and *(b)* Sandra Jean.[948]

---

[942] 1900 U.S. census, Butler County, Ohio, pop. sched., Middletown, ED 21, p. 2.

[943] 1910 U.S. census, Defiance County, Ohio, Defiance, ED 5, dwelling 107, family 112.

[944] 1900 U.S. census, Butler County, Ohio, pop. sched., Middletown, ED 21, p. 2. 1910 U.S. census, Defiance County, Ohio, Defiance, ED 5, dwelling 107, family 112.

[945] 1900 U.S. census, Butler County, Ohio, pop. sched., Middletown, ED 21, p. 2. 1910 U.S. census, Defiance County, Ohio, Defiance, ED 5, dwelling 107, family 112.

[946] 1900 U.S. census, Butler County, Ohio, pop. sched., Middletown, ED 21, p. 2.

[947] 1910 U.S. census, Defiance County, Ohio, Defiance, ED 5, dwelling 107, family 112. Trubey manuscript, 55.

[948] Trubey manuscript, 55.

GENERATION FOUR 189

346. vii. FLORENCE AUGUSTA TRUBEY, born 6 September 1904;[949] married Peter Siler on 4 May 1925, by whom two children were born: *(a)* Marie, and *(b)* Virginia.[950]

347. viii. unknown, born between 1900 and 1910.[951]

100. Barevias Augustus[4] **Trubey** (John[3], Daniel[2, 1]) was born on 25 February 1860[952] in Jewell, Defiance County, Ohio.[953] The 1880 Federal Census reveals that a visitor in the household enumerated immediately after Barevias's household is the woman he wed two years later.[954] Barevias married **Zeruia C. Goodenough** in Defiance County, Ohio, on 15 February 1882.[955] Zeruia, born 19 September 1861 in

---

[949] 1910 U.S. census, Defiance County, Ohio, Defiance, ED 5, dwelling 107, family 112. Trubey manuscript, 55.

[950] Trubey manuscript, 55.

[951] Trubey manuscript, 55, claims eight children born to this couple. The 1900 Census confirms that Carrie was then the mother of five children total, all of whom were then living.

[952] Barevias Augustus Trubey, death certificate no. 49-052029 (1949), California Department of Health Service, Sacramento.

[953] Barevias Augustus Trubey obituary, *Long Beach Press-Telegram*, Long Beach, California, page A-4, transcribed from microfilm roll X43: (July 1-15, 1949), California State Library.

[954] 1880 U.S. census, Defiance County, Ohio, pop. sched., Richland Twp., ED 231, p. 22; National Archives micropublication T9, roll 1011: she is listed here as "Cerugia."

[955] Marriage records, Defiance County, Ohio, Volume 2 (1861-1885), 484; FHL microfilm 1977639. Officiated by B. W. Slagle.

Ohio,[956] was the daughter of William Edwin Goodenough.[957]

Barevias was in the creamery business by 1900,[958] and moved his family to Montana by 1917 where he remained until his wife's death on 18 February 1936 in Forsyth, Rosebud County, Montana.[959] Barevias's interest in his family's history led to his correspondence with and interviewing of various family relatives, the result of which was the Trubey manuscript which serves as the basis for this work. Barevias died in Long Beach, California, where his youngest child resided, on 3 July 1949.[960]

---

[956] Zeruia C. Trubey, death certificate (no registration number), photocopy of the Clerk and Recorder's copy of the Montana Bureau of Vital Statistics' standard certificate furnished by Rosebud County, Forsyth; copy in possession of compiler.

[957] Trubey manuscript, 56. A William and Mary Goodenough were located in the 1860 Federal Census of Defiance County (Noble Twp., p. 346), but this was prior to Zeruia's birth. No entry was found for William in the 1870 Federal Census schedules of Richland, Adams, Defiance or Noble Townships in Defiance County, but an entry for Edwin and Martha Goodenough in the town of Defiance — with an 8-yr-old "Xenia" in their household — likely pertains to William Edwin Goodenough (p. 21/38).

[958] 1900 U.S. census, Defiance County, Ohio, pop. sched., Delaware Twp., Sherwood Village, ED 9, p. 3; National Archives micropublication T623, roll 1263.

[959] Trubey manuscript, 56. Zeruis C. Trubey, Montana death certificate (no number).

[960] Barevias Augustus Trubey, California death certificate no. 49-052029.

GENERATION FOUR 191

The children of Barevias Augustus[4] Trubey and Zeruia C. Goodenough:

348. i. FLORA MAE[5] TRUBEY, born on 17 May 1883, in Richland Twp., Defiance County, Ohio.[961] She married Charles R. Smith on 15 March 1902. The children of this union were *(a)* Marjorie Ray, *(b)* Noma Mildred, *(c)* William Barevias, and *(d)* Clarence Charles.[962] Living in Sherwood, Ohio, in 1949.[963]

349. ii. JOHN EDWIN TRUBEY, born 2 March 1886 in "North Richland Twp.," Defiance County, Ohio.[964] John worked for the Baltimore and Ohio Railroad and the Northern Pacific.[965] He married Addie Gail Anderson of Forsyth, Montana, in June 1910, by whom he had two children prior to his death on 21 December

---

[961] Fayne E. Harter, compiler, *Birth Records of Defiance County, Ohio, July 1, 1867 - December 19, 1908* (1973), 1391; photocopy furnished by the Allen County Public Library, Ft. Wayne, Indiana. Trubey manuscript, 56. 1900 U.S. census, Defiance County, Ohio, Delaware Twp., Sherwood Village, ED 9, p. 3.

[962] Trubey manuscript, 57. Fuller treatment of their four children given on that page.

[963] *Long Beach Press-Telegram*, 4 July 1949.

[964] *Birth Records of Defiance County*, 1391. John Edwin Trubey, death certificate no. 98, photocopy of the Clerk and Recorder's copy of the Montana Bureau of Vital Statistics' standard certificate furnished by Rosebud County, Forsyth; copy in possession of compiler.

[965] Trubey manuscript, 58.

1918;[966] *(a)* Ray Edwin, born 24 June 1912, and *(b)* Lloyd Elton, born 10 April 1914.[967]

350. iii. LYDIA RUTH TRUBEY, born 26 July 1891 in Noble Twp., Richland County, Ohio,[968] where she married William Edward Walker on 28 June 1916.[969] Living in Albany, Oregon, in 1949.[970]

351. iv. MYRON AUGUSTUS TRUBEY, born 7 May 1896, in Noble Twp., Defiance County, Ohio;[971] married Venus Ross of Cleveland, Ohio, on 5 April 1917, to whom four children were born: *(a)* James Wayne, *(b)* Frances Louise, *(c)* Gloyd Orland, and *(d)* Richard Myron.[972] Living in South Gate, California, in 1949.[973]

352. v. THEODORE WAYNE TRUBEY, born 7 February 1902 in Sherwood, Defiance County, Ohio; married Mrs. Margaret (Hooper) James in Casper, Wyoming, on 27 September 1930, both of whom performed as

---

[966] John Edwin Trubey, Montana death certificate no. 98.

[967] Trubey manuscript, 58-59; fuller treatment given on those pages.

[968] *Birth Records of Defiance County*, 1391. Trubey manuscript, 56. 1900 U.S. census, Defiance County, Ohio, Delaware Twp., Sherwood Village, ED 9, p. 3.

[969] Trubey manuscript, 56 and 60.

[970] *Long Beach Press-Telegram*, 4 July 1949.

[971] *Birth Records of Defiance County*, 1391. 1900 U.S. census, Defiance County, Ohio, Delaware Twp., Sherwood Village, ED 9, p. 3. Trubey manuscript, 56 and 61.

[972] Trubey manuscript, 61.

[973] *Long Beach Press-Telegram*, 4 July 1949.

GENERATION FOUR 193

musicians.[974] Living in Long Beach, California, in 1949.[975]

101. Justin Alonzo[4] **Trubey** (John[3], Daniel[2, 1]) was born 1 October 1861 in Defiance County, Ohio.[976] Justin married **Sarah J. Kimberly**[977] (daughter of James Kimberly and Esther J. Barringer)[978] in

---

[974] Trubey manuscript, 56 and 62.

[975] *Long Beach Press-Telegram*, 4 July 1949.

[976] 1900 U.S. census, Defiance County, Ohio, pop. sched., Richland Twp., ED 17, p. 3, enumeration date 7 June; National Archives micropublication T623, roll 1263: gives Justin's birth data as October 1863, but this conflicts with his age recorded therein as 37 [would have been 36]. Trubey manuscript, 63.

[977] 1910 Miracode, Washtenaw County, Michigan, Ann Arbor, ED 113, visitation number 64; National Archives micropublication T1268, roll 224: shows Justin's mother-in-law Esther Kimberly in household. Other evidence of Sarah's maiden name as Kimberly follows.

[978] 1900 U.S. census, Defiance County, Ohio, pop. sched., Richland Twp., ED 17, p. 3; National Archives micropublication T623, roll 1263. 1860 U.S. census, Defiance County, Ohio, pop. sched., Richland Twp., p. 317 (Esther in household of Absolam and Sarah Bearinger) and p. 318 (James in household of John and Anna Kimberly); National Archives micropublication M653, roll 947. 1870 U.S. census, Defiance County, Ohio, pop. sched., Richland Twp., p. 21/172 (Sarah J. in household of James and Esther); National Archives micropublication M593, roll 1195. 1880 U.S. census, Defiance County, Ohio, pop. sched., Richland Twp., ED 231, p. 6 (Sarah still in household of James and Esther); National Archives micropublication T9, roll 1011.

194   DANIEL TRUBEY OF FRANKLIN COUNTY, PENNSYLVANIA

Defiance County, Ohio, on 1 September 1887.[979] Sarah was born in Ohio in December 1866[980] or 1867.[981]

Justin was working as the proprietor of a grocery store in Defiance County in 1900,[982] but removed his family to Ann Arbor, Michigan, by 1910, where his last child was born. Both Justin and his wife were living in 1920, and the Trubey manuscript indicates that Justin died in December 1933.[983]

The children of Justin Alonzo[4] Trubey and Sarah J. Kimberly:
353.   i.   CLAUDIUS EUGENE[5] TRUBEY, born 18 March 1888 in "North Richland Twp.," Defiance County, Ohio;[984] he was last known to be living at his parents' residence at 436 South 3rd Street in Ann Arbor in 1920.[985]

---

[979] Marriage Records, Defiance County, Ohio, Volume 1 (1885-May 1892), 173; FHL microfilm 1977640.

[980] Trubey manuscript, 63.

[981] 1900 census gives December 1867; her ages in 1910 (42) and 1920 (52) also support a December 1867 birth date. 1900 U.S. census, Defiance County, Ohio, Richland Twp., ED 17, p. 3. 1910 Miracode, Washtenaw County, Michigan, Ann Arbor, ED 113, visitation number 64. 1920 Soundex, Washtenaw County, Michigan, Ann Arbor, ED 131, p. 20, National Archives micropublication M1568, roll 261.

[982] 1900 U.S. census, Defiance County, Ohio, Richland Twp., ED 17, p. 3.

[983] Trubey manuscript, 64.

[984] *Birth Records of Defiance County*, 1391. 1900 U.S. census, Defiance County, Ohio, Richland Twp., ED 17, p. 3. Trubey manuscript, 63.

[985] 1920 Soundex, Washtenaw County, Michigan, Ann Arbor, ED 131, p. 20.

GENERATION FOUR   195

354. ii.   MARY LEONA TRUBEY, born 5 September 1890 in Ohio;[986] she married Chauncy O. Rodgers at Ann Arbor on 12 November 1913. Four children were born to them: *(a)* Marian Evelyn, 13 April 1915; *(b)* Harry Franklyn, 7 July 1918; *(c)* Jane Elizabeth, 12 June 1924; and *(d)* Betty Ruth, 10 December 1925.[987]

355. iii. HAROLD DORWIN TRUBEY, born 25 July 1896, in Richland Twp., Defiance County, Ohio.[988] His marriage to Elsie Laura April as given in the Trubey manuscript (p. 65) is corroborated by the 1920 Census,[989] as is the first of his three children: *(a)* Dorwin Melvin, 28 March 1918; *(b)* Robert Emanuel, 28 January 1925, and *(c)* Barbara Jane, 21 July 1932.[990]

356. iv.   MILDRED FAY TRUBEY, born 20 May 1902, in Richland Twp., Defiance County, Ohio;[991] she married 21 September 1921, Harold I. Simpson, by whom three children were born: *(a)* William Robert,

---

[986] 1900 U.S. census, Defiance County, Ohio, Richland Twp., ED 17, p. 3. Trubey manuscript, 63-64.

[987] Trubey manuscript, 64; further information given here.

[988] *Birth Records of Defiance County*, 1391. 1900 U.S. census, Defiance County, Ohio, Richland Twp., ED 17, p. 3. Trubey manuscript (pages 63 and 65), erroneously lists "1895" as his birth year.

[989] 1920 Soundex, Washtenaw County, Michigan, Ann Arbor, ED 131, p. 20.

[990] Trubey manuscript, 65; further information given here.

[991] *Birth Records of Defiance County*, 1391. Trubey manuscript, 63 and 65. 1910 Miracode, Washtenaw County, Michigan, Ann Arbor, ED 113, visitation number 64.

21 September 1922; *(b)* James Norman, 18 January 1924; and *(c)* John Richard, 17 July 1929.[992]

357. v. MARGUERITE LOIS TRUBEY, born 1 August 1910;[993] she married Franklin Richard Gervick on 12 July 1941. One child was born to this couple by the time the Trubey manuscript was compiled: Richard Trubey Gervick, 16 April 1942.[994]

102. Ambrose Enyart[4] Trubey (John[3], Daniel[2, 1]) was born 5[995] September 1863[996] purportedly in Defiance County, Ohio. He was married there on 28 April 1887 to **Catherine Osborn**[997] (daughter of David Osborn and Catherine Hull).[998] Catherine was born in Ohio in August 1867.[999]

---

[992] Trubey manuscript, 65.

[993] Trubey manuscript, 63 and 66. 1920 Soundex, Washtenaw County, Michigan, Ann Arbor, ED 131, p. 20.

[994] Trubey manuscript, 66.

[995] Trubey manuscript, 67.

[996] 1900 U.S. census, Defiance County, Ohio, pop. sched., Richland Twp., ED 17, p. 2; National Archives micropublication T623, roll 1263. Trubey manuscript, 67.

[997] Marriage records, Defiance County, Ohio, Volume 1 (1885 - May 1892), 149; FHL microfilm 1977640.

[998] 1870 U.S. census, Defiance County, Ohio, pop. sched., Richland Twp., p. 5/164; National Archives micropublication M593, roll 1195. 1880 U.S. census, Defiance County, Ohio, pop. sched., Richland Twp., ED 231, p. 15; National Archives micropublication T9, roll 1011. *Henry County, Ohio*, 3: 235.

[999] 1900 U.S. census, Defiance County, Ohio, Richland Twp., ED 17, p. 2.

GENERATION FOUR 197

Ambrose appears to have farmed his entire life in Defiance County, where he and his wife were last known to have been living in 1920.[1000]

The children of Ambrose Enyart[4] Trubey and Catherine Osborn:
358. i. EMMET ELLSWORTH[5] TRUBEY, born 31 December 1887 in "North Richland Twp.," Defiance County, Ohio;[1001] he married Mary Ann Minsel on 14 June 1909, to whom two children were born: *(a)* Ermah Udette, 14 October 1910, and *(b)* Ambrose Ellsworth, 9 July 1917.[1002]
359. ii. HOWARD ALONZO TRUBEY, born 17 August 1889; died 15 September 1911.[1003]
360. iii. ALVA MORRIS TRUBEY, born 11 September 1891 in "North Richland Twp.," Defiance County, Ohio;[1004] last known to have been living in 1920.[1005]

[1000] *Ibid.* 1920 Miracode, Defiance County, Ohio, Richland County, ED 22, p. 3; National Archives micropublication M1581, roll 427.

[1001] *Birth Records of Defiance County*, 1391. Trubey manuscript, 67. 1900 U.S. census, Defiance County, Ohio, Richland Twp., ED 17, p. 2.

[1002] Trubey manuscript, 67.

[1003] *Ibid.*

[1004] *Birth Records of Defiance County*. 1391. Trubey manuscript, 67. 1900 U.S. census, Defiance County, Ohio, Richland Twp., ED 17, p. 2.

[1005] 1920 Miracode, Defiance County, Ohio, Richland County, ED 22, p. 3.

361. iv. ETHEL DONELDA TRUBEY, born 27 December 1898 in Richland Twp., Defiance County, Ohio;[1006] last known to have been living in 1920.

103. Joseph Andrew[4] Trubey (Daniel[3, 2, 1]) was born 13 November 1853[1007] near Huntington, Indiana.[1008] Joseph was married in Jewell County, Kansas, on 13 June 1875 to **Saphronia Day**.[1009] Saphronia

---

[1006] *Birth Records of Defiance County*, 1391. 1900 U.S. census, Defiance County, Ohio, Richland Twp., ED 17, p. 2. 1920 Miracode, Defiance County, Ohio, Richland County, ED 22, p. 3. Trubey manuscript, p. 67, erroneously lists "29 December 1896."

[1007] Daniel Trubey pension.

[1008] Trubey manuscript, 69; birth date here also agrees with pension version. Joseph's birthplace as Indiana is also confirmed by 1860 U.S. census, Henry County, Ohio, pop. sched., Bartlow Twp, p. 251; National Archives micropublication M653, roll 947. 1870 U.S. census, Henry County, Ohio, pop. sched., Bartlow Twp., p. 246/3; National Archives micropublication M593, roll 1195. His son William's entry in 1900 U.S. census, Trinity County, California, pop. sched., Douglas Twp. and city, ED 189, p. 2, dwelling and family 50; National Archives micropublication T623, roll 115. 1910 Miracode, Santa Cruz County, California, ED 122, visitation #440; National Archives micropublication T1261, roll 244.

[1009] Desire Tobey Sears Chapter NSDAR, compiler, *Jewell County [Kansas] Marriage Records*, Volume 1 (DAR GRC 1941?), 19: Vol. A: 93. Gives names as Joseph A. Truly (age 21) and Safronier J. Day (age 21).

was born 12 August 1853[1010] in Virginia;[1011] her parentage is not known. Federal Census information indicates that this couple removed to Arkansas shortly after their marriage, where their two children appear to have been born, yet their 1880 Census entry there could not be located in the Soundex. The family migrated to California by 1900, and was last known to have been living in Santa Cruz in 1910.[1012] Joseph died 11 September 1933, and his widow Saphronia was yet living in 1941.[1013]

The children of Joseph Andrew[4] Trubey and Saphronia J. Day:

362. i. WILLIAM JOSHUA[5] TRUBEY, born 4 March 1877 in Arkansas; he married Mary Rodgers in 1898,[1014] and was last known to be living in Trinity County, California, in 1900, working as a "placer miner."[1015] Although no child appears in their 14 June 1900 household, the Trubey manuscript states that they had one child, Andrew Franklin, born sometime in 1900.[1016]

[1010] Trubey manuscript, 69.

[1011] 1910 Miracode, Santa Cruz County, California, ED 122, visitation #440. Her son William's entry in 1900 U.S. census, Trinity County, California, Douglas Twp. and city, ED 189, p. 2.

[1012] 1910 Miracode, Santa Cruz County, California, ED 122, visitation #440.

[1013] Trubey manuscript, 69.

[1014] 1900 U.S. census, Trinity County, California, Douglas Twp. and city, ED 189, p. 2. Trubey manuscript, 69.

[1015] 1900 U.S. census, Trinity County, California, Douglas Twp. and city, ED 189, p. 2.

[1016] Trubey manuscript, 69.

363. ii. ADDIE E. TRUBEY, born 10 January 1880 in Arkansas;[1017] she was employed as a music teacher in Trinity County, California, in 1900.[1018] Addie married Harry Thompson Grubb on 10 August 1902, and had one daughter, Edna Ethel Grubb, born 4 June 1903.[1019]

104. Mary Jane[4] Trubey (Daniel[3, 2, 1]) was born 9 September 1855 in Henry County, Ohio.[1020] When a small child, Mary Jane removed with her parents to Jewell County, Kansas,[1021] where on 3 May 1874 she was first married to **William T. Pilcher**[1022] (son of Joshua Pilcher and

---

[1017] 1900 U.S. census, Trinity County, California, Douglas Twp. and city, ED 189, p. 2, gives her birth data but not her relationship to head of household [and brother] "William Truby." Trubey manuscript, 69-70.

[1018] 1900 U.S. census, Trinity County, California, Douglas Twp. and city, ED 189, p. 2.

[1019] Trubey manuscript, 70.

[1020] "Mrs. M. Taylor" obituary, *Grand Junction Daily Sentinal* [place of publication not given], 23 July 1939, p. 11; copy provided by the Colorado Historical Society, 1300 Broadway, Denver, Colorado, in possession of compiler. This month, year, and place supported by the 1900 U.S. census, Colorado, Delta County, pop. sched., Precinct 3, ED 15, p. 3; National Archives micropublication T623, roll 122. 1860 U.S. census, Henry County, Ohio, pop. sched., Bartlow Twp., p. 251; National Archives micropublication M653, roll 985.

[1021] *Grand Junction Daily Sentinal*, 23 July 1939.

[1022] DAR, *Jewell County Marriages*, 1: 13: cites original record in Vol. A: 60, William T. Pilcher (age 24) and Mary J. Truby (age 19).

GENERATION FOUR 201

Philadelphia Beer).[1023] William was born circa 1849 in Jo Daviess County, Illinois.[1024]

Although the Trubey manuscript does not provide any detail on Mary Jane Trubey's life, a more recent manuscript gives a good deal of information.[1025] William and Mary Jane had two children in their 1880 household in Mitchell County, Kansas,[1026] and the recent Trubey manuscript identifies three additional children born to this family,[1027] which removed to Colorado in 1882.[1028] Mary joined the Seventh Day

---

[1023] Belleville Chapter (Illinois) DAR, compiler, *Marriage Register, St. Clair County, Illinois, 1807-1845* (DAR GRC 1924-25), 33: Joshua Pilcher and Philadelphia Beer, 17 November 1836. 1850 U.S. census, Jo Daviess County, Illinois, pop. sched., Wapello Precinct, p. 202 (William age 1); National Archives micropublication M432, roll 111. [Anonymous], *The History of Jo Daviess County, Illinois, Containing a History of the County, its Cities, Towns, etc.* (Chicago: H. F. Kett, 1878), 764-765, furnishes more data on this Pilcher family's history.

[1024] 1850 U.S. census, Jo Daviess County, Illinois, Wapello Precinct, p. 202 . 1880 U.S. census, Mitchell County, Kansas, pop. sched., Glen Elder, ED 179, p. 4; National Archives micropublication T9, roll 389. Lucille Jackson Vernon's *Pilcher Family History* (Lexington, N.C.: Young Graphics, no date), 161, gives William's full date of birth as 3 May 1849; no source of proof is given, although it is stated that Patricia Ann (Pilcher) Lee of Kaysville, Utah, compiled the information for this "miscellaneous" Pilcher. This publication also gives William's middle name as Taylor.

[1025] 1962 Trubey manuscript, 31-33.

[1026] 1880 U.S. census, Mitchell County, Kansas, Glen Elder, ED 179, p. 4.

[1027] 1962 Trubey manuscript, 31.

[1028] *Grand Junction Daily Sentinal*, 23 July 1939.

Adventist church shortly after their arrival there, and remained affiliated with this denomination until her death.[1029]

Following William's death in Delta County, Colorado, on 23 December 1891,[1030] Mary married (2) **Andrew T. Taylor** on 13 January 1894 in nearby Montrose County, Colorado.[1031] In 1900, Andrew T. Taylor was employed at the Hidden Treasure Mining and Tunnel Company in Hinsdale County, Colorado,[1032] whereas Mary headed the family household in Delta County, listing her status as "married," and her occupation as "farming."[1033] Traditional information indicates she served as "the doctor for the whole country...she carried

---

[1029] *Ibid.*

[1030] Arkansas Valley Chapter (Colorado) DAR, compiler, *Death Records of Delta, Delta County, Colorado, 1884-1900 and Tombstone Inscriptions, Cemetery Records, Tincup, Gunnison County, Colorado, 1869-1905* (DAR GRC 1984), 7. Vernon's *Pilcher Family History*, p. 161, gives 22 December 1891.

[1031] John Williams Lynn, compiler, *Montrose County, Colorado, Marriage Records, 1883-1900* (Grand Junction, Colo.: a Desert Hill Book by Lynn Research, 1984), 10. However, Mary Jane's obituary gives groom's name as *Robert* Taylor.

[1032] 1900 U.S. census, Hinsdale County, Colorado, pop. sched., Precinct 3, ED 42, page 11-A, line 10; National Archives micropublication T623, roll 124: Andrew (age 49) born in January 1851 in Illinois, father born in Kentucky, mother in Virginia, employed as "mill table tender," and married five years. A scan of the unindexed 1910 Census schedules of Crawford, Precinct 3, of Delta County uncovered a different Andrew D. Taylor who was not this man, and the Soundex to Colorado's 1920 Census did not include Andrew, Mary, or Ellsworth Taylor.

[1033] 1900 U.S. census, Colorado, Delta County, Precinct 3, ED 15, p. 3.

Dr. Kellogg's doctor book in a flowered cloth bag, and went whenever any one called for her, day or night."[1034]

Mary Jane died 22 July 1939 at the Palisade, Colorado, home of her daughter Mrs. J. I. Hampton,[1035] and is said to be buried beside her first husband William T. Pilcher in the cemetery at Crawford, Colorado.[1036] The date and place of Andrew T. Taylor's post-1900 death are unknown.

The children of Mary Jane[4] Trubey and William T. Pilcher:

364. i. JOSEPH LOUIS[5] PILCHER, born 23 August 1877 in Kansas;[1037] he was married on 6 March 1899 in Delta County, Colorado,[1038] to Stella Contessi McKessin. Their children were *(a)* Cecil Louis, born 15 July 1900, *(b)* Eva Gladys, born 8 September 1901, and *(c)* Merle Eugene, born 30 December 1909.[1039] Joseph was not mentioned as one of Mary's surviving sons in 1939.

365. ii. DANIEL FRANKLIN PILCHER, born 7 April 1880 in Kansas;[1040] married at Durango, La Plata County,

---

[1034] 1962 Trubey manuscript, 31.

[1035] *Grand Junction Daily Sentinal*, 23 July 1939. Vernon's *Pilcher Family History*, p. 161, claims Mary Jane died in Grand Junction, Colorado.

[1036] 1962 Trubey manuscript, 33.

[1037] 1880 U.S. census, Mitchell County, Kansas, Glen Elder, ED 179, p. 4. 1962 Trubey manuscript, p. 31, for full birth date.

[1038] DAR, *Delta County Marriages*, 69.

[1039] 1962 Trubey manuscript, 31.

[1040] 1880 U.S. census, Mitchell County, Kansas, Glen Elder, ED 179, p. 4. 1962 Trubey manuscript, 31-32.

Colorado, on 2 July 1907 to Elsie May Parker[1041] by whom four children were born: *(a)* Delbert Eugene, born 16 May 1908, *(b)* Oren, 18 February 1910, *(c)* Agnes Iola, 1912, and *(d)* Woodrow, 30 September 1916.[1042] Mary's obituary gives his 1939 residence as Mancos, Colorado.

366. iii. ETHEL MAUDE PILCHER, born 24 May 1885 in Kansas;[1043] married at Crawford, Montrose County, Colorado, on 25 December 1904 to Joe I. Hampton,[1044] and died 14 October 1960 leaving no children.[1045]

367. iv. WILLIAM EDWIN PILCHER, born 3 December 1888, died January 1889.[1046]

368. v. DAVID EUGENE PILCHER, born 12 April 1890 in Colorado;[1047] married at Ouray, Ouray County, Colorado, on 24 December 1914 to Mary Ellen "Ella"

[1041] Colorado Marriage Record Report #50152, La Plata County; FHL microfilm 1690120. Robert S. Clements, County Judge, officiating.

[1042] 1962 Trubey manuscript, 32. Vernon's *Pilcher Family History*, p. 161, gives Agnes's full date of birth as 19 October 1912.

[1043] 1900 U.S. census, Colorado, Delta County, Precinct 3, ED 15, p. 3. 1962 Trubey manuscript, 31-32.

[1044] Colorado Marriage Record Report #857, Montrose County; FHL microfilm 1690084. J. D. Smith, J.P., officiating.

[1045] 1962 Trubey manuscript, 32.

[1046] The only source mentioning this child is the 1962 Trubey manuscript (p. 31), although Mary Jane's 1900 Census entry does indicate that one of her six children died before 1900.

[1047] 1900 U.S. census, Colorado, Delta County, Precinct 3, ED 15, p. 3. 1962 Trubey manuscript, 31 and 33.

Rathmell,[1048] by whom seven children were born: *(a)* Lola Ruth, born 7 October 1915, *(b)* William, 10 November 1916, *(c)* Alice Margaret, 12 May 1918, *(d)* Eugene David, 5 August 1920, *(e)* Mary Jane, 22 June 1925, *(f)* Kathryn Elaine, 10 May 1928, and *(g)* Hazel Lorraine, 22 December 1932.[1049] David resided in Telluride, Colorado, in 1939.

The child of Mary Jane[4] Trubey and Andrew T. Taylor:
369. i. ELLSWORTH TAYLOR, born July 1894[1050] or January 1895[1051] in Colorado. He is not mentioned as a surviving son in Mary's 1939 obituary. No further information.

105. John Allen[4] Trubey (Daniel[3, 2, 1]) was born 13 January 1858[1052] probably in Henry County, Ohio.[1053] John was married on 6 October

---

[1048] Colorado Marriage Record Report #[blank], Ouray County; FHL microfilm 1690120. W. G. McConnell, minister, officiating.

[1049] 1962 Trubey manuscript, 33.

[1050] 1962 Trubey manuscript, 33.

[1051] 1900 U.S. census, Colorado, Delta County, Precinct 3, ED 15, p. 3.

[1052] Daniel Trubey pension.

[1053] 1860 U.S. census, Henry County, Ohio, pop. sched., Bartlow Twp., p. 251; National Archives micropublication M653, roll 985. 1870 U.S. census, Henry County, Ohio, pop. sched., Bartlow Twp., p. 246/3; National Archives micropublication M593, roll 1221. 1900 U.S. census, Mitchell County, Kansas, pop. sched., Glen Elder, ED 83, p. 2; National Archives micropublication T623, roll 491.

1881 in Jewell County, Kansas,[1054] to **Sarah A. Morgan**, who was born in October 1863 in Illinois.[1055]

John remained in Kansas, and was farming in Glen Elder, Mitchell County, in 1900. John's death date is not known, but his sister Mary (Trubey) Pilcher Taylor's 1939 obituary mentions her surviving brother "J. A. Trubey" of Iola, Kansas, who should be this man.[1056] John's wife Sarah is said to have died on 13 February 1952.[1057]

The children of John Allen[4] Trubey and Sarah A. Morgan:

370. i. JESSE FREEMAN[5] TRUBEY, born 27 April 1883;[1058] he married Mabel Irene Sample on 8 October 1906, to whom six children were born: *(a)* Lester Charles, born 18 January 1908, *(b)* Marie Leha, 26 August 1909, *(c)* Beulah, 21 October 1913, *(d)* Rita Esther, 22 March 1915, *(e)* Amos Calvin, 18 September 1923, and *(f)* Ila Dorlean, 15 August 1927.[1059]

371. ii. CARRIE LOVENA TRUBEY, born 13 June 1887 in Kansas;[1060] she married Clarence A. Hogeland on 22 December 1909, by whom two children were born: *(a)* Vesta Lovena, born 20 September 1912, and

---

[1054] DAR, *Jewell County Marriages*, 1: 82: cites original record as Vol. B: 19, J. A. Truby (age 23) and Sarah A. Morgan (age "?").

[1055] 1900 U.S. census, Mitchell County, Kansas, Glen Elder, ED 83, p. 2.

[1056] *Grand Junction Daily Sentinal*, 23 July 1939.

[1057] 1962 Trubey manuscript, 27; place not given.

[1058] 1900 U.S. census, Mitchell County, Kansas, pop. sched., Glen Elder, ED 83, p. 2. Trubey manuscript, 71.

[1059] Trubey manuscript, 71.

[1060] 1900 U.S. census, Mitchell County, Kansas, pop. sched., Glen Elder, ED 83, p. 2. Trubey manuscript, 71-72.

GENERATION FOUR 207

(b) Raymond Clarence, 19 October 1915. Carrie died 27 March 1937.[1061]

372. iii. LORAINE "LARENA" ESTHER TRUBEY, born 22 March 1896 in Kansas;[1062] she married Leonard C. Kidney on 30 April 1917, by whom two children were born: *(a)* Donald Leonard, born 18 August 1918, and *(b)* Margaret Adeline, 25 September 1924.[1063]

373. iv. LEILA ETHEL TRUBEY, born 24 February 1898 in Kansas;[1064] she married Joseph Bratten on 21 June 1930, by whom two children were born: *(a)* Paul Joseph, born 28 October 1932, and *(b)* Dorlean Lavon, 25 June 1937.[1065]

374. v. CHESTER EDWIN TRUBEY, born 5 August 1899 in Kansas;[1066] he married (1) Elsie Cook on 17 March 1924, by whom a daughter, Dona Rose, was born on 13 January 1927.[1067] By a second marriage, a son, Tony, was born in Great Falls, Montana.[1068]

[1061] Trubey manuscript, 72.

[1062] 1900 U.S. census, Mitchell County, Kansas, pop. sched., Glen Elder, ED 83, p. 2. Trubey manuscript, 71-72.

[1063] Trubey manuscript, 72.

[1064] 1900 U.S. census, Mitchell County, Kansas, pop. sched., Glen Elder, ED 83, p. 2. Trubey manuscript, 71-72.

[1065] Trubey manuscript, 72.

[1066] 1900 U.S. census, Mitchell County, Kansas, pop. sched., Glen Elder, ED 83, p. 2. Trubey manuscript, 71-72.

[1067] Trubey manuscript, 72.

[1068] 1962 Trubey manuscript, 28.

106. Lewis Francis[4] **Trubey** (Daniel[3, 2, 1]) was born on 2 June 1859[1069] or 1860[1070] in Henry County, Ohio. Lewis was married in Mitchell County, Kansas, on 1 November 1885 to **Lavina "Vinnie" Amanda Dudley a.k.a. Ferguson**.[1071] A published genealogy places the birth of Lavina (and her twin sister) in Rock Creek, Mitchell County, Iowa, on 29 March 1867, to parents Robert Bennett Dudley and Livona Jane Childs.[1072]

This couple was not found in Federal Census records of Colorado, although at least two of their children were born there between 1890 and 1898,[1073] and it was noted that an Elder L. F. Trubey performed an 1895 marriage in Colorado's Delta County.[1074] In 1900, this family

---

[1069] 1860 U.S. census, Henry County, Ohio, Bartlow Twp., p. 251, lists "Francis" as age 1 on 30 July 1860.

[1070] Daniel Trubey pension.

[1071] Mitchell County Marriage Book C: 88; photocopy provided by District Court, Beloit, Kansas. This record shows the wedding took place at Daniel Trubey's residence, with A. G. Moffett, J.P., officiating. No other Mitchell County marriage seen for a Ferguson groom and Dudley bride, nor tombstone for a Ferguson giving a circa 1885 death date. A descendant explained Vinnie was unofficially adopted by a Ferguson family after the deaths of her parents, thus accounting for that surname in her marriage record.

[1072] Denis P. Edeline, *Dudley Family of Iowa* (Arcata, Iowa: 1976), 4 and 28; FHL microfilm 0982186. No mention is made therein of a Mr. Ferguson adopting or marrying Lavina.

[1073] 1900 U.S. census, Floyd County, Iowa, pop. sched., Charles City, ED 89, p. 13-B, Isabell Street; National Archives micropublication T623, roll 431. 1910 Miracode, St. Louis County, Missouri., St. Louis City, ED 435, visitation #219; National Archives micropublication T1270, roll 254.

[1074] DAR, *Delta County Marriages*, 47: 28 Dec 1895, F. Snideman and Carrie A. Sees, both of Delta.

resided in Charles City, Floyd County, Iowa, where Lewis was recorded as a "preacher."[1075] In 1907, L. F. and Vinnie gave their residence as Oakland, Shawnee County, Kansas.[1076] By 1910, they had relocated to St. Louis,[1077] and resided in Largo, Florida, by 1939.[1078] Lewis died 25 January 1942.[1079] Vinnie reportedly died on 24 February 1951, at Largo, Pinellas County, Florida.[1080]

The children of Lewis Francis[4] Trubey and Lavina Amanda Dudley a.k.a. Ferguson:[1081]

[1075] 1900 U.S. census, Floyd County, Iowa, Charles City, ED 89, p. 13-B. Unfortunately, the enumerator listed "unknown" over most of the categories for this family (and no others) on this schedule page, noting only the family members' relationships, that Lewis and "Vurnie" were married, and that Vurnie was the mother of three children, all of whom were living (although other records show two additional children had been born and had died by this date).

[1076] L. F. and Vinnie A. Trubey granted power of attorney by his father Daniel Trubey in the latter's "Declaration for Pension Under the Act of February 6, 1907" signed by all parties on 17 March 1907, as found in "Daniel Trubey Pension (Co. D, 55th Ohio Infantry), application 441384, certificate 351986," Civil War and Later Pension Files, Records of the Veterans Administration (Record Group 15), National Archives, Washington, D.C.

[1077] 1910 Miracode, St. Louis County, Missouri., St. Louis City, ED 435, visitation #219.

[1078] *Grand Junction Daily Sentinal*, 23 July 1939.

[1079] Trubey manuscript, 73.

[1080] *Dudley Family of Iowa*, 4 and 28.

[1081] 1900 U.S. census, Floyd County, Iowa, Charles City, ED 89, p. 13-B. 1910 Miracode, St. Louis County, Missouri., St. Louis City, ED 435, visitation #219. Trubey manuscript, 73.

375. i. WILLIAM MAHLON⁵ TRUBEY was born 16 October 1886; died 24 November 1894.
376. ii. MYRTLE EDNA TRUBEY, born 21 May 1889 in Colorado; she married Harry Karl Martens on 25 May 1913 in St. Louis, Missouri.[1082] Their children were *(a)* Hilda Emma Grace, born 10 April 1914, *(b)* Nellie A., 13 August 1915, and *(c)* Berhend Henry, 9 February 1917.
377. iii. JAMES CYRENUS TRUBEY, born 25 February 1893; died 14 November 1894.
378. iv. LEWIS EDWARD TRUBEY, born 16 February 1898 in Colorado; married Muriel Osborn on 7 May 1917. Their children include *(a)* Lewis Merle, born 24 February 1918, *(b)* Charles Francis, 20 November 1923, *(c)* Shirley Maxine, 29 January 1925, *(d)* Lovina Amanda, 28 September 1926, *(e)* William Leslie, 16 October 1928, and *(f)* Myrtle Carolyn, 24 November 1930.
379. v. EMMA GRACE TRUBEY, born 25 January 1900 in Iowa; married Mr. Schee on 28 June 1922. Their children include *(a)* Leland Burlette, born 23 October 1923, *(b)* Virginia Arnell, 30 September 1925, *(c)* Evelyn Lenore, 15 October 1930, and *(d)* James Robert, 29 April 1937.

107. Melissa Ann⁴ Trubey (Daniel³, ², ¹) was born 29 January 1862[1083] in Henry County, Ohio.[1084] After her family removed to Mitchell

---

[1082] 1962 Trubey manuscript, 29.

[1083] Daniel Trubey pension.

[1084] 1870 U.S. census, Henry County, Ohio, pop. sched., Bartlow Twp., p. 246/3; National Archives micropublication M593, roll 1221. 1880 U.S. census, Mitchell County, Kansas, pop. sched., Glen Elder, ED 179, p. 4; National Archives micropublication T9, roll 389. 1900 U.S. census, Montrose County, Colorado, pop. sched., Precinct 7, ED 78, p. 38; National Archives micropublication T623, roll 127.

GENERATION FOUR

County, Kansas, Melissa was married there, at Beloit, on 25 February 1885 to **Benjamin F. Hutchinson** of Jewell County, Kansas[1085] (son of David Hutchinson and Eliza Jane Malone).[1086] Benjamin was born in January 1860,[1087] likely in Dodson Township, Highland County, Ohio.[1088]

After the birth of two children in Kansas, this family removed to Montrose County, Colorado, where Benjamin worked as a farmer in

---

[1085] Bernice Myers Chapman and Douglas Chapman, *Mitchell County [Kansas] Marriages*, Volume I, 1870 to 1896 (No place: no publisher, 1983), 108: cited as Book C: 50, by M. M. Rowley, Probate Judge.

[1086] The 1962 Trubey manuscript, p. 34, states that Benjamin was born in Lynchburg, Ohio, in 1860. 1860 U.S. census, Highland Co., Ohio, pop. sched., Dodson Twp., p. 143/71, dwelling 1040, family 1015; National Archives micropublication M653, roll 986: David Hutchuson (25, born Ohio), Eliza (26, Ohio) and Benjamin (4/12). David N. and Jane N. McBride, compilers, *Marriage Records of Highland County, Ohio, 1805-1880* (Ann Arbor, Michigan: Edwards Letter Shop, 1962), 121 (David Hutcheson & Eliza Jane Malone, 10 January 1858) and 148 (Benjamin Malone & Sally Burnett, 1829). Eliza appears to be the daughter of Benjamin Malone and Sally Burnett, per the latter's divorce action abstracted in David N. and Jane N. McBride's *Common Pleas Court Records of Highland County, Ohio (1805-1860)* (Ann Arbor, Mich.: The Edwards Letter Shop, 1959), 192.

[1087] 1900 U.S. census, Montrose County, Colorado, Precinct 7, ED 78, p. 38.

[1088] This is where his family resided when he was four months old (1860 U.S. census, Highland Co., Ohio, Dodson Twp., p. 143/71).

1900.[1089] Benjamin died in Santa Rosa, California, on 6 August 1946, and Melissa died there on 10 July 1951.[1090]

The children of Melissa Ann[4] Trubey and Benjamin F. Hutchinson:

380. i. DAVID GUY[5] HUTCHINSON, born 1 September 1886[1091] or 1887[1092] in Kansas. He married Margery Lillian Kennedy on 28 April 1909 at Palisade, Colorado.[1093] Their two children were *(a)* Rolland Keith, born 4 March 1910, and *(b)* Lillian Esther, 6 February 1912.[1094]

381. ii. MABEL HUTCHINSON, born 15 October 1888[1095] or 1889[1096] in Kansas; she married Samuel Swindler. Mabel died 27 February 1956, and her husband on 10 September 1963.[1097] No known children.

[1089] 1900 census indicates Kansas birthplaces for David Guy and Mabel only.

[1090] 1962 Trubey manuscript, 34.

[1091] Trubey manuscript, 75.

[1092] 1900 U.S. census, Montrose County, Colorado, Precinct 7, ED 78, p. 38.

[1093] 1962 Trubey manuscript, 34.

[1094] Trubey manuscript, 75. 1962 Trubey manuscript, 34-35.

[1095] Trubey manuscript, 75.

[1096] 1900 U.S. census, Montrose County, Colorado, Precinct 7, ED 78, p. 38.

[1097] 1962 Trubey manuscript, 35.

GENERATION FOUR 213

382. iii. HARRY O. HUTCHINSON, born 9 October 1890 in Kansas[1098] or October 1891 in Colorado.[1099] No known children born to Harry and his wife Guinevere DeFehr, whom he married 10 August 1928 in Oakland, California.[1100]

383. iv. GEORGE ANDREW HUTCHINSON, born 10 December 1892 in Colorado; he married Madge Cecile Service in Meeker, Colorado, on 20 December 1916; two children were born to them: *(a)* Nancy Marie, born 28 October 1917 in Palisades, Colorado, and *(b)* Maybelle Melissa, 5 August 1919 also in Palisade, Colorado.[1101]

384. v. BENJAMIN FRANKLIN HUTCHINSON, born 3 December 1898;[1102] he married Verda L. Holloway in Sebastopol, California, on 25 June 1921. Their children were *(a)* Wilbur E., born 3 April 1922, and *(b)* Wilma L., 26 February 1929, both born in Sebastopol.[1103]

385. vi. HAZEL HUTCHINSON, born 25 January 1901;[1104] she

[1098] Trubey manuscript, 75.

[1099] 1900 U.S. census, Montrose County, Colorado, Precinct 7, ED 78, p. 38.

[1100] Trubey manuscript, 75. 1962 Trubey manuscript, 35.

[1101] 1900 U.S. census, Montrose County, Colorado, Precinct 7, ED 78, p. 38. Trubey manuscript, 75. 1962 Trubey manuscript, 35.

[1102] 1900 U.S. census, Montrose County, Colorado, Precinct 7, ED 78, p. 38. Trubey manuscript, 75.

[1103] Trubey manuscript, 75. 1962 Trubey manuscript, 35.

[1104] Trubey manuscript, 75. 1920 Soundex, Mesa County, Colorado, ED 98, p. 13; National Archives micropublication M1552, roll 30: Hazel, age 17, in household of Benjamin F. and Melissa A.

married Harry Chinnock[1105] by whom were born *(a)* Dorothy Eloise, born 29 October 1928, and *(b)* E. Romayne, born 2 July 1931.[1106]

109. David Cyrenus[4] **Trubey** (Daniel[3, 2, 1]) was born 4 October 1866[1107] in Henry County, Ohio. David married 9 November 1892 in Jewell County, Kansas, **Lulie A. Pratt**[1108] (daughter of J. R. and Omira M. Pratt).[1109] Lulie was born 19[1110] September 1871 in Iowa.[1111]

David allegedly worked as a photographer in his early life; "when his family became of such proportions, he turned to farming."[1112] Yet he was listed as a farmer as early as 1900, when only three children

---

Hutchinson (along with her brother Benjamin F., age 21).

[1105] 1962 Trubey manuscript, p. 36, corrects spelling of surname which appears as "Chimock" in the Trubey manuscript (p. 75).

[1106] 1962 Trubey manuscript, 36. Note that a third child Hazel mentioned in the Trubey manuscript (p. 75) is not mentioned here.

[1107] Daniel Trubey pension.

[1108] DAR, *Jewell County Marriages*, 2: 62: cites original record as Vol. C: 402, D. C. Truby (age 26) and Lula A. Pratt (age 21).

[1109] 1880 U.S. census, Jewell County, Kansas, pop. sched., Calvin Twp., ED 130, p. 8; National Archives micropublication T9, roll 384.

[1110] Trubey manuscript, 76.

[1111] 1900 U.S. census, Jewell County, Kansas, pop. sched., Calvin Twp., ED 44, p. 9; National Archives micropublication T623, roll 483.

[1112] Trubey manuscript, 76.

GENERATION FOUR 215

were in his household.[1113] Daniel's family remained in Kansas until about 1919, when they removed to the Platte River near Shelton, Nebraska,[1114] and removed again in 1923 to Ocala, Florida. Daniel and Lulie followed their daughter Ethel (a nurse) to Hendersonville, North Carolina, where Daniel died on 9 June 1944, and Lulie on 21 January 1962.[1115]

The children of David Cyrenus[4] Trubey and Lulie A. Pratt:
386. i. ETHEL G.[5] TRUBEY, born 9 October 1893 in Kansas;[1116] she married E. V. Poole on 3 September 1927 at Ocala, Florida, to whom was born a son Dalton H., on 14 February 1929.[1117]
387. ii. CLARENCE O. TRUBEY, born 11 May 1895[1118] in Kansas; he married (1) Helen Richert on 8 May 1919; one child died at birth, and a son Orville was born 5 November 1921. After Helen's death on 12 November 1921, Clarence married (2) Elizabeth

---

[1113] 1900 U.S. census, Jewell County, Kansas, Calvin Twp., ED 44, p. 9.

[1114] 1920 Soundex, Buffalo County, Nebraska, ED 49, p. 17; National Archives micropublication M1573, roll 87.

[1115] 1962 Trubey manuscript, 41. Mary Jane (Trubey) Pilcher Taylor's 1939 obituary (*Grand Junction Daily Sentinal*, 23 July 1939) gives the residence of her brother D. C. Trubey as East Flat Rock, North Carolina.

[1116] 1900 U.S. census, Jewell County, Kansas, Calvin Twp., ED 44, p. 9. 1920 Soundex, Buffalo County, Nebraska, ED 49, p. 17. Trubey manuscript, 76.

[1117] 1962 Trubey manuscript, 38.

[1118] 1900 U.S. census, Jewell County, Kansas, Calvin Twp., ED 44, p. 9, gives May 1894 which cannot be correct if his older sister were born in October 1893. Trubey manuscript, 76.

		Voth on 7 April 1923. Their children include *(a)* Betty Jean, born 13 February 1924, *(b)* Merlin Delmar, 6 August 1925, and *(c)* Norman Dalton, 27 December 1926.[1119]
388.	iii.	HAZEL TRUBEY, born 14 November 1897; died 9 September 1898.[1120]
389.	iv.	FLOYD L. TRUBEY, born 6 December 1898 in Kansas;[1121] he married Mae Miller on 30 May 1931 at Delta, Colorado.[1122] Their children include *(a)* Frederick LeRoy, born 7 May 1932, *(b)* Norman Lee, 14 July 1934, *(c)* David Clarence, 30 December 1936, *(d)* Ione Luanne, 29 April 1938, died 27 May 1938 *(e)* Gladys Carol, 29 June 1939, and *(f)* Jewelle Lucille, 6 October 1942.[1123]
390.	v.	FLORENCE T. TRUBEY, born 4 October 1900 in Kansas;[1124] she married W. V. Greene on 31 May 1930 at Hendersonville, North Carolina, by whom

---

[1119] Trubey manuscript, 76-77. 1962 Trubey manuscript, 38.

[1120] Trubey manuscript, 76. No other evidence seen for this child, although the 1900 census corroborates that one of Lula's four children died prior to 1900 (1900 U.S. census, Jewell County, Kansas, Calvin Twp., ED 44, p. 9).

[1121] 1900 U.S. census, Jewell County, Kansas, Calvin Twp., ED 44, p. 9. 1920 Soundex, Buffalo County, Nebraska, ED 49, p. 17. Trubey manuscript, 76-77.

[1122] Colorado Marriage Record Report #4153, Delta County; FHL microfilm 1690143.

[1123] Trubey manuscript, 78. 1962 Trubey manuscript, 39.

[1124] 1920 Soundex, Buffalo County, Nebraska, ED 49, p. 17. Trubey manuscript, 76 and 78.

GENERATION FOUR 217

one daughter was born: Novella Yvonere, on 3 January 1936.[1125]

391. vi. VIOLET A. TRUBEY, born 7 July 1902 in Kansas;[1126] married A. V. Acuff on 31 August 1929 at Largo, Florida. Their three children include *(a)* Loretta, born 17 February 1932, *(b)* Norma Lee, 2 April 1933, and *(c)* Roy Sylvanus, 21 October 1939.[1127]

392. vii. EUGENE C. TRUBEY, born 4 October 1905 in Kansas;[1128] married Mattie Lee Johnson on 3 July 1927 at Fort Valley, Georgia. Two children: *(a)* Mary Ann, born 19 February 1926, and *(b)* Janey Lee, 15 June 1928.[1129]

393. viii. ARTHUR R. TRUBEY, born 30 April 1908 in Kansas;[1130] married Alma Abeney at Hendersonville, North Carolina (date not given). Their children: *(a)* Claude, born 8 April 1929, *(b)* Dennis Lavaun, 5 August 1930, and *(c)* Gail, 1 May 1931.[1131]

394. ix. VERNON TRUBEY, born and died 31 July 1911.[1132]

[1125] Trubey manuscript, 78.

[1126] 1920 Soundex, Buffalo County, Nebraska, ED 49, p. 17. Trubey manuscript, 78.

[1127] Trubey manuscript, 78.

[1128] 1920 Soundex, Buffalo County, Nebraska, ED 49, p. 17. Trubey manuscript, 78.

[1129] Trubey manuscript, 78.

[1130] 1920 Soundex, Buffalo County, Nebraska, ED 49, p. 17. Trubey manuscript, 78.

[1131] Trubey manuscript, 78.

[1132] Trubey manuscript, 76.

110. George A.[4] **Trubey** (Daniel[3, 2, 1]) was born 22 November 1872[1133] in Kansas.[1134] He married at Beloit, Mitchell County, Kansas, on 20 June 1900, **Mary B. Altimus**[1135] (daughter of J. D. and S. J. Altimus).[1136] Mary was born January 1878 in Kansas.[1137]

George and Mary appear to have lived most of their married life in Mitchell County, Kansas, although this family's 1920 Census entry reveals that one of their children, son Vernon, was born in Oregon circa 1915.[1138] George was not mentioned among other surviving brothers of Mary Jane (Trubey) Pilcher Taylor in her 1939 obituary, but tombstone inscriptions from Glenwood Cemetery in Glen Elder Township,

---

[1133] Daniel Trubey pension.

[1134] 1880 U.S. census, Mitchell County, Kansas, pop. sched., ED 179, p. 4; National Archives micropublication T9, roll 389.

[1135] Mitchell County Marriage Book D: 168; photocopy provided by the District Court, Beloit, Kansas. Married by J. S. Allen, Probate Judge.

[1136] 1880 U.S. census, Mitchell County, Kansas, pop. sched., Glen Elder Twp., ED 179, p. 3; National Archives micropublication T9, roll 389: Mary (age 2) last child in household; parents (age 41 and 39 respectively) both born in Pennsylvania. 1900 U.S. census, Mitchell County, Kansas, pop. sched., Glen Elder Twp., ED 83, p. 5; National Archives micropublication T623, roll 491: Mary (22) residing with her widowed mother "Susany" (60), with "farm hand" (and Mary's future husband) George Trubey also in the household.

[1137] 1880 U.S. census, Mitchell County, Kansas, Glen Elder Twp., ED 179, p. 3. 1900 U.S. census, Mitchell County, Kansas, Glen Elder Twp., ED 83, p. 5.

[1138] 1920 U.S. census, Mitchell County, Kansas, pop. sched., Glen Elder Township, ED 108, p. 10-A, 14 January; National Archives micropublication T625, roll 540.

GENERATION FOUR 219

Mitchell County, Kansas, show he died in 1944, and his widow Mary died in 1959.[1139]

The children of George A.[4] Trubey and Mary B. Altimus:[1140]

395. i. RUTH[5] TRUBEY, born 19 August 1904; married Roy Van Wey on 30 July 1924. Children include *(a)* Virgil, 1 August 1924; *(b)* Virginia, 10 January 1928; and *(c)* Marjory, 29 March 1932.
396. ii. unknown, died before 1910.[1141]
397. iii. unknown, died as an infant in 1908.[1142]
398. iv. BERNADENE TRUBEY, born 5 September 1909; married Austin Neifert on 29 September 1935. Their child named Dennis, born 17 May 1938.
399. v. KENNETH D. TRUBEY, born 1 June 1912; married Monsolete Alcorn on 5 July 1937. Their child named Kenneth Doye, born 18 June 1938.
400. vi. VERNON C. TRUBEY, born 7 September 1914; married Genevieve Stiles on 3 August 1933. Their daughter named Joyce L., born 20 May 1934.

[1139] North Central Kansas Genealogical Society, *Kansas, Mitchell County Cemeteries*, Volume I (Cawker City, Kans.: by the Society, 1981), 84; FHL microfiche 6010655.

[1140] Trubey manuscript, 79-80. 1920 U.S. census, Mitchell County, Kansas, pop. sched., Glen Elder Township, ED 108, p. 10-A, for all but Marguerite.

[1141] 1910 U.S. census, Mitchell County, Kansas, pop. sched., Glen Elder, Glen Elder Twp., ED 100, p. 2-A, dwelling and family 34, 18 & 19 April; National Archives micropublication T624, roll 448.

[1142] North Central Kansas Genealogical Society, *Kansas, Mitchell County Cemeteries*, I: 84, buried beside parents. 1910 census also confirms death of two children by that date (1910 U.S. census, Mitchell County, Kansas, Glen Elder, Glen Elder Twp., ED 100, p. 2-A).

401. vii. DALE H. TRUBEY, born 30 March 1919; married 17 March 1956 to Edna M. Casner; son Darrell D., born 12 January 1957.[1143]

402. viii. MARGUERITE L. TRUBEY, born 25 July 1922; married Marshall Beal on 20 June 1941. Their children include *(a)* Karl W., born 23 August 1950, *(b)* Kent, born 2 May 1953; and *(c)* Kevin, born 19 May 1954.[1144]

111. Melissa[4] **Yantiss** (Nancy[3] Trubey, Daniel[1, 2]) was born 30 September 1851 in Huntington, Indiana.[1145] She was married in Richardson County, Nebraska, on 9 November 1871 to **Emanuel D. Heyde**[1146] (son of George Heyde and Leah Grass).[1147] Emanuel Heyde was born 6 April 1842 in Cumberland County, Pennsylvania,[1148] and

---

[1143] 1962 Trubey manuscript, 42.

[1144] 1962 Trubey manuscript, 42.

[1145] Richardson County Marriage Book 1870-1872, p. 128, #541, Office of the County Court, Falls City, Nebraska; photocopy in possession of compiler. This record lists birth and parentage information for bride and groom.

[1146] Richardson County Marriage Book 1870-1872, p. 128.

[1147] *Ibid.* 1850 U.S. census, Cumberland County, Pennsylvania, pop. sched., Upper Allen Twp., p. 11; National Archives micropublication M432, roll 772: George "Heyd" (age 55), Leah (42), and, among others, Emanuel (7). George was born in Lancaster, Pa., and Leah in Cumberland County, Pa., according to E. D. Heyde's death certificate in his pension file.

[1148] Emanuel D. Heyde passport application #11322, 21 January 1898, Passports Volume 861, Records of the Department of State (Record Group 59), National Archives, Washington, D.C. This passport application describes Emanuel as a grain dealer living in Lebanon, Kansas, going abroad for less than one year; he was age

GENERATION FOUR

saw nine months service at the end of the Civil War, as a corporal in Co. I of the 200th Pennsylvania Infantry.[1149]

This couple apparently resided in North Dakota between 1885 and 1893, as that is the birthplace listed for their two surviving children in Federal Census records.[1150] Further, Emanuel appeared as a resident of Hunter, Cass County, North Dakota, in June 1890.[1151]

Emanuel worked as a grain dealer, and listed that as his occupation when he applied for a passport in 1898 to travel to Jerusalem with brother-in-law Landon Yantiss.[1152] The Trubey manuscript claims that the family removed to Illinois in 1901, and gives the death dates for Melissa as 23 April 1932 and for Emanuel as 25 January 1935, with interment for both in the Silver Creek Cemetery in Richardson County, Nebraska.[1153]

55, 5' 7" tall, with a beard and moustache, black and gray hair, gray eyes, dark complexion, broad forehead, oval face and aquiline nose. Applying the same day was his brother-in-law Landon Yantiss.

[1149] Emmanuel D. Heyde Pension (Co. I, 200th Pennsylvania Infantry), application 1120054, certficate 1047541, Civil War and Later Pension Files, Records of the Veterans Administration (Record Group 15), National Archives, Washington, D.C.

[1150] 1900 U.S. census, Smith County, Kansas, pop. sched., Lebanon City, ED 175, p. 8; National Archives micropublication T623, roll 501. The 1880 Soundex for Nebraska does not list this family under "E. D.," "Em(m)anuel," or even [his father] George Heyde.

[1151] 1890 Special Census of Union Veterans and their Widows, Cass County, North Dakota, P. O. Hunter, ED 26, Supervisor's District 116, house and family 144; National Archives micropublication M123, roll 59.

[1152] Occupation documented by Emanuel D. Heyde passport application and 1900 U.S. census, Smith County, Kansas, Lebanon City, ED 175, p. 8.

[1153] Trubey manuscript, 82.

222 DANIEL TRUBEY OF FRANKLIN COUNTY, PENNSYLVANIA

The children of Melissa[4] Yantiss and Emanuel D. Heyde:[1154]

403. i. CARRIE[5] D. HEYDE, born 17 December 1872; died 2 May 1876.
404. ii. GEORGE JACOB HEYDE, born 20 July 1876; died 8 July 1877.
405. iii. [female] HEYDE, born 8 September 1878; died two or three days after birth.
406. iv. BESSIE JANE HEYDE, born 4 February 1885 in Hunter, North Dakota;[1155] married (1) Dr. Ernest A. Hendricks in Bond County, Illinois, on 8 June 1910 by Jeremiah Adams, M.G.;[1156] married (2) Mr. Delveese; died 9 August 1931 at Shawnee, Oklahoma; buried at Silver Creek Cemetery in Richardson County, Nebraska.[1157]

[1154] Children's full names and full dates of birth and death taken from their father's 2 January 1915 questionnaire in his pension file.

[1155] 1900 U.S. census, Smith County, Kansas, Lebanon City, ED 175, p. 8.

[1156] Evelyne McCracken, compiler, *Bond County, Illinois, Marriage Records, 1894-1915* (Greenville, Ill.: Bond County Genealogical Society, 1985), 91: Dr. Ernest A. Hendricks, 26, born Chepultepec, Alabama, s/o Joseph F. and Nancy S. (Nunelly) Hendricks, to Bessie J. Heyde, 25, b. Hunter, S.D. [sic], d/o E. D. & *Melisa* (Yantis) Heyde, married 8 June 1910 by Jeremiah Adams, MG. *Bond County, Illinois, Birth Index 1866-1915* (Greenville, Ill.: Bond County Genealogical Society, 1986), 99 (no Heydes listed herein, and only the following post-1910 Hendricks births: Mary Margaret, 4-2-1911, 5: 533 and Lela May, 6-1-1913, 6: 144).

[1157] "Family Record of John Wesley Stump of Long Island, Kansas," *Our Family, Its Record and Guide to Greatness and Honor* (No place: no publisher, no date), 17; found in NSDAR File Case folder entitled "Stoner, Abraham — Pa.; b. abt. 1745-6, d. 9-_-1824, Franklin County, Pa.," NSDAR Library, Washington, D.C. Photocopy in possession of compiler. The top margin of page 17

GENERATION FOUR   223

407. v. EDNA DAKOTA HEYDE, born 11 October 1892 or 1893 in North Dakota;[1158] died 13 December 1953.[1159]

113. Landon[4] **Yantiss** (Nancy[3] Trubey, Daniel[2, 1]) was born on 26 November 1854 in Indiana.[1160] Landon was married in Richardson County, Nebraska, on 8 January 1876 to **Mary Merriam**[1161] (daughter

---

contains data on Bessie, noting that Bessie's "daughter died after her 1st husband passed away."

[1158] 1900 U.S. census, Smith County, Kansas, Lebanon City, ED 175, p. 8, gives "1893;" Emmanuel D. Heyde pension questionnaire gives "1892."

[1159] Death date from NSDAR membership records, Organizing General's Office.

[1160] Landon Yantis passport application #11323, 21 January 1898, Passports Volume 861, Records of the Department of State (Record Group 59), National Archives, Washington, D.C. This application describes Landon as a farmer residing in Nebraska, age 43, 5'9" tall, with a moustache, oval face and chin, round forehead, dark brown hair, blue eyes, dark complexion and a prominent nose. He indicated his intent to return to the U.S. within one year's time. See his brother-in-law Emanuel Heyde's passport application of the same date.

[1161] Richardson County Marriage Book 1: 398, #955, Office of the County Court, Falls City, Nebraska; photocopy in possession of compiler. Only Landon's parents are identified on this license.

of Henry Merriam and his first wife Esther Folansbee),[1162] who was born on 8 February 1854,[1163] probably in Dane County, Wisconsin.[1164] Landon and his family remained in Richardson County, Nebraska, where he worked as a farmer.[1165] Landon and his brother-in-law Emanuel D. Heyde both applied for passports on 21 January 1898, and it is said that they traveled to Jerusalem in "1908" to visit Daniel

---

[1162] 1860 U.S. census, Dane County, Wisconsin, pop. sched., Medina, p. 41/647; National Archives micropublication M653, roll 1403: shows Mary (age 6) in household of Henry L. (39, born Ohio) and step-mother Eliza M. Merriam, and [grandparents] Joel and Sylvia Merriam (both 74, born in Connecticut). Mary appears in Charles Henry Pope's *Merriam Genealogy in England and America* (Boston: by the compiler, 1906), on page 334 under her father Henry's listing (entry #690), and her lineage as given there includes Revolutionary War pensioner Amasa Merriam (entry #147). Other census entries for Henry Merriam include 1850 U.S. census, Dane County, Wisconsin, pop. sched., Medina, p. 422; National Archives micropublication M432, roll 995. 1900 U.S. census, Richardson County, Nebraska, Liberty Twp., ED 146, p. 10; National Archives micropublication T623, roll 938. The only Folansbee entry found in the 1850 Census of Wisconsin (Columbia County, p. 134) was a Joseph Folansbee household which did not contain a 19-year-old Esther who would become Henry Merriam's wife, as described in the *Merriam Genealogy*.

[1163] 1900 U.S. census, Richardson County, Nebraska, Liberty Twp., ED 146, p. 10. *Merriam Genealogy*, 334.

[1164] 1850 U.S. census, Dane County, Wisconsin, Medina, p. 422. 1860 U.S. census, Dane County, Wisconsin, Medina, p. 41/647.

[1165] 1880 U.S. census, Richardson County, Nebraska, pop. sched., Liberty Precinct, p. 12; National Archives micropublication T9, roll 754. 1900 U.S. census, Richardson County, Nebraska, Liberty Twp., ED 146, p. 10.

GENERATION FOUR

Yantiss "who had gone there two years previous; both claims appear to ten years off."[1166]

At some time before 1900, this couple adopted a daughter who appears in the census of that year as Bessie, born June 1886 in Nebraska, to Pennsylvania-born parents. This may be Landon's niece Bessie Stump [see #415], who is listed in their 1910 household in Phillips County, Kansas, by that name and as their "niece."[1167]

Landon and Mary apparently died just months apart in Long Island, Phillips County, Kansas; Landon on 18 January 1935, and Mary on 10 May 1935.[1168]

The children of Landon[4] Yantiss and Mary Merriam:
- 408. i. JUDSON[5] YANTISS, born October 1876 in Nebraska;[1169] no further information.
- 409. ii. DEWITT YANTISS, born September 1877 in Nebraska;[1170] no further information.
- 410. iii. unknown; died before 1900.

[1166] Trubey manuscript, 82-83. See Daniel Yantiss's entry for further information.

[1167] 1910 Miracode, Phillips County, Kansas, ED 144, visitation #42; National Archives micropublication T1265, roll 144.

[1168] John Wesley Stump family record. However, no photocopies of the pages covering John Wesley Stump's siblings, parents, or grandparents were in this file.

[1169] 1880 U.S. census, Richardson County, Nebraska, Liberty Precinct, p. 12. 1900 U.S. census, Richardson County, Nebraska, Liberty Twp., ED 146, p. 10.

[1170] *Ibid.*

115. Daniel D.[4] **Yantiss** (Nancy[3] Trubey, Daniel[2,1]) was born about July 1859[1171] likely in Huntington County, Indiana, where his parents married in 1851 and resided in 1860. Sol C. Stump, Minister of the Brethren Church in Richardson County, Nebraska, performed the 31 January 1886 wedding uniting Daniel and **Lillie A. Meyers**[1172] (daughter of Joseph H. Meyers and Maggie Johnson).[1173] Lillie was born circa 1865 in Illinois.[1174]

Although the Trubey manuscript entry on Landon Yantiss implied that Daniel went to Jerusalem circa 1906, the entry on Daniel states the year of his emigration as 1896. That date is corroborated by the family record belonging to sibling Elizabeth (Yantiss) Stump, which states that Daniel went "to Jerusalem Palestine in 1896."[1175] However, no passport

---

[1171] 1860 U.S. census, Huntington County, Indiana, pop. sched., Polk Twp., P. O. Antioch, p. 90, 21 June; National Archives micropublication M653, roll 267 (Daniel 10 months old). 1870 U.S. census, Richardson County, Nebraska, pop. sched., Township 2, Range 16, Falls City, p. 6/175; National Archives micropublication M593, roll 832 (Daniel age 10). 1880 U.S. census, Richardson County, Nebraska, pop. sched., Ohio Prct., ED 311, p. 30; National Archives micropublication T9, roll 754 (Daniel age 20).

[1172] Richardson County Marriage Book 3: 64, #2436; Office of County Court, Falls City, Nebraska; photocopy in possession of compiler. Full names of the bride and groom's parents are given, although Daniel's mother is incorrectly identified as "N. *Johnson*" [*sic*: Trubey].

[1173] Richardson County Marriage Book 3: 64. 1880 U.S. census, Richardson County, Nebraska, pop. sched., Barada Pct., ED 311, p. 21; National Archives micropublication T9, roll 754: Joseph "Myers" (45, born Pennsylvania); Maggie (37, born Canada), and, among others, Lillie (15, Illinois).

[1174] Lillie's approximate birth date and place supported by her marriage license, and her 1880 Census entry.

[1175] John Wesley Stump family record.

GENERATION FOUR

application was found for Daniel D. Yantiss,[1176] nor were records of his family's presence found in selected U.S. Consular records of Jerusalem.[1177]

Daniel Yantiss died from a stroke of apoplexy with kidney complications on 17 June 1910 in Jerusalem, and was buried there in "the American Colony Cemetery on Mt. Scopus."[1178] No death date is known for his wife Lillie.[1179]

[1176] Registers and Indexes for Passport Applications, 1810-1906, General Records of the Department of State (Record Group 59); National Archives micropublication M1371, roll 7. Volumes 5 and 6 examined, covering all of 1896.

[1177] Viz., Record of Passports 1867-98, 1913-1914, 1921-1928 (two volumes), Register of Children of American Parents 1910-1916 (one volume), Miscellaneous Correspondence Received and Sent January 1904-July 1912 (1910 volumes 011A and 012), Probate Record and Register of Wills, 1910-1929 (one volume "235") all for the U.S. Consulate - Jerusalem, Records of the Foreign Service Posts of the Department of State (Record Group 84), National Archives, Washington, D.C.

[1178] "Report of a Death of An American Citizen (Form No. 192)," 6 August 1910, Consular Service U.S.A., Jerusalem, General Records of the Department of State (Record Group 59), Decimal File 1910-1929 (file 367m.113-L66), National Archives, Washington, D.C. This report states that all of Daniel's family were members of the American Colony, and were with him at his death. It also states that Daniel's death "information, inventory, accounts, etc., [were] recorded in Miscellaneous Record Book, No. 5, page 46." Daniel's death report was not filed at the time it was written, but was discovered "in moving the consular offices" and was forwarded to Washington, D.C., on 5 October 1910.

[1179] Trubey manuscript, 83. John Wesley Stump family record.

The children of Daniel D.⁴ Yantiss and Lillie A. Meyers:

411.   i.   [male]⁵ YANTISS; "...this man and his family came to the States in July 1938 and now [1940s] are in California."¹¹⁸⁰
412.   ii.   [female] YANTISS; yet living in Jerusalem in the 1940s.¹¹⁸¹
413.   iii.   [female] YANTISS; yet living in Jerusalem in the 1940s.¹¹⁸²

117. Mary Elizabeth⁴ Yantiss (Nancy³ Trubey, Daniel²⋅¹) was born 25 November 1863 at Antioch, Huntington County, Indiana.¹¹⁸³ At the age of 19, "Lizzie" was married in Richardson County, Nebraska, on 1 November 1883 to **John Wesley Stump**¹¹⁸⁴ (son of Sol C. Stump and Magdalena Petrey).¹¹⁸⁵ The couple was married by Rev. J. W. Taylor, with both fathers serving as witnesses.

John Stump was born on 25 April 1860 four miles south of Eldorado, Preble County, Ohio, and moved to Nebraska in 1871. He taught school in Silver Creek, Richardson County, from 1876 until 1884, when he worked in the hardware and implement business in Verdon, Nebraska, adding harness and saddlery goods in 1898. John engaged in the banking business from 1909 to 1912, after which the couple removed to Kansas, residing in Long Island and Glen Elder. John died 4 May 1931 in Nebraska, and was buried at Long Island,

---

¹¹⁸⁰ Trubey manuscript, 83.

¹¹⁸¹ *Ibid.*

¹¹⁸² Trubey manuscript, 83.

¹¹⁸³ John Wesley Stump family record.

¹¹⁸⁴ Richardson County Marriage Book 2: 431, #2022, Office of the County Court, Falls City, Nebraska; photocopy in possession of compiler. Full names of both parents given.

¹¹⁸⁵ Richardson County Marriage Book 2: 431.

GENERATION FOUR 229

Kansas, on 6 May 1931.[1186] No death date is known for Elizabeth, who appears to have survived her husband, both of whom were residing on a farm near Orleans, Harlem County, Nebraska, when he died.[1187]

The children of Elizabeth[4] Yantiss and John Wesley Stump:[1188]

414. i.   QUINTON S.[5] STUMP, born July 1885 in Nebraska; no further information.
415. ii. BESSIE ETHEL STUMP, born September 1886 in Nebraska. Bessie resided in her uncle Landon Yantiss's household in 1910 in Phillips County, Kansas;[1189] no further information.
416. iii. GRACIE STUMP, born 9 May 1888, died 25 September 1888.[1190]
417. iv. JENNIE STUMP, born July 1891 in Nebraska; no further information.
418. v.   CLARENCE STUMP, born June 1894 in Nebraska; no further information.
419. vi. GEORGIA STUMP, born September 1896 in Nebraska; no further information.

[1186] John Wesley Stump family record, 18.

[1187] John Wesley Stump family record. Trubey manuscript, 84.

[1188] Parentage and birth data for all children taken from their 1900 Census entry, with the exception of Grace, whose sources of proof are cited separately.

[1189] 1910 Miracode, Phillips County, Kansas, ED 144, visitation #42.

[1190] Trubey manuscript, 85. 1900 U.S. census, Richardson County, Nebraska, pop. sched., Liberty Twp., ED 146, p. 2; National Archives micropublication T623, roll 938: "Lizza's" entry shows one of her six children was deceased by 1900.

121. John Frederick⁴ Mohn (Rebecca³ Trubey, Daniel[2, 1]) was born March 1854 in Indiana.[1191] The Trubey manuscript contained little data on John, except to relate that he "was married and had a couple of children," and that he died in Peru, Indiana.[1192] Marriage records of Huntington County, Indiana, reveal that on 23 September 1888, John married **Mrs. Sarah C. (Jones) Bradshaw/Brachter/Bracker**,[1193] who was born in February 1859 in Indiana to Simon Jones of Scotland and M. Scott of Pennsylvania.[1194] Two of Sarah's children, Charles E. and Rosa Bradshaw, were identified as John's step-children in 1900. Sarah was then listed as the mother of nine children, eight of whom were living; it is not known to which union the then-deceased child had been born.

[1191] 1860 U.S. census, Huntington County, Indiana, pop. sched., Huntington Twp., p. 28/211; National Archives micropublication M653, roll 152. 1870 U.S. census, Huntington County, Indiana, pop. sched., P. O. Polk, p. 1; National Archives micropublication M593, roll 325. 1880 U.S. census, Huntington County, Indiana, pop. sched., Polk Twp., ED 201, p. 21; National Archives micro-publication T9, roll 285. 1900 U.S. census, Wabash County, Indiana, pop. sched., Noble Twp., ED 121, p. 2; National Archives micropublication T623, roll 410.

[1192] Trubey manuscript, 87.

[1193] Ruth M. Slevin, *Huntington County, Indiana, Marriage Records, 1883 - 1900*, Volume 2 (1970), Grooms, pages 12 (Bracker) and 59 (Brachter), and *Index to Supplemental Record of Marriage Transcript, Huntington County, Indiana, 1882 - 1920, Volume 1, Letters A - K Inclusive* (typescript: Indiana Works Progress Administration, 1942), page "BRA-BRA" (Bradshaw) and "JOH-JUT."

[1194] 1900 U.S. census, Wabash County, Indiana, Noble Twp., ED 121, p. 2. *Index to Supplemental Record of Marriage Transcript, Huntington County, Indiana, 1882 - 1920, Volume 1, Letters A - K Inclusive*, page "BRA-BRA" (Bradshaw) and "JOH-JUT."

GENERATION FOUR

John was listed as a day laborer living at 217 East Elm Street in Wabash in 1900. John's death was recorded in Miami County, Indiana, occurring on 12 March 1932, at age 77, and his wife died there also on 1 October 1935 at age 76.[1195]

The children of John Frederick[4] Mohn and Mrs. Sarah C. (Jones) Bradshaw:

420. i. VON F.[5] MOHN, born 18 March 1891 in Huntington County, Indiana;[1196] no further information.

421. ii. GEORGE W. MOHN, born 14 July 1892 in Huntington, County, Indiana;[1197] no further information.

422. iii. "LIZZIE" B. MOHN, born January 1894 in Indiana; no further information.

423. iv. JESSIE M. MOHN, born 16 February 1896 in Huntington County, Indiana;[1198] no further information.

424. v. [twin; female] MOHN, born 16 February 1896 in Huntington County, Indiana;[1199] no further information.

425. vi. EDITH M. MOHN, born March 1898 in Indiana; no further information.

[1195] Charles Wagner, editor, *Index to Official Death Records: Miami County, Indiana, 1921-1974* (Evansville, Ind.: Unigraphic, 1980 [1978?]), 129.

[1196] *Index to Birth Records, Huntington County, Indiana, 1875 - 1920 Inclusive Volume 2 Letters M-Z* (typescript: Indiana Works Progress Administration, 1942), 24.

[1197] *Ibid.*

[1198] *Ibid.*

[1199] *Ibid.*

122. Mary Jane[4] Mohn (Rebecca[3] Trubey, Daniel[2, 1]) was born 21 November 1856 in Indiana.[1200] A history of Huntington County, Indiana, states that she was married on 21 July 1878 to **John I. Dille** (son of Ichabod Dille and Mrs. Rebecca [Havens] Brooks).[1201] John Dille graduated from the law department of Indiana's state university in 1877, and was employed as an attorney in 1880 and 1887.[1202] The Dille's were residing in Minnesota by 1909, as evidenced by the 1909 obituary of Mary Jane's mother. John was yet employed there as an attorney with Dille, Hoke, Krause & Faegre in 1920.[1203] John is said to have died in 1933; no death date is known for Mary Jane.[1204]

[1200] Trubey manuscript, 87. 1880 U.S. census, Huntington County, Indiana, pop. sched., Huntington city, ED 206, p. 35; National Archives micropublication T9, roll 285: Mary age 23.

[1201] *History of Huntington County, Indiana* (Chicago: Brant & Fuller, 1887), 474-475. George Earl Dille, Josephine Kaye Dille and Earl Kaye Dille, *The Dille Family, Three Hundred Years in America,1664-1964* (Marceline, Mo.: Walsworth Publishing Co, 1965), 78 (entry F7: "John Ichabod Dille, b 11-18-1857; m 7-21-1979 [sic] Mary J. Mohn. To Minn."). John's Dille ancestry back to John Dille (1645-1684) of Woodbridge, New Jersey, appears on pages 74, 77, and 78.

[1202] *History of Huntington County, Indiana*, 474-475. 1880 U.S. census, Huntington County, Indiana, Huntington city, ED 206, p. 35.

[1203] [Title page missing], 1920 Minneapolis city directory, 563; NSDAR Library. 1920 Soundex, Hennepin County, Minnesota, Minneapolis, ED 171, p. 1, 2009 Humboldt Avenue South; National Archives micropublication M1569, roll 33.

[1204] Trubey manuscript, 87.

GENERATION FOUR

The children of Mary Jane[4] Mohn and John Ichabod Dille:

426.   i.   DESSIE B.[5] DILLE, born 31 March 1879 in Indiana;[1205] living in Minneapolis in 1920.[1206] No further information.
427.   ii.   CHESTER B. DILLE, born 31 July 1880 in Indiana;[1207] no further information.
428.   iii.   EVA R. OR THERESA DILLE, born 28 January 1882 in Huntington County, Indiana;[1208] said to have married Archibald Y. Lyon, who was born 21 April 1873.[1209]
429.   iv.   MAYME P. DILLE, born 24[1210] or 27 February 1885 in Huntington County, Indiana;[1211] no further information.

[1205] Trubey manuscript, 87. *History of Huntington County, Indiana*, 475. 1880 U.S. census, Huntington County, Indiana, Huntington city, ED 206, p. 35: Dessie age 1.

[1206] 1920 Soundex, Hennepin County, Minnesota, Minneapolis, ED 171, p. 1.

[1207] Trubey manuscript, 87. *History of Huntington County, Indiana*, 475. Not found under his own name in the 1900 Soundex to Minnesota census records.

[1208] *Index to Birth Records, Huntington County, Indiana, 1875 - 1920 Inclusive, Volume 1, Letters A-L Inclusive* 127. See also Trubey manuscript, 87, and *History of Huntington County, Indiana*, 475.

[1209] Trubey manuscript, 87; no marriage date or place given.

[1210] *Index to Birth Records, Huntington County, Indiana, 1875 - 1920 Inclusive, Volume 1, Letters A-L Inclusive*, 127.

[1211] Trubey manuscript, 87. *History of Huntington County, Indiana*, 475.

430. v. ARNOLD F. DILLE, born 8 January 1887 in Huntington County, Indiana;[1212] died six months later.[1213]

125. Daniel Andrew[4] **Mohn** (Rebecca[3] Trubey, Daniel[2,1]) was born on 15 June 1864 in Indiana.[1214] He was married on 18 March 1885 in Henry County, Ohio, to Mary J. Hancock,[1215] daughter of David H. and Roxanna [—?—] Hancock.[1216] Mary (who also appears in records as "May") was born in the spring of 1860, probably in Delta, York Twp., Henry County, Ohio.[1217]

[1212] *Index to Birth Records, Huntington County, Indiana, 1875 - 1920 Inclusive, Volume 1, Letters A-L Inclusive*, 127.

[1213] Trubey manuscript, 87.

[1214] Trubey manuscript, 87. 1870 U.S. census, Huntington County, Indiana, P. O. Polk, p. 1. 1880 U.S. census, Huntington County, Indiana, Polk Twp., ED 201, p. 21.

[1215] *The 1st Marriage Records of Henry County[,] OH[,] 1847-1898* (Warsaw, Ind.: Scheuer Publications, 1992), no pagination; marriages records arranged alphabetically, first by grooms then by brides: Daniel Mohn & Mary J. Hancock, 18 March 1885, 5: 212 [no Hancock grooms].

[1216] 1860 U.S. census, Fulton County, Ohio, pop. sched., York Twp., Delta, p. 298/60, 18 June; National Archives micropublication M653, roll 965: Mary J. age 3/12. 1880 U.S. census, Henry County, Ohio, pop. sched., Napoleon Corporation, ED 112, p. 1; National Archives micropublication T9, roll 1032: Mary J. age 19.

[1217] 1860 U.S. census, Fulton County, Ohio, York Twp., Delta, p. 298/60.

GENERATION FOUR 235

The births of two of Daniel and Mary's children are recorded in Huntington County, Indiana,[1218] although the family appears to have settled in Ohio around 1889.[1219] Daniel and his brother Charles were both listed as barbers in the 1897 city directory of Toledo, Ohio; the 1898 directory listed "Mohn, Daniel A. *(aged 40), died March 5, 1898.*"[1220] This pre-1900 death is corroborated by his mother Rebecca's 1900 Census entry and her 1909 obituary.[1221] The Toledo city death register confirms Daniel died of "tubercular laryngitis," and that he had resided in the city for five years; he was buried in Waterville, Ohio.[1222]

[1218] *Index to Birth Records Huntington County, Indiana, 1875 - 1920 Inclusive, Volume 2, Letters M - Z,* 24: 11 May 1885, male child (Book H-2: 22), and on 5 March 1887, female child (Book H-3: 24). The first child died five hours after birth, per *Index to Death Records, Huntington County, Indiana, 1882 - 1920 Inclusive Letters A-Z,* (TS: Indiana Works Progress Administration, 1942), 197, cited as recorded in Book A-1: 100. The identity and fate of the second child are not known.

[1219] 1910 U.S. Census, Lucas County, Ohio, pop. sched., Toledo, Precinct I, ED 44, page 3A, 819 Lagrange; National Archives micropublication T624, roll 207, gives "Ohio" as the birthplace of Dessie.

[1220] *Toledo City Directory...1897* (R. L. Polk & Co., 1897), 899, and *Toledo City Directory...1898,* 940, Library of Congress, U.S. City Directories 1882-1901, rolls 8 and 9, Microform Reading Room, Washington, D.C; agrees with Trubey manuscript, 88.

[1221] In 1900, Rebecca was listed in the census as the mother of eight children, five of whom then survived, and five children were mentioned in her 1909 obituary.

[1222] Daniel A. Mohn entry, Toledo Register of Deaths, 95, no. 32, 5 March 1898; FHL microfilm 1672031. No obituary was located by the staff of the Toledo - Lucas County Public Library in issues of *The Toledo Blade* newspapers nor by the staff of the River Bluffs Regional Library in issues of St. Joseph, Mo., newspapers.

The 1899 and 1900 Toledo city directories list "May" as the widow of Daniel,[1223] yet she was not indexed in the 1900 Soundex of Ohio, nor of Missouri where her brother-in-law Charles G. Mohn had removed by 1901. May's entry in the Ohio 1910 Federal Census indicates she was the mother of four children total, two of whom were then living; daughters Ella and Dessie resided in the 1910 household.[1224]

May remained in Toledo as the widow of Daniel until at least 1915,[1225] after which her whereabouts are unknown.

The children of Daniel Andrew[4] Mohn and Mary "May" J. Hancock:
431. i. [male] MOHN, born 11 May 1885, Huntington Co., Indiana;[1226] died five hours later.[1227]

Bluffs Regional Library in issues of St. Joseph, Mo., newspapers.

[1223] *Toledo City Directory...1899*, 1642: dressmaker, 1203 W. Bancroft, and *1900*, 1081: dressmaker, house 2286 Smead Avenue. The Trubey manuscript concurs that Daniel was married, but does not identify his wife nor does it indicate whether Daniel left surviving heirs.

[1224] 1910 U.S. Census, Lucas County, Ohio, Toledo, Precinct I, ED 44, page 3A. May's entry indicates she had a British-born father and Ohioan mother; the 1880 Census entry of her family indicates it was her Hancock *grand*father who was born in England; her father David is recorded as being born in Ohio in both the 1860 and 1880 Census.

[1225] *Toledo City Directory...1915*: "Mohn, May M (wid Daniel) h 712 Michigan." Not listed in 1916, 1918, or 1920 directories reviewed at Library of Congress.

[1226] *Index to Birth Records Huntington County, Indiana, 1875 - 1920 Inclusive, Volume 2, Letters M - Z*, 24: 11 May 1885, male child (Book H-2: 22).

[1227] *Index to Death Records, Huntington County, Indiana, 1882 - 1920 Inclusive Letters A-Z*, 197, cited as recorded in Book A-1: 100.

GENERATION FOUR 237

432. ii. ELLA M.⁵ MOHN, born 5 March 1887, Huntington County, Indiana.¹²²⁸ Ella was yet single and residing in her mother's Toledo, Ohio, household on 16 April 1910.
433. iii. DESSIE B. MOHN, born circa 1889 in Ohio; she was working for an electrical company in Toledo, Ohio, on 16 April 1910.¹²²⁹
434. iv. unknown; died before 1910.

131. Effie Savilla⁴ Scofield (Mary Ann³ Trubey, Daniel²,¹) was born 11 June 1863 in Ohio.¹²³⁰ Effie was married on 9 January 1887 in Henry County, Ohio, to **Abraham Lincoln Lose**¹²³¹ (son of Abraham

---

¹²²⁸ *Index to Birth Records Huntington County, Indiana, 1875 - 1920 Inclusive, Volume 2, Letters M - Z*, 24: 5 March 1887, female child (Book H-3: 24). Ella's 1910 census entry confirms she was 23 years old by April 1910, which perfectly matches the child born on this date in Huntington County, Indiana.

¹²²⁹ 1910 U.S. Census, Lucas County, Ohio, Toledo, Precinct I, ED 44, page 3A.

¹²³⁰ 1870 U.S. census, Henry County, Ohio, pop. sched., Flat Rock Twp., P. O. Florida, p. 7; National Archives micropublication M593, roll 1221. 1880 U.S. census, Henry County, Ohio, pop. sched., Flat Rock Twp., P. O. Florida, ED 115, p. 29; National Archives micropublication T9, roll 1032. 1900 U.S. census, Henry County, Ohio, pop. sched., Flat Rock Twp., ED 24, p. 12; National Archives micropublication T623, roll 1286. Trubey manuscript, 89, gives middle name and actual day of her birth.

¹²³¹ Henry County Marriage Book 6: 53, Probate Judge, Napoleon, Ohio; photocopy in possession of compiler.

Lose and Caroline [—?—]).[1232] Abraham was born in December 1865 in Ohio.[1233]

"Link" Lose was working as a farmer in Flat Rock Township, Henry County, Ohio, in 1900, at which time this couple had four children. Effie was yet living (residence not given) on 14 March 1941; her husband's death information is not known.[1234]

The children of Effie Savilla[4] Scofield and Abraham Lincoln Lose:
- 435. i. INEC [INEZ?] C.[5] LOSE, born September 1889 in Ohio;[1235] no further information.
- 436. ii. MARY P. LOSE, born June 1892 in Ohio; no further information.
- 437. iii. DONALD A. LOSE, born April 1895 in Ohio; no further information.
- 438. iv. "HELLEN" C. LOSE, born July 1897 in Ohio; no further information.

135. Charles Russell[4] Long (Elizabeth[3] Trubey, Daniel[2, 1]) was born 13 July 1869 probably in Flat Rock Township, Henry County, Ohio.[1236]

[1232] 1880 U.S. census, Henry County, Ohio, pop. sched., Flat Rock Twp., ED 115, p. 28; National Archives micropublication T9, roll 1032.

[1233] 1900 U.S. census, Henry County, Ohio, Flat Rock Twp., ED 24, p. 12.

[1234] Trubey manuscript, 89.

[1235] 1900 U.S. census, Henry County, Ohio, Flat Rock Twp., ED 24, p. 12.

[1236] 1870 U.S. census, Henry County, Ohio, pop. sched., Flat Rock Twp., P. O. Florida, p. 22; National Archives micropublication M593, roll 1221. 1880 U.S. census, Henry County, Ohio, pop. sched., Flat Rock Twp., ED 115, p. 26; National Archives micropublication T9, roll 1032. 1900 U.S. census, Henry County, Ohio, pop. sched., Monroe Twp., ED 30, p. 4; National Archives micropublication T623, roll 1286. 1910 U.S. census, Henry County,

GENERATION FOUR

Charles was married in Henry County, Ohio, on 26 March 1890 to **Josephine Heckler**[1237] (daughter of Philip Heckler and Lucy A. Sprough), who was born in July 1868, probably in Vernon Township, Crawford County, Ohio.[1238]

In 1910, Charles was working as a farmer.[1239] Charles died 18 December 1942; no death information is known for his wife Josephine.[1240]

Ohio, pop. sched., ED 34, visitation #98; National Archives micropublication T624, roll 1198. *Henry County*, 3: 191. Trubey manuscript, 91.

[1237] Henry County Marriage Book 6: 309, Probate Judge, Napoleon, Ohio.

[1238] 1880 U.S. census, Henry County, Ohio, pop. sched., Monroe Twp., ED 116, p. 5; National Archives micropublication T9, roll 1032. 1860 U.S. census, Crawford County, Ohio, pop. sched., Vernon Twp., p. 157; National Archives micropublication M653, roll 951. Jane Fisher, compiler, *Crawford County [Ohio] Court Records* (Galion, Ohio: no publisher, not dated), 133: Philip Heckler m. Lucy A. Sprough, 10 October 1855. 1850 U.S. census, Crawford County, Ohio, Vernon Twp., 344 (Philip Hecker in birth family at age 15) and 345 (Lucy Ann "Sprow" in birth family at age 16); National Archives micropublication M432, roll 671.

[1239] 1910 U.S. census, Henry County, Ohio, ED 34, visitation #98.

[1240] Trubey manuscript, 91.

240   DANIEL TRUBEY OF FRANKLIN COUNTY, PENNSYLVANIA

The children of Charles Russell⁴ Long and Josephine Heckler:[1241]

439. i.   FLOYD. F.⁵ LONG, born December 1890 in Ohio; resided in parents' household in 1910.[1242] No further information.
440. ii. MAUD LONG, born circa 1901 in Ohio;[1243] no further information.
441. iii. HARMAN LONG, born circa 1902 in Ohio;[1244] no further information.
442. iv. NELLIE LONG, born circa 1907 in Ohio;[1245] no further information.

136. Herman⁴ Long (Elizabeth³ Trubey, Daniel²,¹) was born 1 April 1872[1246] or 1873,[1247] likely in Henry County, Ohio. A history of Henry County states that Herman married **Frances Menninger**[1248] (possibly

---

[1241] 1910 U.S. census, Henry County, Ohio, pop. sched., ED 34, visitation #98, states only four children born to Josephine by that date.

[1242] 1900 U.S. census, Henry County, Ohio, Monroe Twp., ED 30, p. 4. 1910 U.S. census, Henry County, Ohio, ED 34, visitation #98.

[1243] 1910 U.S. census, Henry County, Ohio, ED 34, visitation #98.

[1244] *Ibid*. Insofar as Charles had a brother He̱rman, this son's may have been Herman rather than Harman.

[1245] *Ibid*.

[1246] Trubey manuscript, 91.

[1247] 1900 U.S. census, Crawford County, Ohio, pop. sched., Bucyrus, ED 4, p. 2, East Mansfield St.; National Archives micropublication T623, roll 1251.

[1248] *Henry County*, 3: 191.

GENERATION FOUR

the daughter of Henry Menninger and Frances [—?—]).[1249] The census suggests a circa 1903 marriage date for this couple.[1250]

In Bucyrus, Herman was employed as a "locomotive fireman" in 1900, and as a "saloon keeper" in 1910.[1251] However, the county history states that Herman ran a shoe shop, an occupation confirmed by his entry in the 1920 Census.[1252] It is not known when Herman and his wife Frances died.

[1249] 1880 U.S. census, Hamilton County, Ohio, pop. sched., Delhi Twp., ED 89, p. 13; National Archives micropublication T9, roll 1022: Henry (39, born Ohio), wife Frances (37, born Ohio), and, among others, Fannie (age 6, born Ohio). 1900 U.S. census, Hamilton County, Ohio, pop. sched., ED 291, p. 15; National Archives micropublication T623, roll 1282: Frances Menninger (born April 1875 in Ohio) in household of Henry Batterman. In 1910, Herman Long's wife Frances was listed as being age 30, and with both parents' birthplaces recorded as Germany. Thus, it is not reasonable to assume that Herman's wife was the Hamilton County Frances Menninger without further evidence. 1910 U.S. census, Crawford County, Ohio, pop. sched., Bucyrus, ED 10, visitation #210; National Archives micropublication T624, roll 1163.

[1250] 1910 U.S. census, Crawford County, Ohio, Bucyrus, ED 10, visitation #210.

[1251] 1900 U.S. census, Hamilton County, Ohio, ED 291, p. 15. 1910 U.S. census, Crawford County, Ohio, Bucyrus, ED 10, visitation #210.

[1252] *Henry County*, 3: 191. 1920 U.S. census, Crawford County, Ohio, pop. sched., Bucyrus, ED 9, p. 4, 513 Warren Street; National Archives micropublication T625, roll 1358.

The child of Herman⁴ Long and Frances Menninger:[1253]
    443. i. JOHN⁵ LONG, born circa 1907 in Ohio, living in Bucyrus in 1920.[1254] No further information.

137. Carey May "Nettie"⁴ Long (Elizabeth³ Trubey, Daniel[2, 1]) was born in 1875 or February 1876,[1255] likely in Henry County, Ohio. Although she was listed in the 1880 Census as "Carey M.," she appeared as Nettie or "Nellie" on subsequent census rolls.[1256] Nettie married circa 1898 **John Palmer Blank** (son of Amos Blank and

---

[1253] In 1910, Frances was listed as the mother of "0" children, "1" of whom was then living. It is not known whether this is an enumerator's error or an indication that their one listed son John was adopted.

[1254] 1910 U.S. census, Crawford County, Ohio, Bucyrus, ED 10, visitation #210. 1920 U.S. census, Crawford County, Ohio, Bucyrus, ED 9, p. 4.

[1255] 1900 U.S. census, Henry County, Ohio, pop. sched., Napoleon Twp. and city, ED 32, p. 6; National Archives micropublication T623, roll 1286. Trubey manuscript, 91, which gives only "1875."

[1256] 1900 U.S. census, Henry County, Ohio, Napoleon Twp. and city, ED 32, p. 6. 1910 U.S. census, Henry County, Ohio, pop. sched., ED 28, visitation #238; National Archives micropublication T624, roll 1198. 1920 Soundex, Henry County, Ohio, Harrison Twp., ED 54, p. 3; National Archives micropublication M1581, roll 32.

Emma J. Clifford).[1257] "Pal" Blank was born on 12 January 1875 in Sandusky County, Ohio.[1258]

Although listed as a farmer and stock raiser in a Henry County history, Pal was recorded as a "machine agent" in the 1900 Census.[1259] Pal died 18 December 1935, and Nettie on 5 June 1947.[1260]

[1257] [Anonymous], *Commemorative Biographical Record of the Counties of Sandusky and Ottawa, Ohio* (Chicago: J. H. Beers & Co., 1896), 202-203: John P. Blank, born 12 January 1875. 1880 U.S. census, Sandusky County, Ohio, pop. sched., Woodville Twp., ED 87, p. 21; National Archives micropublication T9, roll 1064: Amos (39, born Ohio), Emma (32, born Ohio), and, among others, Palmer (5, born Ohio). For Clifford ancestry, see 1850 U.S. census, Huron County, Ohio, pop. sched., New Liberty Twp., p. 674; National Archives micropublication M432, roll 697: Henry (age 23), Sophronia (26), Emma (1). Elyria Chapter, Daughters of the American Revolution and Genealogical Workshop, Lorain County Historical Society, *Marriages, Lorain County, Ohio, 1824-1865* (Elyria, Ohio: no publisher, 1980), 24. G. Frederick Wright, *A Standard History of Lorain County, Ohio*, II (Chicago and New York: The Lewis Publishing Co., 1916), 1028-1030. This surname appears as "Clepherd" in this family's early vital records of Tyringham, Massachusetts.

[1258] *Sandusky County*, 203.

[1259] 1900 U.S. census, Henry County, Ohio, Napoleon Twp. and city, ED 32, p. 6.

[1260] *Henry County*, 3: 191.

The children of Carey May "Nettie"[4] Long and John Palmer Blank:

 444. i. FRANCES C. OR E.[5] BLANK, born 12 May[1261] or April 1898.[1262] She is said to have married Otto W. Heiss in 1916, by whom she had *(a)* William Palmer, born 1917, *(b)* Marolyn J., born 1919, and *(c)* Rita, born 1930.[1263]

 445. ii. KATHRYN J. BLANK, born 1909;[1264] she married Lester Knepper in 1936, and had children *(a)* John David, and *(b)* Jane A.[1265]

 446. iii. HELEN A. BLANK, born 1912 in Ohio;[1266] "married Richard Himel in 1937 and lives in Michigan."[1267]

141. Nettie E.[4] **Carr** (Catherine[3] Trubey, Daniel[2, 1]) was born in August 1874 in Ohio.[1268] After the separation of her parents, she

---

[1261] *Henry County*, 3 :191.

[1262] 1900 U.S. census, Henry County, Ohio, Napoleon Twp. and city, ED 32, p. 6.

[1263] *Henry County*, 3: 191; more detail on their spouses and children given there.

[1264] *Henry County*, 3: 191; "Catharine's" age was omitted from the 1910 Census enumeration of her family, but appears as "10" in the 1920 Soundex.

[1265] *Henry County*, 3: 191; limited additional information given there.

[1266] 1920 Soundex, Henry County, Ohio, Harrison Twp., ED 54, p. 3: age 7.

[1267] *Henry County*, 3: 191.

[1268] 1900 U.S. census, Buchanan County, Missouri., pop. sched., St. Joseph, ED 62, p. 21; National Archives micropublication T623, roll 842. 1880 U.S. census, Defiance County, Ohio, pop. sched.,

GENERATION FOUR   245

removed with her mother and siblings to St. Joseph, Buchanan County, Missouri, where she was married on 27 April 1892 to **Edward Graves**,[1269] who was born in Missouri.[1270] In 1900, a divorced Nettie Graves resided in her mother's household along with her daughter. A search for her possible divorce case in Buchanan County, Missouri, was inconclusive.[1271]

Nettie's occupation in 1900 was "candymaker," and she was yet living in 1906 when her mother Kate Carr listed her as a daughter, then age 31, on a Civil War pension document.[1272]

Defiance city, ED 233, p. 46; National Archives micropublication T9, roll 1011. The birth date of "18 March 1876" as given on her father Frank B. Carr's Civil War pension application does not appear correct vis-à-vis her ages on the above census records. Frank B. Carr furnished those birth dates when he was no longer living with his family, and, therefore, may not have given correct information.

[1269] Buchanan County Marriages, Volume J (1891-1893): 186, license no. 196; FHL microfilm 1004806. Officiated by James Mitchell, J.P.

[1270] His daughter's 1900 census entry gives Missouri as his birthplace. No Edward Graves was located in the 1900 Soundex of Missouri, although a male "E. V. Groves" was listed therein as a 36-year-old carpenter who was a patient at the Ensworth Hospital and Medical College on North 7th Street in St. Joseph; this man was born in March 1864 in Missouri to a New York father and a Maine mother (ED 53, p. 21, line 17).

[1271] Letter from Circuit and Deputy Clerks of Buchanan County, 18 October 1984, reported that only one Graves case was found, to wit, *Josie Graves vs. Nelson Graves* dated "March 14, 1998" [sic], which was dismissed for want of prosecution on "February 17, 1990" [sic].

[1272] Frank B. Carr Pension (Co. D, 124th Ohio Infantry), application 901216, certificate 701028; Kate Carr widow's application 827155, certificate 607618, Civil War and Later Files,

The child of Nettie E.[4] Carr and Edward Graves:
447. i. MOLLIE[5] GRAVES, born November 1894 in Missouri;[1273] no further information.[1274]

Records of the Veterans Administration (Record Group 15), National Archives, Washington, D.C.

[1273] 1900 U.S. census, Buchanan County, Missouri., St. Joseph, ED 62, p. 21.

[1274] A Buchanan County, Missouri, marriage record index was checked for Mollie's possible marriage (FHL microfilm 1004801); a Mary E. Graves married a James Moore on 3 November 1909, but this bride purportedly over 18 whereas Mollie was then just 15 years old (Book Z: 238, no. 1055; FHL microfilm 1004814).

Appendix A

PREFACE

Somebody may want to know the reason for compiling this historical Biography of this line of the Trubeys.

In 1922 or about that time, I had a letter from Mr. Ralph A. Trubey asking about the Geneology of his people. Previously he had written Alvah P. Trubey of Dover, Ohio, who referred him to me. At that time nobody knew very much about the subject, but I having lived *cotemporary* with my Grandfather, Daniel Trubey, and thru my father, John Trubey, fell heir to my father's and Grandfather's records. Though somewhat sketchy, I found much information when sifted and allocated, left some fact to build on.

It seemed no one knew who our fore-father was. My Grandfather said he did not know, as his father died when Grandfather was about 10 years old. We were at a loss as how to find out, but when my Daughter, Mrs. Lydia Ruth Walker and I went back to Ohio from Montana in 1936, we were sent to the old Trubey homestead in Stark County, Ohio, to Mr. Ellsworth Trubey, son of Jacob M. Trubey. As we were talking over the Geneology line he said, "perhaps you would like to look over the record in the old family Bible." I replied, "sure I would be glad to." He brought out his father, Jacob M. Trubey's Bible. There was the name Jacob Trubey, Jacob M. Trubey's father, son of Jacob Trubey. Mr. Clarence Trubey of St. Paris, Ohio has the record at this time.

The History would have been more complete except for the inattention of those asked and their neglect to reply to questions of family lore. I traveled several thousand miles and interviewed a large number of the Kin for the facts revealed and and through this book.

B. A. Trubey, Author

Genealogy and History of Trubey Family from its first entry into the United States of America.

JACOB TRUBEY, our ancestor, according to tradition, and two brothers of Hesse Cassel of Germany (but formerly of Switzerland) came to America as Hessian soldiers in the Revolutionary War, as soldiers of the British army, to fight against the American people. They arrived sometime in the year of 1777 and fought under the command of General Burgoyne, who was defeated and surrendered to General Gates of the American Army on October 17th, 1777.

When he was discharged from the British Army, he remained in this country. He settled near Waynesboro, Pennsylvania, where he married a German woman by the name of Mawk or Mak or in the English pronounced Mock. (First given name no known.)

(No account of the two brothers is available.)

Jacob Trubey, (the first Jacob Trubey) was the father of four children, three sons and one daughter, named as follows:

David Trubey 1
Nancy Trubey 3
Jacob Trubey 2
Daniel Trubey 4
-my grandfather-

Jacob Trubey (the first) essayed, a visit to the old country when my grandfather, Daniel Trubey, was nine or ten years old, but took sick and died before he could make the visit.

DAVID TRUBEY

David Trubey, the first son of Jacob Trubey was born in the year of 1787. The exact date is unknown. Birth took place in Franklin County, Pennsylvania. The date he married is not known and neither is his wife's maiden name known. They were the parents of four children, two boys and two girls.

Andrew Trubey
David M. Trubey
Mary Catherine Trubey
Susan Trubey

He emigrated to Ohio in about the year of 1817 or soon after. He settled in Tuscarawas County, Ohio. There his son Andrew was Professor in Scio College in or near Canal Dover of that county.

David Trubey departed this life on March 10th, 1862 in his 75th year.

PROFESSOR ANDREW TRUBEY

Professor Andrew Trubey, first son of David and Mary Trubey was born at Waynesboro, Franklin County, Pa., on November 22, 1814. He emigrated with his parents to Tuscarawas County, Ohio, where he grew to manhood and was educated in German and English. He was professor of those languages in Scio College in or near New Philadelphia, Ohio.

He was married to Mary Ann Barbara Taylor of the same town and county. She was born Jan. 16, 1815. To them were born six children, 4 boys and 2 girls, viz:

Mary Ann	Aug. 10, 1834
John Taylor	Feb. 5, 1837

    died on Sept. 19, 1845, at the age of 8 years, 7 months, and 14 days.

Lydia Catharine Trubey	Jan. 11, 1839
David Morton Trubey	Apr. 27, 1841
Abraham Musser	Apr. 20, 1843
Andrew Hanibel Trubey	Feb. 6, 1845

    departed this life on July 2, 1845, aged 4 months and 26 days.

Prof. Andrew Trubey was interested financially in coal lands in the vicinity in which he lived. He left this world of strife and toil Feb. 4, 1848[,] at the early age of 33 years, 2 months, and 9 days.

His wife, Mary Taylor Trubey, followed him on May 20, 1850[,] at the age of 35 years, 3 months, and four days, leaving four of the children orphans.

Appendix A

MARY ANN TRUBEY, eldest daughter of Andrew and Mary Taylor Trubey, was married to Mr. Henry Sprain on August 10, 1856[,] at Bolivar, Ohio. They were the parents of twelve children, viz: Sophia, Clark, Lydia, Mary, Mina, Martha, Jennie, Philip, Emma, Abraham, Bessie and Ida.

Jennie, Bessie, and Ida, at this date Dec. 1941 are the only survivors of this large family.

Mary Ann Trubey Sprain departed this life February 22, 1916[,] at the ripe old age of 81 years, 6 months, and 12 days.

The Sprains were residents of Van West Co, Ohio. The three surviving sisters are citizens of Ohio City, Ohio.

LYDIA CATHARINE TRUBEY was wedded to Philip Profit, to whom three children were born names: Charles, Margaret, and Mary. Charles is deceased having been a mail carrier at the time of his death. Lydia Catherine T. Profit passed on in *Spet*. 1875.

DAVID MORTON TRUBEY enlisted in Union Army in 1862 and was stricken with typhoid fever and died at Shiloh, Miss., During battle at that place. He was not married, died at the age of 20 years, 11 months, and 20 days, on April 22, 1862.

ABRAHAM MUSSER TRUBEY

ABRAHAM MUSSER TRUBEY, the second son of Professor Andrew Trubey and Mary Taylor Trubey, was born in Tuscarawas County, Ohio, near Canal Dover, on April [2?]0th, 1843. He passed away at his home in Rockford, Mercer County, Ohio on Dec. 31, 1917, aged 74 years 8 months, and 11 days. His parents died when he was quite small, five years of age. When 18 years old he enlisted in the 46 O.V.V.I. from *Vanwest*, Ohio and served through the entire period of the Civil War, being honorably discharged in 1865. He was wounded in his left leg at the Battle of Shiloh.

On May 11, he was joined in wedlock to Miss Mary Frysinger, daughter of Nathan and Jane Frysinger. To this union were born eight children three of whom with the wife and mother preceded the father and husband to the better world. The five remaining children are Mrs. J. B. Fair, Miss Lida Trubey of Rockford, *Miss* B. H. Sidle of Groven Hill, Ohio, Prof. Ralph S. Trubey of Fargo, N.D. and Attorney Reginald R. Trubey of Rockford, Ohio. Two grand children, Mary Helen Trubey, and Mary Margaret Fair.

APPENDIX A 253

LIDA TRUBEY, daughter of A. M. and Mary Trubey was born at Rockford Ohio on June 9th, 1887 and is a graduate of Rockford high school, and Battle Creek Sanitarium (Battle Creek, Mich) With a Bachelor of Science degree. She is a Registered Nurse now at Leighton Hotel in Los Angeles, California.

MINNIE, sister of Lida was born at Rockford, Ohio, March 19, 1886 and is married to Benjamin Harrison Sidle and lives in Wooster Ohio on a farm. She has a boy and two girls.

Another sister, Bertha Victoria passed away at her brother Ralph's home at Lidgerwood, North Dakota, where he was city Superintendant of Schools. She was 49 years old. She had one son who died in infancy and one daughter who is the wife of Dr. James Croushore, Detroit, Michigan, and she is Mary E. Croushore, aged 41 at this date January 5th, 1942. Three others brother and sister died in infancy, named Nathan, Jennie and Rollie.

RALPH ARCHIBOLD TRUBEY

RALPH ARCHIBOLD TRUBEY, son of Abraham M. and Mary F. Trubey, was born in Rockford, Ohio, on February 18, 1891. He was married to Alma Porter, who was born Dec. 9, 1892, on Aug. 4, 1915. Five children were born, viz:

Mary Helen	Sept. 14, 1916
Reginald Porter	May 1, 1916
Richard Arnold	July 22, 1920
Robert Nathan	April 25, 1922
Dorothy Ann	April 27, 1925

Mr. Trubey, after finishing his high school education at Rockford, attended Ohio Weslyan College at Delaware, Ohio, working his way thru by his own efforts such as washing dishes, waiting table, selling cleaning fluid and silver polish, which he made himself in the summer.

After graduation in 1912 from this Ohio Weslyan, he worked as a sugar chemist at Paulding, Ohio, remaining there until Jan. 1913. He then went to Lidgewood, North Dakota as a teacher and subsequently became Supt. and remained there 11 years. He worked part time as a life insurance man and became State Manager of the Guardian Life Insurance Company of N.Y. in Oct. 1922.

For extra curricular activities, he was president of the Lions Club at Lidgewood and later district governor for the States of Minn., N.D., S.D., and the Provinces of Alberta, Saskatchewan, and Manitoba. In 1938 he was potentate of El Zagal temple of Fargo, N.D. For 20 years he was president of the School Men's Club, known as the Chancellors Club; also president of the Community Welfare Association for three years and for twenty years president of the Red River Valley Council of Boy Scouts, and was on the county board of the Red Cross and chairman of the county boards of the U.S.O. and chairman of the State Citizens Committee of higher education.

APPENDIX A

REGINALD REYNOLD TRUBEY

REGINALD REYNOLD TRUBEY, son of Abraham M. and Mary Frysinger Trubey was born at Rockford, Mercer Co, Ohio on May 25, 1895. Grew up there, and graduated from Rockford High School and finished a Law Course at the University of Cincinnati Law School in May 1917. Joined the Navy in World War and was stationed on the U.S.S. Salem, which was a Submarine chaser. He was promoted to the rank of Ensign and served throughout the war.

He then set up a Law practice in Lima, Ohio, following his discharge. He was assistant Prosecuting Attorney, when he promoted the Art Kraft Sign Co., which is today one of the largest of its kind in the world. It is located in Lima, Ohio. Since then he has helped organize three different Davidson Enamel Plants. One at Connersville, Indiana, one at Lima and one at Clyde, Ohio, which he is operating himself. Four years ago he merged the Veos tile with te letter plant and both are being operated under the same foof. He has one adopted child.

MARY CATHARINE TRUBEY

MARY CATHARINE TRUBEY, second daughter of David Trubey, was born in Tuscarawas County, Ohio on August 12, 1822.

She was married to John Taylor Trimble. To them were born four children, two sons and two daughters, Namely:

D. A. Trimble
T. B. Trimble
Caroline Trimble Munday
Mrs. Trimble Taylor

D. A. and the sisters preceded Mrs. Trimble into the future world. Her Husband John Taylor Trimble was lost at sea in the year 1850.

Mrs. Trimble passed on in the year 1919 in her 97th year at the home of her grand-daughter in Fremont, Indiana. Burial was at LaGrange Indiana. Services by Rev. V. L. DeBow of the Methodist Episcopal Church at LaGrange, of which she was the oldest member.

APPENDIX A

DAVID M. TRUBEY, SECOND

DAVID M. TRUBY, son of David Trubey, was born in Tuscarawas County, Ohio on January 7, 1825. He was married to Mary Smutz. To them were born four sons and two daughters, viz:

Jacob Andrew	Aug. 26, 1846
David A.	April 19, 1848
Joseph D.	Jan. 12, 1854
George W.	Oct. 13, 1856

The two daughters' names and birthdates are unknown.

Mary Smutz Truby, wife of David M. Truby died on July 18th, 1884.

Mr. Truby married again, the name and time not available.

David M. Truby died on April 8th, 1894 aged 68 years, 3 months and one day.

His second wife died about one year later.

JACOB A. TRUBEY

JACOB A. TRUBEY, son of David M. and Mary Trubey was born August 26th, 1846, in Tuscarawas County, Ohio. He lived in Wells County, Indiana after accompanying his parents to Steuben County, Indiana. He there enlisted in the Union Army, in which he served eighteen months. Shortly after the was he was married to Malissa Wyland. To this union were born seven children. Those who are living are:

>David N. of Woodland, Illinois.
>Mrs. Wilson Maddox of Uniondale, Indiana.
>Mrs. J. W. Nicholson of Markle, Indiana.
>Freeman A. A. Trubey of Markle, Indiana.
>Levi J., Ira amd Chancy preceded their father to the better world.

Mr. Trubey was a member of the Trinity Church of God and a loyal worker in that Denomination. He always lived a worthy life, as a soldier and a Christian and a civilian. He was a member of Company A of the Forty-Fourth Indians Volunteer Infantry. He died at his home in Markle, Indiana, on January 18, 1918. The funeral was at his brother Joseph B. Truby's home in LaGrange, Indiana. Service by Rev. DeBow of the Methodist Episcopal Church. Burial in Greenwood Cemetery at LaGrange. He was aged 71 years, 4 months and 22 days.

Melissa his wife was born on August 25th, 1845 and departed this life on August 10th, 1922, aged 76 years, 11 months, 15 days.

DAVID NORVIN TRUBEY

David Norvin Trubey, son of Jacob and Melissa Wyland Trubey, was born November 14, 1867 in LaGrange, Indiana. His boyhood days were spent in Indiana and Kansas. He married Anna Elizabeth Kleemyer, who was born May 12, 1893 in Hanover, Germany.

To them were born five boys and one girl,

Andrew H.
Ernest Freeman
John
Laurence
Doris Marguerite
Harold Vane

DAVID NORVIN TRUBY

DAVID NORVIN TRUBY, first son of Jacob A. and Melissa Wyland Truby, was born in LaGrange Indiana on November 14, 1867. He spent his boyhood days in Indiana. Left home, or as he expresses it, ran away from home when 16 years of age. Met and married Miss Anna M. Klemeyer in the year of 1888. Miss Klemeyer was born in Walla, Germany on May 4, 1871.

To them were born 6 children, five boys and 1 daughter, named as follows:

Andrew H.
Ernest Freeman
John
Laurence
Doris Marguerite
Harold Vane

Mr. Truby came to Bloom, now Chicago Heights, Cook County, Illinois. Worked on a farm four years, then started to work in maintainance Dept. of P. R. railroad, where he put in 48 years, being retired in 1937 on account of age. His wife died October 17, 1936.

Mr. Truby clears up a long extended mystery regarding why David M. Trubey dropped the letter E from his name making it spell David M. Truby. According to David N. David M. was living in Ohio in the late 40's or early 50's and had got in debt, a debt that he could have been imprisoned for, so he left Ohio for Indiana and thought he would be safer by changing the spelling of his name. As it turned out, three of his sons adopted the later version, but one retained the former, viz, David A. whose sons Carl of Seattle, Washington and Oscar Dallas of Augusta, Michigan and three other children remained with the old version.

David N. lives at Woodland, Illinois and is in his 80th year at this writing March 1944.

LEVI J. TRUBY

LEVI J. TRUBY, second son of Jacob Andrew and Melissa Truby was born April 28th, 1869. ~~Sh~~He is dead, but the date is unknown.

Ira M. third son was born September 27th, 1876. He died August 13th, 1879.

FREEMAN ANDREW fourth son was born Sept. 6th, 1879. See his history on another page.

CHANCEY J. fifth son was born March 22nd., 1881. He died October 13, 1881.

EMILY first daughter was born February 1st, 1871. She married a Mr. Maddox. She lives in Markle, Indiana at this date.

MARY TRUBEY NICHOLSON second daughter was born May 5th, 1872. She married John Nicholson May 27th, 1900. No children were born to this union. They reside in Markle, Indiana.

FREEMAN ANDREW TRUBY

FREEMAN ANDREW TRUBY, fourth son of Jacob A. and Melissa Weyland Truby, was born Sept. 6th, 1879. He married Alice G. Cavitte on June 20, 1902. Three children were born to them, viz:

Paul D. Truby	July 7, 1904
Gladys Evelyn	May 29, 1906
Ethela Helen T. Merkey	Aug. 29, 1911

PAUL D. Married to Grace Fruit on August 24th, 1927. They have two children:

Max Truby	Aug. 23, 1931
Carole Truby	March 22, 1936

ETHELA HELEN TRUBY wedded Mr. Merkey. One child was born to them on April 22, 1942 named Karen Elaine Merkey.

APPENDIX A

DAVID A. TRUBEY

DAVID A. TRUBEY, second son of David M. Trubey was born April 19th, 1848. He was married to Miss Mary Elizabeth Summers (Born Nov. 11, 1846) on October 24th, 1875. To them were born five children, viz;

Oscar Dallas	Aug. 15, 1878
Effie Pearl Johnson	Apr. 14, 1880
Wilma V. Charles	March 16, 1882
Frederick Hobart	Oct. 13, 1886
Carl Trubey	May 17, 1890

David A. died March 10th, 1925, aged 78 years, 10 months, 21 days.

Mrs. Mary Elizabeth Trubey died July 14, 1917, aged 70 years, 9 months, 3 days.

FREDERICK was married and had three children, viz:

Caroll	July 1916
Cecil	June 1918
Mary E.	July 14, 1920

He departed this life October 16, 1934 at the age of 46 years and 3 days.

OSCAR DALLAS TRUBEY

OSCAR DALLAS TRUBEY, son of David A. and Elizabeth Summers Trubey, was born August 15th, 1878. He was married to Miss Lulu Piper on December 11, 1903. To them were born nine children consisting of five girls and four boys, viz;

Gladys May	Dec. 15, 1904
Effie	Aug. 3, 1905
Elizabeth Jackson T.	May 10, 1906
Frederick T.	March 28, 1909
Paul	Aug. 10, 1911
Wilma Autman	Apr. 12, 1916
Helen Torrey	Jan. 19, 1922
Harold Trubey	June 25, 1928
Harry Trubey	Jan. 25, 1937

Oscar D. Trubey lives on a farm near Augusta, Michigan.

FREDERICK in the army was accidentally killed at Fort Lewis, Washington. He was married and was 33 years of age.

APPENDIX A

EFFIE TRUBEY JOHNSTON

EFFIE TRUBEY JOHNSTON was married and was the mother of three children, viz;

Wayne Johnston	Dec. 4, 1906
Dorothy Johnston Williams	July 5, 1908
Frances Johnston Healey	Jan. 14, 1912

Effie Trubey Johnston died Dec. 6, 1922 at the age of 42 years, 7 months and 22 days.

WILMA V. is married to Mr. L. J. Charles. They have two children.

Cecil Harold Charles	June 7, 1903
Mary Elizabeth	Nov. 10, 1920

Mary Elizabeth is married to Mr. Ven Meer.

CARL E. TRUBEY is married to Lettie. They have no children. They live in Seattle, Washington.

JOSEPH D. TRUBEY

JOSEPH D. TRUBEY, third son of David M. and Mary Smutz Trubey was born January 12th, 1854. He was married to Miss Mary Moissett on July 1st, 1882. She was born on March 2, 1861. No children were born to this union.

Joseph D. passed on October 8th, 1934, at the age of 80 years, 8 months, 26 days.

The wife, Mary Trubey is still living at this date, at LaGrange, Indiana.

GEORGE W. TRUBY

GEORGE W. TRUBY, fourth son of David M. and Mary Smutz Truby, was born on Oct. 31, 1856. He married Hannah Slack on Oct. 31st, 1880. Three children were born to them, viz;

Cletura	Oct. 17, 1881
Hazel	Aug. 7, 1888
George Lester	April 12, 1886

Cletura was married to a Mr. Schadre. She passed on a few years later, time and age not known. She was a graduate nurse.

Hazel was married to Mr. Charles Routsong on Oct. 28, 1911. To this union six children were born, viz;

George William
Ruth Arlene
Retha Marie
Lois Rowena
Ester Leona
Wava Keturah

Mrs. Routsong's address is LaGrange, Ind. George Lester wedded Blanche Landahl.

George W. Truby died Aug. 23, 1838, aged 80 years, 7 months, 22 days.

JACOB TRUBEY, the Second

Jacob Trubey, the second son of Jacob Trubey, was born at Waynesboro, Pennsylvania, Franklin County, December 25th, 1789. He was married to Mary Welty, who was born February 2nd, 1801. To them was born;

Nancy T.	June	6th, 1818
Jacob Mobley	May	7th, 1820
Samuel T.	Nov.	9th, 1822

Jacob Trubey emigrated from his native state of Pennsylvania to Stark County, Ohio in 1823, taking up his abode on the farm in Sugar Creek Township, Ohio, which was later owned by his son Jacob M. Trubey. The land was partially cleared at the time it came into his possession, and a hewed log house was on the place into which they resided until a more substantial structure could be erected. He only lived about twelve years after his advent into this Stark County, dying at the early age of about forty five years, on March 1st, 1835. He was a very prominent man in his township, holding office of Justice of Peace, and had so long been numbered among its leading citizens, that the news of his death came as a personal calamity to his many acquaintances. At his death he left his wife, and three children, viz; Nancy, Jacob M., and Samuel. Mary Welty Trubey, his wife, died September 13th, 1851.

JACOB M. TRUBEY

Jacob M. Trubey, son of Jacob and Mary Welty Trubey, was born in Franklin County, Pennsylvania, May 7th, 1820. At about three years of age in 1823, he moved with his parents to a farm in Sugar Creek Township, Stark County, Ohio. He was reared upon the farm and assisted his father in doing all kinds of work that the pioneers of that time engaged in.

His education was conducted in the common school of his boyhood days, which did not offer as good facilities for acquiring learning as those of the present day, but he made the most of his advantages and by reading and close observation made up for his early *deficiences* in that line.

When he was fifteen years of age, his father died, and being the eldest of the two only sons, the responsibility of carrying on the farm rested upon him.

On December 12th, 1844 he married Miss Eliza, daughter of Nicholas D. and Mary A. Swan. To them was born a family of seven children;
    Ferdinand and Isabella died in infancy.
    Mary Ann married Josiah Jones, having lived twenty nine years.
The four surviving are;
    Nathan
    Harmon
    Esdras
    Freeman

Mrs. Trubey possessed that culture of mind and kindness of heart, which won for her the esteem of the entire community, and at her death, which *occured* June 14th, 1858, she was greatly mourned.

The lady whom our subject chose for his second wife, December 15th, 1858, was Elizabeth Pherson, who was born in Stark County, February 24, 1833 and was the daughter of Theophilus

JACOB M. TRUBEY #2

and Eliza Pherson. Of the eight children born of this union of Mr. and Mrs. Trubey, five survive who bear the respective names of;
    Ellsworth J.
    Jenna Etta, now Mrs. Samuel Muskof
    Asa H.
    Ira T.
    Alva P.
    Priscilla and Luella May died in infancy.
    Rollin L. died at the age of six days wanting twenty four years.

    Our subject was one of the most progressive citizens of the County, and as farming was his life work, he was thoroughly informed, regarding the peculiar qualities of soil. Having prospered in life, he was able to surround his family with all attainable comfort and luxuries, and bestow upon his children excellent educational advantages. He owned quite a number of farms, most of which are located in LaGrange County, Indiana.

    Politically, he belonged to the Republican party and was always greatly interested in politics, keeping well informed of the issue of the day and the bearing of public events upon state and nation. For three years he held the office of County Commissioner. In Sugar Creek Township, where he lived from early childhood, he filled the position of Trustee and for eighteen years in succession was elected Justice of Peace, during which time he solemnized the marriage contract of fifty-two parties. For twenty one years was commissioned as Notary Public, and in each and every position demeaned himself with credit and proved himself master of it. As a manager of business and a financier his ability was known and conceded par excellence hence, as administrator and executor, he settled no less than ten estates, and by unanimous choice was appointed to adjust and settle up several affairs, largely dry goods stores, which he accomplished to the perfect satisfaction of all concerned.

JACOB M. TRUBEY #3

Religiously, he was in sympathy with the Church of Christ, and with this religious denomination, he joined early in life. Although his life throughout had been devoted to the greatest care and strictest attention to his work and business, nevertheless, he has traversed the American continent from coast to coast and visited most of the principal places of historical interest.

Jacob M. Trubey died May 25, 1902, aged 82 years and 18 days.

(This information was taken from the biography of Jacob M. Trubey, written for the *occassion* of his seventieth birthday.)

APPENDIX A   271

NATHAN TRUBEY

Nathan Trubey, first son of Jacob M. and Eliza Swan Trubey, was born on Nov. 29, 1847 in Stark County, Ohio.

He married Melissa Knepper on Sept. 24, 1876. She was born Nov. 9, 1855.

To them were born;

```
Jacob M. Trubey            Nov.  4, 1877
Elva Terra Trubey Kuns     June 27, 1879
Myrtle Mae Trubey Kirk     Nov.  4, 1881
Mary Winona Trubey Van Eman Apr. 29, 1884
Nebbie Don Trubey          Jan. 24, 1887
Allie Trubey               Sept.20, 1891
Robert B. Trubey           Nov. 13, 1894
Selma Ruth Trubey Goodman  July  2, 1901
```

Elva Terra Trubey Kuns died Aug. 4, 1933.
Nebbie Don Trubey died June 27, 1910.
Allie Trubey died Oct. 21, 1892.

Nathan Trubey died October 3, 1907. His wife, Melissa died Nov. 16, 1930.

HARMON TRUBEY

Harmon Trubey was the second son of Jacob M. and Eliza Swan Trubey. He was born in Stark County, Ohio on Sept. 2, 1850. His wife, Anne May Augustine Trubey was born on January 9, 1861. They were married March 2, 1876 by Rev. Kanaga.

Unto this union was born eight children, whose name are;

Melvin Jay	June 16, 1878
Daisy Odella	Oct. 11, 1881
Elda Martha	June 18, 1883
(Elda died on April 18, 1885)	
Jennie Blanche	Oct. 6, 1885
William Cole	Oct. 28, 1893
(William died August 11, 1896)	
Sylvester Brice	Sept.15, 1897
Wilda Gale	Oct. 2, 1899
(Wilda died on February 15, 1901)	
Golda Oneida	June 20, 1901

Harmon Trubey died on December 25, 1904, aged 54 years, 3 months and 23 days.

MELVIN JAY, first son of Harmon Trubey, was married on June 8, 1917 at Grants Pass, Oregon to Mary Olive Diller. To them was born one daughter, Doris Oneida, who was born on Nov. 27, 1919, and one son, Forest Cole, who was born on Sept. 24, 1924. Mr. Melvin Trubey is an attorney-at-law, and real estate broker in Portland, Oregon. The daughter is a very successful music teacher as well as a school teacher.

DAISY ODELLA TRUBEY, first daughter of Harmon Trubey, was married to Erastus DeWitt Ott. They live in *Massilon*, Ohio and are the parents of three sons, viz;

Myron Dwight	July 2, 1907
Warren Franklin	Apr.21, 1909
Edward Bryce	Aug.29, 1915

APPENDIX A

ERASTUS DEWITT OTT

Erastus DeWitt Ott was born July 22, 1877. He married Daisy Odella Trubey on February 12, 1906. To them were born three sons;

Myron Dwight	July 2, 1907
Warren Franklin	April 21, 1909
Edward Bryce	Aug. 29, 1915

MYRON DWIGHT OTT

Myron Dwight Ott, first son of E. D. and Daisy Odella Trubey Ott was born July 2nd, 1907. He married Mary Catharine Ray on July 29, 1929. The following three children were born to them;

Robert Ray	Nov. 19, 1930
Marylin Louise	Sept. 25, 1932
Jane Blanche	Feb. 16, 1937

WARREN FRANKLIN OTT

Warren Franklin Ott, second son of E. D. and Daisy Odella Trubey Ott, was born April 21, 1909. He married Dorothy Mitchell Brandberg on August 10, 1937. One daughter has blessed this union;

Dorothy Louise	June 10, 1941

EDWARD BRYCE OTT

Edward Bryce Ott, third son of E. D. and Daisy Odella Trubey Ott, was born August 29, 1915. He married Ethel Marie Daniels on April 10th, 1935.

APPENDIX A 275

JENNIE BLANCHE TRUBEY

Jennie Blanche Trubey, daughter of Harmon and Anne May Augustine Trubey was born on Oct. 6, 1885. She was joined in holy matrimony to Benjamin F. Fairless at *Pittsburg*, Pennsylvania.

To them one son was born;

Blaine Fairless

Mrs. B. F. Fairless departed from this life on Sept. 29th, 1942 at the age of 56 years, 11 months and 23 days. She was a very talented woman. She wrote a book and was also an artist of good repute.

SYLVESTER BRICE TRUBEY

Sylvester Brice Trubey, third son of Harmon and Anna Mae Trubey was born in Stark Co., Ohio on September 15, 1897 and La La Trubey, his wife, was born March 24, 1897. They had one son, Dale Trubey who was born on December 13, 1928.

GOLDIA ONEDIA TRUBEY

Goldia Onedia Trubey, daughter of Harmon and Anna Mae Trubey was born on June 20, 1901. She was united in marriage to Oscar E. Barkey in Canton, Stark County, Ohio on June 25, 1916. To this union were born two daughters;

Charity June	March 8, 1920
Gloria Marie	Dec. 6, 1922

ESDRAS B. TRUBEY

Esdras B. Trubey, third son of Jacob M. and Eliza Swan Trubey, was born June 18, 1852, and was married to Mary Ann Sheline of Beach City, Ohio, who was born Jan. 9, 1854.

Born to this union was one girl and one boy.

Eliza Cassandria Trubey   Jan. 2, 1878
David Jacob Trubey   Mar. 27, 1881

Neither of the twain ever married. The home was suddenly saddened by the mother and wife Mary Ann, passing on Oct. 30, 1881.

On Nov. 9, 1882, the father, Esdras B. was married to Lizza Jane Williamson, who was born Aug. 5, 1850 and who passed on Jan. 28, 1898. To this union were born one daughter and one son viz;

Eunice Bessie   Aug. 2, 1885
  at Minneapolis, Minn.
  married Dr. John M. Luttenberger of
  Chicago, Ill, who passed on Jan. 7, 1941
George Esdras   May 11, 1888

He was born at Minneapolis, Minn. and was married to Clara C. Myer on June 19, 1908 at Circleville, Ohio. Two children were born to this union. George Esdras passed away March 8, 1914 at the age of 25 years, 9 months and 27 days.

Esdras B. Trubey was again married in Apr. 1902, to Mrs. Luella B. Marchand, who passed away a little more than two years later leaving no children.

Then on Sept. 4, 1910 he again was married to Miss Rose Lewallyn, who still lives. No children were born to this union.

Esdras B. passed on June 23, 1917, aged 65 years and 5 days.

FREEMAN SWAN TRUBEY

Freeman Swan Trubey was the son of Jacob M. and Eliza Swan Trubey. He was born in Stark County, Ohio on May 23, 1858. He was united in marriage to Anna Mary Minich on March 1, 1885. To this union were born six children.

    Roxis Belle   Feb. 3, 1886
    William Albert   May 20, 1888
    Infant in March 1889 who passed on soon unnamed.
    Nathan Ray   Oct. 31, 1890
    Cor Jacob and Dor Esdras Feb. 24, 1893
        (twins)

Dor Esdras passed on about the age of two and one half years.

Anne Mary Minnich Trubey, wife of Freeman S. passed on November 6, 1926. Freeman passed on March 27, 1937 at the age of 78 years, 10 months, and 4 days.

WILLIAM ALBERT TRUBEY

William Albert Trubey, first son of Freeman S. and Anna Mary Minnich Trubey, was born May 20th, 1887 in LaGrange, Indiana. He married Bessie Belle Sisson on Sept. 16th, 1908. Born to this union were four children;

    Kenneth Devere   Oct. 27, 1910
    Lloyd William   Dec. 18, 1913
    (who passed on Jan. 24, 1919 at the age of of 6 years, 1 month and 6 days.)
    Monroe S.   July 25, 1916
    (He married Dorothy Corson on Feb. 22, 1941)
    Homer Ray   Dec. 9, 1920
     (He married Mary Ellen Newman on Jan. 11th, 1941)

Kenneth D. was married to Olivia Markley Sept. 29th, 1932 and to them were born five children as follows;

    Lowell Kenneth   March 2, 1935
    Paul Myron   July 8, 1936
    Julia Ellen   April 11, 1938
    Max William   May 18, 1939
    Mark Lee   Feb. 10, 1941

William Albert Trubey died Sept. 29, 1941 at the age of 53 years, 4 months and 9 days.

NATHAN RAY TRUBEY

Nathan Ray Trubey, second son of Freeman S. and Anna Mary Minnich Trubey, was born Oct. 31, 1890 and was married to Avah Gooden. She was born Oct. 31, 1893. They were married Feb. 24, 1915. They have two children, one daughter and one son,

    Nellie Virginia   Jan. 2, 1916
    Russell Norris   June 27, 1921

Mr. Trubey farmed eleven years and then took the Civil Service examination in 1923. He was appointed Substitute Clerk and carrier of mail service in LaGrange, Indiana, serving in that capacity for 19 years. He is now regular city letter carrier. He was born and raised in LaGrance County, Indiana.

Virginia Trubey was married Oct. 20, 1941 to Wilbert M. Reed of Huntington, Indiana, who is a Corporal in U. S. Army. Virginia is a deputy Auditor, 1942 being her sixth year at this position.

COR JACOB TRUBEY

Cor Jacob Trubey, son of Freeman S. and Mary Minnich Trubey, was born at LaGrange, Indiana on February 24, 1893.

He married Lulu Belle Anderson.

Born to this union was one son,

Stanley Rodgers Trubey.

APPENDIX A

ELLSWORTH E. TRUBEY

Ellsworth E. Trubey, first son of Jacob M. and Elizabeth Pherson Trubey was born in Stark County, Ohio on Nov. 27, 1861.

He was married to Satira Eunice Killgore. To this union one son was born.

Clarence Trubey, now of St. Paris, Ohio.

Ellsworth E. departed this life on Sept. 27, 1941, aged 79 years, 10 months and 2 days.

IRA T. TRUBEY

Ira T. Trubey, son of Jacob M. and Elizabeth Pherson Trubey, was born in Stark County, Ohio, on July 26th, 1870.

He married Airie McFarron. Two sons and two daughters were the fruit of this union.

Daniel Trubey of Birmingham, Alabama.
Lester Trubey
Joyce Trubey
Nellie Trubey

JENNIE ETTA TRUBEY MUSKOPF

Jennie Etta Trubey Muskopf, daughter of Jacob M. and Elizabeth Pherson Trubey, was born June 16, 1864 in Stark County, Ohio.

She was married to Samuel Muskopf on June 2, 1887. To this union four children were born; three sons and one daughter.

Marcellus A. Muskopf   Jan. 5, 1889
His present address is 2544 Fraymore Rd, University Heights, Cleveland, Ohio.

Emma Mildred   May 7, 1890
She married H.B. Ward, Lake View, New York

Homer A.   Jan. 31, 1904
He is at home yet.

Glen William   March 22, 1906
Died Aug. 19, 1907

Mr. Samuel Muskopf was born Sept. 17, 1861 and died Sept. 12, 1912, aged 51 years, less 5 days.

ASA HARVEY TRUBEY

Asa Harvey Trubey, son of Jacob and Elizabeth was born in Stark County, Ohio on May 13, 1868. Married to Ida Elnore Wolf, on August 1, 1891. Born Feb. 7, 1873, died March 9, 1929.

To them six children were born:

Jennie Ethel	June	8, 1892
Charles Otha	Dec.	10, 1893
Asa Alvah Dead	Oct.	12, 1896
Albert Jason	Jan.	9, 1900
Robert Henry	Jan.	17, 1904
Carl Harrison	June	5, 1908

(He died at the age of 11 months.)

ETHEL TRUBEY

Ethel Truby, born at LaGrange, Indiana June 8, 1892, was married to Leon Maynard on Jan. 20, 1916. They separated on June 6, 1932.

On May 19, 1934 she was united in marriage to John Burton Webber. They live in Detroit, Michigan, 3620 Wabash Avenue.

CHARLES OTHA TRUBEY

Birthplace at La Grange, Indiana, born on Dec. 10, 1893. Was married Aug. 1, 1915. One daughter born on Sept. 22, 1917. Was separated Feb. 2, 1927.

Married a second time on July 4, 1935 to Myrtle Little of Alpena, Michigan. Their address at present is 2644 Myrtle St., Detroit, Michigan.

ALBERT JASON TRUBEY

Born Jan 9, 1900 at Bronson, Michigan. Married March 16, 1926 to LaReine Curby of Buffalo, New York.

Four children blessed this union;

June Ethel	March 9, 1928
Elnore LaReine	April 2, 1929
Lillian May	Sept. 16, 1932
Joice Mable	June 22, 1935

This family lives at Holly Road, Grand *Blance*, Michigan.

ROBERT TRUBEY

Born Jan 17, 1904 at Stroh, Indiana. On April 16, 1931 he married Flossie McPhee of Alpena, Michigan. No children born up to Sept. 26, 1942.

Robert is living at 514 Towas St., Alpena, Michigan.

APPENDIX A   285

ALVAH P. TRUBEY

Alvah P. Trubey was born March 31, 1876.

He married Emma B. Caler. Emma, his wife, died *Spetember* 23, 1942.

Children born to them were;

Paul Perlee	June 1, 1904
Mary E. Trubey Keener	Dec. 27, 1905
Dwight Willis	Jan. 20, 1908
Ruth Trubey Render	June 22, 1912
Raymond Charles	Nov. 24, 1919

Alvah P. Trubey died Nov. 17, 1941, at the age of 65 years, 7 months and 16 days.

ALVAH P. TRUBEY

Alvah P. Trubey was born March 31, 1876.

He married Emma B. Caler. Emma, his wife, died Sept. 23, 1942.

Children born to them were;

Paul	
Mary	Dec. 27, 1905
Dwight	
Ruth	
Ray	Nov. 18, 1920

Alvah P. Trubey died Nov. 17, 1941, at the age of 65 years, 7 months and 16 days.

CHRISTIAN WELTY

Christian Welty was born in Franklin County, Pennsylvania on March 3, 1788, and died at *Massilon*, Ohio on December 29, 1875. He was the husband of Nancy Trubey Welty, who was born in Franklin County, Pennsylvania in the year of 1791. Christian Welty at the time of decease was aged 87 years, 3 months and 26 days.

DANIEL TRUBEY

Daniel Trubey was born August 8th, 1793, at Waynesboro, Franklin County, Pennsylvania. He was married to Mary Stoner of Hagarstown, Maryland on the 12th day of June 1817. Mary Stoner was born March 25, 1799. They were married by the Reverend Johnathan Rolanser of the Reformed Church.

To them were born eleven children, five boys and six girls. Eight were born at Waynesboro, Franklin County, Pennsylvania and three at Stark County, Ohio. The names and date of births are as follows;

Susan Trubey, born at Waynesboro, Pa.
March 1, 1818

David Trubey, born at Waynesboro, Pa.
Nov. 24, 1819

John Trubey, born at Waynesboro, Pa.
Oct. 2, 1821

Daniel Trubey, born at Waynesboro, Pa.
June 7, 1824

Nancy Trubey, born at Waynesboro, Pa.
Sept. 4, 1826

Rebecca Trubey, born at Waynesboro, Pa.
Dec. 15, 1829

Samuel Trubey, born at Waynesboro, Pa.
Jan. 22, 1831

Mary Ann Trubey, born at Waynesboro, Pa.
April 9, 1833

Abraham Trubey, born at Stark County, Ohio
July 20, 1835

Elizabeth Trubey, born at Stark County, Ohio
Nov. 19, 1838

Catherine Trubey (or Kate) born at Stark County
July 7, 1843

DANIEL TRUBEY

Daniel Trubey emigrated from Franklin County, Pennsylvania to Ohio in 1834 and settled in Stark County, Ohio. Later he moved to near Antioch, now Andrews, Huntington County, Indiana, where he lived until the year of 1866 when he and grandmother came to live in one of our houses on the John Trubey farm in Defiance County, Ohio and lived there until after grandmother had a stroke in the fall of 1874 when they broke up housekeeping and grandfather went to live with his daughter, Mrs. Catherine Carr. Grandmother went to live with another daughter, Mrs. Nancy Yantiss in Nebraska. Grandfather lived until October 8th, 1875 when he died, aged eighty two years and two months. He was buried at Independence cemetery, near Defiance, Ohio. Grandmother died at her daughter's house in the year of 1875 at Mrs. Nancy Yantiss's house. She was buried in Silver Creek cemetery, Richardson County, Nebraska, aged 75 years and 8 months and 23 days.

290   B. A. TRUBEY MANUSCRIPT

SUSANHA OR SUSAN TRUBEY

Susan Trubey, the oldest child of Daniel and Mary Trubey was born March 1st, 1818, at Waynesboro, Franklin County, Pennsylvania. She was married three times, first to a Mr. Hunt, to whom were born three children, all girls, named; Mary, Minerva, and Nancy.

After Mr. Hunt's demise, she was married to Mr. McCullick (given name not known) to them was born one daughter, named Ella.

After Mr. McCullick's death she again married a Mr. Bell (given name unknown).

MARY HUNT married a Mr. Stuart to whom were born the following children, named; Harry, James, William, and Elizabeth. After Mr. Stuart's demise, she married John Dixon to whom was born George, Nellie, and Clarabelle.

MINERVA HUNT was a spinster, but married late in life and only lived a short while after. Her husband's name is not known by the writer. Nothing further is known of her. She lived about a year with us, John Trubey, her uncle and his family.

NANCY HUNT married William Jones of Huntington County, Indiana, moved to Clay Center, Clay County, Kansas about year of 1870. Nothing further is abailable about them.

ELLA McCULLICK Nee Terhune was about sixteen or eighteen years old when she came to Ohio and worked for mother (Mrs. John Trubey) then afterwards for her Aunt Elizabeth Long, going back to Indiana. She was married to Edward Terhune. I have no information that there were any children, but rumor is that there was one daughter.

ARABELLE SERENA TRUBEY

Arabelle Serena Trubey, first child and daughter of David and Keziah Klinker Trubey, was born May 20, 1846 in Hancock County, Ohio.

Was married to Elmer P. Shepherd on April 9th, 1868. Three children were born to this union, viz;

Clarence Carlton	Jan. 10, 1874
Grace D.	Sept. 5, 1877
Earle I.	Jan. 27, 1879

Mrs. Arabelle S. Shepherd departed this life on August 20, 1901, aged 55 years and 3 months.

The Shepherds moved to Kiowa, Kansas in 1879, while the Indians were raiding the early settlers. Elmer P. Shepherd held the office of Sheriff for a number of years at Kinsley, Kansas in Edwards County.

CLARENCE CARLTON SHEPHERD

First son of Elmer P. and Arabelle S. Trubey-Shepherd was born Jan. 10, 1874 in St. Joseph County, Michigan. Was married to Tyrannus Goe Morton. One child was born to them, Robert Earle Shepherd on March 11, 1927. The mother passed on Dec. 24, 1933. Clarence C. passed on on Aug. 24, 1940, aged 66 years, 7 months and 15 days.

GRACE D. SHEPHERD MARTIN

Was born Sept. 5, 1877 in St. Joe County, Michigan. Was married to Tono E. Martin on Oct. 31, 1915. Three children were born to this union, viz:

Samuel Page	Feb. 13, 1917
Maubelle	Sept. 10, 1918
Tono S.	May 6, 1921

Tono Shepherd died July 24, 1921, aged two months and 18 days.
Samuel P. Martin is in Civil Service and Engineers at Ft. Sill, Oklahoma.

EARLE I. SHEPHERD

Second son of Arabelle Trubey and Elmer P. Shepherd was born July 27, 1879. He married Miss Anna Sherman. Their home is 1602-4th St., LaGrand, Oregon.

DAVID TRUBEY

David Trubey, the first son of Daniel and Mary Trubey, was born at Waynesboro, Franklin County, Pennsylvania, November 24th, 1819. He came with his parents to Stark County, Ohio about the year of 1834, where he grew up to manhood. He was married to Keziah Katherine Klinker in the year 1845. She was from Barrs Mills, now Beach City, Stark County, Ohio.

To them were born four children, viz;

Arabella Serena	May 20, 1846
Erastus Seabury Trubey	March 16, 1848
Mary Catherine	Aug. 17, 1850
William David	Jan. 26, 1855

David Trubey died Oct. 10, 1855, aged 35 years, 11 months and 16 days.

ERASTUS TRUBEY

Erastus Trubey, the son of David Trubey, was joined in wedlock to Martha Dawson Liddle on November 25, 1874 at Colon, Michigan. The children of this union were:

Halla Belle	Aug. 17, 1875
Valerie Anita	April 18, 1882

Mr. Trubey was a farmer and stockman, buying and selling stock all his life. He was divorced from his wife in the year 1893. He married a second time, name and time unavailable. Mr. Trubey died March 1925 at Colon, Michigan and was buried at Jackson, Michigan, having lived seventy-eight years.

HALLE BELLE TRUBEY

Halle Belle Trubey, the daughter of Erastus Trubey, was married to James Hirst, on August 11, 1906 at Camden, New Jersey and they lived in Vineland, New Jersey until they moved to California in 1910 and have lived there ever since. Unto this union were born:

47

Edgar Delalia   April 19, 1908
   (He died May 5, 1918)
Martha Helene Hirst   Aug. 27, 1910
   (Married on Feb. 20, 1930 to Edward Burroghs
Thompson. They have one son.)
David Edward, who was born on March 4, 1935
James Vincent Hirst, son of Halle B., was born
Oct. 20, 1912.

Halle Laveda Hirst, daughter of Halle Hirst,
was born March 12, 1915.

VALERIE ANITA TRUBEY

The second daughter of Erastus S. Trubey
was born April 18, 1882 and was married to Mr.
William Homer Walker. To them was born four
sons:
William H. Walker
Robert Walker
Francis Walker
Joseph Walker

MARY CATHERINE TRUBEY

The second daughter of David and Keziah
Trubey was born in 1850 at Hancock County,
Ohio and was married to Jasper A. Vanetta.
They have two sons:
LaVern Vanetta
Virgil Vanetta

ARABELLA SERENA TRUBEY

The oldest daughter of David and Keziah
Trubey, was married to Elmer P. Shepherd, on
April 9, 1868. They emigrated to Kiowa, Kans.
in the year of 1879 while the Indians were
raiding the early settlers. The had three
children, viz:
   Clarence Clair Shepherd was born Jan. 10,
1874 in St. Joseph, Michigan. He died August
24, 1940. He was buried Thursday, August 29,
1940 in Valley View Cemetery, Garden City, Kans.
aged 66 years, 7 months and 15 days.

48

APPENDIX A 295

    Grace D. Shepherd Martin, daughter of Elmer P. and Arabella Trubey Shepherd was born Sept. 5, 1877 in St. Joseph County, Mich. Married Tono E. Martin on Oct. 31, 1915. He was born in Champaign County, Illinois on Jan. 28, 1868. Two children blessed this union:

Samuel Page Martin	Feb. 13, 1917
Maribelle Martin	May 6, 1921

E. P. Shepherd, father of Grace D. Martin, was Sheriff and also Surveyor of Edwards Co., Kansas for a number of years.

    Earl I. Shepherd born July 27, 1879 at Kiowa County, Kansas. Married Anna Shermer about 1912.

    Maribelle Martin married E. Lester Elmore Dec. 28, 1941. Home at 1515 N. Topeka, Wichita, Kansas[.]

WILLIAM DAVID TRUBEY

William David Trubey, the youngest son of David and Keziah Trubey was born January 26, 1855 in Hancock county, Ohio. Before settling down in life, he traveled quite a lot through Ohio, Indiana, Michigan, Kansas and Nebraska, meeting with uncles, aunts, and cousins, where he was welcomed as a good companion and friendly fellow. On September 19, 1891, he was married to Eurannah Haas of Colon, Michigan, to whom two children were born.

    George William   May 1, 1893
    Mystia Nafeesie T. Farnsworth April 11, 1896

William David Trubey passed away on March 11, 1899, at the age of 44 years, 1 month and 15 days.

APPENDIX A

LYMAN TRUBEY

Lyman Trubey was born in Carey, Ohio. His wife's name was Adah. They were the parents of five children, viz;

Nina Lawhead,	Upper Sandusky, Ohio
Carl	Loraine, Ohio
Milton	Carey, Ohio
Gladys T. Schuman	Wixon, Indiana
Emma T. Cheesbrough	Fenton, Michigan

JOHN TRUBEY

John Trubey, the second son of Daniel and Mary Trubey, was born October 2, 1821 at Waynesboro, Pennsylvania. The family being poor, he was bound out when a lad, and learned the wagon makers trade. When his time was out, becoming of age, he came to Ohio, to where his parents and family had moved. The great canal system was being built going through Canal Dover where he took to boating and also boated on the Wabash and Cincinnati branches. Here he met his first wife, Sarah Jane Daugherty in or near Trenton, Ohio, Butler County. They were married March 23, 1851, to whom one son was born May 21, 1852 named Nathan John Trubey. The mother fell asleep eight days later on May 29, 1852, aged 24 years 9 months and 3 days.

After this marriage to Miss Daugherty, he set up a wagon making shop in Florida, Ohio, where he worked at his trade for several years.
Sarah Jane Daugherty was born Aug. 26, 1827.

Later, sometime in the year 1855 or 1856 he married Miss Jane Morse, who died November 4, 1857 at the age of 25 years, 1 month, and 28 days. No children were born to them.

He was again married to Miss Lydia Moore of Trenton, Butler County, Ohio.

When they left Florida, Ohio and moved to a farm at Jewell, Defiance County, Ohio, where the three sons were born, named:
Barevias Augustus
Justin Alonzo
Ambrose Enyart

During the years of 1864 and 1865 of the Civil War, he moved to Defiance, Ohio and worked at his trade of making wagons. In the spring of 1866, he moved back to the farm, he and his wife living the rest of their lives there. The wife died on June 26, 1894 and he followed her on March 18, 1897.

Mr. Trubey was a prominent fruit man. In

1870 he planted the first peach orchard of budded fruit in Defiance County. The orchard contained six hundred trees and also had six acres of apple orchards and one and one-half acres of pears.

It was through his efforts that a railroad stop was made, first called Rosebud on the Wabash Railroad. The name was changed when the post office Jewell was established as there was already one post office named Rosebud. He was highly respected and had many friends in the community in which he lived.

LYDIA MOORE TRUBEY

Lydia Moore Trubey (our mother) was born in Butler County, Ohio, November 29, 1823. She was the eleventh child of a family of thirteen, having two brothers younger than she. She was a sufferer on account to chronic rheumatism for many years. She was a faithful believer in God and his son Jesus Christ. Having no information of the family of note. All we have is her father and mother's birth dates and also their deaths and the birth and names of her brothers and sisters, which we give for the benefit of our branch of the family.

Lewis Moore, our grandfather was born in Sommerset, New Jersey, August 16, 1778, and died in Butler County, Ohio, May 8, 1859, aged eighty one years. He was married to Susannah Enyart on July 2, 1804 in Butler County, Ohio. To them were born thirteen children, viz:

Annie Moore	June	6, 1805
Rufus Enyart	March	18, 1807
Infant son		1808
Eliza	Dec.	17, 1809
Sarah	Oct.	15, 1811
Elias	Oct.	5, 1813
Amy	Nov.	2, 1815
Anthony Benezetti	Nov.	5, 1817
Reuben	Oct.	14, 1819
Samuel	Jan.	13, 1822

53

Lydia	Nov. 29, 1823
Stephen Gard	Nov. 12, 1825
Alphonso Ellwood	April 5, 1828

Susannah Enyart Moore died at Arcola, Illinois December 19, 1872, aged 86 years, 5 months and 14 days.

    Lewis Moore and wife in their childhood both emigrated to Ohio, coming down the Ohio River in flat boats some time before the year of 1804. Mother Trubey used to relate how perilous it was for her father and mother to come down the Ohio because of outlaws prowling and Indians. I do not know whether she referred to her father's or mother's journey as it was related to her by one or both of them.

    Benjamin Enyart was born May 28, 1741 in New Jersey. He was married to Joana Tombs, who was born February 29, 1747. Unto them were born eleven children:

Samuel Enyart	Aug. 4, 1765
Sarah	Dec. 18, 1766
Hannah	Jan. 28, 1769
Mary	Dec. 29, 1770
Perses	May 7, 1773
Rufus	Feb. 11, 1775
John	March 17, 1777
David	July 15, 1778
Rachel	Sept. 18, 1781
Cornelius	Nov. 9, 1783
*Susannah (grandmother)	July 5, 1786*

APPENDIX A

NATHAN JOHN TRUBEY

Nathan John Trubey, son of John A. and Sarah Jane Daugherty Trubey, was born in Florida, Henry County, Ohio on May 21, 1852. His mother dying a few days later, he was taken by his grandmother to Butler County, Ohio, to be raised. When 18 or 19 years of age his grandmother Daugherty died. He then came home to his father's at Jewell, Ohio and helped on the farm for a couple of years, then struck out for himself and worked as a farm hand near Lafayette, Indiana. He met and was married to Miss Nettie Ely of near Lafayette, Indiana. Differences arising between them, they separated. No children were born to this union. He then married Miss Lillian Gilbert of Hicksville in Sept. 1887. To this union one son was born, Roy Trubey. After a disagreement they separated. Later he met and married Miss Carrie Virginia Gilbert, who was born April 29, 1871 in West Virginia. They were married at Athens, Ohio, Sept. 4, 1889. To this union were born eight children, all of them now dead, except those mentioned below.

    John Earl Nathan
    Edith Roselle
    Ida Belle
    Florence Augusta
    Albert Sidney   March 5, 1902

Nathan John Trubey departed this life on June 7, 1933 at the age of 81 years and 17 days.

Carrie V. Trubey, widow of Nathan John Trubey passed away on October 14, 1943 at the age of 72 years, 5 months and 15 days.

FLORENCE AUGUSTA TRUBEY, was born Sept. 6, 1904. Married Peter Siler on May 4, 1925. Two children blessed this union.
    Marie   August 22, 1925
    Virginia   Dec. 27, 1926

ALBERT SIDNEY TRUBEY was married in 1925 to Loretta Dudlow. Two children were born,
    Richard
    Sandra Jean

BAREVIAS TRUBEY

Barevias Augustus Trubey, the first son of John and Lydia Moore Trubey, was born near Jewell, Defiance County, Ohio, on February 25, 1860. He grew up on the farm on which he was born, except two years during the Civil War, when they lived in the city of Defiance, Ohio. He received nearly all his schooling in the rural schools. In the year 1882, on February 15, he was joined in holy wedlock in Defiance, Ohio, with Zeruia Corolin Goodenough, with whom he lived fifty-four years and three days, when she departed this life for the better world. On February 15, 1932, he celebrated his Golden Wedding Anniversary.

Barevias was engaged in farming until the year 1898 when he moved with his family to Sherwood, Ohio. Here he was engaged in the creamery business, also the hay business. In 1904 he bought one half interest in a shoe business, finally owning the whole stock. In 1906, he merged it with grocery and dry goods business until the year 1914. When failing in business, he carpentered awhile and also helped in the other stores of the town. Finally he sold his property and migrated to Montana in the year of 1917 and homesteaded 160 acres near the now town of Colstrip, first moving on to his son John's homestead, which he tilled for several years. In 1920, having built a house he moved to his own claim, which he improved. In October 1929, the wife, on account of rheumatism felt unable to do the work on the farm, they moved to Forsyth, Montana where they lived until her demise. She had attained the age of 75 years and 5 months, living the longest of any of her family except her father William Edwin Goodenough who lived ninety-three years.

Unto this union were born five children.
Flora Mae	May	17, 1883
John Edwin	March	2, 1886
Lydia Ruth	July	26, 1891
Myron Agustus	May	7, 1896
Theodore Wayne	Feb.	7, 1902

APPENDIX A 303

At this writing Barevias Trubey is in good health and able to travel, which he has done extensively for the past five years, (Nov. 1940).

THE CHILDREN OF BAREVIAS AND ZERUIA C. TRUBEY

FLORA MAE TRUBEY, first daughter of B. A. and Zeruia C. Trubey was born on May 17, 1883 in Defiance County, Ohio. She moved with her parents to Sherwood, Ohio in the year of 1898. She finished her education in Sherwood High School. Flora Mae married Charles R. Smith on March 15, 1902. To this union were born two daughters and two sons:

Marjorie Ray	April 20, 1904
Noma Mildred	July 31, 1907
William Barevias	May 8, 1911
Clarence Charles	Dec. 9, 1913

They still live on the farm on which they set up housekeeping thirty-nine years ago.

Marjorie Ray Smith McCavitt, daughter of Flora Mae Trubey Smith and Charles R. Smith, was born on April 20, 1904 near Sherwood, Ohio. She married Dale A. McCavitt, who was born March 12, 1902, on July 16, 1927. One son has blessed this union; and one daughter:

Lyndon James	May 13, 1929
Noma Ione	March 5, 1932

JOHN EDWIN TRUBEY

John Edwin Trubey, the first son of B. A. and Z. C. Trubey was born March 2, 1886 on a farm in Defiance County, Ohio. He grew up partly on the farm and in Sherwood, Ohio, of the same county. He received his education there. He began railroading when seventeen years of age as fireman on the Baltimore and Ohio Railroad at Garrett, Indiana. He worked on that road for two or three years, then he transferred to Pennsylvania at *Pittsburg*, Pennsylvania. He then went to Montana in the year of 1908, where he became engineer on the Northern Pacific. On June 30, 1910 he married Miss Addie Gail Anderson of Forsyth, Montana.

Two sons were born to this union:

Ray Edwin	June	24, 1912
Lloyd Elston	April	10, 1914

John Edwin Trubey died December 21, 1918 at the age of 32 years, 9 months and 19 days. He was highly esteemed by his fellow railroad employees and was their representative in the Montana legislature for getting favorable legislation for railway workers, for that he was very successful.

LLOYD ELTON TRUBEY

LLOYD ELTON TRUBEY, the second son of J. E. TRUBEY and ADDIE GAIL TRUBEY was born on April 10 1914 at Forsyth, Montana. He was married to Wanona I. Welch of Lander, Wyoming on June 30, 1936.

A daughter and son were born to this union.

SHARON KAY born in Glendale, Calif. P. and G. hospital May 11, 1942 Monday at 6:59 p.m.

DON EDWIN born in Los Angeles Calif. Queen of Angels hospital November 1, 1946 at 8:43 p.m.

This union was dissolved by divorce in 1953. Filed in March 1952 by LLOYD ELTON TRUBEY and the final degree being granted on July 2, 1953.
       Glendale, Calif.

LYDIA RUTH TRUBEY

Lydia Ruth Trubey, second daughter of Barevias A. and Zeruia C. Goodenough Trubey, was born in Defiance County, Ohio on July 26, 1891. She was married in Defiance, Ohio to William Edward Walker on June 28, 1916. W. E. Walker was born April 14, 1888. They have one adopted son, Maxwell Trubey Walker, who was born November 27, 1909.

They lived for a while in Ohio and Michigan, then in 1918 they migrated to Montana, eventually residing in Forsyth, Montana where they lved 15 years. In the winter of 1941 they made a trip west through Washington and Oregon. Mr. Walker is now employed by the Government at Camp Adair in the Post Engineers Division. They reside at 1616 E. Front St., Albany, Oregon.

MAXWELL TRUBEY WALKER was married at Forsyth, Montana to Mildred Helen Griggs on Sept. 2, 1939. His wife was born April 14, 1918. One son has blessed this union.

James Duane   May 6, 1943

Maxwell Walker was employed in various bakeries for a period of several years, but after moving to Oregon in 1942 he was employed in the Plywood factory at Lebanon, Oregon, and is, at present, still working there.

MYRON AUGUSTUS TRUBEY

Myron Augustus Trubey, the second son of Barevias and Zeruia Trubey, was born in Defiance County, Ohio, May 7, 1896. He grew up in Sherwood, Ohio then found a job in Cleveland, Ohio. Here he met Venus Ross, to whom he was married on the fifth day of April, 1917. They resided in that city until the year of 1932 when they moved to the vicinity of Los Angeles, California. Unto this union was born four children, one daughter and three sons.

James Wayne	Feb. 26, 1920
Frances Louise	Oct. 31, 1923
Gloyd Orland	Feb. 13, 1928
Richard Myron	July 27, 1934

The mother, Venus, was born Aug. 18, 1900

THEODORE WAYNE TRUBEY

Theodore Wayne Trubey, third son of B. A. and Zeruia C. Trubey was born in Sherwood, Defiance County, Ohio on February 7, 1902. He came with his parents to Montana in 1917 where he finished his educatino in Forsyth, Montana. Adopting a musical career as his work he became an expert at the piano. On September 27, 1930 he was married to Mrs. Margaret Hooper James in Casper, Wyoming. She was born in Illinois on January 5, 1900, and is also a fine musician. They have itinerated through ten or twelve of the western and Pacific states under the name of Margaret and Wayne.

APPENDIX A 309

JUSTIN ALONZO TRUBEY

Justin Alonzo Trubey, second son of John and Lydia Moore Trubey, was born in Defiance County, Ohio, near the town of Jewell, on Oct. 1st, 1861. He grew up on the farm where he was born. Attended the district schools of Richland township, Defiance County, Ohio. He helped on the farm until his majority, then took a Business course at Fayette Ohio Business College. Worked as Brakeman on the Nickel Plate Railroad for a short while. Also was engaged in Apriary or Bee Business with Israel Parker for several years. Afterwards with his brother A. E. Trubey, in 1887 they took over the home farm and operated it for four or five years. J. A. then withdrew from the farm and went to Norwalk, Ohio and worked on the Wheeling and Lake Erie Railroad as Brakeman for a short season. He then returned to the farm until the spring of 1897, when he purchased the Elliott stock of goods in Jewell where he done business for about eight years. In 1909 he came to Ann Arbor and engaged in the Ice Cream and Cafe business both wholesale and retail.

Subsequently he was joined in wedlock on Sept. 1887 to Miss Sarah Jane Kimberly of Jewell, Ohio. She was born Dec. 1, 1866. To them were born five children, two boys and three girls, namely:

Claude Eugene	March 18, 1888
Mary Leona	Sept. 5, 1890
Harold Dorwin	July 25, 1896
Mildred Fay	May 20, 1902
Marguerite Lois	Aug. 1, 1910

Mr. Trubey held the Post office as Postmaster for a little over nine years, at Jewell, Ohio. He belonged to the Masonic order and was a member of the Trinity Lutheran Church and lived a good christian life with faith in Jesus Christ as his Savior.

Justin Alonzo Trubey left this world of turmoil and strife on Dec. 16, 1933 at the age of 72 years, 2 months and 15 days.

MARY LEONA TRUBEY, oldest daughter of Justin Alonzo and Sarah Jane Kimberly Trubey, was born at Jewell, Ohio on Sept. 5, 1890. She married Chauncy O. Rodgers at Ann Arbor, Michigan on Nov. 12, 1913. Mr. Rodgers was born in Gallia County, Ohio on Oct. 21, 1884. To this union were born three girls and one boy, viz:

Marian Evelyn	April 13, 1915
Harry Franklyn	July 7, 1918
Jane Elizabeth	June 12, 1924
Betty Ruth	Dec. 10, 1925

Marian Evelyn Rodgers was married to George Geal Nov. 11, 1933. Children born to this union are:

Marilyn Eva	July 3, 1934
Roger William	May 28, 1939

Harry Franklin was married to Miriam Evans. One child has been born to them:

Gary Alan	Nov. 18, 1941

Jane Elizabeth married Albert Thomas on November 1, 1941. A premature baby was born to them on Feb. 1, 1942 and died March 5, 1942.

APPENDIX A

HAROLD DORWIN TRUBEY

Harold Dorwin Trubey, second son of Justin A. and Sarah Jane Trubey was born in the home on the home farm near Jewell, Ohio, on July 25, 1896. Received most of his education in Ann Arbor, having come *their* with his parents.

He was married to Miss Elsie Laura Aprill in Monroe, Michigan on April 9, 1917. Miss Aprill was born Feb. 3, 1896. To them were born two sons and one daughter, viz:

Dorwin Melvin	March 28, 1918
Robert Emanuel	Jan. 28, 1925
Barbara Jane	July 21, 1932

Harold *is* a candy and ice cream maker for a number of years, working for his father, then the McDonald Co. at date Sept. 20, 1942.

Dorwin Melvin Trubey was married to Agnes Vosnik on Sept. 5, 1937. They have two children:

Marguerite Ann	April 6, 1938
Russell Dorwin	Nov. 22, 1940

MILDRED GAY TRUBEY

Mildred Fay Trubey, second daughter of J. A. and Sarah J. Trubey, was born in Jewell, Ohio, May 20, 1902. She came with her parents to Ann Arbor when about seven years of age. Was educated in Ann Arbor schools. She was wedded to Harold I. Simpson Sept. 21, 1921, who was born July 9, 1900. To them were born three sons, viz:

William Robert	Sept. 21, 1922
James Norman	Jan. 18, 1924
John Richard	July 17, 1929

MARGUERITE LOIS TRUBEY

Marguerite Lois Trubey, third daughter of J. A. and Sarah Jane Trubey was born Aug. 1, 1910 in Ann Arbor, Michigan. She was married to Franklin Richard Gervick on July 12, 1941. They have one son:

Richard Trubey Gervick   April 16, 1942

APPENDIX A   313

AMBROSE ENYART TRUBEY

Ambrose Enyart Trubey, the third son of John and Lydia Moore Trubey was born September 5th, 1863 near Jewell, Ohio, Defiance County, Ohio. He was married to Catherine Osborn on April 28th, 1887. To this union were born three sons and one daughter, named:

Emmet Ellsworth	Dec. 31, 1887
Howard Alonzo	Aug. 17, 1889
(he died Sept. 15, 1911)	
Alva Morris	Sept. 11, 1891
Ethel Donelda	Dec. 29, 1896

Ambrose E. has lived all his life in Defiance County, Ohio. He was township clerk of Richland Township for a number of years. He was also Secretary of Jewell Grain Company both of which he served with honor and faithfulness.

EMMETT ELLSWORTH TRUBEY, son of Ambrose E. and Catharine Osborn Trubey was born Dec. 31, 1887 in Jewell, Defiance County, Ohio. He was married to Mary Ann Minsl June 14, 1909, and to them was born one daughter and one son:

Ermah Udette	Oct. 14, 1910
Ambrose Elsworth	July 9, 1917

Ermah U. was wedded to Lenwood B. West on May 26, 1928. They have one daughter named:

Eileen Mary	Oct. 6, 1929

Mr. Lenwood B. West was born Feb. 6, 1905.

Ambrose Elsworth was married to Jeanne Davidson on Oct. 26, 1940. The wife was born Feb. 25, 1919.

67

DANIEL TRUBEY

Daniel Trubey was the third son of Daniel and Mary Stoner Trubey. He was born June 7, 1824 in Franklin County, Pennsylvania. He settled in Henry County, Ohio. He was drafted for the Civil War and served to the end. He sold his property in Henry County and moved to Nebraska and raised a crop in 1872. In the fall of 1872, he went to Kansas. While he was in Nebraska, he rented a home from Uncle Jake Yantiss (his brother-in-law). He first lived in Jewell County, and in a few years went to the adjoining County, which was Mitchell. He was a member of the Seventh Day Advent Church, and lived a christian life.

He was married November 14, 1852 to Esther Drusilla Heath. Unto this union were born eight children, six boys and two girls, viz:

Joseph Andrew	Nov. 13, 1853
Mary Jane	Sept. 9, 1855
John A.	Jan. 13, 1858
Lewis Frances	June 2, 1860
Melissa Ann	Jan. 29, 1862
Daniel A.	June 2, 1864
David C.	Oct. 4, 1866
George A.	Nov. 22, 1872

Daniel Trubey died September 10, 1910 at the age of eighty-six years, three months, and three days.

Esther Drusilla Heath, his wife, was born July 17, 1831. She departed from life on Oct. 11, 1903 at the age of seventy-one years, and three months.

APPENDIX A

JOSEPH ANDREW TRUBEY

Joseph Andrew Trubey, first son and child of Daniel and Esther Heath Trubey, was born in Indiana near Huntington, on November 13, 1853. He later moved with his parents to Henry County, Ohio, where he lived and grew up. When eighteen years of age, he with his parents emigrated to Nebraska and Kansas in the year of 1872. On June 13, 1875 he was married to Miss Saphronia Day, who was born August 12, 1853. To them two children were born:

William Joshua	March 4, 1877
Addie E.	Jan. 10, 1880

Joseph Andrew lived in California where he was foreman in a Smelter. Afterwards he moved to Santa Cruz, California where he engaged in poultry raising. Having more than 1000 white leghorn hens at a time.

Joseph Andrew passed from this mortal strife on September 11, 1933, at the age of 79 years, 9 months and 28 days.

Saphronia Trubey, his wife, is still living. On November 5, 1941, was 88 years old.

WILLIAM JOSHUA TRUBEY, only son of Joseph Andrew and Saphronia Day Trubey, was born on March 4, 1877. He married Mary Rodgers on May 20, 1898. One son blessed this union, viz:

Andrew Franklin   1900.

ADDIE E. TRUBEY GRUBB, only daughter of Joseph Andrew Trubey was born January 10, 1880. She was married to Harry Thompson Grubb, Aug. 10, 1902. To them were born one daughter:

    Edna Ethel Grubb   June 4, 1903

Addie E. Trubey Grubb lives at Angwin, California.

Edna Ethel Grubb married a Mr. Williamson on January 1, 1922. One daughter was born to this union, in San Francisco, California.

    Dorothy Marrian Williamson Sept.17, 1923

Edna Ethel was born in Oakland, California.

APPENDIX A

JOHN ALLEN TRUBEY

John Allen Trubey, second son of Daniel and Esther Trubey, was born in Henry County, Ohio, on January 13, 1858. He moved with his parents to Nebraska, then to Glen Elden, Kansas in the year of 1872. There he met Sarah Adaline Morgan, who was born October 6, 1863, and they were joined in holy wedlock on Oct. 6, 1881. To them were born two sons and three daughters, viz:

Jesse Freeman	April 27, 1883
Carrie Lovena	June 13, 1887
Loraine Esther	March 22, 1896
Leila Ethel	Feb. 24, 1898
Chester Edwin	Aug. 5, 1899

JESSE FREEMAN TRUBEY

Jesse Freeman Trubey, the first son of John A. and Sarah A. Morgan Trubey, was born April 27, 1883 and was married to Mabel Irene Sample on October 8, 1906. To them were born six children, names as follows:

Lester Charles	Jan. 18, 1908
Marie Leha	Aug. 26, 1909
Beulah	Oct. 21, 1913
Rita Esther	March 22, 1915
Amos Calvin	Sept. 18, 1923
Ila Dorlean	Aug. 15, 1927

Lester Charles was married to Nonomie Stringer on September 4, 1932.

Beulah Trubey was wedded to Alvin W. Doubt on September 18, 1931.

CARRIE LOVENA TRUBEY

Carrie Lovena Trubey, first daughter of John A. and Sarah A. Trubey was born June 13, 1887 and was wedded to Clarence A. Hogeland on December 22, 1909. To this union were born one son and one daughter, named:

Vesta Lovena	Sept. 20, 1912
Raymond Clarence	Oct. 19, 1915

Vesta Lovena died January 20, 1926. The mother, Carrie Lovena, passed away on March 27, 1937, at the age of 50 years, 2 months and 14 days.

LORAINE ESTHER TRUBEY

Loraine Esther Trubey, second daughter of John A. and Sarah A. Trubey was born in Kansas on March 22, 1896. She was married to Leonard C. Kidney on April 30, 1917. To this union were born two children.

Donald Leonard	Aug. 18, 1918
Margaret Adeline	Sept. 25, 1924

LEILA ETHEL TRUBEY

Leila Ethel Trubey, third daughter of John A. and Sarah A. Trubey, was born February 24, 1898. She was married to Joseph Bratten, June 21, 1930. Two children blessed this union.

Paul Joseph	Oct. 28, 1932
Dorlean Lavon	June 25, 1937

CHESTER EDWIN TRUBEY

Chester Edwin Trubey, second son of John A. and Sarah A. Trubey was born in Kansas, Aug. 5, 1899 and was wedded to Miss Elsie Cook, March 17, 1924. One child was born to this union.

Dona Rose Trubey	Jan. 13, 1927

APPENDIX A

LEWIS FRANCIS TRUBEY

Lewis Francis Trubey, son of Daniel and Esther Heath Trubey, was born June 2, 1860 in Henry County, Ohio. When he was twelve years old, he moved with his parents in the year of 1872 to Nebraska and then to Kansas where he grew to manhood and was married on Nov. 1, 1885 to Lovina Amanda Dudley, who was born March 29, 1867. To them were born five children, three sons and two daughters, viz:

    William Mahlon   Oct. 16, 1886
      deceased Nov. 24, 1894, at the age of 8 years, 1 month, and 8 days.

    Myrtle Edna   May 21, 1889
    James Cyrenus   Feb. 25, 1893
      departed from this life Nov. 14, 1894 at the age of one year, 8 mo., and 19 days.

    Lewis Edward   Feb. 16, 1898
    Emma Grace   Jan. 25, 1900

Lewis Francis Trubey died Jan. 25, 1942, aged 81 years, 7 months and 23 days.

MYRTLE EDNA TRUBEY was joined in wedlock on May 25, 1913 to Mr. Martens. Their children:

    Hilda Emma Grace   April 10, 1914
    Nellia A.   Aug. 13, 1915
      not married to date
    Berhend Henry   Feb. 9, 1917
      not married to date

Hilda Emma Grace is married to Patrick Jenovese and they are both doctors. They were married May 25, 1938 and live in Los Angeles, California.

LEWIS EDWARD TRUBEY, son of Lewis Francis Trubey, married Munil Osborn on May 7, 1917. Six children blessed this union, viz:

Lewis Merle	Feb.	24, 1918
Charles Francis	Nov.	20, 1923
Shirley Maxine	Jan.	29, 1925
Lovina Amanda	Sept.	28, 1926
William Leslie	Oct.	16, 1926
Myrtle Carolyn	Nov.	24, 1920

EMMA GRACE TRUBEY

Emma Grace Trubey Schee was born January 25, 1900, and married June 28, 1922. She is the mother of four children.

Leland Burlette	Oct.	23, 1923
Virginia Arnell	Sept.	30, 1925
Evelyn Lenore	Oct.	15, 1930
James Robert	Apr.	29, 1937

MELISSA ANN TRUBEY

Melissa Ann Trubey, second daughter of Daniel and Esther Heath Trubey was born Jan. 29, 1862 in Henry County, Ohio. When ten years old, she moved with her parents to Nebraska and then to Kansas, where she grew up to womanhood. She was joined in Holy Matrimony to B. F. Hutchison on February 25, 1885.

To this union were born six children, four boys and two girls.

MELISSA ANN TRUBEY

MELISSA ANN TRUBEY, second daughter of Daniel and Esther Heath Trubey, was born in Henry County, Ohio, January 29, 1862. She moved with her parents in 1872 to Nebraska, then to Kansas where she grew to womanhood. She was joined in Holy Matrimony to Benjamin F. Hutchinson on February 25, 1885. To this union were born six children, four boys and two girls, viz:

David Guy Hutchinson, born Sept. 1, 1886. He married Lillian Kennedy. They have two children, Rolland and Esther Hutchinson Holloway.

Mabel Hutchinson Swindler, born in Kansas on Oct. 15, 1888. Married Samuel Swindler. No children were born to this union.

Harry O. Hutchinson, born in Kansas on Oct. 9, 1890. Wedded Guinivieve De Fehr. No children were born to this union.

George Hutchinson, born December 30, 1892. He married Madge Service. Two children were born to them, namely,

Nancy "married"
Maybelle

Benjamin Franklin Hutchinson was born Dec. 3, 1898. He married Verda Holloway on June 25, 1921. Two children blessed this union,
Wilbur Edgar born April 3, 1922
Wilma Lorraine born Feb. 26, 1929

Hazel Hutchinson was born January 25, 1901. She married Harry Chimock. They have three children:
Dorothy Elois
Romayne
Hazel

DAVID C. TRUBEY

David C. Trubey, fifth son of Daniel and Esther Heath Trubey, was born on June 2, 1866, in Henry County, Ohio. He went with his parents to Nebraska and Kansas in 1872, where he grew to manhood. On November 9, 1892, he was joined in Holy Wedlock to Miss Lulie A. Pratt, who was born Sept. 19, 1871. To this union nine children were born, viz:

Ethel G.	Oct.	9, 1893
Clarence O.	May	11, 1895
Hazel Trubey	Nov.	14, 1897
she died Sept. 9, 1898.		
Floyd L.	Dec.	6, 1898
Florence J.	Oct.	4, 1900
Violet A.	July	7, 1902
Eugene C.	Oct.	14, 1905
Arthur R.	April	30, 1908
Vernon Trubey	July	31, 1911
he passed away the same day.		

Mr. Trubey was a photographer in his early life. When his family became of such proportions, he turned to farming, to give his children a wholesome and healthy living, close to nature and close to God. He also taught Vocal Music in his community, and worked in his community for its welfare and advancement in good Citizenship.

ETHEL G. TRUBEY, eldest daughter of David and Lulie A. Trubey was born Oct. 9, 1893. She was joined in wedlock on Sept. 3, 1927 to E. V. Poole of Occola, Florida. They had one son,

Dalton H. Poole   Feb. 14, 1929

CLARENCE O. TRUBEY, first son of David C. and L. A. Trubey was born in Mitchell County, Kansas at Glen Elder, on May 11, 1895. Here he grew up, finished high school, and was graduated from Hill Academy at Downs, Kansas in 1915.

He taught the district school near his home

APPENDIX A 323

near Glen Elder in winter of 1915 and 1916, and in 1916 and 1917 he attended the Clinton German Seminary at Clinton, Missouri. From May 28, 1918 to July 25, 1919, he was in the army at Camp Lewis, Washington. May 8, 1919, he was married to Miss Helen Richert and both taught school together the following winter. The next year he went to college taking a pre-medical course, expecting to become a Doctor. But because of his wife's death, his finances precluded his fulfillment of desire and caused him to return to the profession of teaching. Then continued in that work for 20 years, being principal for eighteen of the twenty years, at this date Oct. 1941, Mr. Trubey is beginning his eighth year as Principal of Kern Academy at Shefton, California.

Mr. Trubey received his A. B. degree at Pacific Union College at Angwin, California. He also has ½ a Conservatory Course in Music besides his regular college work. Among other subjects he has taught Chorus, Band, Orchestra, and directed Church Choirs.

His first child, a daughter, died at birth, the second, a son, Orville by name, was born Nov. 5, 1921, by a Caesarean operation. The mother, Helen, surviving the ordeal one week. Then she passed on, Nov. 12, 1921.

On April 7, Mr. Trubey was again married to Elizabeth Voth. Three children were the fruit of this union.

Betty Jean	Feb. 13, 1924
Merlin Delmar	Aug. 6, 1925
Norman Dalton	Dec. 27, 1926

All of the above named children are accomplished Musicians under the direction of their father.

FLOYD L. TRUBEY, second son of D. C. and L. A. Trubey, was born Dec. 6, 1898. He married Mae Miller on May 30, 1921 at Delta, Colorado.

77

They have four children, viz:

Freddy Roy	May 7, 1932
David Clarence	Dec. 30, 1936
Norman Lee	July 14, 1934
Gladys	June 29, 1939

FLORENCE J. TRUBEY, daughter of D. C. and L. A. Trubey, was born Oct. 6, 1900. She was wedded to W. V. Greene on May 31, 1930, at Hendersonville, North Carolina. One daughter was born to them.

Novella Yvonere	Jan. 3, 1936

VIOLET A. TRUBEY, daughter of D. C. and L. A. Trubey was born July 7, 1902 and was married to A. V. Acuff on August 31, 1929, at Largo, Florida. Three children were born to this union, viz:

Loretta	Feb. 17, 1932
Norma Lee	Apr. 2, 1933
Roy Sylvanus	Oct. 21, 1938

EUGENE C. TRUBEY, third son of D. C. and Lulie A. Trubey was born Oct. 4, 1905 and was married to Mattie Lee Johnson on July 3, 1927, at Fort Valley, Georgia. Two daughters were born to this union.

Mary Ann	Feb. 19, 1926
Janey Lee	June 15, 1928

ARTHUR R. TRUBEY, fourth son of D. C. and L. A. Trubey was born April 30, 1908. He was wedded to Alma Abeney at Hendersonville, North Carolina. They are the parents of three children.

Claude Trubey	April 8, 1929
Dennis Lavaun	Aug. 5, 1930
Gail	May 1, 1931

GEORGE ABRAHAM TRUBEY

George Abraham Trubey, sixth son of Daniel and Esther Heath Trubey was born in Kansas on Nov. 22, 1872. He was married to Mary Bella Altimus, June 20, 1900. Mrs. Mary Bella Trubey was born January 7, 1878. To them were born three sons and three daughters, viz:

Ruth	Aug. 19, 1904
Bernardene	Sept. 5, 1909
Kenneth D.	June 1, 1912
Vernon C.	Sept. 7, 1914
Dale H.	March 30, 1919
Marguerite L.	July 25, 1922

RUTH TRUBEY was married to Roy Van Wey on July 30, 1924. Mr. Van Wey was born July 24, 1897. They are the parents of three children, viz:

Virgil	Aug. 1, 1924
Virginia	Jan. 10, 1928
Marjory	March 29, 1932

BERNARDENE TRUBEY was married Sept. 29, 1935 to Austin Neifert, who was born July 12, 1910. To date March 1942, one son blesses this union, namely:

Dennis	May 17, 1938

KENNETH D. TRUBEY was married to Monsolete Alcorn on July 5, 1937. She was born April 25, 1918. Who to date March 1942 have one son:

Kenneth Doye	June 18, 1938

VERNON C. TRUBEY married Genevieve Stiles on August 3, 1933. She was born April 24, 1915. They are the parents of one daughter, namely:

Joyce L.   May   20, 1934

Dale H. and Marguerite L. Trubey are both single.

NANCY TRUBEY

Nancy Trubey was born in Franklin County, Pennsylvania on September 4, 1826, the second daughter of Daniel and Mary Trubey. At the age of eight years, with her parents, she moved to Stark County, Ohio, in the year of 1834. Then in the year 1847, with her parents, she went to Huntington County, Indiana. In the year of 1849 she was married to Jacob Yantiss. After about eighteen years of marriage, they then moved to Nebraska in the year of 1867.

Unto this union eight children were born.

Melissa	Daniel D.
George W.	infant daughter who
Landon	died at birth.
Joseph Jackson	Elizabeth
Effie Deloris	

Nancy Trubey Yantiss's death was caused by an accident. Mr. and Mrs. Yantiss had been to the cemetery to fix up Grandma's and their daughter Effie's grave. On their way home, the horse became frightened, throwing her out on her head unconscious. She died on Sept. 30, 1992 at the age of sixty-six years and twenty-six days. She was buried in Silver Creek cemetery, Richardson County, Nebraska.

JACOB YANTISS

Jacob Yantiss was born Oct. 8, 1817 in Frederick County, Maryland. He lived in Guernsey County, Ohio and then moved to Indiana in 1847. He was married to Nancy Trubey in 1849 and they moved to Nebraska in 1867. He had two sons by a former marriage named John I. and Theudas. John Yantiss was in the Civil War with Abraham Trubey and died a year after he did.

Jacob Yantiss died at the age of seventy-nine years, six months and eight days, on April 16, 1897.

THE CHILDREN OF JACOB AND NANCY TRUBEY YANTISS

MELISSA YANTISS, the first child of Nancy and Jacob Yantiss was born in Huntington County, August 29, 1851. With her parents she moved to Nebraska in 1867 and in the year of 1871 she was married to E. D. Heyde on November 9. They moved to Kansas, then to North Dakota, then to Smith County, Kansas, then to Illinois in 1901. She died April 23, 1932 and was buried in Silver Creek cemetery. To this union were born four girls and one boy. Her children are all gone except the youngest daughter who is a nurse in Saint Louis, unmarried. E. D. Heyde died Jan. 25, 1933, at the age of 93 years and 10 months. The Heyde family all rest in Silver Creek cemetery.

GEORGE W. YANTISS, the second child of Nancy Trubey Yantiss and Jacob Yantiss was born in Huntington County, Indiana, on March 1, 1853. With his parents, he moved to Nebraska in 1867. He moved to Smith County, Kansas in 1873, then to Sheridan County, Kansas in 1901. His occupation was cattle raising and farming. He was never married. He died in Long Island, Kansas (at his niece's Mrs. Bessie Young's) at the age of 83 years, six months and six days, on January 7, 1937. Funeral services at the M. E. Church. Interment in Long Island cemetery beside his brother Joe, with whom he lived most of his life and who preceded him in death only a few years.

LANDON YANTISS, the third child of Nancy Trubey Yantiss and Jacob Yantiss, was born in Huntington, Indiana, November 26, 1854. With his parents he moved to Nebraska in 1867. In 1901 he moved to Long Island, Phillips County, Kansas, and was married to Mary Merriam on Jan. 8, 1876. Born to this union were three sons, one dying in infancy. The eldest son died in 1937. They were all members of the M.E. Church. In 1908 he made a trip to Jerusalem Palestine in company with his brother-in-law E. D. Heyde to see the country and historical places of our Lord and Savior and to see his brother Daniel, who had gone there two years previous. He departed this life January 18, 1935 at the age of 80 years, 1 month, and 20 days.

JOSEPH JACKSON YANTISS, the fourth child of Nancy Trubey Yantiss and Jacob Yantiss was born June 26, 1857 in Huntington County, Ind. With his parents, he moved to Nebraska in 1867, to Smith County, Kansas in 1890. He then moved to Sheridan County in 1900. He never married. He and George lived together most of their lives until about two years before his passing when he came to Norton to be close to medical aid. He died at Norton, Kansas, June 23, 1934. He was buried in Long Island cemetery. Funeral was from the M. E. Church.

DANIEL D. YANTISS, the fifth child of Nancy Trubey and Jacob Yantiss, was born in Huntington County, Indiana on July 29, 1859, and with his parents moved to Nebraska in 1867. He then moved to Smith County, Kansas in 1890. In 1896 he went to Jerusalem Palestine. He married Lilly Meyers at Verdon, Nebraska. Three children were born to this union, one son and two daughters. He died June 17, 1910 in Jerusalem Palestine. The son of this man and his family came to the States in July 1938 and now are in California. His daughters and family are still in Palestine and they never lost their citizenship.

THE SIXTH CHILD was a daughter and died at birth, June 10, 1861.

ELIZABETH YANTISS, the seventh child of Nancy Trubey Yantiss and Jacob Yantiss, was born Nov. 25, 1863, in Huntington County, Ind. and with her parents moved to Nebraska in 1867. On November 1, 1883 she was married to J. W. Stump at Falls City, Nebraska. She moved to Phillips County, Kansas in 1913. In 1920 she went to Glen Elder, Mitchell County, Kansas, to care for Uncle Abe Trubey the rest of his life. In 1930 she and her husband went back

83

to Phillips County, and in March 1931 they moved to a farm in Harlem County, Nebraska, where her husband passed away May 4, 1931. Unto this union were born two sons and four daughters.

EFFIE DELORIS YANTISS, the eighth child of Nancy Trubey Yantiss and Jacob Yantiss, was born January 14, 1866 in Huntington County, Indiana. With her family, she moved to Nebraska in 1867. She was never married. She died at the age of twenty-five years, six months, and twenty-seven days and was buried in Silver Creek cemetery, Richardson County, Nebraska. She was a member of the M. E. Church.

QUINTON SYLVESTOR STUMP

Quinton Sylvestor Stump, son of J. W. and Elizabeth Stump, was born at Verdun, Nebraska, July 17, 1885. He finished high school in the same town, then began clerking in a general store. He was a member of the Congregational Church. He was married to Miss Nellie Cunningham at Verdun, Nebraska in Oct. of 1906. An infant son, who died at birth, was born to this union. Quinton passed away January 23, 1912 of Pleura Pneumonia at the age of 26 years 6 months and 6 days. He was buried in Verdun Cemetery by the side of his infant son.

BESSIE ETHEL STUMP

Bessie Ethel Stump, daughter of J. W. and Elizabeth Stump, was born at Verdun, Richardson County, Nebraska on the 20th day of September of 1886. She completed her education at high school at Verdun, in her 16th year. She attended Business College at Falls City, Neb. in 1907 and 1908. She attended W. N. College at Shenandoah, Iowa in 1910 and taught school in 1910 and 1911. She worked in a telephone office for five years. She united with the Congregational Church at Verdun, and was married to Ira C. Young of Long Island, Kansas on March 15, 1911 at her parents' residence at Verdun. Two daughters were born to this union, viz:

    Ruth
    Inez
    Their vocation was a vanity store.

GRACIE STUMP

Gracie Stump, third child of J. W. and Elizabeth Stump was born at Verdun, Nebraska on May 9, 1888, and died Sept. 25, 1888, aged four months and 16 days. She was buried in Silver Creek Cemetery.

JENNIE ESTHER STUMP

Jennie Esther Stump, fourth child of J. W. and Elizabeth Yantiss Stump, was born at Verdun,

Richardson County, Nebraska on July 1, 1891. She united with the Congregational Church at Verdun, Nebraska on Easter Sunday in 1905. She finished high school in her 14th year. She worked in telephone office for several years and later was made manager for one year, then clerked in a general merchandise store for three years. Later, she moved to Long Island, Kansas, where she was married to Mr. William H. Reece of Long Island. His occupation was farming. No children were born to this union.

CLARENCE ALBERT STUMP

Clarence Albert Stump, fifth child of J. W. and Elizabeth Yantiss Stump was born at Verdun, Richardson County, Nebraska on the 22nd day of June in 1894. He completed his high school education at Verdun, later moving to Long Island, Kansas, from which place he enlisted in the World War. Serving his country overseas throughout the duration of the war, and returning from the war, he was married to Wilma Halderman of Long Island, Kansas. On June 23, 1923, one son, Gerald Stump, was born to this union. Mr. Stump is engaged in farming and is substitute mail carrier.

GEORGIA DELORIS STUMP

Georgia Deloris Stump, sixth child of J. W. and Elizabeth Yantiss Stump was born at Verdun, Richardson County, Nebraska on the 9th day of September 1896. She attended and completed her education at the same place and was a member of the Congregational Church at Verdun. Later, she changed to the Methodist Church at Long Island, Kansas. She worked in a printing office in 1912 and 1913 at Long Island and taught two terms of school. She was married to Harry W. Porfser of Long Island, Kansas on March 29, 1916. A daughter, Lucille, and a son, Loyle, were born to this union. Mr. Porfser is engaged in farming.

APPENDIX A 333

REBECCA TRUBEY

Rebecca Trubey, the daughter of Daniel and Mary Trubey, was born December 15, 1829. She was married to John Mohn in the year of 1852. To them were born three sons and three daughters.

John Frederick	March 25, 1854
Mary Jane	Nov. 21, 1856
Elizabeth	March 5, 1859
Amanda Catherine	Dec. 28, 1861
Daniel Andrew	June 15, 1864
Charles Godfrey	Oct. 24, 1867

John Frederick Mohn was married and had a couple of children. Record of them is not obtainable. John Frederick is dead, exact date is not mentioned. He died in Peru, Ind.

Mary Jane Mohn was married to John Dille, July 21, 1878. John Dille was born Nov. 18, 1857. To this union were born five children.

Dessie B.	March 31, 1879
Chester B.	July 31, 1880
Eva R.	Jan. 28, 1882
Mayme P.	Feb. 27, 1885
Arnold F.	Jan. 8, 1887
(he died 6 months later)	

Eva Dille was married to Archibald Y. Lyon. Mr. Lyon was born April 21, 1873. John Dille passed on about the year 1833.

Elizabeth Mohn was married to Alexander Hazen on June 12, 1897, and passed away on November 12, 1922, leaving no children.

Amanda Catherine Mohn was married. The date and name are unknown. Her husband and children are dead. She lives at present, Jan. 12, 1941 in Los Angeles, California.

87

Daniel Andrew Mohn was married, and was a barber in Florida. He died March 5, 1898 in Toledo, Ohio at the age of 33 years, 8 months, and 20 days.

Charles Godfrey Mohn married and has no children. He lives at present in Inglewood, California.

John Mohn was born in Baden Baden, Germany in the year of 1818 and died May 17, 1895 in his seventy seventh year.

Rebecca Trubey Mohn died June 19, 1909 at the age of seventy-nine years, 6 months, and four days.

SAMUEL TRUBEY

Samuel Trubey was born in Waynesboro, Franklin County, Pennsylvania, the fourth son of Mary and Daniel Trubey, on January 22, 1831. He enlisted in the Union army in 1861 at the age of thirty years. He became missing and was never heard of afterwards.

APPENDIX A 335

MARY ANN TRUBEY

Mary Ann Trubey, the daughter of Daniel and Mary Trubey was born April 9, 1833. She was married to Andrew J. Schofield on March 21, 1853. To this union were born five children.

Helen Susanna	April 10, 1854 died Oct. 1, 1862
Nelson Edgar	Feb. 28, 1856 died June 20, 1864
Elizabeth Jane	May 10, 1858 died Sept. 19, 1862
Mary Emily	Aug. 23, 1861 died Sept. 12, 1862

Effie Savilla Scofield was born June 11, 1863 and was married to Abraham Lincoln Lose on January 9, 1887. She was the mother of three daughters.

Effie is the only child living of A. J. and Mary Ann Trubey Scofield at this date, March 14, 1941.

Mary Ann Trubey Scofield died on September 15, 1865 in Florida, Ohio at the age of 32 years, 5 months and six days.

ABRAHAM TRUBEY

Abraham Trubey was born July 20, 1835 in Stark County, Ohio, the youngest son of Mary and Daniel Trubey. He was the ninth child. When twelve years of age, with his parents, he moved to Huntington County, Indiana. In his early life, he taught school in the State of Indiana. In 1861, he enlisted in the Union army and served the entire duration of the Civil War. In 1871 he homesteaded in Jewell County, Kansas, spending the remainder of his life in that state. On August 10, 1887, he was united in marriage to Mrs. M. M. Knight, who died in 1915. He was converted and united with the Free Methodist Church in 1895, and continued a faithful member until death. He was a loyal and consistent christian, deeply interested in the work of the Lord, to which he gave liberally. His last public testimony, just before he died was clear and definite as to the saving grace of God and as the end drew near, he expressed himself willing and ready to go. He died April 20, 1922 at the age of eighty-six years and nine months at the home of Mr. and Mrs. J. W. Stump of Glen Elder, Kansas, with whom he lived for over two years.

He was a man who loved to travel. In 1913 he and his wife made a visit to relatives in Ohio. In 1916, after his wife's death he made another trip to Ohio. In 1918, he made a visit to Montana to his nephew, B. A. Trubey. He was a member of the G. A. R. and attended most of the annual conventions. He was a very intelligent and friendly person and all those loved him with whom he came in contact.

ELIZABETH TRUBEY

Elizabeth Trubey was the fifth daughter of Daniel and Mary Trubey and was born in Stark County, Ohio on November 19, 1838. She was married to George Eebolt Long on December 19, 1858. To this union were born seven children,

```
William Henry              March 15, 1860
George (died in infancy)   May   21, 1863
Franklin                   March 29, 1865
  (died about 1868 or 1869)
Charles Russel             July  13, 1869
  (he died Dec. 18, 1942, aged 73 yrs, 5
  mo. and 5 days)
Herman                     April  1, 1872
Nettie and twin brother              1875
```

Mrs. Elizabeth Trubey Long died July 27, 1878 at the age of 39 years, 8 months and 8 days.

Mr. G. B. Long, after marrying again died February 26, 1898.

CATHARINE TRUBEY

Catharine Trubey was born in Stark County, Ohio July 7, 1843. She married Frank B. Carr on June 5, 1869. They were married by Rev. W. V. Thomas, a Baptist minister. Five children were born to them, two sons and three daughters.

Charles R.	1871
E. William	Aug. 8, 1874
Nettie	
Eugenie	Apr. 15, 1877
Pansy	

Catharine Trubey Carr departed this life on November 15, 1914 at Denver, Colorado at the age of 71 years, 4 months and 8 days.

APPENDIX B 339

[Letter #1]

7 Aug 1847

David Truby
Finlay, Hancock Co., Ohio

Dear Brother,

I am now have the opportunity to inform you that we are all well at present for as I know except myself I have had the ague about five days. Every day before I got it stopped and I hope when these few lines will come to hand that they may find yours all enjoying good health. And John has come back from the West the first of June last and he has been boating a boat two weeks and then he and I got to building a coalboat [canal boat?] for Mr. Hunt and have commenced it the 20th of June and finished on the 28 of July and a few days before it got done I was taken sick with the ague and haven't been doing anything since. And I was living at Mr Hunt's and I don't know what kind of work I get at next and I sometimes think that I will buy a boat and go boating so I don't know what I will get at next and maybe I may take the notion of coming out there to see <u>they</u> folks and the country and I have sold my colt to Harvey Hunt for $55 for his note due the first of October and the note that you have against me Mother want to have let it go towards that money et [?] you got from her if you will and she would like to know what you are agoing to <u>due</u> about it and we would take up you would sent us a answer as soon as you can. We would like to know all about the country whether <u>they</u> would be a good chance to buy land or not. Mother is talking of coming out there to live with you and if she gets her third she wants to buy herself a home and <u>the</u> haven't got my money, only two hundred dollars and Kindler won't pay the rest not until the mortgage is settled. Mother won't give <u>they</u> deed till she gets her third. Father, he is still <u>they</u> same old sixpence over he could not catch up as he thought he could so he put out down to Sugar Creek as I spose you knew that they had moved to Mr. Hunt's. John went down to Sugar Creek and Rebecca and Elizabeth and Abraham is to Welty's yet. I believe as this is all that I have to write at present. Daniel Trubey

David Truby

Brother and sister, I would like to see you very much. I have no particular <u>knews</u> to write to you and I would like to know how you are getting along and how you like the country. Be this time and I would like to know how your <u>dauter</u> [Arabella] is getting along. I am still living to Mr. Hunt's yet and still remain single yet it appears that some folks was good deal alarmed about me getting married. It is very sickly again I have nothing more in particular at present. I hope you will write soon, so I remain your affectionate sister, my best respects to you all.
Nancy Trubey.

APPENDIX B 341

[Letter #2]

David Trubey, near Ft. Finlay, Hancock County, Ohio
postmark Bolivar, Ohio, Sept 9, year not visible
"In haste" written in circle at bottom

                                                                Stark County, Ohio
                                                                September 5, 1847
                                                                    (Bolivar)

Dear brother and sister,

We will again write to yours hoping that we may be honored enough this time to receive an answer as we have not heard from you by letter more than once which was last winter and that be answered in about three days after receiving it and should answered it sooner but delayed in consequence of our son's Cullen's health as we have stated to you. We <u>where</u> well satisfied to hear from you and that you both liked the country and the anecdote about the turkeys etc which was cheering news to us and on the head of the excitement of your entertaining letter, we wrote of all subjects to you that we thought would be entertaining to you and hoped an answer speeedily but all in vain up to the present. And the cause we do not know, whether from a non-reception or neglect or disrespect but God forbid it not to be through the last mentioned objection. The last we heard from you was about four weeks ago from Absalom Klinker stating that he received a letter from you and that yours <u>where</u> enjoying your natural health and pleased with the country and your little daughter could walk and talk and if we are are not <u>mistaking</u> (Laney?) received a letter from you this summer. You know James is married and your father Trubey sold his farm last spring and intends to move to Henry County, Ohio, and that your father's family is out at Hunt's and cannot move in consequence of them not getting their down money on their farm and that John is back from the West and intends to come out and see you this fall and we calculate to come out this fall if possible but not short of eight weeks from now and we have too much work to leave as Father is building a house this summer and is not near finished yet. And if we come we will bring our cloth along as you know from our letter that we have your cloth since last fall. Relations, we are well at present, our father Welty, too, and of Father Klinker we have not heard for a month. James and wife <u>where</u> well last week, no late news from Absalom or D. Trubeys move than Elizabeth is living with us this summer and

Abraham with Father Welty's and Aunt Mary is as delirious again as she was eight years ago. Now for about two weeks but the remainder of her family is well. But our country is becoming to be sickly this fall. There are a number of cases of chill and intermitting fevers but not many deaths so far but we hope these few lines will find you in good health and spirit. Now as for your boat affairs, we wrote to you that we visited brother and Weaver that they could not pay last fall and that my authority for collecting your money was not sufficient as it was verbal and not written and we wrote to you that if we should collect it, you should send an order but no letter or order appeared. Father Welty went to clear land in June and inquired concerning your money and Hunt told him it was ready and we were still looking for an order but no order came yet. Finally, last week I went out on purpose from a (__) to see what could be done. I discovered that Wheeler and Company hold the boat now and Weaver runs her and brother keeps grocery and I went to Wheeler and Company and they say that they will settle agreeable with the article on an order from you to me specifying that it is for money due on the boat to you, and as soon as I present such authority I can settle but no sooner. Now you may do as you think best. Come yourself or send me an order enclosed in a letter with your name on it.

As for our moving out this fall it is by no means likely, but our coming to visit is likely unless sickness breaks in on us and destroys our calculations as many are sick and daily ( ) taken down. Crops: wheat with us is not good in quantity but mostly in quality, corn is ordinary, oats good, market wheat in Bolivar from 95-98 cents per bushel.

Please do not forget us as we would like to hear from yours, monthly if possible. We cannot contrive why you do not write to us as we answer (each?) you soon. Now I want to know in your letter about the boat. I think it advisable to have it all tended to now as the money may be had but it could not of been had much sooner. No more at present. Then my respects to ( ) brother and our respects and immortal love to you all in family.   J. T. Welty and Phianna

APPENDIX B 343

[Letter #3]

August 7, 1849

Respected brother and sister,

I will inform you at this present time that we are all well at present and I hope when these few lines come to hand they will find you all in the same blessing. I have no particular news to write to you. I have not heard from you so long I thought I must write to you to know how you are getting along. I presume you have heard before now that we have got to Indiana. I had a letter from Daniel last week and he wrote that they were all well. He is afarming now. Father deeded his land to him for maintaining the family. He wrote that the wheat crop failed very much, that he would not get more than they sowed, red sead [?], but the rest of the crops pretty well. Mr. Hunt's wheat turned 8 bushels to 30. Their ___ summer we have ___ this summer it has been quite healthy this summer but the cholera is raging it has got within 8 miles of us and it is very __ bad in Huntington that is 30 miles. I will live to Mr. Hunt's yet, I have been teaching school this summer but it is out now. About a half a mile from home. I like <u>they</u> country very well but girls' wages are not much, from 50 cents to 75. Rebecca has gone to Henry County. I would like to know what you named your son [Erastus]. We have a mile and a half to town. I have nothing more at present but if you will answer these few lines speedily, pleased to excuse my handwriting and spelling. Direct your letter to Montpelier, Blackford County, Indiana. So I remain your respected sister, Nancy Trubey.

P.S. I was in a great hurry when I wrote this.

344   LETTERS

[Letter #4]

Wayne Township, March 10, 1851
Tuscarawas County

Dear David and Keziah,

I received your favor of January last stating that you were all well in compliment I say that we are all well. I was at Welties last week. They are all well. I saw Absalom, they are all well. Our country was not very healthy. Some death took place. Father Swigert died in November, David Wimer (preacher) died about four weeks ago. John Wimer, Esq., died about two weeks ago. Both Wimers were struck with the palsy.

You said in your letter you wished help to buy that land of Absalom's joining you. I gave him the letter to read and __ [?] to him that I would pay him $100 for you next June. He said he would <u>wright</u> to you. If business goes well with me, I may able to give you $50 more next year. I wish to say something about that Brought affair, I think I said that Brought had paid my tax two years out of that money that he had collected of Bowers, it is only one year. I have got through with that land affair with Mr. Bose and Gerber. Mr. Gerber came in and paid me my damage and I paid Bose so all is settled. Nothing new of any importance. Eliza and Catherine [Starner?] were married some time ago. George Nicholas has been unwell since last fall. It is supposed he is consumpted. McFarling merchant at Sandyville is broke up has mad quote it smash [?] of some $40,000. I saw Abraham Taylor since your last and spoke to him concerning that land. He concluded he would be willing to go in for equal share. You must have something done with that land, have the taxes paid and see that the timber is not destroyed. I suppose they think you and James live handy, etc. I wish you and James would go and look at it before your next and say what you think about it. It may be that I will buy Taylor out if he wishes to sell. Still dingle along alone, no help yet, hands ask high wages. Market prices: thread/72, corn/37, teynac/31 [?], butter/10, eggs/[?]. In conclusion, I have thought to stop hoping that you may prosper and your children may be a blessing to you and me. Mother gives her compliments to you all.   Jacob Klinker

to David Trubey

N.B. I told James in his letter I wrote to him that he should write to me how he was likely to get along with his payments. Just put him in mind of it. J.K.

LETTERS

[Letter #5]

Wayne Twp, Tuscarawas County
December 18, 1851

Dear David and Keziah,

I received your favor sometime since which gave me satisfaction to learn that you are all well. I have detained time hoping to see Absalom or Phianna or [Abraham?] Taylor but all in vain. I myself am so much confined to my business that I cannot leave home but in whole I think it good policy to put it off until spring that is saying the sale of Levias' land the offer of George Brought is a sloe [?] one. Land will not fall in price in your country. Absalom told me when I saw him last that he was agoing to pay you a visit in the spring and so says your letter. On his way he is going to see Joanna etc. You complain that Absalom has flew the track in your land bargain. You or I must be mistaken to the price that was talked of. I have it $350 whole sum.

You say your wheat has done poor. My advice to you in farming is to try your luck in corn, rain [?], pork and seep [?] on going for cheese. You said nothing about the concern of Brought, neither did James, in the money lost; answer, we have no special news. I sold my pork on foot, my pork and beef will amount to $100, my wool and sheep last spring amounted about to the same. I have on hand about 1,000 bushels of wheat. Hold on for higher market. I have not many debts, I have no hand, had none since the 12th of August, work hard, feel stout, content and go ahead. I gave up some $50 this fall on your account, thinking you would come to a contract (died on the second Tuesday of October last, that much celebrated K/Coon Weggary. His remains were buried most honorable way. Chaplet to preach his funeral Reuben Wood hymn, "Long live the Constitution, long live equal rights with the people, etc." Peace to his ashes).

I calculate to give you $50 more next spring in case you buy land. Nothing more, we are all well hoping this may find you all well. My respect and compliments of Mother to you all. Forget not to tell James and his wife that we are all well. If it [I?] could be in your presence, say all and see you and your little ones run and play it would be consolation for me. I still remain, once you <u>loose</u> me you will face [?] the loss of a friend. May that day be postponed.   Jacob Klinker
David Trubey

APPENDIX B 347

[Letter #6]

Mr. Daniel Trubey, Florida, Henry County, Ohio
postmarked Huntington, Ind., June 24 [no year]

[hole in letter] June 25, 1852

Dear brother,

I can inform you that we are all well and hoping these few lines will find your ones ( ) same. I received your letter as a lamentation over the loss of my sister-in-law [Sarah Jane (Dougherty) Trubey] for altho I never saw her and hope she is at rest, it is the way we all must go, how [?] soon we do not know. You stated in your letter that John was agoing to get Mother to nurse the child and if she is I think she would better come home with it. Rebecca and Nancy says the would give it suck and if John wants me to keep house for him I will do so or else I will go to Hunt's and Elizabeth won't stay by herself so I think you better send Mother or Catherine home. I will stand good for Father that he will use her as well as lays in his power. He has quit drinking and wants to join church. Therefore, he wish to see Mother. Weary lad but for I do not know [?] and what is to be done we do not know. We are out of meat and the cow is almost dry and Father is run out of powder and lead and money, too, or else he would shoot squirrels. I want you to do something soon, either eat meat or fish [?]. We got $2 with our canociser [?] order and he would [?] gone us no more until he wrote to you and if you know the reason why Mother did not write to me let me know and send me a letter as soon as possible. Your affectionate sister, Mary Ann Trubey.

[Letter #7]

Florida July 5, 1852

Dear brother,

I take my pen in hand to inform you that my folks are well at present but I myself, I feel unwell. I quit work today at noon. I have helped to frame a barn since I was to your house and have commenced to work on a warehouse and it will take us about 4 weeks to get through with it and then I have John's house to finish up. I don't think that I can come out to help you to harvest but I would like to come and hep you all if I could if it could be so but I hope you and James will get along well without me. I must tell you what reason I did not write sooner. I had wrote to Maryann and Susan Hunt and I wanted to hear from them before I would write to you so as I could tell you how they was all getting along but I only got one letter and that was from Maryann and it stated that they was all well at that time and she stated in her letter that Father wanted Mother to come home to live with him. And if she would he would join the Dunkard Church if she would come home but I don't think she will go home. John got a letter from Jacob Oller and it stated that they was all well at time. David Snively got home the 21 of May, John had one letter from his wife's folks and it stated that they hahe __ [?] as well at that time but I hope that those few [lines] comes to hand that they may find your all enjoying good health.

John's traded his land warrant of 4 rom [?] land for 160 acres of land it lays Beaver Creek. He tells me he would not take $400 for it. I want you to write soon as you can. No more at present but remain your affectionate brother, Daniel Trubey.

David Trubey

APPENDIX B

[Letter #8]

[Envelope addressed:] Mrs. Keziah Trubey, Adrian, Seneca County
[3 cent stamp, postmarked Massillon]

Massillon, Stark County
March 5, 1857 [?]

Dear sister,

I take my pen to inform you that we are all well hoping these lines may find you the same. I received your letter March 4, you wished to know whether John Zimmerman is coming to work for you, this question I cannot answer from here. Say I think not. You wish I would tell you what to do, I would say to you employ the one you menion [mention?] or someone else as Father or John has had plenty of time to inform you of their intention. I will write to Father but my writing to him need not hinder you from hiring someone. ~~As soon as you employ~~ Figuring from your letter, hands are as [?] there as they are here. I am sorry that you suffered so much loss [?] with us. Matters and things are about the same as when you was here. I am ~~sorrow~~ sorry that you and sister are not agree, the only two brothers or sisters in the family living neighbors [?]. Please write frequent how you are getting along. I must close. I want to deposit these lines in the office today. My wife is cutting carpet rugs and Permelia is churning and ain't get any butter. As for those <u>faternes</u> it would delay this letter too long to dram them off. Your affectionate brother, Absalom Klinker

Keziah Trubey

350   LETTERS

[Letter #9]

Franklin Township,
Tuscarawas County,
February 26, 1858

Dear daughter,

Sunday last Welty and Fianna was with me the first I have heard of you since Pipian [Phianna?] was returned home. She says that you are in a state of <u>confution</u> and despair about your home matters and that you wish me to give you some advice. If I was with you or near you I would say you should listen to my words, as it is I will say it few words but do not leave your home now, stay where you are, third, take care of that you have got, if you leave your home all will go to sonass [someone?] if you do not stay where you are you will find someone occupying your seat and you will be a wandering widow without a home and last of all they will have the care that you ought to have and they will look out of your window and you may look in, etc.

Phianna says you have six horses I think you should sell all but two cows two horses and then go in for sheep. Sheep are always easier tended than any other stock. If you will go in for sheep and be careful to get young stock such as 1 and 2 year old 150 sheep will net you $200 and that if worked right will be clear. Sow one small field of wheat, plant two or three acres in corn, sow 4 or 5 or 6 acres oats and feed your sheep oats in [?] the sheep in winter. If you go in the sheep business, I will give you instructions. You likely might trade one horse off for sheep, likely two. I have 200 sheep, I should not like to do without that number. Fianna says you wished to buy [__?] my lot in Hancock County and you wish to build on that and clear. Strange, what should you do in the woods and think you cannot live on your cleared up farm and all to you have take the second thought and <u>wey</u> matters well. P. says you like the folks better in Hancock than where you are, this may be all fancy by the time you would get there and fixed, those esteemed friends may be dead and gone or moved off and you would have swapped your apple orchard for a sycamore such as they are.

Ph. says you are almost out of debt so shall have you the more to stay where you are and try your luck on sheep as the punsipee s___ [?] you will find it will work easy. Welty is not well, he is better. Phianna talks of going to buy them tombstone sarn [?]. I heard from Absalom, all well. I got a letter from James dated December, all well. His wheat crop was poor, the cause s___ fusing out and the rust. Miscellaneous news ____ Mrs. Liver Boses <u>ded</u>. She had the cancer and dropsy, three children of Mr. Klek family dead in two days. Complaint, the croup. No news in our place we are all well. How I will get along tune well talk. There is some corn to husk yet. Our corn was hurt with the ____. My paper is poor, my pen does not work well. I will stop in saying that remain your friend. Why do you not write if you wish to hear from us.

Jacob Klinker

Keziah Trubey

[Letter #10]

Franklin Township
January 24, 1859
Tuscarawas County

Dear daughter,

With due admiration I acknowledge the receipt of your letter yesterday with some apology for not writing to me on account of some news being received by you. Singular that so much change should take place with you that you could not inform me even to change your name and apologize that the news had reach me. If you could not write you would be excusable. As you have made your bed so you must lie. You say you wish to buy that lot of land joining Smelser and are willing to pay $1,000 for it, $400 down. You say nothing about the payments, I should like to have $500 down. Say in your next what you can do conveniently and you shall have the lot if my wife will sign the deed. I think she will.

You say something about school. Our school will not last more than five or six weeks anymore at Welty's I know the chance is poor [Jacob T.?] Welty sells to Bolivar and pays for his schooling. As for Absalom's school, I know nothing, it is one mile from his house. As for my coming out this winter, is out of the question. I have nobody hired, one boy and myself do the chores. If I want anything done, I hire by day. Work seems to go hard with me. News about this place is not bad though there is some deaths occasionally, many old people have died in this our country not neighbors. George Starner is buried this day. I have no news our folks as far as I know they are well. Our winter is almost all rain and mud. It is cold today, hay is plenty, corn is scarce, oats is poor, and scarce potatoes are 50 cents per bushel, wheat 1.10 whit red [?] $1, oats 40/50, corn 50.

As you have become a step-mother, I hope that you are aware that is to be a step-mother is something delicate. You have heard and seen enough so that I shall not say much to you only I wish to hear that you shine like apples of gold in pictures of silver amongst the cross step-mothers. I remain as forevermore your father, Jacob Klinker

Keziah Morgan

Appendix B

Joseph Morgan, By way of your letter, I make some acquaintance with you as you say you have become my son-in-law. I hope you will act the part of a man toward your wife and a father towards her children and a gentleman at large and hoping that you and your family, as they are brought together will have peace and plenty. As for myself, I hope that I may have the pleasure of seeing you and with a friendly meeting at some future day. Jacob Klinker

Joseph Morgan

LETTERS

[Letter #11]

Bolivar July 27, 63

Dear sister and family,

I promised you a letter last week but I thought it better policy to defer until now as Father Klinker took worse the latter part of last week and so I thought it best to wait and see if he would rally again or not. Phianna and I stayed with father last Thursday night and Allman and I went over on Saturday afternoon and returned Sunday afternoon and found him very poorly indeed. He is hardly able to articulate ( ) as to be understood. He does a good part of his talking by motions and he has not rallied any and neither do I think he ever will although he eats some food but his system is about used up. He is indescribably poor and is confined to his bed and must be helped in moving to any position. He has his spitting and throwing up as ever but his food stays better now that what it did some few days ago. In short, I think he is running down very fast this last week, but how long he will live I am unable to say but I think him weak enough to die any day although he may live a week or two. But I think if you wish to see him alive you would do well in coming forthwith. James came Sunday afternoon to your father's in company with Absalom's wife. He intends to stay until father changes. I sent you $5 in the last letter and promised to send the balance in this but I am not certain you got your five so I thought I would defer until I know better.

We had a very dry time since Arabella left, both in season and company but along by Father Klinker's rain was tolerably plenty but our corn looked very well for not having any rain but our pasture is all dried up.

We etc all the folks interesting you are well [?]. Morgan the rebel general of the Indiana gurilies [guerillas?] has invaded Ohio and has caused a great deal of fear and excitement but we learnt today that Morgan was captured last night some miles below New Philadelphia. It was reported that they were in Zoar but it is not true but business is suspended on many of our farms today as they called on every able-bodied man yesterday in the whole neighborhood for soldiers. They applied twice yesterday for Allman and I still refused and they got mad

APPENDIX B 355

at me for not letting him go so about 2 o'clock last night a body of men came to my residence and fired about 10 or 12 shots close to the house and left. Who they were and where they went we do not know. I want to hold Allman at the risk of my life. Phianna, Allman, Elvira, and John went to Father Klinker's this night.

Goodbye sister and family until I am further posted. I and Jake occupy our house this night.

J. T. Welty

[Letter #12]

Signal Camp, Georgetown, D.C.
April 10 [or 11; year not given]

Friend Belle,

I promised to write to you before I left and I will fulfull it now. I like camp life very well as far as I have tried it, it goes better than I expected it would. We have not much to do and that suits me exactly. But then there is some things I do not like, like one thing, bored, and the other is the duty. There is not much of the latter, however. Our camp is situated on the heights of Georgetown. It is one of the nicest places ever was. We can see all over the great city of Washington. It is a beautiful city. The capitol can be seen plainly from here. It is not much nicer than the state house at Columbus, Ohio. We are right at the edge of Georgetown, it is not much of a place by the side of Washington. There is the grandest raceway around here on the (__) I ever saw. There are covered with evergreens and (__) all look nice in the evening when the setting sun throws his long rays through them. There I like to wander off of the noisy crowd, and I think of the happy days of yore where we used to be schoolmates and friends together, but, alas, they are gone. Perhaps never to return but I for one hope they will and that we may all be permitted to enjoy each other's company again. If army life was all as good as it is here I would be perfectly satisfied. But enough of this, this will be of very little interest to you and I will stop, for I am writing too long a letter, it will tire you to read it. I do not want you to forget the photograph you promised me. I would like to have one from all the girls in Posert [?] run. I will exchange with you if you wish it. No more at present but remain your sincere friend, Curt - no belle.

P.S. I want you to answer this as soon as possible for I am tired of waiting to hear from someone around there. Excuse this for I am writing in a very (__) place and (__) at best a very (__) written but you need not look at the writing. Direct to Signal Camp, Georgetown, DC.

C. B. Hare

APPENDIX B 357

[Letter #13]

Lone Tree, Ill.
Saturday, February 1, 1868

Dearest Belle,

Again I take my grente [? pen to] address you. I received your last missive yesterday. I want to go to a sale and go home today so I will not have very much time to talk to my love. Oh, if school was only out now I could soon be with you. By one more week in school and then I don't think I can finish up business re as to get off the next week. School is out but will come soon as possible.

You can prepare till I come. Not take me very long don't think. I was somewhat surprised at the success of the Lutheran Church. They got some that needed religion very much but Belle why don't you go to tent ward [?] or me leave because P. may be hard-hearted. I must close this. Love to hear from you very much but don't think you had better write any more as the letter might be deferred and come after I have left and I don't want that to be the cause but if you write at all address as family Milo, Bureau County.

Love, please excuse this faas [?] writing. I will come to see you after while then won't have to write. Goodbye, love, Elmer

[Letter #14]

Mendon, Michigan
March 18, 1878
Monday morn

Dear Mother and all,

We are going to pack for Kansas today. Send [sent?] a box of goods with bureau in with Charlie Liddle which will start tomorrow. He hired a car and we will not go until next week sometime. I want you to leasure [?] and get here so as to ( ) all. How I would like to see Erastus first. The women are all helping me get myself ready to leave. My cashed [?] done ere we go. Collard [?] says Saturday take it. The Weavers tonight forty yards, want to leave feather beds, one or two, with you ( ) pack rest in barrels that don't go with Charlie L. Don't know where in Kansas we will stop yet. I would like ever so much to see Van Nette ere we go. Tell him to come along. Be sure and not forget your close line [clothesline?]. I dreamed you did. Now write as soon as get this. Please do. No more, ever yours, Belle S.

APPENDIX B

[Letter #15]

Mendon, Sept 12, '79

My dear daughter Belle,

I rest [?] we received a card or a letter from you aWednesday, I was just getting ready to thrash Thursday, I could hardly work after I read it. I wanted you to come right away, now come as soon as you get able and we will dry some apples for you and make some apple butter if we haute [have?] enough. What is the use to stay there and lose your cattle. Get them away as soon as can. You must not ride on the wagon, it will ruin you. Mary will surely go up if she hears you are acoming home. She is poorly again, her health is still worse. I wish you could come now. I was down to Erastus when I heard news about your baby boy [Earl Irvin Shepherd]. I was so surprised I could hardly believe it. Eras didn't. I tell you the truth, I am glad I did not know it but my dear girl what narrow escape you did make. Now do be careful of yourself. I don't see how Mary can live clhe [? she?] is getting poorer every day of her life. She wants to see you so bad, you must go and see right away. I guess I will send for her. I just come home three weeks ago, I was sick there, something like the flux, but am well again. Van Nette come with me to south. Send to see about his machine, but only stayed two days and went home. Lyman has an ugly cough. I hate that; he don't like his cough either. I fear it is again to be fatal. I have so much trouble, I won't write much more, expect to see you before long. The crops were better in Ohio and much then ever was known [?]. Brayton 47 1/2 bushels of wheat per acre on three acres, baker 900 bushels on 18 acres...James had 65 acres, don't that beat cances [?]. I will tell you the rest when I see you. We are sowing wheat now. If you are able, don't wait to wash a dress but by no means ride on a wagon like you did last fall. Write as soon as you rec[eive] this if you don't come yourself. Bring your babe with you.

[top of page, upside down] Clarence, your <u>aunta</u> says she is agoing to steal one of your ma's babies. She thinks it will be you. Write soon, from your mother.

[Letter #16]

Ottawa, Kansas
April 28, 1892

Mrs. Bell Shepherd

Dear madam,

Don't know if this will meet with favor or not but thought I could do you a favor for the sake of old times. Hear E.P. is going to sue for a divorce. Also to appeal the suit, if you want to know how he slandered you, you can write to Ella and get a letter she has in her possession. You could easy prosecute him for slander. But burn this and don't tell them I wrote you. You can let on to Ella that you had heard he wrote to E.M. and ask her if she knows anything about it. But for the sake of old times, don't say a word ~~xzxzx~~ I have written to you at all for I did swear in my wrath that I never would write you again and if you write Ella, don't mention it. Sorry you are to have any more trouble and hope you may prosper in all your undertakings. If any of them knew I wrote you, they would not like it, but Ella would like for you to have the letter. Had to send to the postmaster at Mendon for your address. Yours truly, M.C.L.

Index 361
(Names and Place-names)

Abeney
  Alma 217, 324
Acuff
  A. V. 217
  Loretta 217
  Norma Lee 217
  Roy Sylvanus 217
  Violet A. (Trubey) 217, 324
Adams
  Jeremiah, M.G. 222
Adrian, Ohio 181, 349
Alabama
  Birmingham 164, 281
Albany, Ore. 192, 306
Alberta, prov. of 254
Alcorn
  Monsolete 219, 325
Allen
  J. S. 218
  Sarah Catherine (Kochenderfer) 176
Allman
  Margaret (Clark) 117
  Nicholas 116
  Sarah E. 44, 116
Alpena, Mich. 163, 284
Altimus
  J. D. 218
  Mary B. 72, 218, 325
  S. J. (-?-) 218
Ambs
  Charlotte 185

Anderson
  Addie Gail 191, 304
  Lulu 156, 280
Angwin, Calif. 316
Ann Arbor, Mich. 194, 309, 310, 311, 312
Antioch, Ind. 228
April
  Elsie Laura 195, 311
Arbaugh
  Benjamin Harrison 114
  Caroline Harriet 42, 115
  Catherine Ann 42, 105
  David Franklin 42, 106, 112
  Dennis 114
  Elizabeth J. E. 42, 110
  Elsie 114
  John 17, 41
  Maud 114
  Nancy Ellen (Fry) 42, 112
  Samantha J. 42, 103, 111
  Susan 114
  Susannah (Trubey) 17, 41
  William A. 43
Archer
  Mary 107
Arcola, Ill. 300
Arkansas 199
  Carlisle 144
  Duvall's Bluff 107

  Little Rock 107
  Lonoke Co. 144
Ashland Co., Ohio 121, 135, 140, 141
Athens Co., Ohio 187
Athens, Ohio 301
Atkinson
  Abel 107
  Margaret Ann 106
  Mary (Archer) 107
  Matilda 107
Augusta Cemetery, Mich. 131, 132
Augusta, Mich. 131, 260, 264
Augustine
  Anne May - see Mary Anne
  Martha Jane (Cole) 148
  Mary Anne 54, 147, 272
  William 148
Autman
  Wilma (Trubey)? 264
Baden Baden, Germany 334
Baird
  Catherine 135, 141
Baker
  Mr. 359
Baltimore and Ohio Railroad 191, 304

INDEX

Baptist Church,
  Ohio 338
Barberton
  Methodist
  Episcopal
  Church, Ohio
  94
Barberton, Ohio
  94
Bare
  Bertha (-?-)
  130
  Charles 130
  Clarence 130
  David 130
  Jacob 48, 129
  Mary 130
  Mary C.
  (Trubey) 48,
  128
  Permelia
  (Canon) 129
Barkdoll
  Jacob 7-9
Barkey
  Charity June
  150, 275
  Gloria Marie
  150, 275
  Golden Oneida
  (Trubey)
  150, 275
  Oscar E. 150,
  275
Barringer
  Absolam 193
  Esther J. 193
  Sarah (-?-) 193
Barrs Mills, Ohio
  293
Batterman
  Henry 241
Battle Creek
  Sanitarium
  253
Battle Creek,
  Mich. 132,
  253

Bavaria 100
Beach City, Ohio
  87, 145, 151,
  180, 276,
  293
Beal
  Karl W. 220
  Kent 220
  Kevin 220
  Marguerite L.
  (Trubey)
  220
  Marshall 220
Bear - see Bare
Bedford Co., Va.
  103
Beer
  Philadelphia
  201
Bell
  James 25, 60,
  290
  Susan (Trubey)
  Hunt
  McCullick
  25, 56, 290
Beloit, Kans. 211,
  218
Bercedoll - see
  Barkdoll
Berkel
  Joanne (Van
  Nette) 183
Bettis
  Jacob, Jr. 6, 8
  Jacob, Sr. 7
Bingham
  Mary 170
Birmingham, Ala.
  164, 281
Black
  John 10
Blackford Co.,
  Ind. 57, 59,
  72, 343
Blank
  Amos 242

Carey May
  "Nettie"
  (Long) 83,
  242
  Emma J.
  (Clifford)
  243
  Frances C./E.
  244
  Helen A. 244
  John Palmer
  83, 242
  Kathryn J. 244
  Pal - see John
  Palmer
Bleakney
  William 6
Bloomfield, Ind.
  126
Bolckow, Mo. 72
Bolivar, Ohio 86,
  101, 341,
  342, 354
Bond Co., Ill. 222
Books
  Henrietta 157
Bornes
  John 7
Bose
  Mr. 344
  Mrs. Liver (?)
  351
Bose Cemetery,
  Ohio 152
Boulder, Colo.
  111
Bourns
  John 7, 8
Bowers
  Helen 95
  Henry 38
  Henry A. 94
  Laura 95
  Mr. 344
  Nettie (Welty)
  38, 94
  Raymond 95

INDEX

Brachter/Bracker - see Bradshaw
Bradshaw
  Charles E. 230
  Rosa 230
  Sarah C. (Jones) 77, 230
Branch Co., Mich. 130, 161, 183, 184
Brandberg
  Dorothy Mitchell 274
Brannon
  Mary A. 38, 95
Bratten
  Dorlean Lavon 207, 318
  Joseph 207, 318
  Leila Ethel (Trubey) 207, 318
  Paul Joseph 207, 318
Brayton
  Mr. 359
  William 63
Brethren Church 226
Bretz
  Carmen (Van Nette) 183
Bristow, Okla. 107
Bronson, Mich. 284
Brooks
  Rebecca (Havens) 232
Brought
  George 346
  Mr. 344
Brown
  Minnie 49, 134, 171

Browns Creek Cemetery, Kans. 27
Buchanan Co., Mo. 75, 84, 245
Bucyrus, Ohio 241
Buffalo, N.Y. 162, 284
Bulharz
  Lewis A., J.P. 136
Bureau Co., Ill. 174, 357
Burgoyne
  General 248
Burguffeln, Germany 1
Burnett
  Sally 211
Bushnell
  Idabella (Taylor) 116
  William 116
Butler
  John 46
Butler Co., Ohio 66, 82, 186, 298, 299, 301
Cain
  Hannah L. 154
Caler
  Emma Belle 55, 165, 285, 286
  George 165
  Susannah Elizabeth (Mase) 165
California 293, 329
  Angwin 316
  Glendale 305
  Inglewood 80, 334

Long Beach 190, 193
Los Angeles 79, 253, 305, 307, 319, 333
Oakland 213
San Francisco 104, 316
Santa Cruz 199, 315
Santa Rosa 212
Sebastopol 213
Shafter 323
South Gate 192
Trinity Co. 199
Camden, N.J. 180, 293
Camp Adair, Ore. 306
Camp Lewis, Wash. 323
Campbell Co., Va. 103
Canal Dover, Ohio 163, 249, 298
Caney, Kans. 113
Canon
  Permelia 129
Canton, Ohio 87, 275
Carey, Ohio 173, 297
Carlisle, Ark. 144
Carns
  J. B., Rev. 154
Carr
  Catherine (Trubey) 24, 27, 80, 81, 83, 289, 338
  Charles H. 85, 338
  E. 69
  Eugenie E. 85, 338

INDEX

Franklin B. 27, 83, 338
Nettie E. 85, 244, 338
Pansy 85, 338
William A. 85, 338
Cascade, Kans. 113
Casner
  Edna M. 220
Casper, Wyo. 192, 308
Cass Co., N.D. 221
Casteel
  Ida Mae 71
Cavitte
  Alice G. 262
Celina, Ohio 102
Champaign Co., Ill. 295
Champion Hill, Miss. 138
Chaplet
  Rev. 346
Charles
  Cecil Harold 265
  L. J. 132, 265
  Mary Elizabeth 265
  Wilma V. (Trubey) 131, 132, 263
Charles City, Iowa 209
Chattanooga, Tenn. 101, 103
Chautauqua Co., Kans. 113
Cheesbrough
  Emma (Trubey/ Morgan) 297

Chicago Heights, Ill. 260
Chicago, Ill. 153, 276
Chickamauga, Ga. 103
Childs
  Livona Jane 208
Chinnock
  Dorothy Eloise 214, 321
  E. Romayne 214, 321
  Harry 214, 321
  Hazel 321
  Hazel (Hutchi(n)son) 213, 321
Choctaw Nation 84, 104
Church of Christ 270
Church of the Brethren ("Dunkard") 2, 46, 348
Circleville, Ohio 153, 276
Civil War 67, 69, 76, 83, 86, 88, 97, 101, 103, 107, 110, 113, 118, 119, 124, 126, 135, 138, 141, 173, 221, 251, 252, 258, 298, 302, 314, 327, 334, 336, 354, 356
Clark
  Margaret 117
  May 183

Clay Co., Kans. 167, 290
Clements
  Robert S., Hon. 204
Cleveland Iron Mining Company 33
Cleveland, Ohio 87, 160, 192, 307
Clifford
  Emma J. 243
  Henry 243
  Sophronia (Merrill) 243
Cline
  Frank B. 153
Clinton, Mo. 323
Cochran
  John 7
Coe
  Frieda 183
Coldwater, Mich. 183
Cole
  Amos 138
  Martha Jane 148
  Nancy (-?-) 138
  Sophrona Hester D. 51, 138
Colon, Mich. 179, 180, 183, 184, 293, 296
Colorado 78, 111, 205, 213
  Boulder 111
  Crawford 203
  Delta 216, 323
  Delta Co. 34, 202, 203, 208
  Denver 84, 338

INDEX

Durango 203
Fort Collins 150
Hinsdale Co. 202
La Plata Co. 203
Larimer Co. 150
Mancos 204
Meeker 213
Montrose Co. 202, 204, 211
Ouray Co. 204
Palisade 203, 212
San Miguel Co. 71
Telluride 205
Colstrip, Mont. 302
Comanche Co., Kans. 174
Congregational Church, Nebr. 331, 332
Connecticut 136
Cook
  Elsie 207, 318
Cook Co., Ill. 44, 118
Corson
  Dorothy 278
Coughran
  John 10
Council Grove, Kans. 107
County Down, Ireland 31
Cox/Cocks
  Sarah A. 119
Crawford
  Edward 11
Crawford Co., Ohio 239

Crawford Co., Pa. 77
Crawford, Colo. 203
Creek Co., Okla. 107
Creek Nation 107, 109
Crites
  Jacob 111
  John 111
  Rebecca 110
Croushore
  James, Dr. 253
  Mary Margaret (Fair?) 253
Cumberland Co., Pa. 2, 220
Cunningham
  Nellie 331
Curby
  LaReine 162, 284
Dalton Cemetery, Ohio 36, 93, 96
Dalton, Ohio 93, 96
Dancer
  Catherine 51, 140
  John 140
  Margaret (Huston) 140
Dane Co., Wisc. 224
Daniels
  Ethel Marie 274
Davault
  Michael 7, 8
Davidson
  Jeanne 313
Davis
  Minnie (Brown) 171

Day
  Saphronia 70, 198, 315
DeBow
  V. L., Rev. 256, 258
DeFehr
  Guinevere 213, 321
Defiance Co., Ohio 24, 67, 83, 139, 186, 189, 191, 193, 196, 197, 289, 298, 302, 303, 304, 306, 307, 308, 309, 313
Defiance, Ohio 139
Delaware, Ohio 254
Delta Co., Colo. 34, 202, 203, 208
Delta, Colo. 216, 323
Delta, Ohio 234
Delveese
  Bessie Jane (Heyde) Hendricks 222
  Mr. 222
Denver, Colo. 84, 338
Detroit, Mich. 162, 253, 283, 284
Dickey
  Sarah 66
Dille
  Arnold F. 234
  Chester B. 233, 333

Dessie B. 233, 333
Eva R. 233, 333
Ichabod 232
John I. 77, 232, 333
Mary Jane (Mohn) 77, 232, 333
Mayme P. 233
Rebecca (Havens) Brooks 232
Dille, Hoke, Krause & Faegre law firm 232
Diller
 Mary Olive 149
 Olive 272
District of Columbia
 Georgetown 356
Divorces
 Bare, Jacob 129
 Hills, Mary Caroline (Trimble) Mundy 124
 Malone, Benjamin 211
 Mohn, Amanda Catherine 79
 Morgan, Keziah (Klinker) Trubey 64
 Shepherd, Arabella Serena (Trubey) 175

Staffeldt, Eurannah (Hass) Trubey 184
Terhune, Edward 169
Trubey, Erastus Seabury 179
Trubey, Lloyd Elton 305
Trubey, Nathan John 186, 301
Dixon
 Clarabelle 61, 290
 George 61, 290
 John 61, 290
 Mary A. (Hunt) Stewart 61, 290
 Nellie 61, 290
Dotts
 Thomas 38
Doubt
 Alvin W. 317
 Beulah (Trubey) 317
Dougherty
 Nathan 66
 Sarah (Dickey) 66, 301
 Sarah Jane 25, 66, 298, 347
Dover, Ohio 247
Drake
 Harriet (Triplett) Filson 121
 James L. 121
 Mary 44, 121
 Susannah (Hayward) 121
Drube
 Daniel iv
 Johann 1

Johann Daniel 1
Dudley
 Lavina Amanda 70, 208, 319
 Livona Jane (Childs) 208
 Robert Bennett 208
Dudlow
 Loretta 188, 301
Durango, Colo. 203
Dutchess Co., N.Y. 33
Duvall's Bluff, Ark. 107
East Flat Rock, N.C. 215
Edwards
 Barbara J. 138
 Daisy A. 138
 Go[l?]die M. 137
 Harrison Royal 137
 Joel A. 51, 136
 Lester A. 137
 Mary Margaret (May) Huston 51, 135
 Nancy 137
 R(e)ubin A. 137
 William S. 137
Edwards Co., Kans. 174, 291, 295
Eldorado, Ohio 228
Elmore
 Maribelle (Martin) 295
Ely
 Nettie J. 68, 186, 301

INDEX 367

England 96
Englehart
   Hannah 2
English Lutheran
   Church, Ohio
   88
English Prairie
   Brethren
   Church, Ind.
   47
Enterprise, Ore.
   103
Enyart
   Benjamin 300
   Cornelius 300
   David 300
   Hannah 300
   Joanna (Tombs)
     300
   John 300
   Mary 300
   Perses 300
   Rachel 300
   Rufus 300
   Samuel 300
   Sarah 300
   Susannah 67,
     299, 300
Erbprinz Regiment
   (Hereditary
     Prince) ii, iv
Evans
   Miriam 310
Fair
   Bertha V.
     (Trubey)
     102, 252,
     253
   J. B. 102, 252
   Mary Margaret
     252
Fairless
   Benjamin F.
     150, 275
   Blaine 150,
     275

   Jennie Blanche
     (Trubey)
     150, 275
Fairmont
   Cemetery,
   Colo. 84
Falck
   Amanda
     (Mohn) 78
   John F. 78
Falls City, Nebr.
   73, 329, 331
Fargo, N.D. 252,
   254
Farnsworth
   Charles
     Reginald
     185
   Mystia Nafeesie
     (Trubey)
     185, 296
   Mystia Nafeesie
     185
Fayette Co., Pa.
   45, 144
Fenton, Mich.
   297
Ferguson - see
   Dudley
Fields
   George 8
Filson
   Harriet
     (Triplett)
     121
Finlay, Ohio 339
Finney Co., Kans.
   177
First Methodist
   Church,
   Nebr. 73
First Presbyterian
   Church, Ohio
   61
Fisher
   Carl B. 98
   Eliza 173

   Goldie (Sprain)
     98
Fitch
   Betsy (Perrin)
     Patterson
     179
Flint, Ind. 125,
   126
Florida
   Largo 209,
     217, 324
   Ocala 215, 322
   Pinellas Co.
     209
Florida, Ohio
   141, 185,
   298, 335,
   348
Floring
   Elizabeth M.
     119
Floyd Co., Iowa
   209
Folansbee
   Esther 224
Foreman
   Frederick 4
Forsyth, Mont.
   302, 304,
   305, 306,
   308
Fort Collins, Colo.
   150
Fort Finlay, Ohio
   341
Fort Lewis, Wash.
   264
Fort Sill, Okla.
   292
Fort Valley, Ga.
   217, 324
Franklin Co., Pa.
   ii, v, 11, 14,
   15, 18, 21,
   31, 50, 51,
   56, 61, 65,
   68, 72, 74,
   80, 249, 250,

INDEX

267, 268, 287, 288, 289, 290, 293, 314, 327
Frederick Co., Md. 35, 73, 327
Frederick, Md. iii, iv
Free Methodist Church, Kans. 336
Fremont, Ind. 123, 256
Freymire Elizabeth 159
Fruit Grace 262
Fry Nancy Ellen 42, 112
Frysinger Jane (Ryan) 102, 252
Mary M. 41, 101, 252
Nathan 102, 252
Gaines Martha M. 26, 336
Gallatin Co., Mont. 143
Gallia Co., Ohio 310
Garden City, Kans. 177, 294
Garrett, Ind. 304
Gates General 248
Geal George 310
Marian Evelyn (Rodgers) 310
Marilyn Eva 310

Roger William 310
Georgetown, D.C. 356
Georgia 118
Chickamauga, battle of 103
Fort Valley 217, 324
Gerber Mr. 344
German Baptist Church, Ind. 47
German Reformed Church, Md. and Pa. 13, 288
Germany 97, 98, 159
Baden 75
Baden Baden 334
Burguffeln 1
Hanover 259
Hesse Cassel ii, 248
Kammerbach ii
Walla 260
Gervick Franklin Richard 196, 312
Marguerite Lois (Trubey) 196, 312
Richard Trubey 196, 312
Gilbert Lillian A. 68, 186, 301
Susana (-?-) 186
Virginia Carrie 68, 187, 301
W. P. 186
Glass Valentine 8, 10

Glen Elder, Kans. 206, 228, 317, 323, 329, 336
Glendale, Calif. 305
Glenwood Cemetery, Kans. 218
Goe Tyrannus 177, 292
Gooden Avah 156, 279
Goodenough William Edwin 190, 302
Zeruia C. 68, 189, 302
Goodman Mr. (-?-) 147
Selma Ruth (Trubey) 147, 271
Graham Anna T. 30
Charles H. 30
Grand Blanc, Mich. 162, 284
Grand Junction, Miss. 101
Grant Robert L. 87
Grants Pass, Ore. 149, 272
Grass Leah 220
Graves Edward 85, 245
Mollie 246
Nettie E. (Carr) 85, 244
Great Falls, Mont. 207

INDEX

Greene
  Florence J.
    (Trubey)
    216, 324
  Novella
    Yvonere 217
  W. V. 216, 324
Greenwood
  Cemetery,
  Ind. 47, 48,
    118, 127,
    128, 134,
    258
Griggs
  Mildred Helen
    306
Grimm
  Catharine 82
Groner
  Mary 20, 56
Grover Hill, Ohio
  252
Grubb
  Addie E.
    (Trubey)
    200, 316
  Edna Ethel
    200, 316
  Harry
    Thompson
    200, 316
Grundel
  Hannah 82
Guernsey Co.,
  Ohio 327
Gunn
  Catharine 82
Hachenberg
  Col. ii
Hagerstown, Md.
  18, 288
Halderman
  Wilma 332
Hampton
  Ethel Maude
    (Pilcher)
    204
  Joe I. 204

Hancock
  David H. 234
  Mary J. 79,
    234
  Roxanna (-?-)
    234
Hancock Co.,
  Ohio 62, 65,
    172, 178,
    181, 183,
    291, 296,
    350
Hanover, Germany
  259
Hare
  Curtis B. 174,
    356
Harlem Co., Nebr.
  229, 330
Harris
  Mary M. (-?-)
    144
  William 144
Hass
  Eurannah 65,
    183, 296
  George B. 183
  Rachel (Narber)
    183
Havens
  Rebecca 232
Hays
  Sarah J. 33
Hayward
  Susannah 121
Hazen
  Alexander 77,
    333
  Clarissa
    Elizabeth
    (Mohn) 77,
    333
  Eliza (McGuin-
    ness) 77
  Samuel Wilder
    77
Heacock
  Alfred, Dr. 19

Healey
  Frances
    Johns(t)on
    265
Heath
  Capt. 40
  Esther D. 25,
    69, 314
  Joseph 69
  Mary (-?-) 69
Heckler
  Josephine 83,
    239
  Lucy A.
    (Sprough)
    239
  Philip 239
Hei/High
  Mr. 97
Heiss
  Frances C./E.
    (Blank) 244
  Marolyn J. 244
  Otto W. 244
  Rita 244
  William Palmer
    244
Hendersonville,
  N.C. 215,
  216, 217,
  324
Hendricks
  Bessie Jane
    (Heyde) 222
  Ernest A., Dr.
    222
Henry Co., Ohio
  25, 50, 64,
  66, 71, 81,
  82, 135, 138,
  140, 141,
  185, 200,
  205, 208,
  210, 214,
  234, 237,
  238, 240,
  242, 301,
  314, 315,

INDEX

317, 319,
320, 321,
322, 341,
343, 347
Hess
  Henry 22
  Hesse Cassel,
    Germany ii,
    248
Heuer
  Mystia Nafeesie
    (Farnsworth)
    185
Heyde
  Bessie Jane
    222
  Carrie D. 222
  Edna Dakota
    223
  Emanuel D.
    74, 220, 224,
    328, 329
  George 220
  George Jacob
    222
  Leah (Grass)
    220
  Melissa
    (Yantiss) 74,
    220, 328
Hicksville, Ohio
  301
Higgins
  John 62
Highland Co.,
  Ohio 211
Hills
  William 123
Himel
  Helen A.
    (Blank) 244
  Richard 244
Hinkel
  Gasper 7-9
  Jasper 6, 8
Hinsdale Co.,
  Colo. 202

Hirst
  Edgar Delalia
    180, 294
  Halle Belle
    (Trubey)
    180, 293
  Halle Laveda
    180, 294
  James 293
  James K. 180
  James Vincent
    180, 294
  Martha Helene
    180, 294
Hoffman
  Mr. 97
Hogeland
  Carrie Lovena
    (Trubey)
    206, 318
  Clarence A.
    206, 318
  Raymond
    Clarence
    207, 318
  Vesta Lovena
    206, 318
Holinger
  Philip 7
Holloway
  Amey A. 104
  Catherine
    Elizabeth
    104
  Emma L. (-?-)
    105
  John Tipton
    105
  Lillian Esther
    (Hutchi(n)-
    son) 321
  Nora Louetha
    105
  Pheby Keziah
    104
  Pleasant 103
  Samantha J.
    (Arbaugh)

    42, 103,
    111
  Samaria (-?-)
    104
  Susan Caroline
    105
  Verda L. 213,
    321
  William 42,
    103, 111,
    113
  William
    Barkdoll
    105
Holly Springs,
  Miss. 101
Holmes Co., Ohio
  51
Hooper
  Margaret 192,
    308
Horn
  Elias 7
Houston - see
  Huston
Howells
  Ida (Welty) 37
  John H. 37
Hubert
  Matthew 46
Hughes
  Ellen (-?-) 121
  Lewis D. 121
Hull
  Catherine 196
Hunt
  Asa Harvey 25,
    57, 61, 290,
    339
  George D. 61
  Harvey A. 58
  Mary A. 60,
    290
  Minerva 57,
    60, 290
  Mr. 343
  Nancy Maria
    61, 166, 290

INDEX

Susan (Trubey) 25, 56, 72, 290, 348
Hunter, N.D. 221
Huntingdon Co., Pa. iii
Huntington Co., Ind. 22, 26, 72, 74, 81, 127, 133, 226, 228, 230, 232, 289, 290, 327, 328, 329, 330, 336
Huntington, Ind. 198, 279, 343, 347
Huston
 Alsetta F. (May) 51, 141
 Catherine (Baird) 135, 141
 Frank B. 142
 Jeremiah 51, 135
 Jeremiah Sr. 135, 141
 Lewis R. 137
 Louisa J. "Susanna"? 137
 Lusetta 142
 Margaret 140
 Mary Margaret (May) 51, 135
 Nancy M. 142
 Philip 51, 141
 Samuel D. 137
Hutchi(n)son
 Benjamin F. 70, 211, 320, 321
 Benjamin Franklin 213, 321
 David 211
 David Guy 212, 321
 Eliza Jane (Malone) 211
 George Andrew 213, 321
 Guinevere (DeFehr) 213, 321
 Harry O. 213, 321
 Hazel 213, 321
 Lillian Esther 212, 321
 Mabel 212, 321
 Madge Cecile (Service) 213, 321
 Margery Lillian (Kennedy) 212, 321
 Maybelle Melissa 213, 321
 Melissa Ann (Trubey) 70, 210, 320, 321
 Nancy Marie 213, 321
 Rolland Keith 212, 321
 Verda L. (Holloway) 213, 321
 Wilbur E. 213, 321
 Wilma L. 213, 321
Ice
 Rebecca (-?-) 83
Iden
 Arminda 73
Illinois 206, 221, 226, 308, 328
 Arcola 300
 Bond Co. 222
 Bureau Co. 174, 357
 Champaign Co. 295
 Chicago 153, 276
 Chicago Heights 260
 Cook Co. 44, 118
 Jo Daviess Co. 201
 Lone Tree 357
 Mendon 359, 360
 Milo 357
 Winnetka 180
 Woodland 127, 258, 260
Independence Cemetery, Ohio 24, 68, 289
Indiana 46, 108, 110, 113, 146, 148, 223, 230, 260, 296, 315, 327, 343
 44th Ind. Inf. 124, 126
 58th Ind. Inf. 110
 101st Ind. Inf. 103, 110, 118, 119
 142nd Ind. Inf. 88
 152nd Ind. Inf. 124

372 INDEX

Antioch 228
Blackford Co.
  57, 59, 72,
  343
Bloomfield 126
Flint 125, 126
Fremont 123,
  256
Garrett 304
Huntington
  198, 220,
  279, 343,
  347
Huntington Co.
  22, 26, 72,
  74, 81, 127,
  133, 226,
  228, 230,
  232, 289,
  290, 327,
  328, 329,
  330, 336
Jay Co. 58
Kendallville
  126
Lafayette 186,
  301
Lagrange 88,
  118, 128,
  256, 258,
  259, 266,
  278, 279,
  280, 283,
  284
Lagrange Co.
  29, 44, 47,
  49, 53, 88,
  117, 121,
  122, 126,
  127, 129,
  133, 154,
  161, 269
Markle 127,
  258, 261
Miami Co.
  170, 231
Montpelier 343
Noble Co. 122

Peru 230, 333
Randolph Co.
  103
Steuben Co.
  44, 123, 124,
  126, 258
Stroh 162, 284
Tippecanoe Co.
  186
Uniondale 128,
  258
Wabash 118,
  231
Wells Co. 16,
  41, 44, 46,
  58, 103, 110,
  111, 115,
  119, 166,
  169, 258
White Co. 33,
  34
Wolcottville
  122
Indians 300
Inglewood, Calif.
  80, 334
Iola, Kans. 206
Iowa 210, 214
  Charles City
    209
  Floyd Co. 209
  Mitchell Co.
    208
  Rock Creek
    208
Ireland 96
  County Down
    31
Isenberger
  Catherine iii
Ithnier
  Magdalena 144
Jackson Co., Mich.
  177
Jackson, Mich.
  177, 180,
  293

James
  Margaret
    (Hooper)
    192, 308
Jay Co., Ind. 58
Jenovese
  Hilda Emma
    Grace
    (Martens)
    319
  Patrick 319
Jerusalem 221,
  226, 328
Jewell Co., Kans.
  26, 198, 206,
  214, 314,
  336
Jewell, Ohio 189,
  299, 301,
  309, 310,
  311
Jo Daviess Co., Ill.
  201
Johns(t)on
  Dorothy 265
  Effie (Trubey)
    265
  Effie Pearl
    (Trubey)
    132, 263
  Frances 265
  Robert A. 132
  Wayne 265
Johnson
  Maggie 226
  Mattie Lee
    217, 324
Jones
  Benjamin 166
  Dona [?] J. 169
  Dora 169
  Elizabeth (-?-)
    166
  Ellen 168
  Emma P. 168
  Jessie H. 168
  John W. 168

INDEX

Josiah H. 54, 268
M. (Scott) 230
Mary A.
  (Shore) 167
Mary Ann
  (Trubey) 54, 268
Myrtle M. 168
Nancy Maria
  (Hunt) 61, 166, 290
Oscar B. 168
Rev. J. P. 47
Sarah C. 77
Simon 230
Ulysses S. 168
William 61, 290
William A. 166
Joseph, Ore. 110
Kalamazoo Co., Mich. 131
Kalamazoo, Mich. 175
Kammerbach, Germany ii
Kanaga
  Rev. 272
Kansas 104, 111, 167, 171, 203, 211, 212, 215, 216, 259, 296, 315, 318, 319, 320, 321, 322, 325, 358
8th Kans. Vet. Vol. Inf. 27
9th Kans. Cav. 107
Beloit 211, 218
Caney 113
Cascade 113
Chautauqua Co. 113

Clay Co. 167, 290
Comanche Co. 174
Council Grove 107
Edwards Co. 174, 291, 295
Finney Co. 177
Garden City 177, 294
Glen Elder 27, 206, 228, 317, 323, 329, 336
Iola 206
Jewell Co. 26, 198, 200, 206, 211, 214, 314, 336
Kingman 107
Kiowa 291, 294
Kiowa Co. 295
Long Island 225, 228, 328, 331, 332
Marion Centre 117
Marion Co. 113, 117
Mitchell Co. 70, 201, 206, 208, 210, 218, 314, 322, 329
Montgomery Co. 113
Morris Co. 106, 112, 113
Oakland 209
Ottawa 360

Phillips Co. 225, 328, 329, 330
Republic Co. 126
Shawnee Co. 70, 209
Sheridan Co. 328, 329
Smith Co. 74, 328, 329
Topeka 71
Wichita 295
Kansas City, Mo. 118, 122
Kaylor
  Catherine
    (Dancer) 51, 140
  Samuel 140
Keener
  Mary E.
    (Trubey) 165, 285, 286
  Mr. (-?-) 165
Kellogg
  Dr. 203
Kendallville, Ind. 126
Kennedy
  James 117
  Margery Lillian 212, 321
Kentucky 112
Kidney
  Donald Leonard 207, 318
  Leonard C. 207, 318
  Loraine Esther (Trubey) 207, 318
  Margaret Adeline 207, 318

INDEX

Kilgore
  Henrietta
    (Books) 157
  Satira Eunice
    55, 157, 281
  William B. 157
Kimberly
  Anna (-?-) 193
  Esther J.
    (Barringer)
    193
  James 193
  John 193
  Sarah J. 68,
    193, 309
Kimble
  Levi 60, 290
  Minerva (Hunt)
    60, 290
Kindler
  Mr. 339
Kingman, Kans.
  107
Kintner
  Susanna 151
Kiowa Co., Kans.
  295
Kiowa, Kans.
  291, 294
Kirk
  Mr. (-?-) 146
  Myrtle Mae
    (Trubey)
    146, 271
Kleemyer
  Anna Elizabeth
    259
Klek
  Mr. 351
Klinker
  Absalom 341,
    344, 346,
    349, 352,
    354
  Catherine
    (Schweickert)
    28, 62

  Jacob 28, 61,
    341, 344,
    346, 349,
    351, 352,
    354
  James 62, 341,
    344, 346,
    348, 351,
    354, 359
  Joanna 346,
    349, 354
  John 349
  Keziah 25, 61,
    293, 344,
    346, 349,
    351, 352,
    358, 359
  Mrs. Jacob
    (2nd) 346
  Permelia 349
  Phianna 15, 28,
    89, 342, 346,
    350, 354
Knepper
  Godfrey 143
  Jane A. 244
  John David
    244
  Kathryn J.
    (Blank) 244
  Lester 244
  Magdalena
    (Ithnier) 144
  Mary A. (-?-)
    143
  Mary A.
    (Spankel)
    Young 143
  Melissa 54,
    143, 271
Knight
  Martha M.
    (Gaines) 26,
    336
Knisely
  U. Jesse, M.G.
    86

Kochenderfer
  Sarah Catherine
    176
Krabs
  Henry 8
Kunkel
  Lola Pearl 150,
    275
Kuns
  Dr. (Rev.) 88
  Elva (Trubey)
    145, 271
  Mr. (-?-) 145
Kurtz
  Rev. 18
La Plata Co.,
  Colo. 203
Lafayette, Ind.
  186, 301
LaGrande, Ore.
  112
Lagrange Co., Ind.
  29, 44, 47,
  53, 88, 117,
  121, 122,
  126, 127,
  129, 133,
  154, 161,
  269
Lagrange, Ind. 88,
  118, 128,
  256, 258,
  259, 266,
  278, 279,
  280, 283,
  284
Landahl
  Blanche 266
Laramie, Wyo.
  178
Largo, Fla. 209,
  217, 324
Larimer Co., Colo.
  150
Lawhead
  Nina (Trubey/
    Morgan)
    297

INDEX 375

Lebanon, Ore. 306
Lebold
  Jacob R. 90
  Mary (Merchant) 90
  Mary Amelia 32, 90
Leonhardt
  Bessie (May) 141
  Catharine 141
  Donald 141
  Frank 141
Levias
  Mr. 346
Lewallyn
  Rose 54, 152, 276
Liddle
  Charlie 358
  Gilbert Van Deusen 178
  Martha Dawson 65, 178, 293
  Rebecca Bradley Watson 178
Lidgerwood, N.D. 253, 254
Lincoln Co., Okla. 107
Little
  Myrtle 162, 284
Little Rock, Ark. 107
Lone Tree, Ill. 357
Long
  Armel 82
  Carey May "Nettie" 83, 242
  Charles R. 83, 238, 337
  Elizabeth (Trubey) 27, 81, 82, 290, 337
  Elizabeth (Weaver) 82
  Floyd. F. 240
  Frances (Menninger) 83, 240
  Franklin 83
  George 27, 82, 83, 337
  Hannah (Grundel) 82
  Harman 240
  Herman 83, 240, 337
  John 82, 242
  Josephine (Heckler) 83, 239
  Lavina 82
  Maud 240
  Nellie 240, 337
  Nettie - see Nellie
  Noah 82
  Rebecca (-?-) Ice 83
  Reuben 83
  William H. 83, 337
Long Beach, Calif. 190, 193
Long Island Cemetery, Kans. 328, 329
Long Island, Kans. 225, 228, 328, 331, 332
Lonoke Co., Ark. 144
Loraine, Ohio 297
Los Angeles, Calif. 79, 253, 305, 319, 333
Lose
  Abraham Lincoln 82, 237, 335
  Abraham Sr. 237
  Caroline (-?-) 238
  Donald A. 238
  Effie Savilla (Scofield) 82, 237, 335
  Hellen C. 238
  Inec/Inez C. 238
  Mary P. 238
Loudonville, Ohio 121
Lovell
  E. K., Rev. 67
Lower
  Elias, V.D.M. 151
Lutheran Church, Ill. 357
Luttenberger
  Eunice Bessie (Trubey) 153, 276
  John M., Dr. 153, 276
Lynch
  Marion 84
Lyon
  Archibald Y. 233, 333
  Eva R. (Dille) 233, 333
Mack
  Alexander 2
  family cemetery 11
  Hannah (Englehart) 2
  Jacob 2, 11

Margaret 1, 11, 248
Maria 21
Maddox
  (-?-) (Trubey) 128, 258
  Emily (Trubey) 261
  Wilson 128, 258, 261
Maisch
  Dorothy 100
Malone
  Benjamin 211
  Eliza Jane 211
  Sally (Burnett) 211
Mancos, Colo. 204
Manitoba, prov. of 254
Mann
  John 7
Maple Grove Cemetery, Ohio 164
Marchand
  Luella B. (-?-) 54, 152, 276
Marion Centre, Kans. 117
Marion Co., Kans. 113, 117
Markle, Ind. 127, 258, 261
Markley
  Olivia 278
Marquette Co., Mich. 33
Martens
  Berhend Henry 210, 319
  Harry Karl 210
  Hilda Emma Grace 210, 319
  Mr. (-?-) 319

Myrtle Edna (Trubey) 210, 319
Nellie A. 210, 319
Martin
  Grace Darling (Shepherd) 63, 177, 292, 295
  Maribelle 177, 292, 295
  Samuel Page 177, 292, 295
  Tono E. 177, 292, 295
  Tono Shepherd 177, 292
Maryland 13, 28, 42, 66
  Frederick iii, iv
  Frederick Co. 35, 73, 327
  Hagerstown 18, 288
  Washington Co. 13, 15, 18, 21
Mase
  Susannah Elizabeth 165
Massachusetts
  Tyringham 243
Massillon Cemetery, Ohio 20, 29, 32, 35, 52, 89, 145, 158
Massillon, Ohio 95, 144, 287, 349
Mattern
  Cathrine 16
  George 16

May
  Alsetta F. 51, 141
  Bessie 141
  Carrie M. 140
  Catherine (Dancer) Kaylor 51, 140
  Charles L. 141
  Dora 140
  Frank Lee 139
  George C. 140
  Harrison T. 51, 138
  Jennie 140
  Lewis 20, 50
  Mary Margaret 51, 135
  Max Walter 139
  Nancy (Trubey) 20
  Paul Ernest 139
  Ralph Carey 139
  Samuel W. 51, 140
  Sophrona Hester D. (Cole) 51, 138
Maynard
  Jennie Ethel (Trubey) 161
  Leon 161, 283
Mays
  Anna Bell 109
  Catherine Ann (Arbaugh) 42, 105
  David 107
  Emma J. 110
  Ethel 108
  Isaac Dickenson 106

INDEX 377

Joseph 42, 107
Joseph Archer
 109
Lloyd 108
Margaret Ann
 (Atkinson)
 106
Mary (Archer)
 Atkinson
 107
Minerva (-?-)
 108
Norma Gertrude
 109
Pearl (-?-) 108
Walter Franklin
 108
William Wesley
 106
McAlester, Okla.
 84
McCalmont
 James 9
McCavitt
 Dale A. 303
 Lyndon James
 303
 Marjorie Ray
 (Smith) 303
 Noma Ione 303
McConnell
 W. G., Rev.
 205
McCullick
 Ellen 61, 169,
 290
 Esther (Slusher)
 59
 Henry 25, 58,
 290
 Martha
 (Twibell) 59
 Susan (Trubey)
 Hunt 25, 56,
 290
McDowell
 James 9

McElhenie
 Elizabeth
 (Stinson) 92
 Joe 92
 Selina A. 37,
 92
McFarland
 Hannah E. 71
McFarling
 Mr. (merchant)
 344
McFarren
 Arie L. 55,
 163, 281
 Daniel 163
 Jemima
 (Shettler)
 163
McGuinness
 Eliza 77
McKee
 J., Rev. 92
McKessin
 Stella Contessi
 203
McPhee
 Flossie 162,
 284
McWhinney
 John 31
 Mary Jane 15,
 31, 90
 Nancy (Wolf)
 31
Meeker, Colo.
 213
Mendenhall
 Renie 172
Mendon, Mich.
 174, 182,
 358, 359,
 360
Menninger
 Frances 83,
 240
 Frances (-?-)
 241
 Henry 241

Mentzer
 David 10
Mercer Co., Ohio
 98, 100, 102,
 252
Merchant
 Mary 90
Merkey
 Ethela Helen
 (Trubey)
 262
 Karen Elaine
 262
 Mr. (-?-) 262
Merriam
 Amasa 224
 Esther
 (Folansbee)
 224
 Henry 224
 Joel 224
 Mary 74, 223,
 328
 Sylvia (Stanley)
 224
Merrill
 Sophronia 243
Mertens
 Minnie M. (-?-)
 80
Methodist Church,
 Kans. 332
Methodist
 Episcopal
 Church, Ind.
 256, 258
Methodist
 Episcopal
 Church,
 Kans. 328,
 329
Methodist
 Episcopal
 Church,
 Nebr. 330
Meyers
 Clara A. 116

378   INDEX

Clara C. 153, 276
Joseph H. 226
Lillie A. 74, 226, 329
Maggie (Johnson) 226
Violet (Trubey) 72
Miami Co., Ind. 170, 231
Michigan 244, 296, 306
　Alpena 163, 284
　Ann Arbor 194, 309, 310, 311, 312
　Augusta 131, 260, 264
　Battle Creek 132, 253
　Branch Co. 130, 161, 183, 184
　Bronson 284
　Coldwater 183
　Colon 179, 180, 183, 184, 293, 296
　Detroit 162, 253, 283, 284
　Fenton 297
　Grand Blanc 162, 284
　Jackson 177, 180, 293
　Jackson Co. 177
　Kalamazoo 175
　Kalamazoo Co. 131
　Marquette Co. 33

　Mendon 174, 182, 358
　Monroe 311
　Sherwood 184
　St. Joseph Co. 65, 88, 177, 178, 181, 292, 294, 295
　Sturgis 88, 181
Miller
　Amos 38, 94
　Mae 216, 323
　Mary Gertrude 94
　Michael 4, 7, 9, 10
　Minnie (Welty) 38, 93
　Roger Oscar 94
Miller Cemetery, Ind. 60, 170
Mills
　Emily 126
　Francis 34
　Francis P. 15, 33
　Henry 33
　Mary (Purdy) 33
　Mary Ann (Welty) 15, 32
　Mary Ellen 34
　Sarah J. (Hays) 33
Milo, Ill. 357
Miner
　William 10
Ministers
　Adams, Jeremiah 222
　Carns, J. B. 154
　Chaplet, Rev. 346

　DeBow, V. L. 256, 258
　Jones, J. P. 47
　Kanaga, Rev. (-?-) 272
　Knisely, U. Jesse 86
　Kuns, Dr. 88
　Kurtz, Rev. 18
　Lovell, E. K. 67
　Lower, Elias 151
　McConnell, W. G. 205
　McKee, J. 92
　Preston, J. R. 47
　Rahauser, Rev. Henrich Jonathan 13, 15, 21, 288
　Ritz, Solomon 45
　Skinner, H. D. 179
　Stump, Sol C. 226
　Taylor, J. W. 228
　Thomas, W. V. 83, 338
　Trubey, Lewis Francis 208
　Weaver, H. S. 150
　Wimer, David 344
Minneapolis, Minn. 153, 233, 276
Minnesota 153, 232, 254
　Minneapolis 153, 233, 276

INDEX 379

Minnick
  Anna Mary 55, 154, 277, 278
  Hannah L. (Cain) 154
  William R. 154
Minsel
  Mary Ann 197, 313
Mississippi
  Champion Hill 138
  Grand Junction 101
  Holly Springs 101
Missouri 109, 111, 118
  Bolckow 72
  Buchanan Co. 75, 84, 245
  Clinton 323
  Kansas City 118, 122
  Morgan Co. 44, 117, 121
  St. Joseph 75, 77, 80, 84, 245
  St. Louis 71, 78, 209, 328
Mitchell
  Amos 136
  Edith (Terhune) 171
  James M. 171
  James, J.P. 245
  Mary Margaret (May) Huston Edwards 135
Mitchell Co., Iowa 208
Mitchell Co., Kans. 70, 201, 206, 208, 210, 218, 314, 322, 329
Mock - see Mack
Moffett
  A. G., J.P. 208
  Mary A. 49, 266
Mohn
  Amanda Catherine 78, 333
  Caroline C. 76
  Charles G. 79, 84, 236, 333, 334
  Clarissa Elizabeth 77, 333
  Daniel Andrew 79, 234, 333, 334
  Dessie B. 237
  Edith M. 231
  Ella M. 237
  George W. 231
  Jessie M. 231
  John 25, 74, 75, 333
  John Frederick 77, 230, 333
  John Sr. 75
  Lizzie B. 231
  Mamie - see Amanda
  Mamie Belle 79
  Mary (-?-) 75
  Mary J. (Hancock) 79, 234
  Mary Jane 77, 232, 333
  May (-?-) 236
  Minnie M. (-?-) Mertens 80
  Rebecca (Trubey) 25, 74, 79, 84, 333, 347
  Sarah C. (Jones) Bradshaw 77, 230
  Von F. 231
Moissett - see Moffett
Monroe Co., Ohio 107
Monroe, Mich. 311
Montana 304, 336
  Colstrip 302
  Forsyth 302, 304, 305, 306, 308
  Gallatin Co. 143
  Great Falls 207
  Rosebud Co. 190
Montgomery Co., Kans. 113
Montpelier, Ind. 343
Montpelier, Ohio 118, 120
Montrose Co., Colo. 202, 204, 211
Moore
  Alphonso Ellwood 300
  Amy 299
  Annie 299
  Anthony Benezetti 299
  Elias 299
  Eliza 299
  Lewis/Louis 67, 299
  Lydia 25, 67, 298, 299, 300
  Reuben 299

Rufus Enyart
   299
Samuel 299
Sarah 299
Stephen Gard
   300
Susannah
   (Enyart) 67,
   299
Morgan
   Gen., C.S.A.
   354
   Joseph 64, 353
   Keziah
   (Klinker)
   Trubey 352
   Lyman - see
   Lyman
   Trubey/
   Morgan
   Sarah A. 70,
   206
Morgan Co., Mo.
   44, 117, 121
Morris Co., Kans.
   106, 112,
   113
Morse
   Jane 25, 67,
   298
Morton
   Tyrannus (Goe)
   177, 292
Motter
   Catherine 12,
   15
Mounsey
   Jennie Iness
   171
Mt. Mora
   Cemetery,
   Mo. 76
Mundy
   Alanson 44,
   118, 122,
   123
   Glen 125
   Harry 125

John Allen 125
Lewis 123
Mary Caroline
   (Trimble)
   44, 123, 256
Mertie 125
Nettie Ellen
   125
Polly
   (Stevenson)
   123
William Ellis
   125
Muskopf
   Elizabeth
   (Freymire)
   159
   Emma 160,
   282
   Glen William
   160, 282
   Homer 160,
   282
   Jennie Etta
   (Trubey) 55,
   158, 269,
   282
   John 159
   Marcellus 160,
   282
   Mary
   Magdalena
   (Zintmeister)
   159
   Samuel 55,
   159, 282
Musser
   Mary Ann 38
Myer(s) - see
   Meyers
Napoleon, Ohio
   25
Narber
   Rachel 183
Nashville, Tenn.
   88

Naylor
   Alvira "Ella" N.
   (Welty) 30,
   87
   David 30, 88
   Margaret (-?-)
   88
   Roger Welty
   89
   Thomas 88
Nebraska 289,
   296, 314,
   315, 317,
   319, 320,
   321, 322,
   329
   Falls City 73,
   329, 331
   Harlem Co.
   229, 330
   Orleans 229
   Richardson Co.
   24, 26, 73,
   220, 223,
   226, 228,
   289, 327,
   330, 332
   Shelton 215
   Silver Creek
   228
   Verdon 228,
   329, 331
Nedrow
   (-?-) [female]
   112
   Carrie B. (-?-)
   112
   Elizabeth J. E.
   (Arbaugh)
   42, 110
   Jane 112
   Jesse(y) Wesley
   112
   John 113
   John Allen 111
   John D. [or W.]
   42, 110

INDEX

Joseph Franklin 111
Leona 112
Mary C. 111
Rebecca (Crites) 110
Simon 110
William Henry 112
Neifert
  Austin 219, 325
  Bernadene (Trubey) 219, 325
  Dennis 219, 325
Neilson
  C. N., Mrs. 179
New Jersey 300
  Camden 180, 293
  Somerset 299
  Vineland 180, 293
New Philadelphia, Ohio 151, 354
New York iv, 28, 57, 69, 81, 108
  Buffalo 162, 284
  Dutchess Co. 33
  Lake View, N.Y. 282
  Rochester 43
Newman
  Mary Ellen 278
Nic(o)son
  Luis 105
  Susan Caroline (Holloway) 105

Nicholas
  George 344
Nicholson
  J. W.? 128, 258
  John 261
  Mary (Trubey) 128, 258, 261
Nickel Plate Railroad 309
Noble Co., Ind. 122
North Carolina
  East Flat Rock 215
  Hendersonville 215, 216, 217, 324
North Dakota 222, 254, 328
  Cass Co. 221
  Fargo 252, 254
  Hunter 221
  Lidgerwood 253, 254
Northampton Co., Pa. 62
Northern Pacific Railroad 191, 304
Norwalk, Ohio 309
Oakland, Calif. 213
Oakland, Kans. 209
Ocala, Fla. 215, 322
Ohio 112, 115, 119, 244, 359
  14th Ohio Inf. 141
  23rd Ohio Vol. 121

  46th Ohio Inf. 40, 101
  55th Ohio Inf. 69
  68th Ohio Inf. 25, 135, 138
  124th Ohio Inf. 84
  139th Ohio Inf. 97
  Adrian 181, 349
  Ashland Co. 121, 135, 140, 141
  Athens 301
  Athens Co. 187
  Barberton 94
  Barrs Mills 293
  Beach City 87, 145, 151, 180, 276, 293
  Bolivar 86, 101, 341, 342, 354
  Bucyrus 241
  Butler Co. 66, 82, 186, 298, 299, 301
  Canal Dover 163, 249, 298
  Canton 87, 275
  Carey 173, 297
  Celina 102
  Circleville 153, 276
  Cleveland 87, 160, 192, 307
  Crawford Co. 239
  Dalton 93, 96
  Defiance 139
  Defiance Co. 24, 67, 83,

139, 186, 189, 191, 193, 196, 197, 289, 298, 302, 303, 304, 306, 307, 308, 309, 313
Delaware 254
Delta 234
Dover 247
Eldorado 228
Florida 141, 185, 298, 335, 348
Ft. Finlay 341
Gallia Co. 310
Grover Hill 252
Guernsey Co. 327
Hancock Co. 62, 65, 172, 178, 181, 183, 291, 296, 339, 350
Henry Co. 25, 50, 64, 66, 71, 81, 82, 135, 138, 140, 141, 185, 200, 205, 208, 210, 214, 234, 237, 238, 240, 242, 301, 314, 315, 319, 320, 321, 322, 341, 343, 347
Hicksville 301
Highland Co. 211
Holmes Co. 51

Jewell 189, 299, 301, 309, 310, 311
Loraine 297
Loudonville 121
Massillon 95, 144, 287, 349
Mercer Co. 98, 100, 102, 252
Monroe Co. 107
Montpelier 44, 118
Napoleon 25
New Philadelphia 39, 151, 354
Norwalk 309
Ohio City 251
Paulding 254
Pickaway Co. 153
Preble Co. 228
Richland Co. 192
Rockford 102, 252, 254
Rosebud 299
Sandusky Co. 243
Seneca Co. 63, 124, 182, 349
Sherwood 191, 302, 303, 304, 307
St. Paris 281
Stark Co. 14, 16, 18, 22, 26, 29, 31, 33, 35, 50, 51, 56, 65, 82, 83, 87, 88, 90, 91,

94, 95, 135, 138, 142, 146, 147, 149, 150, 151, 152, 154, 157, 158, 161, 163, 165, 267, 268, 271, 272, 275, 277, 281, 282, 283, 288, 289, 293, 327, 336, 337, 338, 341, 349
Summit Co. 94
Tiffin 182, 183
Toledo 79, 235, 334
Tuscarawas Co. 16, 28, 38, 41, 43, 45, 57, 61, 65, 86, 90, 97, 101, 110, 112, 116, 121, 123, 126, 130, 151, 164, 249, 250, 252, 256, 257, 258, 344, 346, 350, 352
Upper Sandusky 297
Van Wert 41, 252
Van Wert Co. 97, 98, 99, 251
Waterville 235
Wayne Co. 36, 57, 92-95

Williams Co.
44, 120, 122
Wooster 253
Wyandot Co.
23, 63, 65,
173, 183
Zoar 354
Ohio City, Ohio
251
Ohio Weslyan
College 254
Oklahoma
Bristow 107
Creek Co. 107
Ft. Sill 292
Lincoln Co.
107
McAlester 84
Payne Co. 107
Shawnee 222
Oliver
Catherine
Elizabeth
(Holloway)
104
Mr. (-?-) 104
Oller
Jacob 348
Ollig
John 10
Oregon 218, 306
Albany 192,
306
Camp Adair
306
Enterprise 103
Grants Pass
149, 272
Joseph 110
LaGrande 112,
178
Lebanon 306
Portland 149,
272
Wallowa Co.
103, 110,
111

Orleans, Nebr.
229
Osborn
Catherine 68,
196, 313
Catherine (Hull)
196
David 196
Muriel 210,
319
Oswald
George 46
Ott
Daisy Odetta
(Trubey)
149, 272,
273
Dorothy Louise
274
Dorothy
Mitchell
(Brandberg)
274
Edward Bryce
149, 272,
273, 274
Erastus DeWitt
149, 272,
273
Ethel Marie
(Daniels)
274
Jane Blanche
274
Mary Catharine
(Ray) 274
Marylin Louise
274
Myron Dwight
149, 272,
273, 274
Robert Ray
274
Warren Franklin
149, 272-274
Ottawa, Kans.
360

Ouray Co., Colo.
204
Palisade, Colo.
203, 212
Parker
Elsie May 204
Israel 309
Thomas 67
Patterson
Betsy (Perrin)
179
C. L. 180
F. J. 179
Harriet "Hattie"
A. 177, 179
Paulding, Ohio
254
Payne Co., Okla.
107
Pea Ridge, Tenn.
135
Peges?
Henry 10
Pennsylvania 13,
28, 35, 41,
43, 56, 59,
64, 96, 110,
130, 136,
143, 225
200th Pa. Inf.
221
Crawford Co.
77
Cumberland Co.
2, 220
Fayette Co. 45,
144
Franklin Co. ii,
v, 11, 14, 15,
18, 21, 31,
50, 51, 56,
61, 65, 68,
72, 74, 80,
249, 250,
267, 268,
287,
288-290,

384 INDEX

293, 314, 327
Huntingdon Co. iii
Northampton Co. 62
Philadelphia 30
Pittsburgh 150, 275, 304
Waynesboro 248, 288, 293, 298
Perrin
  Betsy 179
  Joseph 179
  Susan (-?-) 179
Peru, Ind. 230, 333
Peter
  Jacob 7, 9
Petrey
  Magdalena 228
Pherson
  Eliza (Tate) 52, 269
  Elizabeth 20, 52, 268
  Theophilus 52, 268
  Philadelphia, Pa. 30
Philip(s)
  J. L. 186
  William 34
Phillips Co., Kans. 225, 328, 329, 330
Physicians
  Heacock, Alfred 19
  Hendricks, Ernest A. 222
  Jenovese, Hilda Emma Grace (Martens) 319
  Jenovese, Patrick 319
  Kellogg, Dr. 203
  Luttenberger, John M. 153, 276
  Ollig, John? 10
Pickaway Co., Ohio 153
Pilcher
  Agnes Iola 204
  Alice Margaret 205
  Cecil Louis 203
  Daniel Franklin 203
  David Eugene 204
  Delbert Eugene 204
  Elsie May (Parker) 204
  Ethel Maude 204
  Eugene David 205
  Eva Gladys 203
  Hazel Lorraine 205
  Joseph Louis 203
  Joshua 200
  Kathryn Elaine 205
  Lola Ruth 205
  Mary Ellen (Rathmell) 204
  Mary Jane 205
  Mary Jane (Trubey) 70, 200
  Merle Eugene 203
  Oren 204
  Philadelphia (Beer) 201
  Stella Contessi (McKessin) 203
  William 205
  William Edwin 204
  William T. 70, 200
  Woodrow 204
Pinellas Co., Fla. 209
Piper
  Lula M. 132, 264
Pittsburgh Landing, Tenn. 124
Pittsburgh, Pa. 150, 275, 304
Poole
  Dalton H. 215, 322
  E. V. 215, 322
  Ethel G. (Trubey) 215, 322
Popejoy
  Gladys 172
Porfser
  Georgia (Stump) 332
  Harry W. 332
  Loyle 332
  Lucille 332
Porter
  Alma 254
Portland, Ore. 149, 272
Pratt
  J. R. 214
  Lulie A. 72, 214, 322
  Omira M. (-?-) 214

INDEX 385

Preble Co., Ohio 228
Preston
  J. R. 47
Pritchard
  Sally 98
Profit
  Charles 101, 251
  Donday [Dorothy?] 100
  Dorothy (Maisch) 100
  Emma ["Mary?"] 101, 251
  John 100
  Lydia Catherine (Trubey) 40, 99, 251
  Margaret "Maggie" 101, 251
  Philip 40, 99, 251
  Susan 100
  Theodore 101
Purdy
  Mary 33
Rahauser
  Rev. Henrich Jonathan 13, 15, 21, 288
Randolph Co., Ind. 103
Rathmell
  Mary Ellen 204
Ratt
  Mary Winona Trubey (Van Eman) 146
  Mr. 146
Rausch
  Rebecca J. 169

Ray
  Mary Catharine 274
Reece
  Jennie (Stump) 331
  William H. 332
Reed
  Michael 9
  Mr. (-?-) 104
  Nellie Virginia (Trubey) 279
  Pheby Keziah (Holloway) 104
  Philip 4, 6, 8, 10
  Wilbert M. 279
Render
  Mr. (-?-) 166
  Ruth (Trubey) 166, 285, 286
Republic Co., Kans. 126
Revolutionary War ii, 110
Richards
  Capt. 25
  Elizabeth (Warner) 35
  John 35
  Mary 15, 35
Richardson Co., Nebr. 24, 26, 73, 220, 223, 226, 228, 289, 327, 330, 332
Richert
  Helen 215, 323
Richland Co., Ohio 192
Rife
  Frederick 144

Ritz
  Solomon, M.G. 45
Rochester, N.Y. 43
Rock Creek, Iowa 208
Rockford, Ohio 102, 252, 254
Rodgers
  Betty Ruth 195, 310
  Chauncy O. 195, 310
  Gary Alan 310
  Harry Franklyn 195, 310
  Jane Elizabeth 195, 310
  Marian Evelyn 195, 310
  Mary 199, 315
  Mary Leona (Trubey) 195, 310
  Miriam (Evans) 310
Rosebud Co., Mont. 190
Rosebud, Ohio 299
Ross
  Venus 192, 307
Routsong
  Blanche (Landahl) 266
  Charles 134, 266
  Ester Leona 266
  George W. 134, 266
  Hazel (Trubey) 134, 266
  Lois 134, 266

386 INDEX

Retha 134, 266
Ruth 134, 266
Wava Keturah 266
Row
  Abraham 13
Rowley
  M. M. 211
Royer
  Daniel 10
  John 10
  Samuel, Jr. 7, 8
Ruff
  John 97
Rural Seminary, Ohio 39
Ryan
  Jane 102, 252
Sample
  Mabel Irene 206, 317
San Francisco, Calif. 104, 316
San Miguel Co., Colorado 71
Sandusky Co., Ohio 243
Sandyville Greenlawn Cemetery, Ohio 91
Santa Cruz, Calif. 199, 315
Santa Rosa, Calif. 212
Saskatchewan, prov. of 254
Savage
  Almon 86
  Maria (Stout) 86
  Mary E. 30, 86
Schaal
  Thelma (Van Nette) 183

Schadle
  Cleturah (Trubey) 134, 266
  George L. 134, 266
Schee
  Emma Grace (Trubey) 210, 320
  Evelyn Lenore 210, 320
  James Robert 210, 320
  Leland Burlette 210, 320
  Mr. (-?-) 210
  Virginia Arnell 210, 320
Schermer
  Anna 178, 292, 295
Schuman
  Gladys (Trubey/ Morgan) 297
Schuyler
  Sarah A. 181
Schweickert
  Catherine 28, 62
  Jacob 344
Scio College, Ohio 39, 249, 250
Scofield
  Andrew J. 335
  Andrew W. 25, 81
  Catharine (Grimm) or (Gunn) 82
  Effie Savilla 82, 237, 335
  Elizabeth J. 82, 335
  Helen S. 82, 335

James E., J.P. 135
Jared 81
Mary Ann (Trubey) 25, 80, 335
Mary E. 82, 335
Nelson E. 82, 335
Susannah (-?-) 81
Scotland 88, 230
Scott
  M. 230
Seattle, Wash. 260
Sebastopol, Calif. 213
Selby
  Luke 117
  Mary A. (-?-) 117
  Mary Ann 44, 117
Seneca Co., Ohio 63, 124, 182, 349
Service
  Madge Cecile 213, 321
Seventh Day Adventist Church, Colo. 201
Seventh Day Adventist Church, Kans. 314
Shafter, Calif. 323
Shawnee Co., Kans. 70, 209
Shawnee, Okla. 222
Sheline
  Cassandra (-?-) 151

INDEX 387

David 151
Mary Ann 54,
    151, 276
Susanna
    (Kintner)
    151
Shelton, Nebr.
    215
Shepherd
    Anna
        (Schermer)
        178, 292,
        295
    Arabella Serena
        (Trubey) 65,
        172, 291,
        294, 358,
        359, 360
    Clarence Clare
        177, 291,
        292, 294,
        359
    Earl Irvin 178,
        291, 292,
        295, 359
    Eliza (Fisher)
        173
    Elmore P. 65,
        173, 294,
        357, 360
    Grace Darling
        63, 177, 291,
        292, 295
    Harriet "Hattie"
        A.
        (Patterson)
        177, 179
    Melba Helen
        178
    Robert Earl
        177, 292
    Sarah Catherine
        (Kochender-
        fer) Allen
        176
    Thomas N. 173
    Tyrannus (Goe)
        Morton 177

Virginia Louise
    178
Sheridan Co.,
    Kans. 328,
    329
Sherwood, Mich.
    184
Sherwood, Ohio
    191, 302,
    303, 304,
    307
Shettler
    Jemima 163
Shiloh, Tenn.
    101, 251,
    252
Shipshewana
    Brethren
    Church, Ind.
    47
Shober
    Francis 7, 8
Shockey
    Jacob 7
Shore
    Mary A. 167
Shroyer
    Jacob 9
Sidle
    Benjamin
        Harrison
        252, 253
    Minnie L.
        (Trubey)
        252, 253
Siler
    Florence
        Augusta
        (Trubey)
        189, 301
    Marie 189, 301
    Peter 189, 301
    Virginia 189,
        301
Silver Creek
    Cemetery,
    Nebr. 24,
    74, 221, 289,

327, 328,
330, 331
Silver Creek,
    Nebr. 228
Simpson
    Harold I. 195,
        311
    James Norman
        196, 311
    John Richard
        196, 311
    Mildred Fay
        (Trubey)
        195, 311
    William Robert
        195, 311
Sisson
    Bessie Belle
        155
Skinner
    H. D. 179
Slack
    Abraham 133
    Hannah (-?-)
        133
    Hannah E. 49,
        133, 266
    Mr. 71
Slagle
    B. W. 189
Slusher
    Esther 59
Slutz
    Charles 19, 20,
        50
Smelser
    Mr. 352
Smith
    Amelia/
        Parmelia A.
        115
    Charles R. 191,
        303
    Clarence
        Charles 191,
        303

INDEX

Flora Mae
  (Trubey)
  191, 303
J. D., J.P. 204
Marjorie Ray
  191, 303
Noma Mildred
  191, 303
William
  Barevias
  191, 303
Smith Co., Kans.
  74, 328, 329
Smutz
  Jacob 45
  Mary 17, 45,
  257
  Mary (-?-) 45
Snively
  David 348
Snowberger
  David 7
  John 10
Somerset, N.J.
  299
South Dakota 254
South Gate, Calif.
  192
Spankel
  Mary A. 143
Sprain
  Abie 98
  Abraham F.
  99, 251
  Elmina 99, 251
  Emma A. 99,
  251
  Goldie 98
  Henry 40, 97,
  251
  Henry Clark
  98, 251
  Ida Florence
  99, 251
  Jane Etta 99,
  251
  Lydia 98, 251
  Martha 99, 251

Mary 98, 251
Mary Ann
  (Trubey) 40,
  97
Maudie 98
Phillip
  Augustus
  99, 251
Sally (Pritchard)
  98
Samantha
  Elizabeth
  99, 251
Sophia Ellen
  98, 251
Sprough
  Lucy A. 239
St. John's
  Evangelical
  Lutheran
  Church, Md.
  18
St. Joseph Co.,
  Mich. 65,
  88, 177, 178,
  181, 292,
  294, 295
St. Joseph, Mo.
  75, 77, 80,
  84, 245
St. Louis, Mo. 71,
  78, 209, 328
St. Paris, Ohio
  281
Staffeldt
  Eurannah
  (Hass)
  Trubey 184
  Rachel 184
  William 184
Stamay/Stamy
  John 6-9
Stanley
  Clyde M. 71
  Sylvia 224
Stark Co., Ohio
  14, 16, 18,
  22, 26, 29,

31, 33, 35,
50, 51, 56,
65, 82, 83,
87, 88, 90,
91, 95,
135, 138,
142, 146,
147, 149,
150, 151,
152, 154,
157, 158,
161, 163,
165, 267,
268, 271,
272, 275,
277, 281,
282, 283,
288, 289,
293, 327,
336, 337,
338, 341,
349
Starner
  Catherine 344
  Eliza 344
  George 352
Stauffer
  Mary C.
  (Trubey)
  Bare 47, 48,
  129
  Peter 48, 129
Stephens
  Peter 10
Steuben Co., Ind.
  44, 123, 124,
  126, 258
Stevenson
  Polly 123
Steward
  Lewis 7
Stewart
  Bardin 60, 290
  Elizabeth 60,
  290
  Henry 60, 290
  James 60, 290

Mary A. (Hunt)
  60, 290
William 60,
  290
Stiles
  Genevieve 219,
    326
Stinson
  Elizabeth 92
Stone Creek
  Cemetery,
  Ohio 38
Stoner
  Abraham 10,
    21, 72, 222
  David 6, 9, 21
  Maria (Mack)
    21
  Mary 12, 21,
    73, 288, 327
  Rebecca 23
Stouder
  John 23
Stout
  Joseph 66
  Maria 86
Stringer
  Nonomie 317
Stroh, Ind. 162,
  284
Stroup
  Charles C. 118
  Helen Ardetta
    (Trimble)
    118
Stump
  Bessie Ethel
    225, 229,
    328, 331
  Clarence 229,
    332
  Elizabeth
    (Yantiss) 27,
    226, 329
  Georgia 229,
    332
  Gerald 332

Gracie 229,
  331
Jennie 229,
  331
John Wesley
  74, 228, 329,
  336
Magdalena
  (Petrey) 228
Mary Elizabeth
  (Yantiss) 74,
  228, 336
Nellie
  (Cunning-
  ham) 331
Quinton S.
  229, 331
Sol C. 228
Sol C., Rev.
  226
Wilma
  (Halderman)
  332
Sturgis, Mich. 88,
  181
Summers
  Catherine (-?-)
    131
  Frances S.
    (Wilson)
    131
  Jacob 131
  John 131
  Mary Elizabeth
    49, 130, 263
  Peter 131
  Sarah (Yoder)
    131
Summit Co., Ohio
  94
Swan
  Eliza 20, 51,
    268
  Enos 143
  Mary A. (-?-)
    51, 268
  Nicholas D.
    51, 268

Swigert - see
  Schweickert
Swihart
  Anna M. 17,
    48
Swindler
  Mabel
    (Hutchi(n)-
    son) 212,
    321
  Samuel 212,
    321
Switzerland 248
Tate
  Eliza 52, 269
Taylor
  Abraham 40,
    344, 346
  Amelia/
    Parmelia A.
    (Smith) 115
  Andrew T. 70,
    202
  Annie D. 116
  Annie D.
    (Taylor) 116
  Calvin G. 116
  Caroline Harriet
    (Arbaugh)
    42, 115
  Clara A.
    (Myers) 116
  David 115
  Eli M. 116
  Ellsworth 205
  Ezra 44, 118,
    119, 124
  Fanny (-?-)
    120
  Franklin 120
  Harrison A.
    120
  I. Freeman 116
  Idabella 116
  Isaac 119
  J. W., Rev.
    228
  John 38, 120

John W. 42, 115
Lauretta 120
Levi 116
Marion B. 120
Mary Ann 17, 38, 250, 252
Mary Ann (Musser) 38
Mary Jane (Trubey) Pilcher 70, 200, 206, 218
Sarah A. (Cox/Cocks) 119
Susan K. (Trimble) 44, 119, 256
Telluride, Colo. 205
Tennessee
  Camp Shiloh 41
  Chattanooga 101, 103
  Nashville 88
  Pea Ridge 135
  Pittsburgh Landing 124
  Shiloh, battle of 101, 251, 252
Terhune
  Bertha 172
  Charles 171
  Clayton 171
  Edith 171
  Edward 61, 169, 290
  Edward Russell 172
  Ellen (McCullick) 61, 169, 290
  Garrett 170
  Gladys (Popejoy) 172
  Grace 172
  Henry 172
  Ida Belle 169
  Jennie Iness (Mounsey) 171
  Mary (Bingham) 170
  Minnie (Brown) Davis 171
  Rebecca J. (Rausch) 169
  Renie (Mendenhall) 172
  William Oscar 172
Tetrick
  Glen M. 112
  Mrs. (-?-) (Nedrow) 112
Texas 105
  panhandle 107
Thomas
  Albert 310
  Jane Elizabeth (Rodgers) 310
  W. V., Rev. 83, 338
Thompson
  Edward B. 294
  Martha Helene (Hirst) 294
Thornsbury
  James 20, 56
  Mary (Welty) Trubey 20, 56
Tiffin, Ohio 182, 183
Tippecanoe Co., Ind. 186
Toledo, Ohio 79, 235, 334
Tombs
  Joanna 300
Tomlinson Cemetery, Ohio 98, 101
Topeka, Kans. 71
Torrey
  Helen (Trubey)? 264
Townsend
  Mr. (-?-) 72
Trayer
  Jacob 130
Trimble
  Cora 122
  David A. 44, 118, 121, 124, 256
  Elizabeth M. (Floring) 119
  Foss S. 119
  Helen Ardetta 118
  John 17, 43, 256
  Mary (Drake) 44, 121
  Mary Ann (Selby) 44, 117
  Mary Caroline 44, 123, 256
  Mary Catherine (Trubey) 17, 43, 256
  Nettie E. 122
  Pearl S. 123
  Sarah E. (Allman) 44, 116
  Susan K. 44, 119, 256

INDEX 391

Thomas
 Barkdoll 44,
 116, 121,
 124, 256
Trinity Church of
 God, Ind.
 258
Trinity Co., Calif.
 199
Trinity Lutheran
 Church, Ohio
 309
Triplett
 Harriet 121
Troy
 Martin 107
Trube
 Andreas ii
 August ii
 Augustin ii
 Jakob ii
Trubey
 Abraham 26,
 288, 327,
 329, 336,
 339, 342
 Abraham M.
 41, 101, 250,
 252
 Addie E. 200,
 315
 Addie Gail
 (Anderson)
 191, 304
 Agnes (Vosnik)
 311
 Albert Jason
 162, 283,
 284
 Albert Sidney
 188, 301
 Alice G.
 (Cavitte)
 262
 Allie 146, 271
 Alma (Abeney)
 217, 324

Alma (Porter)
 254
Alva Morris
 197, 313
Alvah P. 55,
 165, 247,
 269, 285,
 286
Ambrose
 Ellsworth
 68, 197, 313
Ambrose Enyart
 196, 298,
 309, 313
Amos Calvin
 206, 317
Andrew
 Franklin
 199, 315
Andrew H. 259
Andrew Hanibel
 41, 250
Anna Elizabeth
 (Kleemyer)
 259
Anna M.
 (Swihart)
 17, 48
Anna Mary
 (Minnick)
 55, 154, 277,
 278
Arabella Serena
 65, 72, 172,
 291, 293,
 294, 340,
 341, 354,
 356, 357,
 358, 359,
 360
Arie L.
 (McFarren)
 55, 163, 281
Arthur R. 217,
 322, 324
Asa Alvah 162,
 283

Asa Harvey 55,
 161, 269,
 283
Avah (Gooden)
 156, 279
Barbara Jane
 195, 311
Barevias
 Augustus i,
 68, 189, 247,
 298, 302,
 336
Bernadene 219,
 325
Bertha V. 102,
 252, 253
Bessie Belle
 (Sisson) 155
Betsy (Perrin)
 Patterson
 Fitch 179
Betty Jean 216,
 323
Beulah 206,
 317
Carl E. 131,
 133, 260,
 263, 265
Carl Harrison
 163, 283
Carole 262
Caroll 263
Carrie Lovena
 206, 317,
 318
Catherine 24,
 27, 80, 81,
 83, 288, 338,
 347
Catherine
 (Isenberger)
 iii
Catherine
 (Motter) 12,
 15
Catherine
 (Osborn) 68,
 196, 313

INDEX

Cecil 263
Charles Francis 210, 320
Charles Otha 162, 283, 284
Charles William 185
Charlotte (Ambs) 185
Chauncy J. 128, 258, 261
Chester Edwin 207, 317, 318
Clara C. (Myer) 153, 276
Clarence 158, 247, 281
Clarence O. 215, 322
Claude 217, 324
Claudius Eugene 194, 309
Clayton 158
Cleturah 134, 266
Clyde 72
Cor Jacob 156, 277, 280
Daisy Odetta 149, 272, 273
Dale 150, 275
Dale H. 220, 325, 326
Daniel (1750) 1, 3
Daniel (1793/5) 12, 21, 247, 248, 288, 289, 339, 341, 343, 347, 348

Daniel (1824) 25, 68, 81, 288, 314, 339, 341, 343, 347, 348
Daniel A. 71, 314
Daniel F. 164, 281
Darrell D. 220
David (1788) 7, 12, 15, 248, 249
David (1819) 25, 61, 68, 72, 173, 288, 293, 339, 341, 344, 346, 348
David A. 47, 49, 130, 257, 263
David Clarence 216, 324
David Cyrenus 72, 214, 314, 322
David Jacob 153, 276
David Keith 185
David M. 17, 45, 249, 257
David Morton 40, 250, 251
David Norvin 46, 127, 258, 259
Dennis Lavaun 217, 324
Don Edwin 305
Dona Rose 207, 318
Dor Esdras 156, 277

Doris Marguerite 259
Doris Oneida 149, 272
Dorothy (Corson) 278
Dorothy Ann 254
Dorwin Melvin 195, 311
Dwight Willis 166, 285, 286
Edith Roselle 188, 301
Edna M. (Casner) 220
Effie 264
Effie Pearl 132, 263
Elda Martha 149, 272
Elida 102, 252, 253
Eliza (Swan) 20, 51, 268
Eliza Cassandria 153, 276
Elizabeth 27, 81, 82, 288, 337, 339, 341
Elizabeth "Lizzie" (Williamson) 54, 152, 276
Elizabeth (Pherson) 20, 52, 268
Elizabeth (Voth) 215, 323
Elizabeth Jackson 264

Ellsworth J.
55, 157, 247,
269, 281
Elnora LaReine
162, 284
Elsie (Cook)
207, 318
Elsie Laura
(April) 195,
311
Elva 145, 271
Emily 50, 128,
261
Emma 188
Emma Belle
(Caler) 55,
165, 285,
286
Emma Grace
210, 319,
320
Emmet
Ellsworth
197, 313
Erastus Seabury
65, 72, 178,
184, 293,
343, 358,
359
Ermah Udette
197, 313
Ernest Freeman
259
Esdras 54, 151,
268, 276
Esther D.
(Heath) 25,
69, 314
Ethel Donelda
198, 313
Ethel G. 215,
322
Ethela Helen
262
Eugene C. 217,
322, 324
Eunice Bessie
153, 276

Eurannah
(Hass) 65,
183, 296
Eva 134
Ferdinand 54,
268
Flora Mae 191,
302
Florence
Augusta
189, 301
Florence J.
216, 322
Flossie
(McPhee)
162, 284
Floyd L. 216,
322, 323
Forest Cole
149, 272
Frances Louise
192, 307
Freddy Roy
324
Frederick
Hobart 131,
132, 263
Frederick
LeRoy 216
Frederick T.
264
Freeman 55,
154, 268,
277
Freeman A.
128, 258,
261, 262
Gail 217, 324
Genevieve
(Stiles) 219,
326
George 49, 72
George A. 72,
218, 314
George
Abraham
325

George Esdras
153, 276
George Gaylord
185
George Lester
134, 266
George W. 47,
63, 133, 257,
266
George William
185, 296
Gladys 324
Gladys Carol
216
Gladys Evelyn
262
Gladys May
264
Gloyd Orland
192, 307
Golden Oneida
150, 272,
275
Grace (Fruit)
262
Halle Belle
180, 293
Hannah E.
(McFarland)
71
Hannah E.
(Slack) 49,
133, 266
Harmon 54,
147, 268,
272
Harold 264
Harold Dorwin
195, 309,
311
Harold Vane
259
Harry 264
Hazel 134,
216, 266,
322
Helen 264

394 INDEX

Helen (Richert) 215, 323
Homer Ray 155, 278
Howard Alonzo 197, 313
Ida Belle 188, 301
Ida Elnora (Wolf) 55, 161, 283
Ida Mae (Casteel) 71
Ida Martha 20
Ila Dorlean 206, 317
Ione Luanne 216
Ira 164
Ira T. 55, 163, 269, 281
Ira W. 128, 258, 261
Isabella 54, 268
Jacob (1789) 12, 18, 247, 248, 267
Jacob A. 47, 48, 118, 122, 126, 257, 258
Jacob Andrew 17, 38, 249, 250, 252
Jacob M. iii, 20, 23, 50, 51, 247, 267, 268
Jacob Marion 145, 271
James Cyrenus 210, 319
James Wayne 192, 307
Jane (Morse) 25, 67, 298

Janey Lee 217, 324
Jeanne (Davidson) 313
Jennie 253
Jennie Blanche 150, 272, 275
Jennie Ethel 161, 283
Jennie Etta 55, 158, 269, 282
Jesse Freeman 206, 317
Jewelle Lucille 216
John 259
John (1821) 22, 25, 65, 247, 288, 289, 290, 298, 339, 341, 347, 348
John Allen 70, 205, 314, 317
John Earl Nathan 188, 301
John Edwin 191, 302, 304
John Taylor 40, 250
Joice Mable 162
Joseph Andrew 70, 198, 314, 315
Joseph B. 47, 49, 257, 258, 266
Joyce 281
Joyce L. 219, 326

Joyce M. 164, 284
Julia Ellen 278
June Ethel 162, 284
Justin Alonzo 68, 193, 298, 309
Kenneth D. 219, 278, 325
Kenneth Devere 155
Kenneth Doye 219, 325
Keziah (Klinker) 25, 61, 293, 344, 346, 349, 351, 352, 358, 359
LaReine (Curby) 162, 284
Laurence 259
Lavina Amanda (Dudley) 70, 208, 319
Leila Ethel 207, 317, 318
Lester 281
Lester Charles 206, 317
Lester E. 164
Lettie (-?-) 265
Levi F. 127, 258, 261
Lewis Edward 210, 319
Lewis Francis 70, 208, 314, 319
Lewis Merle 210, 320
Lillian A. (Gilbert) 68, 186, 301

Lillian May 162, 284
Lloyd Elton 192, 304, 305
Lloyd William 155, 278
Lola Pearl (Kunkel) 150, 275
Loraine Esther 207, 317, 318
Loretta 324
Loretta (Dudlow) 188, 301
Lovina Amanda 210, 320
Lowell Kenneth 278
Luella B. (-?-) (Marchand) 54, 152, 276
Luella May 55, 269
Lula M. (Piper) 132, 264
Lulie A. (Pratt) 72, 214, 322
Lulu (Anderson) 156, 280
Lydia (Moore) 25, 67, 290, 298, 299
Lydia Catherine 40, 99, 250, 251
Lydia Ruth 192, 302, 306
Lyman - see Lyman Trubey/ Morgan

Mabel Irene (Sample) 206, 317
Mae (Miller) 216, 323
Margaret (Hooper) James 192, 308
Margaret (Mack) 1, 8, 11
Marguerite Ann 311
Marguerite L. 220, 325, 326
Marguerite Lois 196, 309, 312
Marie Leha 206, 317
Mark Lee 278
Martha Dawson (Liddle) 65, 178, 293
Martha Elisabeth 1
Martha M. (Gaines) Knight 26, 336
Mary 128, 258, 261
Mary (Groner) 20, 56
Mary (Rodgers) 199, 315
Mary (Smutz) 17, 45, 257
Mary (Stoner) 12, 21, 73, 288, 327, 339, 347, 348
Mary (Welty) 12, 18, 56, 267

Mary A. (Moffett) 49, 266
Mary Ann 25, 40, 54, 80, 97, 217, 250, 251, 268, 288, 324, 335, 347, 348
Mary Ann (Minsel) 197, 313
Mary Ann (Sheline) 54, 151, 276
Mary Ann (Taylor) 17, 38, 250, 252
Mary Anne (Augustine) 54, 147, 272
Mary B. (Altimus) 72, 218, 325
Mary C. 47, 48, 128
Mary Catherine 17, 43, 65, 181, 249, 256, 294, 359
Mary E. 165, 188, 263, 285, 286
Mary Elizabeth (Summers) 49, 130, 263
Mary Ellen (Newman) 278
Mary Helen 252, 254
Mary Jane 70, 200, 314
Mary Leona 195, 309, 310

Mary M.
  (Frysinger)
  41, 101, 252
Mary Olive
  (Diller) 149
Mary Winona
  146, 271
Mattie Lee
  (Johnson)
  217, 324
Max 262
Max William
  278
Melissa
  (Knepper)
  54, 143, 271
Melissa
  (Wyland)
  48, 126, 258
Melissa Ann
  70, 210, 314,
  320, 321
Melvin Jay
  149, 272
Merlin Delmar
  216, 323
Mildred Fay
  195, 309,
  311
Minnie (Brown)
  Yergin 49,
  134
Minnie L. 102,
  252, 253
Monroe S. 155,
  278
Monsolete
  (Alcorn)
  219, 325
Muriel (Osborn)
  210, 319
Myron
  Augustus
  192, 302,
  307
Myrtle (Little)
  162, 284

Myrtle Carolyn
  210, 320
Myrtle Edna
  210, 319
Myrtle Mae
  146, 271
Mystia Nafeesie
  185, 296
Nancy 347
Nancy (1786)
  12, 13, 248,
  287
Nancy (1818)
  20, 50, 267
Nancy (1826)
  24, 25, 72,
  288, 327,
  340, 343
Nathan 54,
  142, 253,
  268, 271
Nathan John
  68, 77, 185,
  298, 301
Nathan Ray
  156, 277,
  279
Nebbie Don
  146, 271
Nellie 164, 281
Nellie Virginia
  156, 279
Nettie J. (Ely)
  68, 186, 301
Neva 134
Nonomie
  (Stringer)
  317
Norma Lee
  324
Norman Dalton
  216, 323
Norman Lee
  216, 324
Novella
  Yvonere 324
Olive (Diller)
  272

Olivia
  (Markley)
  278
Orville 215,
  323
Oscar Dallas
  131, 132,
  260, 263,
  264
Paul 264
Paul D. 262
Paul Myron
  278
Paul Perlee
  165, 285,
  286
Priscilla 55,
  269
Ralph A. 102,
  247, 252,
  254
Ray Edwin
  192, 304
Raymond
  Charles 166,
  285, 286
Rebecca 25,
  74, 79, 84,
  288, 333,
  339, 343,
  347
Regenal
  [Reginald?]
  103, 252,
  255
Reginald Porter
  254
Richard 188,
  301
Richard Arnold
  254
Richard Myron
  192, 307
Rita Esther
  206, 317
Robert B. 147,
  271

INDEX 397

Robert Emanuel
    195, 311
Robert Henry
    162, 283,
    284
Robert Nathan
    254
Rollie 253
Rollin Lincoln
    55, 269
Rose
    (Lewallyn)
    54, 152, 276
Roxie/Roxia B.
    155, 277
Roy 187, 301
Roy Sylvanus
    324
Russell Dorwin
    311
Russell Norris
    156, 279
Ruth 166, 219,
    285, 286,
    325
Samuel 25, 56,
    288, 334
Samuel J. 20,
    50, 56, 267
Sandra Jean
    188, 301
Saphronia (Day)
    70, 198, 315
Sarah 49
Sarah A.
    (Morgan)
    70, 206
Sarah J.
    (Kimberly)
    68, 193, 309
Sarah Jane
    (Dougherty)
    25, 66, 298,
    347
Satira Eunice
    (Kilgore) 55,
    157, 281

Selma Ruth
    147, 271
Sharon Kay
    305
Shirley Maxine
    210, 320
Stanley Rogers
    156, 280
Susa (-?-) 158
Susan 290
Susan (1818)
    25, 56, 288,
    348
Susannah 17,
    41, 249
Sylvester Brice
    150, 272,
    275
Theodore
    Wayne 192,
    302, 308
Tony 207
Trixie E. (-?-)
    132
Valerie Anita
    180, 293,
    294
Venus (Ross)
    192, 307
Vernon 217,
    322
Vernon C. 219,
    325, 326
Violet 72
Violet A. 217,
    322, 324
Virginia Carrie
    (Gilbert) 68,
    187, 301
Walter 72
Wanona I.
    (Welch) 305
Wilda Gale
    151, 272
William A.
    155, 277,
    278

William Cole
    150, 272
William David
    63, 65, 183,
    293, 296
William Joshua
    199, 315
William Leslie
    210, 320
William Mahlon
    210, 319
Wilma 264
Wilma V. 131,
    132, 263
Zelda M. 164
Zeruia C.
    (Goode-
    nough) 68,
    189, 302
Trubey Brothers
    Stock
    Brockers
    184
Trubey/Morgan
    Adah (-?-) 297
    Carl 297
    Emma 297
    Gladys 297
    Lyman 64,
    297, 359
    Milton 297
    Nina 297
Truby
    Andrew 16
    Cathrine
        (Mattern) 16
    Christopher 16
    Jacob 16
Turner
    Mary C.
    (Nedrow)
    111
Tuscarawas Co.,
    Ohio 16, 28,
    38, 41, 43,
    45, 57, 61,
    65, 86, 90,
    97, 101, 110,

INDEX

112, 116, 121, 123, 126, 130, 151, 164, 249, 250, 252, 256, 257, 258, 344, 346, 350, 352
Twibell
  Martha 59
Twibell Cemetery, Ind. 59
Twins
  Dudley, Lavina & Lavona 208
  Long, Carey May & Reuben 83
  Mohn, Jessie & unknown 231
  Taylor, Eli & Levi? 116
  Trubey, Cor J. & Dor E. 156
  Wilson, (-?-) & (-?-) 109
Tyringham, Mass. 243
U.S. Signal Corps 173
Uniondale, Ind. 128, 258
University of Cincinnati Law School 255
Upper Sandusky, Ohio 297
Valley View Cemetery, Kans. 294
Van Eman
  Arthur E. 146

Mary Winona (Trubey) 146, 271
Van Nette
  Abel 181
  Adair B. 183
  Adair B., Jr. 183
  Carmen 183
  Frieda (Coe) 183
  Jasper 65, 181, 294, 358, 359
  Joanne 183
  Mary Catherine (Trubey) 65, 181, 294, 359
  May (Clark) 183
  Sarah A. (Schuyler) 181
  Thelma 183
  Verne V. 183, 294
  Virgil 294
  Wesley 183
Van Wert Co., Ohio 97-99, 251
Van Wert, Ohio 252
Van Wey
  Marjory 219, 325
  Roy 219, 325
  Ruth (Trubey) 219, 325
  Virgil 219, 325
  Virginia 219, 325
Ven Meer
  Mary Elizabeth (Charles) 265
  Mr. (-?-) 265

Verdon Cemetery, Nebr. 331
Verdon, Nebr. 228, 329, 331
Vineland, N.J. 180, 293
Virginia 64, 199
  Bedford Co. 103
  Campbell Co. 103
  Winchester iv
  Yorktown iii
von Bose
  Regiment iv, 1
von Scheer
  Major Friedrich Henrich iv
Vosnik
  Agnes 311
Voth
  Elizabeth 215, 323
Wabash, Ind. 118, 231
Wakefield
  John 105
  Nora Louetha (Holloway) 105
Walker
  Francis 181, 294
  James Duane 306
  Joseph 181, 294
  Lydia Ruth (Trubey) 192, 247, 306
  Maxwell Trubey 306
  Mildred Helen (Griggs) 306
  Robert 180, 294

INDEX 399

Valerie Anita
 (Trubey)
 180, 294
William Edward
 192, 306
William H.
 180, 294
William Homer
 180, 294
Walla, Germany
 260
Wallace
 Capt. Thomas
  v
Wallowa Co., Ore.
 103, 110,
 111
Walter
 John 7, 8
War of 1812 59
Ward
 Emma
 (Muskopf)
 160, 282
 H. B. 160, 282
Warner
 Elizabeth 35
Washington 133,
 306
 Camp Lewis
 323
 Fort Lewis 264
 Seattle 260
Washington Co.,
 Md. 13, 15,
 18, 21
Waterville, Ohio
 235
Watson
 Rebecca
 Bradley 178
Wayne Co., Ohio
 36, 57, 92,
 93, 94, 95
Waynesboro, Pa.
 248, 267,
 288, 293,
 298

Weaver
 Elizabeth 82
 family 358
 H. S., Rev. 150
 Mr. 342
Webber
 Jennie Ethel
 (Trubey)
 Maynard
 283
 John Burton
 283
Weggary
 K/Coon 346
Welch
 Wanona I. 305
 William, Mrs.
 179
Wells Co., Ind.
 16, 41, 44,
 46, 58, 103,
 110, 111,
 115, 119,
 166, 169,
 258
Welsh
 John 7, 8
Welty
 Abraham 15,
 35
 Almon C. 30,
 86, 354
 Alva McKinley
 93
 Alvin Cullen
 91
 Alvira "Ella" N.
 30, 87, 355
 Anna T.
 (Graham) 30
 Belle H. (-?-)
 87
 Blanche Jenettie
 93
 Charles Henry
 96

Christian 12,
 13, 31, 287,
 341
Cullen 90
Cullen F. 87
Cullen J. 30,
 341
Cullen M. 32
Frank 30
Franklin 38, 95
Gretchen 96
Hazel M. 96
Ida 37
Ina May 38
Iva 37
Jacob 13, 18
Jacob T. 15,
 28, 86, 339,
 342, 350,
 352, 355
James A. 87
John 7, 8, 13,
 15, 18, 31
John Cullen
 30, 355
John J. 91
Lillie 30
Mary 12, 18,
 56, 267
Mary (Richards)
 15, 35
Mary A.
 (Brannon)
 38, 95
Mary Amelia
 (Lebold) 32,
 90
Mary Ann 15,
 32
Mary E.
 (Savage) 30,
 86
Mary Jane
 (McWhin-
 ney) 15, 31,
 90
Minnie 38, 93

INDEX

Nancy (Trubey) 12, 13, 287
Nettie 38, 94
Paulene 96
Perler/Perlee L. 87
Phianna (Klinker) 15, 28, 89, 342, 346, 350, 354
Selina A. (McElhenie) 37, 92
Tilden 37, 91
Walter E. 93
Walter H. 87
Wentling
 John 10
West
 Eileen Mary 313
 Ermah Udette (Trubey) 313
 Lenwood B. 313
West Virginia 187, 301
Weyant
 John 6, 7
Wheeling and Lake Erie Railroad 309
Whipple
 Mr. (-?-) 114
 Susan (Arbaugh) 114
White Co., Ind. 33, 34
Wichita, Kans. 295
Williams
 Dorothy (Johns(t)on) 265

Williams Co., Ohio 44, 120, 122
Williamson
 Dorothy M. 316
 Elizabeth "Lizzie" 54, 152, 276
 George 152
 Mr. (-?-) 316
 Rachel (-?-) 152
Wilson
 Alford E. 109
 Frances S. 131
 James G. 109
 Loren C. 109
 Norma Gertrude (Mays) 109
 Walter F. 109
Wimer
 David, Rev. 344
 John, Esq. 344
Winchester, Va. iv
Winnetka, Ill. 180
Wisconsin
 Dane Co. 224
Wolcottville, Ind. 122
Wolf
 Charles 161
 Ida Elnora 55, 161, 283
 John 31
 Matilda (-?-) 161
 Nancy 31
Woodland Cemetery 180
Woodland, Ill. 127, 258, 260
Wooster, Ohio 253

World War I 255, 332
Wyandot Co., Ohio 23, 63, 65, 173, 183
Wyant
 D. B. 52
Wyland
 Emily (Mills) 126
 Levi 126
 Melissa 48, 126, 258
Wyoming
 Casper 192, 308
 Laramie 178
Yantiss
 Arminda (Iden) 73
 Daniel D. 74, 224, 226, 327, 329
 DeWitt 225
 Effie 73, 74, 327, 330
 Elizabeth 226, 327, 329
 George 74, 327, 328
 Jacob 25, 72, 314, 327
 John I. 327
 Joseph J. 74, 327, 329
 Judson 225
 Landon 74, 221, 223, 327, 328
 Lillie A. (Meyers) 74, 226, 329
 Mary (Merriam) 74, 223, 328
 Mary Elizabeth 74, 228
 Melissa 73, 74, 327, 328

Miss 228
Mr. (-?-) 228
Nancy (Trubey)
  24, 25, 72,
  289, 327,
  347
Theudas 327
Yergin
  Minnie (Brown)
  49, 134
Yoder
  Sarah 131
Yorktown, Va. iii
Young
  Bessie Ethel
    (Stump)
    328, 331
  Inez 331
  Ira C. 331
  Jayson 101
  Mary A. 143
  Mary A.
    (Spankel)
    143
  Ruth 331
Youngstown Iron
  Mining Co.
  34
Zanesville
  Cemetery,
  Ind. 17, 42,
  115
Zimmerman
  Daniel 46
  John 349
Zintmeister
  Mary
    Magdalena
    159
Zoar, Ohio 354

www.ingramcontent.com/pod-product-compliance
Lightning Source LLC
Chambersburg PA
CBHW050833230426
43667CB00012B/1975